Ministry of
Darkness

Ministry of Darkness

How Sergei Uvarov Created
Conservative Modern Russia

LESLEY CHAMBERLAIN

BLOOMSBURY ACADEMIC
LONDON · NEW YORK · OXFORD · NEW DELHI · SYDNEY

BLOOMSBURY ACADEMIC
Bloomsbury Publishing Plc
50 Bedford Square, London, WC1B 3DP, UK
1385 Broadway, New York, NY 10018, USA

BLOOMSBURY, BLOOMSBURY ACADEMIC and the Diana logo are trademarks of
Bloomsbury Publishing Plc

First published in Great Britain 2020

ISBN: HB: 978-1-3501-1669-6
PB: 978-1-3501-1668-9
ePDF: 978-1-3501-1670-2
eBook: 978-1-3501-1671-9

Typeset by Deanta Global Publishing Services, Chennai, India
Printed and bound in Great Britain

To find out more about our authors and books visit www.bloomsbury.com
and sign up for our newsletters.

'his work would have put us back fifty years into bondage ...'
Joseph Conrad

Contents

Figure

Abbreviations

Archive material

GIM   Gosudarstvenyi istoricheskii muzei (State Historical Museum) Moscow

Encyclopedias

BE   Bol'shaya entsiklopedia (pre-1917, undated)

BROKGAUZ   Entsyklopedicheskii slovar', izd. Brokgauz, F.A. i I.A. Efron (St Petersburg 1880–1907)

GRANAT   Entsyklopedicheskii slovar' russkogo bibliograficheskogo instituta Granat (Moscow, undated)

RBS   Russkii biograficheskii slovar' (St Petersburg, 1896–1918)

Collected works

PSS   Polnoe sobranie sochinenii

Introduction

The shock of revolution

At first some Russians were delighted by the French Revolution. When news of the fall of the Bastille reached St Petersburg, the French ambassador, the Comte de Ségur, saw people embracing in the streets. The teenage royal princes, Alexander and Constantine, who had received a liberal education, rushed up to congratulate him on the Nevsky Prospect. But their grandmother Catherine, already a woman of sixty, in her twenty-eighth year on the throne, was less impressed.

The French Enlightenment had intrigued her. It was an intellectual reform movement that championed materialism and natural rights. What it stood for, the power of reason to construct a modern civilization, free from superstition and prejudice and based on a vision of equality, entertained her through endless dreary days in the Venice of the North and provided an antidote to the superficiality of the court. The Enlightenment also did more than entertain the German-born Russian empress. Montesquieu's *Esprit des Lois* had informed the Nakaz, the 'Great Instruction' of 1767, in which she reviewed the laws of her empire and set out the principles on which she wanted her reign to rest. But, having learnt the hard way the business of governing an unruly empire, seeing it through the eyes of a woman born in Europe, she knew emancipatory thinking was not a practical possibility for Russia. That distant admiration for Enlightenment liberalism, in tension with 'learning the hard way' about Russia, will stalk the narrative of this book.

The bigger the hold Enlightenment thought gained, the more the empress who would become known as Catherine the Great felt the need to distance herself from her earlier enthusiasms. Repelled by events in France, she found her eye guided towards England, her future ally against Napoleon. In March 1790, her ambassador in London, Semyon Romanovich Vorontsov, reported that fortunately and to the credit of the English people there was no sign of the revolutionary spirit taking hold there, despite the presence everywhere – and here already he intimated the potential danger to Russia – of 'French apostles ... who preach a metaphysical equality among people which has never existed in any society'.[1] Edmund Burke's *Reflections on the Revolution in France* expressed the widespread anti-revolutionary view in England among the ruling class, when it appeared ten months later. Burke disparaged metaphysical interventions into the art of government, and when the book reached her the following year, Catherine had Vorontsov convey her admiration to the author.[2] Burke, however, rejected the compliment. Conservative he might be, but he was quite sure he and the empress of Russia did not stand in defence of the same cause.

Burke appealed to the power of tradition and the complexity of human nature in action. He argued that no theory of how to govern or how to live should be founded on a mere idea, but on the wisdom of practice. He disdained what happened in France as irresponsible speculation. It was intellectual Jacobinism. Yet at the same time he could clearly envisage a situation where revolution might be justified in the face of real political repression, such as the oppression his Irish kin suffered at the hands of the English. So he was a conservative, but out of a philosophical conviction that had little to do with preserving the interests of the landed and ruling class in England. He was a communitarian who felt that the stability of society was in everyone's interest and of a higher priority than any individual concern. He is perhaps best seen as a top–down utilitarian, with the idea of the common good providing the justification for social and legal constraint. He wrote,

> Government is a contrivance of human wisdom to provide for human wants. Men have a right that these wants should be provided for by this wisdom. Among these wants is to be reckoned the want, out of civil society, of a sufficient restraint upon their passions. Society requires not only that the passions of individuals should be subjected, but that even in the mass and body as well as in the individuals, the inclinations of men should frequently be thwarted, their will controlled, and their passions brought into subjection. This can only be done *by a power outside of themselves*.[3]

Any reader of Burke would have to decide how, given the endlessly diverse wants of individuals, freedom can be managed in an enlightened society.

In 1791 – Burke was right – Russia was not thinking of how to mould the passions of individuals to the common good. It was conservative through the dominant mentality of the nobility, which served the tsar and accepted autocracy as Russia's Orthodox Christian heritage. But what made the

Russian situation peculiar was the way Peter the Great had instrumentalized the nobility as the class to modernize Russia through travel and learning. Their task was to put themselves in contact with the West in order to bring the most innovatory ideas back home. They would help Russian science progress, and in this they would loyally serve their tsar. Their mission was thus twin-headed: to modernize Russia through the spread of knowledge, but not to allow, or encourage, loss of political control.

Though the image of the nobility, after the nobility was freed from obligatory civil and military service in 1762, was of an increasingly indolent class, there were enough hereditary nobles who continued to take the Westernizing task to heart. They wanted to serve Russia out of moral sentiment, and here a certain seriousness took root, encouraged by Catherine II's own great interest in education. Catherine effectively continued Peter the Great's policy of wanting to make Russia more European in the level of its learning, and into that tradition the subject of this book, Sergei Uvarov, was born, in 1786. Was he a Burkean? Perhaps more than most. But his achievement would be to define a unique Russian conservatism that eased the tension between scientific ambition, and hence national prestige, and domestic order.

Psychologically the task would never be easy, for two main reasons. One was the sense of being pulled in contradictory directions that just couldn't be reconciled, as if at once reversing the French Revolution and benefiting from the intellectual advances the Enlightenment brought. The other reason was that like the nobility in Louis XIV's France more than a century earlier the Russian nobility served the monarch herself, or himself, and the confusion of state interests with the personal interests of the sovereign often tended to lead to a sense of unreality and confusion: a feeling that the country couldn't move forward because even its most loyal servants couldn't get their bearings.[4]

The writer, historian, dramatist and traveller Nikolai Karamzin defined the late-eighteenth-century Russian conservatism that Burke objected to when he insisted that, for better, for worse, autocracy was Russia's traditional form of government and should only be tampered with at great risk. 'Autocracy is the Palladium of Russia; on its integrity depends Russia's happiness.'[5] In Russia what mattered were not political institutions but the Enlightenment and virtue of the citizenry, and if autocracy was the means to that end then it was a good enough form of government. When Catherine asked Karamzin to expound his views in a secret 'memoir', and her courtiers upheld this conservatism in the face of the French Revolution, it was not an attitude totally alien to the West. Rather, it was consistent with the mainstream European Enlightenment of a century earlier,[6] and that defensiveness against what counted as progress in the West became another feature of the Russian desire to resist change to autocratic rule.

The nobleman Alexei Vasilievich Naryshkin (1742–1800) wrote in his 1790 pamphlet entitled 'The Thoughts of A Dispassionate Citizen on the Violent Events in France':

> I must confess that my rule in life in all situations has always been that what joins people and reinforces their bond is good; that everything that divides and breaks this bond is evil; and I slavishly subordinate myself to the absolute power (*samovlastie*) of this truth.[7]

Naryshkin clearly stated the Russian conservative position. On the one hand, it was Burkean in its insistence on the wisdom of experience and the need for social coherence. On the other it was specifically Russian, an absolute endorsement of autocracy (*samovlastie*, for which the synonym *samoderzhavie* would become more common), because that was the only way the author could imagine continuing social order in Russia.

A traveller, scholar and writer, Naryshkin delighted in his contacts with the West, especially in France, where he became friends with the veritable pilot of the French Enlightenment, Denis Diderot. Naryshkin's grandest moment in service to his empress was to accompany Diderot on his celebrated, and for Catherine hugely symbolic, visit to Russia in 1773. Here was the embodiment of the French Enlightenment visiting her court and Naryshkin travelled with him in the coach all the way from The Hague to St Petersburg and then lodged him safely and comfortably with his brother Sergei. Ought Diderot to have been impressed? Of course. In some sense the Naryshkins were just what they needed to be for the occasion: they were the Enlightenment in Russia. Alexei was a state councillor, senator and corresponding member of the Academy of Sciences. Both brothers had translated articles from the *Encyclopédie*, edited by Diderot and the mathematician and philosopher Jean le Rond d'Alembert. The encyclopedia was synonymous with the modern advancement of knowledge, and the Naryshkins rejoiced in that. Like Catherine, however, Alexei Vasilievich Naryshkin's familiarity with a more liberal world failed to persuade him that Russia should change its political heart. Like Peter he believed that what Russia wanted from Europe was to mine its science and adapt its learning, but not to borrow the means of what would be its political undoing.

Other leading Russian aristocratic families of the day undoubtedly felt the same way as Naryshkin. The Golitsyns, Sheremetevs and Vorontsovs were three clans in whose libraries a copy of Burke's *Reflections* could also be found. They were deeply affected by what had happened in 1789; they took a great interest in progressive developments in the West, but they could not envisage Russia going down the same path. The Vorontsovs had served Empress Elizabeth, Catherine's mother-in-law.[8] Relatively newly ennobled, within two generations they were towering figures at the court, in the Academy and in foreign chanceries. Alexander Vorontsov was Russian ambassador in England at the age of twenty and rose to be chancellor of Russia. His brother Semyon who took over the London post after him was an outspoken anti-Jacobin who felt at home among English Tories. In Russia these men made minor adjustments to power. But they were never less than loyal to the principle of absolute rule.[9] If there was some unvoiced conflict deep inside them, they were free to live abroad, and, indeed, Semyon spent forty-seven years in England.

Expounding a simpler conservatism, Prince Alexander Nikolaevich Golitsyn (1773–1844) had a career ahead of him steering the nation's religious affairs and thus its conservative politics.[10] His conservatism was not an articulated philosophy but a God-fearing shrinking from the new. The Sheremetevs left a more cultivated mark. One of Russia's most illustrious military families since the sixteenth century, they had over generations become patrons of Russian theatre and music. Nikolai Petrovich Sheremetev (1751–1809) studied the *opéra comique* while in France, and his travels and his musical skills took him more widely abroad. Back home, infected by European dramatic and musical culture, he provided special education for serfs whom he perceived had dramatic talent. But, always, his politics were loyal to the tsar.[11]

But then in 1790 one of them did suddenly speak up in favour of liberty, equality and fraternity. That writer's name was Alexander Radishchev. Educated in Germany, he formed a worldview inspired by the aims of the American and French Revolutions. Having also travelled and studied abroad, which included a period of study at the University of Leipzig, Radishchev felt a wave of horror when he contemplated his own country, and decided to tell a new reading public, and Empress Catherine herself, why. Surely she was not aware of the iniquities in her own realm, he thought. Radishchev was not in his own eyes a revolutionary, but he wanted Russia to respect all its subjects, from the great to the humble. In the light of what was happening in the West, he insisted that the relationship of the common people to the autocrat and the nobility should be reformed on the basis of enlightened law.

Alexei Naryshkin's 'Thoughts of a Dispassionate Citizen on the Violent Changes in France' paid tribute to Catherine's wisdom. But Radishchev's *Journey from St Petersburg to Moscow*, published the same year, absolutely rejected the principles of imperial statecraft if they led to degradation such as any traveller across the country could see. Radishchev's *Journey* was a catalogue of concern for an enslaved people. Every one of its lightly fictionalized pages pleaded for a new sincerity in human dealings in Russia. 'If the law or the sovereign or any power on earth should tempt you to falsehood or to depart from virtue, remain immovably true to it,' insisted an apparition of virtue that appeared to Radishchev's traveller. To that moral sentiment which could have come from Rousseau, Radishchev added his already passionate Russian desire for social justice in an unjust country.

> Remember the coffee in your cup and the sugar dissolved in it have deprived a man ... of rest.
> Madmen, look about you! You are trying to support truth with falsehood, you seek to enlighten peoples with error.[12]

Sentence by sentence, page by page, Radishchev's *Journey* nailed the injustices and errors of Russian society. Its author was suddenly of a new kind in Russia, poised to open up a great gulf between the ruling class and the oppressed people. From the next century the revolutionary intelligentsia would look back in heartfelt admiration.

Radishchev's book, which took a number of years to compile and which took advantage of the author's new freedom to own a private press to print himself, was full of revulsion at the self-satisfied ways of the nobility. Vaguely satirical and reflecting the famous work of Lawrence Sterne, it wished a plague on that post-Petrine class that educated itself with sentimental journeys across Europe but ignored the condition of Russia. To them it said: Stop! There's no need to go abroad to find something interesting to write about. The next time you make that inconvenient journey from Petersburg to Moscow, get down from your carriage and look around at what you see, at the peasants exhausting themselves in the fields to have just enough to live on, after giving their labour six days a week to the feudal lord. But above all *Journey* was indignant at the moral horror of serfdom. 'Black Mud', the title of the last chapter, pointed directly at the way the ruling class traded in human lives and contained the words: 'Oh, wretched fate of many millions! Your end is hidden even from the eyes of my grandchildren.'

Radishchev was arrested on the last day of June 1790, just five months before Burke's *Reflections* appeared in London. As his 'travel' book caused panic in St. Petersburg, almost as much as the French Revolution itself, he had burnt the copies he still had at home. Once he was locked up in the dank, subterranean Peter and Paul fortress, city booksellers were divested of their stock and copies already purchased were confiscated, or they too were incinerated.

Catherine, who sat down with the book for two weeks on end, in order to take it in every detail, noted that the author of *Journey* was 'infected and full of the French madness' and had 'a preference for arbitrary, quasi-philosophical raving'. Radishchev was 'inclined to ill-will' and 'sees everything in a dark and sombre way'. She added, absurdly, 'Our peasants who have good masters are better off than any in the world.' A court interpreted her will and sentenced Radishchev to death.

Yet, surely she was torn over how to handle Radishchev, as her country would always be torn, over how to handle its humanitarian critics. For one thing Radishchev was a former subordinate and long-time favourite of Alexander Vorontsov, Catherine's own chancellor and her most loyal servant. Moreover, did Catherine not want to be known in the West as a friend of Voltaire and Diderot? Why else correspond with the apostles of reason and invite them to Russia? Catherine was the first Russian ruler who knew that a more liberal Europe was watching how she worked with enlightened European ideas. That same Europe puzzled over how she could admire Voltaire but reject reason as the basis for modernizing the governance of her own country. When she studied Radishchev's book personally, making notes sentence by sentence, Catherine seemed to want to prove something to any Western critic who might be watching. She told the officials who would note her comments: 'I do not want to judge him without hearing him, although he judges sovereigns without hearing their justification.'[13] Furthermore, though she had Radishchev sentenced to death, in another of those typical 'liberal' twists which would recur in Russian history after her, she declined to sign the warrant.

The possibility of Catherine's loyalties being torn has rarely been entertained.[14] But was it really to celebrate Russia's victory in the war against Sweden that summer that Radishchev was not executed but sentenced to ten years' exile in Siberia? Was the prisoner, whose noble class actually protected him from corporal punishment, treated relatively kindly for that reason alone? He was spared the need to wear fetters on his legs after the first day's trek, permitted to spend Christmas in Moscow, and once in Siberia allowed to lead a varied life, which would keep him well in mind and body.[15] Catherine acted on representations from Alexander Vorontsov on Radishchev's behalf, but surely she also listened to her own conscience. She did not feel easy contravening laws she had created and values she had publicly espoused.

Like so many Russian leaders after her, Catherine wanted to appear acceptable to the West, while at the same time being driven by a ruthless domestic realpolitik. Her Russia was already torn, like future Russias would be, by the awkward twin goals of cultural prestige abroad and raw power at home.[16]

The Radishchev episode, occurring as it did just after the French Revolution, is one of those hugely symbolic acts in Russian history that would have to have been invented had it not happened. Over the next century and later, the revolutionary intelligentsia would refer back to it as their inspiration and origin. Radishchev even lived up to a certain expectation of martyrdom when he killed himself in 1802, wrongly fearing that he was about to be rearrested. He entered history at the head of the revolutionary tradition, while Catherine stood for autocratic Russia's awkward balancing act between glory abroad and control at home – a balancing act that was itself about to become a political institution.

Russian conservatism redoubled in strength when Louis XVI was guillotined in January 1793. The Russian ruling class was aghast when the risk to its own antiquated notion of Russian stability suddenly became so clear. If a similar upheaval befell Russia and the divinely sanctioned supreme ruler was removed, the country would become ungovernable. In Russia, unlike in France, there was no *tiers état* to step into the role. Russia had no bourgeoisie that could govern in the name of the people. On the occasion of the regicide, therefore, Catherine informed Ségur that, as an aristocrat, she now had no choice but to break off diplomatic relations with France. But it was what she added that was more significant. She declared that Russia would take over the old French order and continue it. 'We are raising the hope of France, and it is these young people who will restore the monarchy,' she said in words that confirmed Russia's political reality after 1789 would be an active striving for counter-revolution.[17]

Old Russian conservatism was in danger from this moment, its more nuanced attitudes poised to disappear in a blind fear of revolution. Possibly the empress was referring to the thousands of French émigrés who had poured into Russia since the upheaval 700 miles away to the west, when she said she would raise them to restore the monarchy. But if she was referring also to her own country her words were startling, because from their utterance could be dated the moment when modern Russia acquired an ideological identity. At the very least, given the way the ethos of the court would be transformed over the next fifty years to defend itself at all costs against revolution, they could be seen as prophetic. That was because, if revolution was an ideology, so was counter-revolution. As ideologies, both were routes to political order by way of intellectual invention. They were about rule by ideas and principles. They were about deducing a set of general values to which individuals could adhere to in order to give their lives meaning – and, as I shall argue in this book, that set of values was, in Russia's case, nationalist and defensive, paradoxically inspired by, but against, the West. It certainly wasn't Burkean.[18]

The French Enlightenment had used the term 'ideology' to look forward to a science of sciences. Diderot would have recognized it as the underlying aim of the *Encyclopédie*. After 1789, however, ideology acquired a meaning which directly connected 'ideas', otherwise known as 'metaphysics', with political revolution. Burke used the term 'metaphysical' in this sense, and so did Napoleon.

It is to ideology, the cloudy metaphysics which, by subtly searching for first causes, wishes to establish on this basis the legislation of peoples, instead of obtaining its laws from knowledge of the human heart and from the lessons of history, that we must attribute all the misfortunes of our fair France.[19]

But ideologists of both a revolutionary and a counter-revolutionary persuasion did not share this negative view. For them the realm of ideas, an extension of the rationalist French passion for *l'esprit de système*, presented a uniquely effective guide to social and political organization in their time, and it was this modern time, suddenly sprung upon it by events in France, that Russia was now about to enter.

Whereas in Burke the French Revolution produced a classic expression of anti-ideology, in Russia it gave birth to ideology. It opened up a world in which ideas in competition with each other would preserve or destroy the social order. It was only in that form that some kind of negotiated conservatism, as opposed to blind stasis and reaction, could occur under tsarist Russian conditions, and, arguably, in Russia under subsequent forms of government too.

Sergei Uvarov was the inventor of that ideology that tried to negotiate a more enlightened Russian future.

1

A childhood close to power

Sergei Uvarov was born on 26 August 1786 and later recalled Empress Catherine's presence at his baptism. She was his godmother.[1] His father was a vice-colonel ('Vitse-Polkovnik') among Catherine's lifeguards: a handsome, carefree man who had risen on the coat-tails of a cousin's military success. The diarist Filip Vigel' thought of Semyon Fyodorovich Uvarov as 'good, honorable, brave and merry'.[2] He was charming and outstandingly musical, able to play the formidable Ukrainian bandura, with its sixty strings, and dance knees-bent, Cossack-style, holding the bulbous, long-necked instrument in one hand. The empress's favourite prince, Potemkin, considered him an ideal courtier and nicknamed him 'Sen'ka the bandura-player', which is how everyone at court came to know him. Potemkin even encouraged Catherine to make Sen'ka' on of her adjutants.[3] But in truth Sen'ka was not at all well-connected. The Uvarov family had entered the tsar's service in the fifteenth century and the name was honourable enough, but the latest representative had few resources in money or kind and no well-placed relatives.[4] So, one might surmise, he relied on being an entertaining companion.

Sen'ka married Darya Ivanovna Golovin in 1784 when he was already forty, and she was said, according to the slanderous habit of the times, to be on the shelf. Darya brought with her a large dowry and on her paternal side an excellent heritage. The Golovins were one of the great aristocratic Russian clans, with their quality enhanced by many good connections made through marriage over the past century and a half of Romanov rule.[5] Her older sister Natalya was married to Alexei Kurakin, a future minister of internal affairs. The family knew that Darya was marrying beneath her status, but everyone could see she was happy.[6]

After their wedding the Uvarovs set up home at the regimental headquarters next door to Catherine's court, where they were waited on by junior ranks. Not long after Sergei was born, they had a grand house built on the newly granited banks of the Catherine canal in the centre of St Petersburg. By the beginning of 1788, Darya was pregnant again. However, the family was already in difficulty. Sen'ka had no talent for business, people said. While talented in music, in life he was unreliable. As soon as he was installed at court, his new importance went to his head. He lost his fear of Potemkin and ruined the company of which Catherine named him vice-colonel. According to that distinguished prince, after a stint under Uvarov all that was left of this highly disciplined unit 'was its outward appearance, and the fact that the grenadiers could sing'.[7] Whereupon, for reasons no one was able to determine, Sen'ka went missing in battle against the Swedes in Finland.[8]

Sergei was not yet even two and the new arrival, his brother Fyodor Semyonovich, was a babe in arms. Darya was left in great financial difficulty. Growing ill with worry, she turned to Alexander Mamonov, Catherine's latest lover, to see if he couldn't persuade the empress to pick up the colossal bill of 70,000 roubles for the house. When only five thousand were forthcoming, Darya had to abandon Dom 101 on the Catherine Canal.[9] The family meanwhile was outraged. Why hadn't she restrained her high-spending husband? Her parents, with evidently all their wealth tied up in land and serfs, the habitual aristocratic lament, were powerless to help. They wondered about their daughter's character. It seemed that she too had been spending wildly.

Darya turned to her sisters in-law, the Kurakins, for help. That was the privilege Sergei ought to have highlighted in any autobiographical sketch. The Kurakin family invited their two nephews to grow up in their extended household, alongside nine *vospitaniki*: boys quasi-adopted for the sake of their education.[10] The situation was not so unusual. The sons of the gentry were often brought up fatherless because of the demands of military service.[11] The illegitimate and the orphaned were readily adopted.[12] But Uvarov was exceptionally blessed by his adoptive family background. Like the Uvarovs the noble line of the Kurakin family went back to fifteenth-century Muscovy. Meanwhile, it owed its present high profile to the distinguished figure of Boris Ivanovich Kurakin (1676–1727). Close to Peter the Great as a government servant and as his brother-in-law, close associate and friend, Boris Kurakin had successfully negotiated the end of the Great Northern War which made Russia a modern European power. He had wit, brains and style, and in the remainder of his life he became Russia's first permanent ambassador abroad in Paris. He was writing a book about his life and times when he died leaving behind seven children from two marriages. One of those seven, Alexander (1697–1749), succeeded him at the mission in France. In turn it was Alexander's son Boris-Leontii Kurakin (1733–64) who became a senator and key economic adviser to Catherine II, and Boris-Leontii's sons Alexander (b. 1752) and Alexei (b. 1759) who took the Uvarov brothers under their wing. Alexei Kurakin – a composer in his spare time, and a man passionate about theatre – was married to Darya's sister Natalya.

Alexei, who was also an expert in banking and finance, took a stern view of Darya'a predicament and counselled her on ways of living economically. He suggested that she live outside the capital to reduce her costs and that she should not borrow any more money if she wished to spare the family further embarrassment. But Darya, energetic and headstrong, was a cultivated woman from the metropolis and the idea of moving to the country where life would have been dreary and ignorant and slow did not appeal. So she patched up the family's existence in Piter, as the northern capital had long been affectionately known, and within a couple of years resumed her presence in society. She has been called 'spoiled and unscrupulous' and accused of conniving to have her sons educated in the Kurakin household,[13] but in another age she may well have been looked upon as a survivor, for she seems to have been a sharp-witted, spirited woman determined to see her sons make good.

The Kurakin aspect of his education ought to have made Sergei Uvarov a liberal. His Kurakin uncles had a remarkable liberal education themselves, supervised by one of the best-known courtiers of Catherine's reign, Nikita Ivanovich Panin.[14] The empress had Panin, who was also head of her Ministry of Foreign Affairs, educate her son Paul after an attempt to secure the encyclopedist d'Alembert failed. The education Panin prescribed included statecraft, familiarity with the ways of the Orthodox church, and knowledge of classical French literature, language and ways. It allowed the idea that civil life – not yet in Russia, but perhaps one day soon – might be grounded on the basis of law. Uvarov, however, ended up being educated at home by a French abbé by the name of Mauguin who had fled the Revolution from his estate in Bordeaux. Mauguin seems to have been a modish choice on the part of his mother. ('Don't send me a Frenchman or a German. I want an abbé,' declared the fashionable woman of the day.[15]) Darya sold two child serfs from her Yaroslavl estates to a female relative on her husband's side of the family to help pay for Mauguin's services.

Very quickly it was apparent Sergei Uvarov was a boy of peerless ability. He could write French with native fluency before his teens. He read La Bruyère on the corrupt, but nicely polished ways of the court of Louis XIV and some minor works of Voltaire. He would always love classical French literature, as much for its language as its content. Mauguin had him read travelogues too, classic versions of The Grand Tour. Radishchev had shown how politically devastating this educative form could be when turned on Russia itself. But Mauguin had Uvarov travel mentally in an earlier and quite different world. *The Letters Sent to His Mother in 1764 From a Journey to Switzerland*, by Stanislas de Boufflers, reflected the interests of the seigneur in women, horses, land, politics and idyllic landscapes. Boufflers, born in 1738, was the grandson of Maréchal Louis Francois de Boufflers, one of the most important men at the

Sun King's court and elected to the Académie française in 1788. Intelligent and well-travelled, the later Chevalier de Boufflers, like many subscribers to the moderate Enlightenment, accepted social inequality as a condition of political stability, and passed that view on to his young Russian reader.

As Uvarov studied, willingly and ably, Charles Mercier-Dupaty's *Lettres sur l'Italie en 1785* also imparted to him something of the history of art. Uvarov had a real connoisseur's bent, and this education was not wasted on him. He later built on his knowledge to become an enthusiastic collector of the great neoclassical sculptor Canova. He loved neoclassical art as he loved neoclassical French literature.

But, again, where was Russia in all of this? Radishchev's point about adapting Lawrence Sterne's *A Sentimental Journey* to Russian conditions was to tell young men of Uvarov's generation that the days for following the arts merely as a pastime in Russia were over. Social issues pressed too hard. Reform was desperately urgent. Still there's no indication Uvarov ever read Radishchev. He grew up to have fine taste in matters that were artistic but morally superficial. Meanwhile, politically he had this great animus against revolution which the abbé Mauguin could only have endorsed.

When he entered public service in August 1801, twelve months earlier than the minimum age of sixteen, it was probably under the influence of Alexander Kurakin. A new tsar had come to the throne in March, and Kurakin had been made vice-chancellor. Some of his peers already found Sergei Uvarov too good to be true. Filip Vigel', the principal diarist of the age mentioned earlier in this chapter, disliked him at first sight: 'One rather handsome boy appeared to me to be entirely insupportable and annoying; he was presumptuous, arrogant, garrulous and, in a loud voice and without any humility whatsoever, deliberated about French literature and theatre.'[16] Vigel' and Uvarov worked alongside each other in the College of Foreign Affairs, soon to be renamed the Foreign Ministry, and went on studying while they worked. Vigel' was homosexual and Uvarov would become a noted bisexual in ruling circles, so perhaps there was always that additional tension between them.

Sergei probably attended the Cadet School in Petersburg, an elite cramming-house run along the lines of a French lyceé, where the curriculum included French, English, German, Latin, Russian and fencing, while at the Ministry his work mainly involved translating.[17]

All the while he was being egged on by his mother, and it was about this time that he began to socialize in earnest in the circles close to the tsar. The Kurakins had enjoyed a close relationship with the previous ruler, Paul I, and after his death the dowager empress Maria Feodorovna became hostess of one of the most important salons of the decade. Darya encouraged her son to win the empress's attention. Alexei Kurakin accused her of compromising her son with her pushiness, but the Uvarovs were undaunted. Sergei was under particular pressure to visit Marya Naryshkin, the tsar's mistress, more often.[18]

The glory of the age, at least for the nobility that created and enjoyed it, was the Franco-Russian house party – lavish merrymaking continued at this party right up until 1917.[19] Similar parties took place in this period in the cosmopolitan salons of Petersburg and in the cosier, more markedly Russian atmosphere of the Moscow houses. (Madame de Stael would find them to be 'tartar material with a French border' when she visited in 1812.)[20] They underpinned the francophone high society that Leo Tolstoy, born in 1828, would portray to the next generations. This was the culture that was so memorably depicted as socializing its way to a complete unsuspected end in Alexander Sokurov's film *Russian Ark* (2002). Uvarov loved the cultural conventions of this extraordinary class, and he shone there, with his talent for amateur dramatics, his ease in several languages and his eloquence about books. Alexei Kurakin had to concede that this Franco-Russian 'Serge d'Ouvaroff' was destined for the heights: 'Ouvaroff will make his way. ... You should know that of all the young men of his age he is the pearl, and not many like him are born.'[21]

The St Petersburg salon of Alexei Nikolaevich Olenin and his wife was the gathering Uvarov singled out, and later he was at pains to say how Russian it was, in fact. Whatever critical thoughts people had in retrospect, he wrote fifty years later, the Olenin salon was peculiarly Russian and of immense value to the nascent arts of the early nineteenth century. Olenin was at once a favourite of the court, a future director of the Imperial Public Library, a book illustrator and an archaeologist. When Uvarov first visited his home on the Fontanka Canal, he was ravished by Olenin's collection of antiquities and dated his own interest in archaeology from that moment. 'Art and literature found a modest but constant refuge in [his] house,' he reminisced.[22] This lively scene of Russian art, literature and learning stoked his patriotic pride from an early age. He wrote: '[Olenin's] ardent love of everything which might lead to the development of Russian talent did much to ensure the success of Russian artists. Kiprensky was discovered and encouraged by him. ... The two Bryulovs did not forget [his] constant support.' Orest Kiprensky would one day paint Uvarov's own portrait, while the (Huguenot) name of Karl Bryullov became famous, and all the more celebrated in Italy, with his spectacular oil painting *The Last Days of Pompeii* (1830–1833). The works of the fabulist Ivan Krylov were read among friends at the Olenin's for the first time. Another important guest was Nikolai Gnedich, the Russian translator of Homer. The dramatist Vladislav Ozerov appeared one day with the manuscript of his play *Oedipus in Athens* (1804) and first rehearsals took place at the Olenins.

Uvarov's claim that modern Russian culture was born in the salons was not wrong. Writers like the court poet Gavrila Derzhavin, Krylov the Russian Aesop, the Romantic poet Vassily Zhukovsky and, eventually, the poet

Alexander Pushkin who was born in 1799, created it. It was literary art that barely touched the life of the ordinary Russian, and until Pushkin the literary language was removed from ordinary speech. But the salon atmosphere of Franco-Russia raised enough men of independent critical thought, with a great interest in a better Russia, to provide the first generation of the Russian intelligentsia.

The Olenin memory was so sweet to Uvarov so many years later, however, because

> despite the menacing events taking place in Europe at the time, politics was not a main topic of conversation, it always took second place to literature. Here it must be observed that not only in Russia but throughout Europe there was a strong impulse towards the development of literature and an inclination towards peaceful intellectual pursuits at the very time when all governments were pushed to the brink of destruction by the shaking of the foundations of civil order and spirit of military campaign.

Uvarov clung vehemently to the idea that art and politics should be separate. The needs of society were not to be discussed in verse. But that was not the future of Russian literature at all.

A foreigner could take a different view of what was of value in those salons. One who observed the Russian houses firsthand was the minor German playwright Georg Reinbeck. Reinbeck taught at the Cadet School and was a sometime tutor to a 'Herr Uvarov'. He knew the Razumovskys and the Dolgorukovs and set two of his plays in such Russian noble households. He wrote, 'Unencumbered by any serious occupation, the Muscovite nobleman, without possessing any extraordinary share of philanthropy or hospitality, is happy to collect around him a circle of individuals, who can give life and variety to the dull uniform scene of good living and idleness.' Particularly foreigners were welcome, he added. 'The Russian nobility cannot upon the whole be termed uncultivated ... but their intelligence is confined simply to matters of fact. It would be vain to look for principles among them, and still less for a definite character. ... Where in fact can men acquire principles and character, who have no other pursuit than the enjoyment of ease and pleasure?'[23] His play set in the Razumovsky household, into which Uvarov eventually married, bore the title *Graf Razumowsky oder Nicht Alles is Falsch, was Glänzt, Russisches Charaktergemälde in 4 Abteilungen* ('Not everything is false that glitters, a Russian character sketch in four parts').

If one were to judge by Uvarov's own character, there would seem to have been much truth in the culture Reinbeck was describing. Uvarov too was not a strikingly individual man. He was educated and intelligent and attracted to things foreign, but he was never known for his principles or his strength of character. He cultivated big names and associated himself with greatness, as if he hoped that some of it would rub off on him through the proximity of names on a page. That this class typified by Uvarov knew French literature but not the literature of its own people outraged Reinbeck, who felt it didn't disturb the Russian nobles themselves at all. This Russia 'appreciated the fine arts as appendages to greatness, rather than as a means of refining and exalting the human mind'. The corollary of that remark must be that the individualism that formed such an important part of the Enlightenment, particularly in the German lands, did not take root in Russia, a country where it was above all political power that wanted to make use of learning. The towering genius of contemporary German literature Johann Wolfgang von Goethe was so fascinated by what Reinbeck had to report that he had lengthy conversations with the tutor who returned so disillusioned from Russia after his thirteen-year stay.

* * *

Uvarov did have a Russian education, but that was in realpolitik, a brutal schooling in the ways of Russian power, fifty years before the European term was invented.[24] In fact the previous tsar, Paul I, had not died naturally; he had been brutally murdered when Uvarov was fourteen. Later in his life he would say it had been a necessary event, but one which should not be discussed. He would pass over Paul in silence in his many writings on the Romanovs. But he must have had cause to reflect on that event when it happened in March 1801.[25]

The best liberal education money, political power and prestige could buy had failed to help the tsarevich Paul, Catherine's son by Peter III. He had a disastrous childhood and became a troubled adult. As part of a long struggle over which branch of Peter the Great's family should succeed to the throne, Elizabeth, Paul's grandmother on his father's side, had removed him from his mother's care almost from birth. Thus when Catherine in her turn overthrew her own husband – Voltaire said Peter III allowed himself to be nudged aside like a child being sent to bed – Paul was left an effective orphan, because he had never bonded with his mother, nor she with him, and soon his father was not only deposed but dead. What was more, rumours abounded, although never proven, that Catherine had had Peter murdered.

Paul as an adult had no capacity for dealing with the world. Knowing his weakness, his mother gave him no hand in the running of state affairs, and he became more and more estranged from practical life. For almost two centuries after his death, historians accepted Catherine's verdict and called her son mad. Today he is seen as having been 'morally abnormal'.[26] He became tsar nevertheless, because in 1796 Catherine fell ill and died suddenly and the faction that supported Paul's son, Alexander, had not garnered enough support.

Once in power, Paul summoned the Kurakins. The three boys had been educated side by side and were friends. Paul made Alexander Kurakin his vice-chancellor, effectively the highest executive post in the land, handling all the monarch's important documents and meeting daily with foreign dignitaries. Alexander handled diplomacy during the time of the directoire, the government of the first French Republic, and Napoleon's rise to power. To Alexei Kurakin went the title of procurator-general, with not only the vital task of reforming fiscal matters but, even more urgently, the legality of government business.

Alexei created the first Auxiliary Bank for the Nobility, an institution designed on a German model to concentrate all that class's financial debts in one place, to make them creditors of the sovereign they served and, altogether, to make their impoverished lives easier. But never had the nobility been so dissatisfied with a ruler as they became with Paul when he set about punishing them for the moral corruption he associated with his mother's reign. Ironically he thought French liberalism had poisoned the nobles.[27]

Even before a year had passed since his coronation in 1797, Paul had issued 48,000 orders regulating bureaucratic and court life.[28] They included what time people should get up, how their houses might and might not be decorated and what styles of clothing were permissible. The tsar's orders banned children from playing in the streets and their parents from using words like the Russian equivalent of *citoyen* and *patrie*.[29] Compulsory military service, a moratorium on foreign travel and study and a ban on the entry of foreigners into Russia and on the import of goods from Western Europe followed.[30] Paul I presided over some of the darkest days Russia had ever registered before the painful absurdities of communist totalitarianism.

As the threat of revolution spreading from France loomed ever larger in the person of Napoleon and his armies in Europe, the emperor's anxieties were carefully nourished by high-ranking French émigrés in the Russian capital, such as Comte de Choiseul-Gouffier and Prince de Nassau-Siegen, and other 'false friends', according to his son's Swiss tutor, Frédéric-César de La Harpe.[31] Paul dismissed around 10,000 officials in government and military posts, which were especially resented. No one knew any longer what were the law. La Harpe said Paul had a good heart and 'had a need to redress the injustices he had had the misfortune to perpetrate'.[32] But his psychological violence against his country and the people around him added a special edge of paranoia to normal Russian harshness. Alexander Herzen was wrong to call Paul's murder 'the only interesting episode of his reign' because it contained the most instructive political tensions, as well as the tragedy of the ruler himself.[33] No Russian ruler before 1917 would go as far in committing himself to a constitution for Russia as did Paul. His teacher Panin had shown him the liberal way.[34] Another of Paul's legacies, almost as if he had read Radishchev's encounter in Lyubani with the peasants who were forced to work six days out of seven not for themselves, was to improve the rights of serfs, who were now required to work for their masters only three days a week.[35] Paul's legacy was a strange mixture of great liberal and moral idealism and extreme despotism, and the nobility, who either missed or didn't care for his concern for social justice, doubly hated him for his contradictions.

But the last straw in conservative Russian eyes was the odd course Paul chose to steer Russia's relations with France. Napoleon's success in Italy in 1797–98, a country where Paul himself had travelled, prompted a late and futile military intervention, as Russia wavered between playing a role as a mediator between other conflicting European powers and becoming involved in direct action. In 1799, persuaded that he was being betrayed by Britain and Austria, his allies in the Second Coalition, he moved to restore diplomatic contact with France.[36]

Alexander Kurakin fell from grace as vice-chancellor at the end of 1799, probably in disagreement over the new policy towards France. Any rapprochement with France was greeted in more conservative Russian circles with horror. He was replaced by Nikita Petrovich Panin (1770–1837), nephew of the liberal figure who had left such a positive stamp on Paul's life. This later, lesser Panin hated all Frenchmen on principle and hoped to subvert the new policy. His disobedience discovered, he was sacked and sent into country exile.[37]

But a moment of justice availed nothing, and now the plotting began in earnest. Nikita Petrovich Panin got together with Count Pahlen, soon to become Paul's last head of the College of Foreign Affairs, and petitioned Alexander for permission to remove his mad father from office. The coup finally went ahead with the plot to kill the tsar on the night of 10/11 March 1801, when a group of disaffected officers, including an Uvarov cousin, broke into the tsar's state apartment and strangled him. Panin was one of the cabal of senior military and government figures from whom they had taken their orders. The twenty-four-year-old Alexander was complicit, but not in the brutal murder that resulted.

Paul embodied ideology as tyranny. His draconian rules ignored what Burke called 'the balances between differences of good; [the] compromises sometimes between good and evil, and sometimes, between evil and evil' which, in the way they comprise life, are 'incapable of definition, but not impossible to be discerned'.[38] But he had also been pushed to become a 'holy fool' in love with a *Polizeistaat* of his own fantasy.[39] In the Russia in which he lived his sickness, instead of being soothed by a culture of common sense, was set ablaze by the paranoia of others.

Now that Paul was dead, the people of Russia once again rejoiced in the streets. Alexander opened the country again, amnestied large numbers of prisoners in jail and reversed his father's dismissals in the civil service and the military. He took new advisers and promised a representative government for Russia and respect for the rule of law. He punished Nikita Petrovich Panin, as he did others involved in his father's death, by rusticating him, this time for the rest of his life. Alexander's own advisers joked, but sincerely, that the new tsar had formed a Committee for Society's Salvation, to make good the evil of the past.

In fact it was a hope, and one that from a Russian point of view climaxed with Alexander's future victory over Napoleon. Uvarov would come of age trying to contribute to this 'new good Russia', as it entered the nineteenth century.

Still something in the experiences of Grand Duke Alexander, now to become Tsar Alexander I, Constantine and Nicholas, who were his brothers, their father Paul, and their future state servant Sergei Uvarov, even when they were children, prepared these Russian boys for sudden changes in the Russian political climate which would make or break their lives and the lives of others. It was the experiences of political violence. For so long Russian sovereigns did not accede to the throne but were hurled on to it, or if they were invited to step up, they stepped up after blood had been spilt. And when they got there they were torn between liberty and order. Uvarov as their loyal subject came to feel that cruel dilemma as a tension between the European culture he loved and the Russian politics he served. He has been described as 'of progressive vision but cautious disposition'.[40] But the divided loyalties within him were so much more intense and potentially tragic.

Every Russian generation, including and after Paul, learnt of European liberalism and the value of progress, but these lessons were never detached from Russia's own furious self-instruction in realpolitik. Alexander's brother Constantine, who avoided power, and the much younger Nicholas, who relished it, were perhaps exceptions. But for Tsar Paul and after him Tsar Alexander, and Alexander's servant Sergei Uvarov, the question they all eventually had to face was what they could do with their knowledge and the hope it inspired, given the condition of Russia.

2

The charm of life abroad

Where was Uvarov to place himself in the new era of Alexander I? The young tsar was neither a died-in-the-wool sybarite nor, unlike his father, 'morally abnormal'. Tutored in Enlightenment and republican values by the Swiss political reformer Frédéric-César de La Harpe, Alexander favoured reform towards a constitutional monarchy in Russia. He was ready to respond positively to the French Revolution, initiating a fifteen-year-long era, from his accession in 1801, that was open-hearted and optimistic. The first half of his reign might be compared with the freedom-loving, progressive years of glasnost and perestroika almost two hundred years later, when communism was ending. Alexander surrounded himself with liberal advisers schooled in the French Enlightenment, the so-called Secret Committee, and under their influence set about improving education, streamlining government and reforming the law. Besides the Kurakins he was advised by the Pole Adam Czartoryski, a man deeply committed to liberal social ideals, and Mikhail Speransky, who had risen from lowly birth – his surname taken from the Latin *sperans*, 'hoping', commonly given to those whose parents were unknown – to become one of the most important administrators in the empire. This was the milieu in which Uvarov perfected the formal stages of his own education. The tsar apparently noticed him at the Naryshkin salon and singled him out as a future education minister.[1]

In 1802 Napoleon's armies defeated the Second Coalition led by Britain, Austria and Russia. The last of the Revolutionary wars was over and the first of the Napoleonic wars yet to begin. Uvarov took advantage of this lull in hostilities and went to Europe. Still technically a Foreign Ministry cadet he went to Göttingen, one of the best and most prestigious universities in Europe, and studied there in 1802–3. His attendance is not confirmed by the university records, but he probably paid for private teaching, which was common practice at a university which drew many wealthy and well-connected students.[2] Russian nobles enrolled most commonly in courses in philology, political science and jurisprudence and about twenty matriculated in the four years before Russia returned to war against France in 1805.[3]

At Göttingen, the Hanoverian school of conservative professors inspired by Burke formulated their arguments against the French Revolution. The Göttingen men rejected the idea that new institutions could be created based on abstract reason and the equality of all men before the law and insisted on traditional monarchy and social hierarchy.[4] Uvarov certainly needed no persuading in this respect. But what caught his attention at the German university was rather more the emerging world of German Romanticism. Goethe told Eckermann of a current of thought that was causing 'the whole world to talk about classicism and Romanticism, which no one thought of doing 50 years ago'.[5] Romanticism was bound up with the philosophy of history, with its central idea of national progress, and the changing values and the new sense of historical possibility Romanticism brought would soon have a huge effect on emerging national cultures across central and eastern Europe. In Jena the philosopher Johann Gottlieb Fichte was already poised to give a series of lectures entitled *Reden an die deutsche Nation*, 'Appeals to the German Nation', in 1808. Historicism and Romantic nationalism would prompt Uvarov to speculate that Russia too was coming into its own as a culture with world-historical significance, and they would do so against the Burkean grain of rejecting abstraction and 'metaphysics' in politics.

One of the most interesting speakers at Göttingen was the elderly August-Ludwig Schloezer, who had taught in Moscow and was well acquainted with Russian history and conditions. He offered a course in Russian history which argued what Uvarov already believed, namely that his country was part of Europe. Moreover, Schloezer also praised Alexander as a most progressive and enlightened tsar, who would be capable of making that European character of Russia real.[6] Part of the new historicism meanwhile was the remarkable German academic revitalization of Classicism from the mid-eighteenth century. At Göttingen, Arnold Heeren taught a celebrated course in ancient history, and Christian Gottlob Heyne lectured in Classics. It was this renaissance of interest in Antiquity, which prompted the constant comparison of the Classical and Romantic worlds, that so struck Goethe. Uvarov pursued his studies in Latin and Greek for their own sake, and his vocation made a strong impression on him, as he followed the latest developments in archaeology which, having made the ancient world so vivid, had sparked the new way of thinking. Uvarov began to think of himself as a scholar building on the legacy of the great J. J. Winckelmann, who had travelled to Greece and Rome and founded the discipline that had transformed the age. But he also began to imagine transplanting Classical studies also to Russia, as part of the foundation, there too, of a new cultural era.[7] Nor finally could he leave German Oriental philology alone either, for there he absorbed the idea that the development of the modern world required a heightened awareness of the common ancient heritage, from Greece and Italy back through Egypt and Mesopotamia to India. Russia, a country poised between East and West, with a language close to Greek, seemed ideally placed to take part in the revolution also in Oriental studies. In all these ways the young student from St Petersburg became focused on the future of Russia as a late-developing nation, while on the aesthetic fringes of his thinking[8] he flirted with the Platonic aesthetic of beauty, truth and goodness, and with Winkelmann's ideal of Greek male beauty. He emerged from Göttingen with five languages to his credit – Russian, French, German, Latin and English – a spiritual-artistic conservative mindset, but a keen sense of new international political opportunity.

Part of what became the enigma of Sergei Uvarov was the enigma of the German idealism he absorbed in Göttingen. Idealism had a different identity from the Romanticism that followed it because it was still an expression of the Enlightenment belief in cosmopolitan rationality. In the German principalities like Goethe's Weimar, and at the university of Jena, where Schiller worked, anxiety generated by the violence of political upheaval in France had sparked the desire to find moral and aesthetic reasons for preferring moderation, and gradualism, to extremism, and these Immanuel Kant, and Schiller, claimed to find in the very configuration of educated human nature. Uvarov was able to place himself at the heart of that conservative yet not illiberal German philosophy that answered 1789 and 1793 and it helped him, because he knew he could never get on with the republican spokesman for the will of the people, Jean-Jacques Rousseau.[9] Schiller, at once poet, philosopher and historian, stressed that to guard against political extremism every man should make aesthetic balance his goal before he tried to improve society. It would not have been difficult for Uvarov to see this as sanction for the *ancien régime* good taste he had learnt from Mauguin, and to believe in his own moderating role as a writer and scholar. It was not how Schiller would generally be received in Russia, where he was taken as a figurehead in the struggle for liberty and equality. But the aesthetic message of German idealism was yet another form of conservatism, and Uvarov attuned himself to it. It was another way of keeping politics and art separate – that facet of Russian life that he had so appreciated at the Olenins – and he would often return to it, albeit in that mannered way of insisting on good taste, as opposed to the political directness of the sans-culottes.

From Göttingen in 1803 Uvarov returned to St Petersburg where he continued to study and work in the Foreign Ministry, but he was soon abroad again. Probably at the encouragement of Alexander Kurakin, the Ministry dispatched him in 1805 as a courier to Naples. This short visit now gave him the chance to add Italy and Italian to his list of accomplishments. In Italy the excavations at Pompeii were underway that had first drawn Winkelmann in

1755. Building on what Olenin had first encouraged in him as a St Petersburg Cadet, Uvarov not only had fresh knowledge of archaeology from his German professors but was following in the footsteps of Winkelmann and Goethe, classicizing first-hand. He read Roman history and equipped himself with a store of useful observations.

One point about Uvarov was that he seemed to have both a Classical and a Romantic soul. In Italy therefore he found he had a German Romantic yearning for the south and an inclination to dream. These tendencies would be quite inappropriate for his political career in Russia, but they weren't falsely affected. More in line with his early initiation into the brutal politics of autocratic power, however, were any lessons he might draw from Italy's contemporary upheaval to the north. He was still in residence or had only recently left when, now as emperor of the French and president of the Italian Republic, Napoleon dissolved that Republic and declared himself king in Milan in the autumn of 1805. Italian lands in Lombardy and Romagna were parcelled up for Bonaparte's relatives to govern. The event stuck in Uvarov's mind to the degree that forty years later he returned in an essay to Napoleon's invasion and intentions.

Meanwhile in St Petersburg his career progressed in his absence. In 1804 he had been promoted to Kamerjunker, a title outside the standard Table of Ranks created by Peter the Great, but designed to recognize the social standing of diplomats.[10] Now in June 1806 his appointment was announced as a secretary to the Vienna embassy. Darya Ivanovna was delighted at the post, promised by Alexander Kurakin in his capacity as ambassador-designate to Austria, and urged her son to make sure of a good salary for his pains.[11]

In the Austrian capital peace had just been settled, once again between France and Russia, after two renewed years of wasteful hostilities. Napoleon had set up a provisional administration in Warsaw and the tsar was anxious after the disaster of Austerlitz and the collapse of his Austrian ally to cut his losses. Uvarov's immediate job was to soothe Austrian apprehension at Russia's move towards the French. By way of recompense for any effort this entailed, he had the social and cultural experience of a lifetime.

Never before had he met so many powerful people who were also distinctive individuals. Since Paris had fallen into the hands of a barbarian, Vienna had become home to France's and Switzerland's most illustrious exiles. The Russian aristocracy arrived on extended visits to be present at the new right place at the right time, along with displaced Poles, Austrian dignitaries and military men and diplomats of every stripe. Vienna had become the centre of continental Europe for conservative writing, money and artistic patronage. Beethoven and Haydn were in residence; music and the arts flourished. The effect was to make Uvarov, 'a young man of fine and lively features, very slim and poised, flitting between the emblazoned salons of the archducal city and partaking of its aristocratic pleasures with infinite ease', feel he had at last found his spiritual home. He stayed for three and a half years in which time he grafted real French roots on to his upbringing. He was noted as speaking and reading excellent French, and combining 'deferential curiosity with impeccable manners and delicate, allusive speech'.[12] He was the perfect product of Russia's effort to restore the France of pre-1789 on its own soil, and now it seemed he could live again in those times with real French men and women.

He exercised an immediate attraction for the octogenarian Prince de Ligne, the aristocrat and military colossus who was familiar with European royalty and had accompanied Empress Catherine of Russia on her 1787 journey to the Crimea. De Ligne was also a writer and traveller and flatteringly invited the young Russian with his excellent literary French to edit his work. As De Ligne guided Uvarov through the transplanted drawingrooms of pre-revolutionary France, Uvarov's reflections emerged so thick and fast that he began to keep a diary.

To sketch the aged Princesse de Lorraine, Comptesse de Brionne, became another way of mourning the old, lost France:

Her arms and legs are paralysed, but her head is still entirely young. It is impossible to imagine greater beauty, more charming conversation, or better manners. Her figure is still fine and magisterial. She is the last relic of the French monarchy and an archive of the century she lived in. When I saw her, I seemed to have been transferred to that old France which no longer exists, which I so much love to study and which is still the source of our heart's delight.[13]

Madame de Stael arrived in the winter of 1807–08, and it was one of the most dazzling seasons anyone could remember. Uvarov divided his time between concerts, galleries, the theatre, balls and amateur dramatics. His acting brought him into frequent social contact with De Ligne, de Stael and the former Austrian foreign minister Ludwig Cobentzl and his wife, and together they formed a troupe to perform French plays. Both the women readily took an interest in De Ligne's 'cher petit'. de Stael took him to listen to Haydn and one Madame Rombecq often invited him to dine. He bubbled with enthusiasm to his mother: 'Yesterday there was a play put on at the house of the Countess Zamoiska. I didn't take part, but the illustrious Madame de Stael, who has been here a month, had a role.' Six days later in mid-February another letter reported that they had staged a play by Marivaux: 'Our Vienna is very good. The Carnival was brilliant. Now we do a play one a week. Yesterday Madame de Stael was in "Le Legs". Opinions were divided, but as far as I was concerned I found her performance excellent in places. Next Sunday we are going to put on "The young Henry V" in which I have a part.'[14] A Russian who impressed Uvarov in Vienna, and on whom he was flattered to make a good impression in return, was the ambassador who retired in 1806, Andrei Razumovsky. Known to posterity as Beethoven's patron, Razumovsky was also a distinguished collector of Italian art and possessed a fine collection of Correggio and Canovas. He lived in Vienna for the rest of his life.

If Uvarov was inspired anew by Razumovsky to start his own collections, Razumovsky set a strange and yet not uncommon example to a young man in his country's service. Though happy to serve his government from afar he never wished to return to Russia. He resembled Semyon Vorontsov, the Russian ambassador to London who rather than return at the end of his assignment stayed in England for the remaining forty-seven years of his life. In 1807 Andrei Kirillovich Razumovsky was most reluctantly leaving office and had decided to stay on to enjoy the city and his palace at leisure. Possibly because he incurred foreign criticism for his politically insensitive sybaritism, Uvarov never paid him tribute in print.[15]

Uvarov himself created an ambivalent impression in his early diplomatic days. It was true he was immediately impressive, but he also left his critics unsure of his real talent and future. Madame de Stael, reading his poetry, thought him superficial. She told him to curb his desire for glory, remarking that 'your talent is worth more than your successes'.[16] What he possessed, now to his advantage, now to his detriment, was a strong sense of his own – and often by implication Russian – superiority. It made him highly critical of his Austrian surroundings. A passage he wrote in his diary, indeed, seemed to turn the tables on any Western critics of Razumovsky and his class:

> The law of primogeniture, by virtue of which practically all wealth is passed on [in Austria] to the eldest son of the family, maintains the inviolability of the great estates. ... But the way these rich men use their wealth is hard to believe. They rarely hold open house, and usually lead a closeted life, vegetating in their huge palaces, smoking and drinking amongst themselves. ... The main reason for this is poor education; everything which elevates and feeds the interests of the spirit is alien to them; they scorn literature and education and indulge their passions for horses and for buying women without restraint. The structure of government is such that they play no part in the spiritual development of society. The aristocracy holds the government in contempt for its obvious weakness whilst the ordinary people are contemptuous of an aristocracy which instead of striving to distinguish itself by its nobility and talents finds pleasure only in the dark sins which have muddied it.[17]

This striking passage shows how education would always bring out Uvarov's seriousness and public commitment. He believed in the cultural responsibility of the educated classes to determine the quality of society, and if he was in Europe to see how this responsibility was being exercised he could say he was already disappointed. Russia might do better. But it is also a passage of almost unconscious Russian cultural self-defence, turning current Western terms of criticism of the Russian nobility back on a Western country. It sounds just like Reinbeck, or, counter-Reinbeck: a patriotic counter-attack against the negative portrait of the Russian nobility that the German who had once been a tutor to a 'Herr Uvarov' had just published in Leipzig. By 'almost unconscious' I mean that we cannot be aware of how nationally self-conscious Uvarov was in writing it. Nor do we know whether he knew the Reinbeck travelogue or the Reinbeck plays with a noble Russian setting – only that those plays were set in households he knew well and that the publication year for the crucial second volume of the *Cursory Remarks on a Journey* was the same as the one in which Uvarov was presently writing.[18] Still the coincidence of the terms of critique is striking. As for the last metaphor, applied to the perceivedly degenerate Austrian aristocracy despised by the 'ordinary people', one can't but remember the last chapter of Radishchev's *Journey*, where the moral mud in Russia had been churned by serfdom. Uvarov could redeem the official image of Russia by finding moral turpitude elsewhere. Moreover, if he was a diplomat by profession, his private thoughts confided to his notebook were already synonymous with what the job of promoting Russian prestige abroad required.

It's striking that Uvarov defended the Russian version of the nobility even as the obsolescent ways of the aristocracy were being widely ridiculed in post-revolutionary Europe. Schiller, for instance, in his *On the Aesthetic Education of Man* (1795) had lamented,

> The cultivated classes, on the other hand, offer the even more repugnant spectacle of lethargy, and of a depravation of character which offends the more because culture itself is its source. I no longer recall which of the ancient or modern philosophers it was who remarked that the nobler a thing is, the more repulsive it is when it decays; but we shall find that this is no less true in the moral sphere. The child of Nature, when he breaks loose, turns into a madman; the creature of civilisation into a knave. That of the mind, which is the not altogether groundless boast of our refined classes, has had on the whole so little of an ennobling influence on feeling and character that it has tended rather to bolster up depravity by providing it with the support of precepts. ... In the very bosom of the most exquisitely developed social life egotism has founded its system.[19]

Thomas Paine, in *The Rights of Man* (1791), declared that 'aristocracy ... whether we view it before or behind, or sideways, or any way else, domestically or publicly, it is still a monster'.[20] Uvarov aged twenty wanted to salvage a good legacy from the ancien regime.

He was deciding who he was in terms of his class and his country. He was looking in Vienna for both positive and negative models of what could unfold from the privilege of high birth, and, indeed, of being Russian. That the Duke of Esterhazy made available none of his wealth to the state struck the young kamerjunker from St Petersburg as wrong, whereas Count Karl Harrach, who became a doctor and treated the poor free of charge, was admirable.

In short Uvarov's Vienna notebook was partly nervous patriotism, sparked by Western criticism of the luxury-obsessed Russian ruling class, and partly the start of what would be the lifelong construction of a morally more positive image for Russia. This was a country that, he envisaged, would retain its nobility, adjutants to the autocracy, and by doing so would build for the social good. With a model of national instruction incorporating the gradualism and traditionalism of Burke and the German Idealist vision of intense individual self-development, Uvarov would try to produce an educated class at once apolitical and committed to serving Russia. Apolitical would mean not indulging in revolution. The reward for that commitment would be the freedom to enjoy the fruits of scientific progress. Russia would flourish that way and Uvarov would personally show how. He would, while retaining the style and privileges of an old-style nobleman, become a leading member of the new educated class.

In Vienna he encountered two men with whom in private he could share his political ideas. They were the fifty-year-old Heinrich Friedrich Karl, Baron vom und zum Stein and the Corsican exile Carlo Andrea Pozzo di Borgo. Pozzo had grown up with Napoleon, while Stein, a Prussian aristocrat, was one of the best products of Göttingen in the 1770s and an ardent social and educational reformer. These men struck Uvarov as 'spiritual aristocrats', a crucial transitory term. It was not because of the circumstances of their birth but by virtue of their good characters that he admired them. They were people of enormous presence, determination and moral fibre. Moreover, both were wholly committed to the overthrow of Napoleon. Uvarov called them 'two men of the elite', and returned to them in an essay many years later.

Pozzo was a diplomat who mainly served the Russian court after he went into exile. From relatively humble circumstances he impressed Uvarov with his judgement and detachment, which he coupled with absolute commitment to his cause. No man made Uvarov more aware of the politics of his day than Pozzo when he urged him to study Napoleon as a unique phenomenon. He pressed Uvarov to study the nature of power and recommended Machiavelli's *Discorsi*. In response, Uvarov observed that Pozzo was possessed by 'a single passion, wholly political and wholly abstract', and was himself 'a man of power'. Together Pozzo and the young Uvarov considered the position of Europe as being at a political watershed. They were concerned where the future lay, and Pozzo particularly swayed the young Russian's thoughts on the political import of the Classical model. Pozzo told Uvarov that for the continent of Europe there were only two great political institutions from which to learn, the Roman Empire and the French monarchy:

> He used to tell me there were only two forms of government in history which warranted study, the Roman Empire and the French monarchy. The new forms of government are not yet developed, and their future depends on the events which are taking place now.[21]

Pozzo said the aristocracy was finished as a hereditary ruling class and that the only answer now was benevolent despotism under a strong monarch. He suggested that for Europe to maintain strong, positive government without concessions to democracy Napoleonic tyranny should be replaced by a Franco-Russian protectorate. Shades of an international protection policy were still present in Uvarov's thinking thirty years later.

But it was through that more sentimental part of himself, that side of him susceptible to German idealism, that Uvarov felt the gentler attraction of Freiherr vom Stein. Together he and Stein mused on the development of ideal, inwardly harmonious men in a mould that would ease the path of political change. Stein conceived of a restored Prussia which while not sacrificing political authority would promote liberal education for all men regardless of origin and give those men – men at least – a voice in government. Uvarov took Stein's educational ideals to heart, and though they were of different nationality and generation, he cherished a bond based on their shared love of Antiquity and Weimar Classicism. When he recalled Stein's theories in later years, Uvarov stressed their utopian aspect and sought to correct the widespread mistaken impression that Stein had been wholly liberal. He pointed out from the vantage point of middle age that Stein's philosophy relied on uncommonly talented men, 'aristocrats of the spirit', if it was to cohere. But as a young man he believed Stein's ideas were workable and it was on the coat-tails of Stein's dreams that he became a liberal reformer in Russian education under Alexander.[22]

Loving both Stein and Pozzo, drawn to liberalism and conservatism simultaneously, Uvarov was in fact a creature of 'zwei Seelen', sharing that difficult condition of having two souls with Goethe's Faust. The new intellectual horizons attracted him, and he was committed to opening up education to a wider social constituency, but political republicanism repelled him. His political ambivalence meant that he could not properly make up his mind, neither about de Stael nor about the brothers Friedrich and August Wilhelm Schlegel, resident in Vienna, because all of them embroiled him in new contradictions over where culture and sensibility were headed in the post-revolutionary age.

de Stael was evidently dangerous to a man of his political views. Her father Jacques Necker as France's Minister of Finance had helped bankroll the American Revolution. He had believed that common people had a right to interest themselves in their country's spending. When Louis XVI dismissed him, that action was said to have prompted such popular outrage that it led to the storming of the Bastille. 'I heard that one evening [de Stael] proved that good taste was a quality worthy of scorn ... that anarchy is only destructive in its results; that France is trying to establish a constitution in the English spirit. ... In these utterances one recognizes the daughter of Monsieur Necker and the spirit of the political club whose python she was ... in the eyes of the Viennese [her father] was not very different from Danton and Robespierre.' He eventually decided 'to enjoy the astonishing breath of her mind, the brilliant impulses of her imagination, and not interrupt her with rational thoughts'.[23]

Part of de Stael's brilliance was undoubtedly to grasp the new cultural spirit in Europe that accompanied political upheaval. Suddenly the feelings of individuals mattered, and were reflected in a new kind of literature. Her insights overlapped with those of the Schlegel brothers, and she learnt from them. Through contrasting definitions of Antiquity and modernity, the Schlegels had analysed the nature of the new sensibility of self-conscious individuals, and the effect was to establish literature, as a reflection of that self-consciousness, as no longer a pleasant diversion for the upper classes but a vital truth-seeking tool on a par with philosophy. August Wilhem Schlegel, whose groundbreaking Berlin lectures of 1801–04 were published in a Viennese journal in 1808, favoured the vigour of Shakespeare and Calderón, and attacked the artificiality of French neoclassicism. He emphasized the genius of the individual artist: the need for the creative soul to go beyond rules. He conceived of literature in such a way, organically, that creative minds the world over were intuiting the truth of nature and humanity's place in nature as part of an ongoing process of self-knowledge. The effect was to dynamize the concept of humanity as a creative force.[24]

As an interpreter in our own time writes, in *De la Littérature considérée dans ses rapports avec les institutions sociales* (1800) 'what interests [de Stael] is modern conscience, it's the link between actions and the life of sentiment, the difficult interior debates, the complexity proper to conflicts which arise between the aspirations of the individual and social constraints'.[25] In her view literature, and again it was world literature that was meant, was progressing as human thought was progressing in search of new rules of life. The new kind of literary work had the power to present to the reader conflicts in which he or she could find reflected their own. Under the influence of Rousseau, de Stael wrote not only about conscience but also about personal pain. Her expectations of literature were deeply serious, and she shared them with her sometime lover and long-term admirer August Wilhelm Schlegel. All three temporary residents in Vienna were extraordinary living intellectual sources. Uvarov borrowed without acknowledgement the Schlegels' sense of the Classical (Southern) and Romantic (Northern) spirits vying and combining to give birth to a vital new culture in the present day. Russian power would be drawn from this elementary dialectic in due course. More immediately Friedrich Schlegel's Orientalist masterpiece *On the Language and Wisdom of the Indians* (1808) helped stimulate the vital interest in the East that Uvarov would take back to Russia.[26]

The difficulty for us is to find that Uvarov sneered at these geniuses personally. As would famously be said of him, he didn't have the heart to go with his mind.[27] de Stael may even have been in love with him briefly, and he didn't behave well. He pretended to comfort her in her much more serious but unhappy love affair with Maurice O'Donnell, an Austrian officer whom she had met in Italy, but he may have deliberately befriended O'Donnell to know more about de Stael. She generously read Uvarov's French poetry and praised his talent. She showed him affection and offered him every help in his pursuit of a literary career and became emotionally dependent. He disappointed her.

> My dear Uvarov, I will not judge you, you are a spoilt child, but sometimes a child of genius. Between you and me there is too great a difference in age for any kind of permanence in friendship, but my interest in you is permanent. Don't forget this evening's dinner. I left Pozzo [di Borgo] when I received your note; every word left out caused me pain.

After she left Vienna Uvarov betrayed her further. He spread gossip about her failure with O'Donnell, and other romantic intrigues. She finally denounced him as a 'Frenchified Russian capable of perfidious falsehoods'[28] and a 'young tartar fop'.[29]

There were other social and erotic intrigues Uvarov was involved in in Vienna. He took Varfolomei Bogolyubov, a colleague from the embassy who was an adopted son of Kurakin, into his confidence, but was later embarrassed by their connection. Bogolyubov became well-known as a sleight-of-hand gossip and social climber, flighty and unreliable.[30] Meanwhile he had another close female acquaintance in the city, Madame Rombecq, who acted as a curious foil to his relationship with de Stael; it was almost as if he set up this alternative relationship as the standard by which he really wanted to be judged. Widely known for an emotional style of behaviour, La Rombecq treated Sergei with motherly intensity and unique vulgarity and brought out his effeminacy.

But in her company – was it because her politics were impeccable since she was well-known for espousing the emigré cause and particularly that of the Tsar? – Uvarov felt happy and relaxed. Their open liaison set everyone talking, but he seems not to have cared, an uncharacteristic turn for a prudent young man. In his diary Uvarov wrote a glowing account of Rombecq's naturalness, originality and freedom of manners, saying how good, generous, soft-hearted and even reasonable she was. He knew her fondness for and loyalty to Russia approached fervour, so he was free to admire her wit. The contrast was striking after his censure of de Stael. Just as his diary entry shifted Reinbeck's criticisms of the Russian nobility to his own vis-à-vis Austria, so the Rombecq affair was also an uncanny mirror image, as if made to recast every one of de Stael's criticisms of himself in a positive light. It was almost as if he wanted to say, this is how we are, in our politics and our personal lives, we Russians, and we are proud of it.[31]

Uvarov by his early twenties was then a genuine educational reformist, inspired by his contacts with liberal German thinking, at the same time as he was a political reactionary in a thoroughly Russian mould. With his smooth and modish exterior, he looked the Romantic part, but his Russian loyalties bound him to reject the natural law that de Stael would have talked about[32] and the Romantic individualism of A. W. Schlegel. The idea of natural law that was the great legacy of Montesquieu, and which we saw at the outset of this story had inspired Empress Catherine, nevertheless continued to be unacceptable in Russia. Though he privately estimated Montesquieu as important and kept his works in his library, such human freedoms as underpinned the United States Declaration of Independence in 1776 and the French Declaration of Rights in 1789 Uvarov publicly turned his back on. As we have already noted, Uvarov was also not an admirer of Rousseau, the greatest revolutionary influence on the culture of sensibility with or without the political revolution of 1789. Yet, in truth, he couldn't get them out of his head, so much he knew the times were changing.

3

Marriage and a Russian career

Napoleon entered Vienna, and Uvarov returned to Russia in the autumn of 1809. He went straight to visit his mother, who lived in the countryside, where she had finally retired. He wanted to rest for a few months as he expected that he would be dispatched to the Paris embassy. But Darya Ivanovna died early in 1810, and the tsar prevaricated over Kurakin's request to have Uvarov transferred to his office. Both were powerful blows.[1] His mother died young and Sergei had been close to her. She had nourished his social competitiveness from an early age and he seems to have inherited her pronounced sensuality. Both mother and son had tales of sexual intrigue told about them in their lives.[2] Yet the greatest blow was financial. Sergei and Fyodor took over the burden of Darya's mortgaged property and heavy debts, and, although the tsar eventually relented, Uvarov could no longer contemplate going abroad. His job in Paris went to a young Baltic German named Karl Nesselrode, who went on to become Alexander I's foreign minister.[3] Uvarov had planned to visit Goethe in Weimar on his way to France, but that plan to enact one of the great literary pilgrimages of the age also had to be abandoned. He was made to realize that despite myriad personal talents a man who came from an unorthodox, impoverished family was vulnerable.

Back in Russia, some people would, in fact, soon see vulnerability as the keynote of his reputation. The always moody, always perspicacious Vigel' told a strange story about how Uvarov kept a portrait of his father Sen'ka playing the bandore on the wall of his office, but yet denied his identity:

> During my brief acquaintance with Uvarov I was surprised to see a picture or a portrait hanging on the wall of his office. It depicted a man about 35, good looking, in simple Russian dress and with a bandore in his hands, but clean shaven and with short hair. In reply to my immodest question he replied drily: 'Oh that's not a real person.' But I found this unreal person remarkably resembled his younger brother Fyodor Semyonovich.[4]

Uvarov could be made to cringe at the reminder of his paternal background. And so he had double reason, financial and social, to better himself through marriage. He proposed to Catherine Razumovsky, elder daughter of the current Minister of Enlightenment Alexei Kirillovich Razumovsky, niece of the former Vienna ambassador Andrei, halfway through 1810, and they were married in September.

It was characteristic of Uvarov already to be more unsure of himself than he need have been. His social and intellectual contemporaries found him exceptionally impressive. A dashing figure, he was not only socially poised, but also scholarly, industrious and had enormous talent and drive, qualities none of which, it was said, were common in Russia. Among those who knew him, his gifts seemed to represent a new Russian epoch, when European learning would be brought home and made to yield fruit on Russian soil. Indeed there was a feeling he alone might alter the Western image of Russia as an intellectual backwater. Alexander Turgenev, who had been abroad himself, also for a time in Göttingen, fell over himself with praise for Uvarov:

> He is a fine chap and a fine poet. His French verse is often as good as Delille's, sometimes it is even better; on top of that he knows German literature so well that he makes me feel ashamed, even in history ... I have come to like [him] very much for his talents and for his splendid education ... You will find him a fine and interesting acquaintance. He loves me and loves German literature and he knows it well.[5]

Alexander Turgenev was a rising liberal[6] figure of the same age and background as Uvarov; together with his brother Nikolai Turgenev, he was interested without reservation in Romantic ideas. He presumed Uvarov was too. In fact Uvarov was one of the very few young men in the Russia of his day who could separate a progressive intellectual outlook from Western-inspired political liberalism. Yet, Turgenev's confusion was understandable, because Uvarov positively acted the Romantic part. In St Petersburg he put into circulation the graceful, world-weary French poems he had been writing since his teens: 'I had everything, now all is gone' and 'My Fate'. He took up the classic theme of whom the gods favoured in another creation, 'On the Advantage of Dying Young', and preciously mourned his youth in 'I have left the home of my fathers'. He also worked in German, claiming to compose 'in the manner of Goethe':

> Dreams of youth, colours of morning, sounds of the lyre:
> Are you gone, silent for ever?
> Life is grave, the future is dark,
> Man must struggle with hostile powers:
> Mother nature creates and destroys eternally.

Turgenev was present when Uvarov penned these lines with the arch-Romantic title 'Longing'. They were sitting in a carriage one Sunday on their way to the Olenins in the country. 'Think of it', Turgenev wrote afterwards, 'a Russian Kammerjunker writing German poetry!'[7]

Vigel' said the success went to his head:

> He was a clever boy by nature, notably quick in his studies, of extraordinary comely appearance, who could write and speak French prose and verse just like a Frenchman; everyone praised him, everyone wondered at him and all that made his head spin.[8]

As to his hasty and profitable marriage, Alexander Yaklovich Bulgakov, privy to the Uvarovs' social circle, was sympathetic. He commented to his brother:

> It's a fine thing and will sort out the affairs of these good lads. I don't think that Serge is marrying for love, nor even out of inclination; for he has never spoken to us of the young woman; I'm sure that he wanted to sacrifice himself for his mother and his brother. They say she's a very nice girl all the same.[9]

Catherine was more than that. She was a woman of excellent family,[10] and she made her husband's fortune. Uvarov received in addition to a wife a substantial dowry and 6,000 serfs. Even better, Andrei Razumovsky was her uncle, and her father, Alexei Kirilovich Razumovsky, held the highest educational post in the land.[11] She loved Uvarov, whom she had met four years earlier, as a man 'in all things perfection' and could not stop talking about him in the weeks before her marriage, but Vigel' couldn't resist twisting the knife, observing how plain she was, as well as being five years older.[12] Whatever Sergei's own feelings, whatever even his sexuality – for he enjoyed many a gay fling – they were married for thirty-nine years and had four children who brought them happiness. Sergei survived Catherine by six years and when she died in 1849 he felt bereft.

Homosexuality was not seen as a vice at the time and indeed Uvarov saw it as a mark of superiority, something he had in common with Winckelmann and Bouterwek. In his introduction to his translations of *The Greek Anthology* with poet Batyushkov, he referred to it as 'the shameful sin to which the Greeks gave their name' but says it generated not only crude expressions but great beauty and tenderness and was part of a more vital and simple sensibility 'ou l'amour sans pudeur n'est pas sans innocence!'[13] Shameless love is not without its own innocence. If any vice was conspicuous in Uvarov it was rather more ambition. His first published essay, hastily finished in 1810, even while his marriage was being arranged, was dedicated to his father-in-law, the Minister of Education. The genial Alexander Turgenev, without drawing any conclusion, merely noted that having begun as a grand scholarly project, this essay, 'Project for an Asiatic Academy' became shorter and more practical in the writing.[14] But when in the same December as his wedding took place Sergei's appointment was announced as Superintendent of the Petersburg Educational District under Razumovsky's Ministry, his formidable rise through marriage could not be ignored. His promotion made him one of the six top men in education in the country, in charge of public instruction and censorship for the capital and the surrounding area, and he received the rank of real state counsellor, the equivalent of major-general in the army. At the same time, the St Petersburg Academy of Sciences, though almost defunct, made him its youngest member.

Against that faint accusation of haste and practicality Uvarov at twenty-four might have said in his defence that he always wanted to make a reputation as a scholar, but that there were so many other calls on his time when he returned to Russia, not least the emergency of the family finances, that he had to take a short cut. Copies of his essay, written in French, were immediately sent abroad to foreign scholars, in the hope that it mattered. But there was now this suspicion that his other aim in life was glory, the vice of which de Stael had accused him.[15]

Always, it seemed, he had a double motive, leaving the historian divided in how to assess his life and work. In fact *Project* was a serious, positive and indeed important work in which Uvarov laid the foundation for Oriental studies in Russia and made possible that passion for the East which for example inspired some of Pushkin's most famous work in the 1820s.[16] He introduced to Russia the immense curiosity about the Eastern roots of Western culture which Friedrich Schlegel's work in philology had stimulated in Europe. At the same time he drew Russian attention to Herder's work of three decades earlier on the growth of languages and cultures. Uvarov was hoping both to further scholarship for its own sake and to enhance Russian prestige. As he put it to Goethe when he sent him a copy: 'It is time Russia took part in the great ferment of ideas and built its culture on the firm ground of the East.'[17] Of that national move into the nineteenth century he was himself to be the embodiment.

Project set out plans for an academy curriculum and the staff to teach it, but it also had admirable philosophical breadth, embracing the total state of contemporary culture and anticipating the tone of much nineteenth-century Russian literary comment on the West. Uvarov declared that Europe was in decay while Russia was just beginning, uncertain of the way ahead but with rich resources. Oriental studies pointed to the means of cultural renewal, and Russia, poised between East and West, seemed uniquely placed to develop them on the world's behalf. Its strength was the direct connection between the Russian and Greek languages. The notion that Russia could rejuvenate the West was an idea Uvarov had gleaned from his Göttingen professors.

They had stressed Russia's closeness to the East through Byzantium. He now stated that advantage clearly in his essay:

Russia has an infinite advantage over the rest of Europe. She can take Greek literature as the foundation of her national literature, and found a wholly original school. She is bound to bind herself to imitating neither German literature nor the French spirit, nor Latin learning. A deeper study of Greek will open an inexhaustible source of new ideas and fertile images for Russia. These will give to history, to philosophy, to poetry, the purest forms closest to the true models. The Greek language is anyway linked with the religion of the Russians and with Slavonic literature which seems to have taken shape according to it ... and Byzantine history has more than one motif of interest for the Russians.[18]

The political implications of *Project* were timely, and Bonaparte called for a report on it. As well as Germany, France and England had done extensive Oriental research in the last fifty years. The German interest was a purely scholarly phenomenon, but France and England had political interests in the East, and under Catherine Russia had acquired ambitions to rival them, which gave Uvarov his national-political cue for expanding Oriental scholarship in Russia.[19] Recent territorial gains from Turkey and Persia had extended the Russian Empire down to the Black Sea and east of it to the Caspian. The whole of the Caucasus was now under the tsar, Georgia having been annexed by Paul I. Beyond these lands lay the possibility of India, now under British control, and China, which Petersburg was also pursuing trade relations with. All these enterprises required better knowledge of the Eastern languages and cultures.[20]

Uvarov's essay was, however, devoted to no one purpose: not scholarship, not Empire-building, not philosophical speculation and not political opportunism. Rather, its form and message suggested that Uvarov was looking at a number of ways in which he might press his erudition into national service and that he believed he had discovered a common Oriental heritage. *Project* in that sense was written to reconcile his European learning with his Russian duties. Blending foreign learning with Russian hopes, it worked on three levels, the ideological, the practical and the personal, and established the mould in which Uvarov would couch his thoughts on education, history and society for the next ten years.

It would always be a balancing act. As Uvarov's first attempt to assemble foreign ideas in a pattern beneficial to Russia, *Project* was essentially a defence of the pre-Revolutionary order, but it had so many inconsistencies that those who read it seriously foresaw disaster ahead for the author. Uvarov strove to keep in balance the order and certainty of the old world, and yet not to be closed to the intellectual adventures of the new, and the result was an unsatisfying hedging of his bets. Under the heading of 'romanesque' thinking, he denounced all that he found politically unsound about Romanticism for the arrogance of its sweeping speculations and called for a return to the authority of the church:

> a metaphysics which supposes facts, and pretends to dissect the most mysterious operations of human understanding will never satisfy the human spirit. All good minds have long been in revolt against this system at once arid and romanesque which reason rejects and which does not seduce the imagination. They have seen at each step in the history of man, traces of a better state, and the evidence of the degeneration of the human race.[21]

Yet – and here was the core of his ambiguity – the very form in which Uvarov presented his argument for tradition rested on the new belief in historicism, the idea that progress was governed by an inner principle of growth, manifesting itself through time. Like a German philosopher measuring the distance between the Classical and the Romantic spirit, he depicted the human race as having moved farther away in time from its divine origins since Antiquity. In line with historicism he extracted from the plotting of these two extreme points, ancient and modern, a pattern for contemporary self-improvement. He believed the ancient tradition, born in the East, mediated through Greece and Rome and carried into modern times by Christianity, would help humanity return to a better existence. He placed his faith in a most modern sense in organic Progress.

Two of his keenest readers objected strongly. The first was the resident Sardinian ambassador in St Petersburg, a formidable critical genius deeply opposed to the free spirit of the *philosophes*, Joseph de Maistre. De Maistre was an active political force in Alexander's Russia, sceptical of all claims of reason and progress, and a brilliant and mischievous encourager of darkness. He claimed to be the only man in the city to have read Uvarov's essay properly and he pounced on its contradictions. Uvarov was courting the very modern, secular, way of thinking he wanted to attack, de Maistre exclaimed. He was rehearsing the idea that history was the progress of the human spirit, which was quite wrong. He should get away from any idea of 'progress' or 'becoming'. 'Man always has the same mind, though it is put to new uses' he declared.

> I admire and I cherish the courage which has made you raise your head above the age in which you live, but, let it be said with the same frankness, your feet are still fairly deeply stuck in that tenacious mud. Believe me,

make a big leap into the age of vigour and draw yourself completely away from there, otherwise you will be loved neither by the Exegetists [German scholars like Herder who reinterpreted the Bible] nor by us. You are in the position of Hercules *in bivio*; make up your mind and keep straight.[22]

Uvarov's reply to de Maistre no longer exists, but it was evidently unyielding and accused the Sardinian envoy of partiality because of his Catholicism. From de Maistre in return came a celebrated blast against German thinking as 'religious sansculottism': Germany had witnessed in philosophy as much of a revolution as France had in politics, and both were detrimental. De Maistre was trying to hold Uvarov back from the nineteenth century, but Uvarov was already halfway there, *in bivio*, where he would stay for the rest of his life, neither a liberal nor a reactionary, but trying to reconcile autocracy and progress.[23]

In hindsight *Project* is a fascinating illustration of what it would cost a 'frenchified' Russian conservative of the eighteenth century to move into the nineteenth, when, if he wanted to retain an open spirit, he would have to widen his vision, and exchange his pleasure in aesthetic and social detail for the broad sweep of moral enthusiasm and a concern with the happiness of the majority. It was a move Uvarov never made, a price he refused to pay, though he could see the necessity of it, and spent the rest of his life talking about preparations to decamp.

Uvarov's other critic, the poet Zhukovsky, took a different tack. After himself translating *Project* into Russian and publishing it in 1811, he wrote to Alexander Turgenev complaining that it showed a fundamental lack of interest in Russia. It was written in French and its tone was too elevated and its content too far removed from ordinary Russian life:

Evidently [Uvarov] shares with many people an unhappy prejudice against all things Russian and is more inclined to be unoriginal in French than to lower his talent to Russian and be an outstanding Russian writer ... I am very far from the crude ecstasies of a Glinka; but what will become of our poor motherland if all of us without exception hold her in contempt and take pleasure only in what is not ours? ... As far as the actual project is concerned, it does honour to its creator, but it can hardly be very useful in Russia. If we already had a high standard of education then I think perhaps we could undertake a study of Asiatic literature with warm interest and genuine profit, but where is our education and scholarship? ... I am virtually certain that if this academy were founded it would be no more than an empty name and that Asiatic literature cannot be attractive to a people which does not yet have a literature of its own, has only a very superficial knowledge of French literature and no idea of Ancient, English or German literature.[24]

It struck Zhukovsky that Uvarov had no attachment to Russia as such. His *patrie* might have been anywhere. Zhukovsky raised the possibility of a Russian who though he was a leading member of the ruling class, felt cold and contemptuous towards his native country. He wondered what kind of Russia would result if such a man forced unattractive, hollow institutions upon an unreceptive people whose sincere desire for self-improvement was frustrated or uncatered for.[25]

Beyond the immediate criticisms of both de Maistre and Zhukovsky, Uvarov also held a fundamental belief which set him against the popular path the nineteenth century was taking. We should note it here for the degree to which it was both old-fashioned and sincerely held. He believed that humanity had fallen from grace, that the French Revolution instantiated that sin against divine order, and that modern times were burdened with the task of reconstruction after 'the bloody excesses committed in the name of the human spirit'.[26] The notion of corruption was as important in his thinking as it was in Rousseau's, and Uvarov felt the opposite to Rousseau, namely that traditional institutions were sacred and the human heart wanting. Combining Christian faith with Platonism he wrote in *Project* of the pure noumenal idea corrupted in the phenomenal world and over the passage of time. He was convinced humanity had fallen from perfection but that great and rare minds, of which his own was one, could begin the re-ascent towards true perception. In any future age threatened with liberty, equality and fraternity he would act as a Platonic Guardian.

The modern age threatened the eclipse of almost everything Uvarov valued: genius,[27] political order, intellectual vigour and respect for deep-seated traditions. It was sapped by inwardness, analysis and populism. In an echo of Gibbon he wrote persuasively that knowledge was being dispersed too widely to support either brilliance or political stability. And yet he was part of that very movement forwards, through a vision of education.

In Russia he would try to create institutions which would transcend the fragilities of European liberalism. Meanwhile for himself he would seek solace in – with very rare exceptions – anything but contemporary culture. He would say, even as Russian poetry entered its first Golden Age, that nowhere else could he meet the rigour, the harmony and the abundance he found in Oriental poetry – that nowhere else could he enjoy in the poetic word such a sensuous immediacy.[28] It was one more tension between his work and his life – one more contradiction – that Russia's emerging literature of social engagement and perhaps also the Russian language it was written in did not interest him.

4

Emancipation or isolation?

Uvarov had been in office ten months as educational superintendent for the St Petersburg district when he submitted proposals to reform gymnasium education in the city. A Classicist himself, he wanted above all to introduce Latin and Greek into the secondary school curriculum. The general aim was to increase scholarly depth and discipline at pre-university level, so he banished from the classroom those philosophical and politico-economic subjects he thought better suited to university teaching, and pared down the number of courses to a core of languages and history. To make these changes effective he projected a more or less simultaneous reorganization of the Pedagogical Institute to improve teacher training. The plans of 1811 laid the foundation for his future work in education.[1]

His approach was both idealistic and practical, and the combination would serve him well over the next thirty years. It was coupled with ideological tact, as he underpinned the liberal curriculum with across-the-board teaching of the Russian language and of Russian Orthodoxy, to please the conservatives. As he realized, his position was difficult. Returning from Europe where he had been praised for his intellect, he found himself serving a society which hardly valued learning for its own sake. Education, though it had begun as a priority area for reform in Alexander's reign, was now ruled over by Uvarov's most unenlightened father-in-law, under the sway of Maistre. The French-speaking Savoyard's 'Cinq lettres sur l'education publique en Russie à M. le Comte Razoumovsky' had condemned freethinking and republican ideals and told the authorities that the spread of knowledge was dangerous to stability in Russia. To give education to the non-noble classes was asking for revolution. Against this policy brochure published in 1810 Uvarov had pitched his own recommendations.[2]

Gentry conservativism and the drain on resources from continued campaigns against Napoleon had hindered educational reform for the past six years, not to mention this latest attempt to frighten an impressionable sovereign. Plans drawn up in 1803–04 by Alexander's Western-inspired liberal advisers, and which potentially opened up all levels of instruction on merit, had not been realized. Mikhail Speransky, often regarded as the father of liberalism in Russia, had been a leading architect of those plans and Uvarov was very much in sympathy with the state secretary's Classicism and pursuit of enlightened monarchy.[3] But even the most moderate openness to the West had begun to run into opposition after 1805, when Russia's defeat at Austerlitz suggested that Alexander didn't have a firm enough hand abroad. So Uvarov trod carefully, first by correcting unworkable aspects of the previous plan, such as an overlarge curriculum, and meanwhile increasing patriotic instruction. He knew if he could satisfy the demands of religion and official patriotism he would be free to increase the quality and extent of public instruction, and he presented plans which were finely balanced to that end.

To put Classics at the centre of modern Russian education was the tool by which he hoped to transplant to Russia the new educational humanism he had encountered in Europe. Since Vienna he had remained in contact with Stein and been in correspondence with Stein's colleague in education, Wilhelm von Humboldt, and these German Idealists, friends and contemporaries of Goethe and Schiller, continued to inspire him. From 1808-10 Humboldt had been director of education and culture in the Prussian Interior Ministry when he helped found the University of Berlin. Wilhelm von Humboldt was an advocate of the minimal state guaranteeing legal freedom to individuals and the rights of property. In education he believed in encouraging a cultural sense of nationality, while the crux of his plan for Prussia was to innoculate it with the Greek spirit. Like Stein he believed education should not be limited by class, censorship should be moderate, and that the best means to build up education was the humanistic, secular gymnasium.[4]

Uvarov believed that the study of Antiquity was thoroughly virtuous, in a way that could not fail to be accepted in Russia, because it brought the twin rewards of wisdom and political obedience. He was always careful to show the political advantages of what he was advocating. Classics taught moderation, responsibility and 'good taste', and might therefore be freely available for educational purposes in an autocratic state.[5] The ideal of taste was crucial to the balancing act Uvarov envisaged for himself and his country. It married the aesthetic idealism of Schiller, itself a balancing act between French liberatarianism and despotic German caution, and Uvarov's own most cherished experiences of enlightened Russian life in the salon of the Olenins. It persuaded him that the growth of an educated populace need not threaten public order. Moreover, he was uniquely poised, with his own education and background, to explain how. 'Ce serait à la fois donner un sage emploi à l'agitation des esprits, et rendre à la civilisation européene l'important service de déterminer les bases de sa généalogie.' ('It would at the same time put to good employ the agitation of minds and hearts and render to European civilization the important service of determining the bases of its genealogy.')[6]

Not a few months passed, however, and Uvarov's first flight of optimism was dashed. By the beginning of 1812 the war, once again against Napoleon, had taken a new turn and now overrode all other considerations. Mikhail Speransky was banished in a court conspiracy against his liberal influence on the tsar.[7] Now the short distance between reform and reaction was also to become the keynote of Uvarov's experience in Russian office. Overnight the scope for the kind of subtle argument he had advanced in *Project* vanished. Torn between political wrangling and military preparations, a Russia seized by defensive chauvinism was now in no mood for enlightened reforms drawn up by a young man who had been educated abroad and was in many ways a foreigner.

Over the next eighteen months therefore Uvarov retreated a little from public life (as, indeed, he had already anticipated in *Project*) and took pleasure in the company of liked-minded friends, mainly foreign scholars living in Russia who, though far from immune, were at least less subject to autocratic whim in the continuing practice of their professional lives. In the first rank stood Professor Friedrich Graefe, an eminent German Classicist with whom Uvarov had taken Greek lessons after his return from Vienna. Graefe was a disciple of Wilhelm von Humboldt's friend, Gottfried Hermann, and he taught Greek at the St Petersburg gymnasium. Uvarov gave three evenings a week to Greek and remained Graefe's pupil for fifteen years. He also put money at Graefe's disposal to buy students the texts they needed. Another member of their circle of enthusiasts for Greek was the Spanish ambassador in St Petersburg, Don Benito Pardo de Figeroa.[8]

Another contact was Christian Friedrich Mattei, a Saxon-born Hellenist teaching at Moscow University. When Mattei died in September 1811 Uvarov wrote a short eulogy, stressing his professional closeness to the scholar who had uncovered previously unknown manuscript treasures in Moscow's Synodal Library. The death notice framed Uvarov's persistent efforts to enhance his reputation by stressing the company he kept, although Mattei turned out to be a bad moral choice, because he was later found to have stolen priceless items from the library.[9] Uvarov was on safer ground with Stein, however, and he was overjoyed when his old friend from Vienna took refuge from Napoleon in St Petersburg.

Almost in an exact reproduction of the cosmopolitan society that had formed in Vienna six years earlier, when in the words of de Stael, the Austrian capital became 'a French island in a Germanic sea',[10] a number of distinguished European political refugees now took refuge in Russia's northern capital. With Stein, who was invited to advise the tsar over Prussia, Uvarov spent many hours reading Tacitus and Thyucidides in a circle of mutual friends who included Moritz Arndt, an energetic traveller and poet who had been deeply roused by Napoleon's march through Europe. Arndt gave himself to the cause of continental rebirth, dependent upon a strong Prussia and came to St Petersburg at Stein's request to be his chief anti-French propagandist.[11]

For Uvarov these were slow-moving times professionally, but stimulating and companionable years for his personal intellectual development. Catherine Uvarov helped entertain her husband's teachers and guests and her house became a focal point for the most distinguished members of the exile community. Only one visitor was obviously not welcome and that was de Stael, who, having arrived in 1812, attended soirees at the Naryshkins and read from her groundbreaking guide to the explosion of German culture over the past half-century, *De l'Allemagne* (1811). de Stael was willing, but she and the 'young tartar fop' had no significant meeting after their quarrel in Vienna. Having privately labelled him a 'treacherous frenchified Russian who told lies',[12] she wrote in a conciliatory spirit to him from Stockholm, 2 May 1813, suggesting he deliberately avoided meeting her. She congratulated him on his successes, looked forward to discussing Russia with him one day and urged him to visit England, but he ignored the overture.[13]

Uvarov began in earnest to entrench himself in a Russia that now took an intensely reactionary turn. In September Napoleon's armies invaded Moscow, had their strength broken in the campaign and retreated at the onset of an unusually cold winter. Russia experienced an ecstatic moral victory which seemed, like the great celebrations of the Orthodox Church, to unite the most powerful and the humblest men in a Russian spiritual cause. The person of the emperor was exalted and divinity thrust upon him for his part in resisting the infidel. Uvarov watched as public life expanded to embrace the growing religious spirit. In 1813, a year of great military effort, the Easter eggs bore the names of the victorious generals Kutuzov and Wittgenstein. The writer, historian and traveller Karamzin and the ageing court poet Derzhavin wrote poems on the expulsion of the French. To relieve war losses the empress founded a Ladies' Patriotic Society, in which Catherine Uvarov and her sister Varvara played prominent roles. The fundamentalists led by Prince Alexander Golitsyn and Alexei Razumovsky founded a Bible Society to propagate the teaching of the Gospels and restore the world to spiritual health, while in court and Masonic circles a passion spread for French mysticism, actively encouraged by the daemonic Maistre. Notwithstanding that the mysticism was of suspect national origin, the climate of irrationality suited Maistre's view of Russia as a place where the people needed to be kept in darkness.[14]

These were insufferable populist times for Uvarov who now increasingly tended to stoical intellectual retreat. He kept up the standard of public loyalty, but with effort. With Maistre and Alexander Turgenev and Zhukovsky he joined the *Colloqium of Lovers of Russian Literature*, founded by the arch-conservative Admiral Shishkov, and he and Turgenev were freemasons and junior directors of the Bible Society. But Uvarov abhorred fanaticism and always preferred contemplation to campaign. He was willing to oppose Bonaparte but not all things French. He was a Christian, but not a zealot. He was a freemason, but then most public men were. A few years later he would revel in sending up the mysteries and rituals of the lodges.

The most constructive idea he had was to start up a propaganda newspaper against Napoleon, encouraged by his experience of Stein's and Arndt's prolific wartime propaganda operation. He envisaged a paper of a few pages for the exiled French community in St Petersburg, which would draw items from the official Russian press comprising 'interesting material for the history of the time'. This would allow him to work in French and publish articles and obituaries on favourite themes and personalities connected with the *ancien régime*, including his own pieces.[15] It was a means to counteract the tendency to tar all Frenchmen with the same brush and Uvarov persuaded his former tutor, Mauguin, to be the editor. The twice-weekly *Conservateur impartial* became the capital's semi-official anti-Napoleon bulletin, vocal in its loyalty to the tsar and its hatred of the French army. At the same time it showcased Uvarov's interest in archaeology, in classics, in education and particularly in the French literature of a more temperate age. It praised de Stael (oddly), published Maistre, and waxed positive over contemporary intellectual Germany (perhaps for that reason.) Alexander Turgenev described it in 1818 under another editor as 'full of obscurantist rubbish'; but in its early days it was the best open attempt Uvarov was involved in to transcend the excesses of his day without causing public offence.[16]

To read the best product of Uvarov's Classical studies, the 'Essay on the Eleusinian Mysteries', which he worked on and published in 1812, is to feel how urgently he wanted to escape from the pressures of this world into the freedom of the study.[17] The exaggerated pressure of Russian reality made him think he was at heart a scholar who had strayed by accident into the world of action, and perhaps that was true. Like *Project*, 'Eleusis' was no more than a sketch of a potential larger work, but its discussion of the ancient Orphic rites and their transmission to posterity provided an occasion to say what religion was, and where the author stood in relation to it. While its scholarly character meant he was unlikely to be held to account for his unsympathetic sentiments towards the present day, it also allowed him to inquire, obliquely, into why such a muddled and muddied Russian public life stood in the way of his reforms.

The period around the third century AD, marking the end of Antiquity and the emergence of the Christian world fascinated Uvarov. It was the period when Neoplatonism developed in Alexandria, and, as philosophy, tended to pass into religion.[18] He distinguished between the nature of early cult worship, which was mysterious, sensual, ecstatic, superstitious and demagogic, and Christianity, which was a purely intellectual faith as he perceived it. He said the Orphic rites, which tried to achieve a point of mediation between man and the divinity, represented unusual refinement for the pre-Christian era. By contrast his descriptions of the lower forms of worship seemed to describe the present day:

> the mysterious practices of barbaric jugglers, whose mission was limited to seizing upon the credulity of a then semi-wild people; and later the adroit charlatans who, with the aid of obscure and alien ceremonies, believed they could prevent the fall of a religion that was crumbling everywhere.[19]

The palliative of scholarship allowed Uvarov to comment on the absurdity of Russian ultra-conservative panic in the face of the collapsed *ancien régime*, which resulted now in an upsurge of superstition and nationalistic fervour, as Old Russia tried to protect itself from liberal and foreign demons.

Uvarov has not passed into history as a social critic or even a writer about Russia. Such eloquence arises in the early 1830s, with the first appearance of Peter Chaadaev in print and with Alexander Herzen and Vissarion Belinsky in the next decade. But, written in Russian, one might imagine the passage just quoted to have come from a young Herzen. 'Eleusis' is a dissenting record of the public impact of 1812 and it is essential for understanding Uvarov's tortured intellectual development.

It showed that Uvarov had modified his views somewhat since his early twenties. He now believed the French Revolution, in its effects, had come to stay. Change was inevitable, also beyond France, only it should come gradually. Gradual change was essential to avoid the ugly confusion in public life that was happening at the time, and which Uvarov's Classical and German mentors equally abhorred. He sought arguments to slow the pace. He'd already tried good taste. Now he simply juggled historicism and providence. Equality and liberty were part of Christian progress, he argued. It was a way of telling potential revolutionaries that violence was not necessary to achieve their aims. Those goals were destined anyway to be realized, in the God-given world that history was unfolding. On the other hand, Uvarov could legitimately add, in a message directed at obscurantists like his Razumovsky father-in-law, that to keep men in superstition and darkness was not Christian:

> The deeper one gets into the study of the ancient religions, the happier one is to be placed in an epoch when the human spirit has risen above this maze of popular cults, without morality and without dignity, it is perhaps the only way in which we have the advantage over the ancients; but it is an immense advantage. The double doctrine [the division of the

Greek mysteries into an esoteric and an exoteric aspect] of the ancients condemned the universe to eternal servitude; while a small number of men enlightened by the most sublime wisdom, penetrated into the highest realms of thought, the multitude languished in miserable blindness, and in its shameful superstitions, maintained with care and artfully adorned by means of all the tricks of the imagination. Every thinking man should consider himself lucky now to have been born in the reign of a purely intellectual religion, equally accessible to the pastor and to Newton, whose character is as divine as its origin. In giving oneself up to these considerations one experiences that sort of satisfaction and pride that an Englishman must feel when he considers the constitution of his country compared with the despotic governments of the Orient, which have this in common with false religions, that they degrade man by corrupting him.[20]

This passage was contained in a footnote to the sixth chapter of the Eleusis essay where it might not be too closely read. Those who did read it, however, would know that the Russian government in Montesquieu's survey of men and institutions in *The Spirit of the Laws* had been labelled Oriental, that was, despotic, while England represented the noble end of the scale. It was Pozzo di Borgo's advice to Uvarov, though others had written it, that the English 'constitution' could not be transplanted to the continent, that the continental countries had to find an equivalent. Accepting the challenge Uvarov leapt upon the possibility of a Russian answer in 'Christianity', or, better, Christianity in Russia with a new enlightened content. It was a concept which, by name at least, ought not to frighten conservatives, while progressives would be happy to see the causes of individual Enlightenment, freedom and dignity espoused.

Such synthesizing skills have been compared to Hegel's and in a different historical scenario one might imagine the doctrinaire left-Uvarovians and the right-Uvarovians enjoying a tug of war over the real meaning of this text, after the master's death. Was it progressive or conservative? For Uvarov it was neither. What it was was a Russian compromise.[21]

He nurtured other quasi-Hegelian thoughts in his next educational proposals, twenty-five years before Hegel would start to become the leading philosopher to influence Russian intellectuals.[22] In 'On the Teaching of History in relation to Popular Education', published in May 1813, Uvarov saw the job of history teachers in Russia to encourage in their most humble pupils a love of their native country and to explain away 'contradictions' as acts of providence. Students with greater intellectual capacity were to be taught philosophy and religion in such a way as to bring peace and order to the mind. If the problem was how to educate the subjects of the tsar without making them politically rebellious or doubtful of God, Uvarov answered that by 'elevating the spirit and educating taste' the right history teaching would induce in students a sense of moderation. To write this essay was 'dry and mundane work' for him personally, but it had to be done.[23]

He suggested that a certain style of history might perturb students with the threat of universal arbitrariness. Therefore an education system based on tapered access, of the kind favoured in enlightened European countries, would be needed. It would make sure that only those minds capable of the plural interpretation of facts would have the opportunity to explore them. In Russia all pupils would learn the facts of Russian history and divinity at secondary schools, but only gymnasium and university courses would introduce universal history, under strict guidance. Teachers were in effect censors, and although Uvarov's theoretical emphasis on patriotism and his 'ladder' policy were only what were to be found, to an equal degree, in French, German and English schools of the day, with progressive intent, in his case the hard-edged theory was inevitably designed to placate ultra-conservative fears of political disorder.[24] Even the rules for using St Petersburg's first public library in 1814 were based on a scala of availability according to age, social position and political trustworthiness.[25]

What would 'universal history' reveal, one might ask, that would be so disastrous in Russia? The answer would be what Uvarov himself discovered during his time abroad, namely that the West had a painfully negative view of Russia, and with that educated Russians might be persuaded to concur. Even the eighteenth-century French poet Jacques Delille, extracts from whose epic work 'Les Jardins' Uvarov had read as a boy with Mauguin, had taken his cue from Montesquieu and written there of Peter the Great's attempts to modernize and Westernize the country:

> Par les hardis travaux, tel le plus grand des czars
> Sut chez un peuple inculte acclimater les arts.
> Heureux, si des mechants l'absurde frenesie
> Ne vient pas en poison changer leur ambrosie.[26]

'The greatest of the tsars with his bold works managed to acclimatize an uncultivated people to the arts. It would be a happy thing if the absurd freneticism of malefactors doesn't come to change that ambrosia into poison.' J. G. Herder, contemporary of Goethe and pioneer of a cultural historicism applied to the development of languages and peoples, was quoted by Uvarov himself as saying a country without its own literary language was undeveloped.[27] August Schloezer, one of Uvarov's teachers at Göttingen, though positively inclined after his prolonged stay in the country, regarded Russia as backward, and Wilhelm von Humboldt placed Russia low down in his planned scheme for a work on cultural anthropology.[28] Foreign expectations of Uvarov himself as a Russian had been low. Friedrich Schlegel was surprised at his erudition, given his origins.[29] The pain of this realization, of how Russia appeared in the Western mirror, was an important factor in Uvarov's experience of Europe, as it would be for generations of intelligent, travelled Russians after him. Having made the decision not to stay abroad, or fate having made it for him, his task was now to try to bring about Westernizing cultural improvements in his tarnished homeland.

Uvarov's ideas immediately seemed to some too sophisticated for Russia. When Schiller's 1795 treatise *On the Aesthetic Education of Man* had attempted to make the link between political moderation and aesthetic finesse, it was a subtle theory, dependent on generosity and imagination. Its Ninth Letter began, 'All improvement in the political sphere is to proceed from the ennobling of character – but how under the influence of a barbarous constitution is character ever to become ennobled? To this end we should have to seek out, presumably, some instrument not provided by the State, and to uncover living springs, which, whatever the political corruption, would remain clear and pure … . This instrument is fine art; such living springs are uncovered in its immortal works.'[30] Indeed Schiller's subtlety was such that he was hardly understood in his own country.[31] Uvarov's kindred proposal in Russia made patriotic realists like Zhukovsky and Karamzin shrug their shoulders. By all means be hopeful, wrote the historian after reading *On Teaching*, but remember all is in the hands of God and the human mind can only propose:

> I commend your zeal and your thoughts. May God grant that a happy outcome of peace will give the government greater means to concern itself with the domestic well-being of Russia in all its aspects! Shall we live to see times of true and lasting creativity and better education founded in a system of national instruction? We have had enough destruction. But I am speaking of what our limited mind sees; the divine mind sees it differently. We poor folk have the right to pray in a drought for rain and for salvation in times of trouble. Cultivate in yourself a desire for the general good and a belief in the possibility that things will get better.[32]

Through most of Alexander's reign Uvarov, however, kept trying to introduce his European-style refinements to Russia. He was this particular kind of foreign-inspired Russian Romantic conservative who was liberal in his attitude to education but highly cautious about political change. His was a rare attempt at a nuanced conservatism in Russia.

One can catch the nuances by comparing him with Karazmin and with Maistre. Maistre, as his power of zealotry over ruling circles reached its zenith, was counselling the tsar and Alexei Razumovsky against any deviation from absolute monarchy and the wisdom of the Bible. He suggested that the Catholic Church was the way to achieve Russian integration into the West and advocated the Jesuit model in Russian education to guarantee political stability. Uvarov the progressive educationalist found himself in opposition to a man who deemed education reducible to three truths: that God created man for society; that the existence of society necessitated government and that every man was obliged to submit himself to government. Maistre said the Russians particularly were not made for science; they should be taught only the Bible, and a minimum of history and some specialist education for the military.[33]

Karamzin meanwhile was urging the tsar to hold fast to Orthodoxy and Russian autocratic traditions. He believed in the institution of the tsar as a patriarch and a father who treated his people benevolently and kept them in order. He emphasized the emotional bond between ruler and ruled, and didn't question serfdom. In 1811 he wrote a secret memorandum to Alexander decrying the introduction of foreign influences to Russia since Peter the Great and urging Russia to rediscover its real historical identity. His unpublished essay heaped anger and scorn on Alexander's policies.[34]

Uvarov's educational plans therefore faced enormous opposition, if Delille's imagined 'malefactors' could turn the tsar from his liberal path.

Some of this conflict became deflected into a debate active throughout the decade as to which way the Russian literary language might or should develop. Language became a way of dealing with the issue of political and social progress indirectly. The extreme camps were the old guard followers of Admiral Shishkov, who clung to the heritage of Church Slavonic, and the rather artificial Karamzinian school, which favoured Gallic models.[35] Uvarov followed neither. Uppermost in his mind was a feeling for original poetic vitality, which he found in ancient Greece, and in the East, and hoped to encourage in Russia. By extension, compared with the reactionary and anti-Western Shishkov, and the arch-conservative Karamzin, he was not at heart a nationalist but a cosmopolitan individualist.

He tried to live what he taught. He recommended and lent to his friends many books in different languages which he regularly procured abroad; he passed on his interest not only in Herder and Friedrich Schlegel, but also in English prose writers and poets who joined the Germans in being much in demand in Russia, His reading was always wide and in 1813–14 included Byron, Scott and Southey.[36] In budding Russian literature he fell in love with Zhukovsky's Romantic poetry, describing his talent in 1813 as 'great and original … superlative'. Zhukovsky was a far better poet than he himself. 'You possess a talent … which attracts you to ideal poetry … from now on … every work [of yours] should newly enlarge the sphere of our language and literature.'[37]

Translation was another area of Russian culture he had a great impact on. Russia needed access to more foreign literature and philosophy to make progress, and Uvarov oversaw the belated translation of the Classical epics into Russian. So that these might make their full impact, he insisted on every effort being made to render the spirit and quality of the original, advising the poet Nikolai Gnedich, for example, to render *The Iliad* in hexameters not the alexandrines of neoclassical convention. As Uvarov wrote to one of his main opponents on the issue, the minor poet Kapnist, it was something he cared about passionately:

> We must try to maintain the impression produced by a reading of [Homer's verses] on all educated minds. We must ... present a sample of the work of Homer in the spirit of the original, with his forms and all the nuances, so that we see before us not Kostrov or Gnedich but Homer – Homer in the purest reflection of his natural beauty, the Homer which captivated the legislator of Sparta, the conqueror of Asia, the wise men of Alexandria, in short all the brilliant host of his admirers in the ancient and the modern world. This is the way the ancients can affect us; but to reach this goal, to spread their beneficial influence, it is imperative to recognise the first rule, that form in poetry is inseparable from the spirit of it, that between the form and the spirit of poetry there exists the same mysterious link as exists between body and soul; that their double-edged influence and action – that of form on thought and thought on form – are so tightly bound that it is impossible in any way to determine their limits, still less to break their unity without sacrificing the one or the other.[38]

As well as being free from nationalist ideology, this was unusual and sensitive criticism for its time in Russia with definite beneficial effect on the growth of a national literature. Uvarov proposed moving away from the French model to develop an indigenous Russian form that might preserve the power of the Greek. He had matured considerably since his objections in Vienna to any innovation that criticized the standards of eighteenth-century literary France. A Russian scholar of the mid-century noted that but for Uvarov 'probably we would never have had an epic metre'.[39] Zhukovsky paid a similar retrospective tribute, acknowledging Uvarov's influence over his own translation of *The Odyssey*.[40]

Uvarov's critical activity encouraged Pushkin's interest in the hexameter and inspired another minor poet, Voeikov, to write a tribute in the same metre in which he called Uvarov, 'the glorious offspring of the Hellenic and Germanic muses'. Voeikov praised the scholar and public servant for not losing his exquisite taste and the poetic spark in his heart under the burden of work.[41]

Yet the pressures of the new age and of public office quickly limited the scope of Uvarov's literary endeavours, as, in the view of a Russian obituarist, had similarly threatened the later career of Delille:

The epoch of 1789 arrived, the revolution which was so fatal to taste and to the republic of letters whose first need is peace; it robbed him of his titles and his fortune and incensed his soul, by nature gentle and sensitive; but it did not destroy his courage; he did not follow the example of a number of writers and embrace these destructive principles. To turn his eyes away from the fearful spectacles it presented by its swift progress, he sought, like a Roman orator, to still his pain in the embrace of literature and friendship.[42]

These words, published in the *Conservateur*, might have been written by Uvarov himself. His hand is evident in the style and choice of many of the pieces, and he had a habit of not signing his contributions. He recognized that a new world was being born in politics, and because he could not foresee a new critical relation of art to politics, it forever limited the positive role he could play in the development of Russian literature. Isolated by his own outstanding classical education, he gave what he could. He would remain for the rest of his life, besides a classical scholar, a unique 'frenchified Russian' writer, for whom more appreciation came from readers and critics in France than from Russia itself.[43]

5

To believe in something different is an effort, a fantasy ...

By 1813 Uvarov felt cut off from the Europe that had nurtured his ambitions. Stein left Russia that year and the intellectual companionship Uvarov had found abroad was not replaced. He dwelt romantically on the possibility of visiting Stein in his German castle once the hostilities were over, but the cosmopolitan, enlightened land where he would feel happy threatened to become a necropolis or increasingly imaginary. In an adroit juxtaposition of the emotional elements at stake he confided to Zhukovsky: 'Even to believe in the possibility of something better in our situation is an effort, a fantasy, an ideal; but to try actually to do something is a Herculean task.'[1]

Uvarov became a dreamer, preferring the company of men who were dead or far away, and believing his choice would be vindicated in a restored cosmopolitan Europe. On how to live in his own country he ignored Karamzin's advice to come down to earth, as he ignored Maistre's not to attempt the difficult balancing act between maintaining political order and furthering enlightenment.

When General Jean-Victor Moreau died in October 1813 Uvarov mourned an apparent like-minded soul, and what he wrote in praise of Moreau seemed to be as much about himself as about this Frenchman who had come over to the Russian side against Napoleon and died a Russian hero:

The times and above all the example of France had taught him that the dreams of a good man must never influence his political conduct ... the entirety of his [Moreau's] character and his life dragged him involuntarily into exalted regions where his spirit dwelt without effort. He found himself in the midst of the finest geniuses of antiquity as in the bosom of his true family. The study of history placed him in continual contact with the best and greatest of men. ... But when he left those sublime regions and that order of things, the eternal glory of humanity, his calm and severe reason took the upper hand again. Profoundly convinced of the need for monarchist government, he reserved for a just a small number of like souls what he called his Imaginary State.[2]

Uvarov too reserved his political ideal for just a few souls. His 'Imaginary State' was the cosmopolitan, humanitarian republic he shared with Stein and Humboldt, a community where every citizen was a spiritual aristocrat. At its centre blazed the ideal of a rounded, individual non-vocational education in which self-reliance, knowledge and understanding transcended status, wealth and background. This in German was the concept of *Bildung*, and it linked military men, bureaucrats, philosophers and poets according to a common ideal.[3]

But Uvarov's frustrations that this ideal was impossible in Russia gathered inevitable momentum, compounded by his separation from Europe and his leaving the diplomatic service. On 18 November 1813 he could no longer resist pouring his heart out to Stein. It was a rare moment of self-dramatization in public, and the emotional counterpoint derived from Uvarov's protestations that he had always been a realist:

There is nothing more ungratifying, or rather, more impossible than these [his duties as educational superintendent]. I am not a dreamer, as you know; I like the world of action and have found myself in it, as it were, since childhood; you know my convictions, my views; despite all that, I have reached a point where I am losing hope, not only that I may do any good, but even that I may stick to the course I have marked out for myself, and from which I will never diverge without sacrificing the things that are most dear to me in the world, honour and health, beliefs which are essential to my wellbeing. Do not think there is the slightest exaggeration in my words. I am so calm that I surprise all those around me, but in my heart there is despair. The state of mind in which people are these days there is no end to the confusion of ideas. Some of them want education which is not dangerous i.e. fire which does not burn; others (and there are more and more of them) heap together in one lump Napoleon and Montesquieu, the French army and French books, Moreau and Rosenkampf, the nonsense of Sch ... [Schelling][4] and the discoveries of Leibniz; in short there is such a chaos of yelling, passions, of parties fiercely opposed to each other and every kind of exaggeration that it is unbearable to look upon for long. People throw words in each other's faces: religion is in danger, the ground of morality has been shaken, this man is a supporter of foreign ideas, this one an Illuminist, a philosopher, a Freemason, a fanatic, and so on. In short it's complete madness.

Every moment you risk compromising yourself or becoming the executive instrument of the most exaggerated passions. In the middle of what depths of ignorance do you find yourself forced to work on knowledge which is being eroded at the foundations and on every side is ready to collapse. That, I agree, is a sad and painful admission; believe me, everything I have said is entirely true. I need to unburden my heart, and I could write on that count a whole book ... I am waiting only for a happier state of affairs, in order to tear myself from the chaos which is choking and crushing me beyond words. I need cleaner air and peace. My health is suffering; my spirit and my morale are growing weak. No one can say I have given in easily to depression. I had so many hopes and illusions, but three years' experience have destroyed them.[5]

The letter to Stein of the autumn of 1813 is a genuinely anguished document and one of the few in Uvarov's lifetime which speaks directly of his private personality. It was written only four days after Catherine's safe confinement and the birth of their first child, Alexandra, but the consolation of family life was not sufficient. He missed Stein; he had lost the company of a fellow Classicist and reformer in Mikhail Speransky, who had been exiled from the capital;[6] and his brother Fyodor was ill. Not knowing what it was to be realistic in the reign of a tsar subsequently known for his dreaminess as 'the Hamlet on the Throne' Uvarov avowed that it seemed impossible for his career to progress. He was pained by the spectacle of seeing ideas he knew well misunderstood in Russia, and exclaimed to Stein in rare exasperation that the tsar could not possibly be aware of so much foolishness as was going on in his capital.[7]

Another factor which lowered Uvarov's morale that autumn and winter was ill health. In fact the whole crisis was prescient of his fate to come over the next forty years, until his death in 1855.[8] Even in his mid-twenties he felt the vulnerability of having a sensitive constitution, which meant his intellectual conflicts would always cause his health and his spirits to suffer. The generally accepted view today of a psychosomatic susceptibility, such as Uvarov had, is that heredity, early childhood, the weakening of an organ by injury or infection, and the symbolic meaning of the organ for the personality concerned – all play their part in causing malady. The evidence for the effect of his constitution on his professional behaviour is circumstantial but compelling. Uvarov's dependence on his mother, his slight build and effeminate manner, his professional malleability and his quest for honours suggest an overall physical and psychological weakness, with a need to be comforted and avoid strain. One can see these needs emerging in his preference for inferior company, his susceptibility to flattery, and his favouritism. Meanwhile it was observed that Uvarov ate and drank with striking moderation.

Uvarov's depression lasted into 1814 despite rays of light emerging on the international political horizon. In mid-winter he wrote with a witty flourish to Maistre that the ideological confusion continued to flourish in Petersburg to the extent that every religious sect took him to be a member of the opposition. He seemed perversely to be enjoying his superiority.[9] But the moods came and went and came again. He had a foreign education in a country which disdained foreignness but had not enough learning of its own. He was an intellectual and a scholar, but now without sufficient access to Western intellectual company or understanding. To try to cope, he could be philosophical or mournful, knowing that his problems were greatly magnified by the war. He could pin his hopes on letters sent abroad. But he couldn't escape the fact he was only half-living.

In these moods he gave into the fashionable temptation to turn inwards. It did not matter whether the object of longing was 'Europe', an Imaginary State, or his personal happiness, for as Novalis once put it: 'In the distance everything becomes romantic.' One might add that nothing near is ever satisfying to men and women in such moods and that for Uvarov the nearest thing to disappoint him was his native land.

He wrote to Goethe even after the coming of peace, on 6 June 1814:

Your friendly letter has cheered me into activity again. It is truly a good thing to follow with courage the course I have undertaken in my fatherland; yet the thorns along this path are too many to count; and all too often the spirit and the mind are under pressure. Although I know very well that life in such circumstances is a long struggle and that I have been steeling myself to face it from the beginning, nevertheless I feel constantly a deep longing for another, freer life, a longing for the land where the lemon trees grow, for friends far away.[10]

The letter referred to two of Goethe's poems, of which 'Mignon', containing the phrase 'longing for the land where the lemon trees grow' had acquired a pathetic private meaning. Italy had been a brief, underexploited part of Uvarov's European tour at the beginning of his twenties, and now in the Romantic spirit he was happy to take that country as a symbol of his lost freedom.

Could such a man be a Russian patriot? Andrei Razumovsky, having made his spiritual home in Vienna amidst the collected artefacts of a preferred culture, had not bothered to consider the question, but Uvarov was bound to tackle it, having returned home, and it was immensely complicated, for, even though Uvarov wanted an enlightened country, he was not devoted to the cultural individuality of the emergent Russian people. That was what

Zhukovsky detected on the evidence of *Project*. Had not Uvarov echoed there Herder's view that a nation is only as close to civilization as its language is perfect, and yet committed that sentiment to paper in a foreign tongue? It seemed the young cosmopolitan could spare Russia little love. He'd absorbed the critical views of Russia of Delille, Monntesquieu, Schloezer, Wilhelm von Humboldt and Friedrich Schlegel, among his immediate acquaintance or points of reference, and de Stael, when she visited in 1812, found it a superficial and anti-intellectual culture, showy and suspicious of ideas.[11]

But in fact Uvarov faced a double difficulty with where to place his emotional loyalties, because the Europe he loved was also vanishing. Had they met when she visited Moscow, de Stael would have been just the mind to explain to her young tartar fop that a Romantic adherence to the land of one's birth was already transforming France, and the German lands, and the emotional lives of the Poles, in their resistance to being crushed by the Russian Austrian and Prussian Empires. Speaking for the new Romantic spirit, she wrote that there could be no *patrie* without that emotional feeling of cultural identity by which men made themselves 'a literary and philosophical homeland'.[12]

Uvarov's feelings were alien to this political Romanticism. He was a patriot because he had ultimate regard for the nation's cultural prestige as a political power. In that he was a Maistrian. Yet again he was emotionally attached to Russia, in that he sincerely wanted it to become a more enlightened country. But he held this view without any devotion to the cultural individuality of the emergent people. And so, as Maistre so brilliantly saw, he was destined to remain *in bivio*, in fact for the rest of his life.

When he spoke of his patriotic duty in private as a young man, he invariably referred to his intellectual isolation. He could do little to help himself. It was not just that he was rationally committed as a European scholar to a 'cold' view of Russia. In his deepest ambitions for himself as a man of letters, he needed to live in an *ancien régime* of the spirit devoted to the primacy of Classical scholarship. He believed in it and it was the area where his talent lay. Had he embarked on a career in Russian *belles lettres* he might have enjoyed no success at all, whereas to date in Europe he had at least been acclaimed for his promise. He associated himself so closely with Goethe, Humboldt and Stein because there was no one in Russia of his time – not yet – who so commanded his admiration, except as a poet Zhukovsky. Also he feared professionally that he might not succeed in Russia, not even as an administrator.

Karamzin might have showed the young Uvarov more understanding than Maistre because he as a Russian could live with his contradictions. Karamzin was a cultured, travelled and European-educated man, known for his nine-volume patriotic history of Russia, still being written while Moscow went up in flames. His work stressed the need for Russia to have autocracy and to cleave to Orthodoxy in eternity. To one of his young disciples Karamzin declared that his ideal form of government was republican but that he could not countenance it for Russia, because republicanism depended on the virtue of its citizens.[13] He constructed his cultural theory on the basis of Russia's impoverished political reality, exactly what Uvarov meant by a 'realist', surely. But Uvarov was still a dreamer, struggling to be realistic.

When peace came, he felt his dream revive. Part of the pathos of his wartime position was that he had been waiting to serve a discriminating monarch. Now came the chance to state, once again, what he believed in. He wrote an essay, 'Alexander and Buonaparte', published in May 1814 in the *Conservateur impartial,* inspired by Chateaubriand, which combined a fascination with these two world-historical figures with a eulogy of Alexander's achievement at defeating the infidel. It hoped for the restoration of a free continent and all that that might bring for commerce and letters. Pushing aside his private pain at the thorny path which made serving his country so difficult, he exulted in how the war had transformed Russia. In particular the mood of the mob became something far nobler than he had experienced:

> Love for the fatherland which penetrated all the classes was exalted to the highest degree. It was a convulsive surge of feeling, a spontaneous crusade whose noble character and brilliant details history will remember.[14]

Alexander, of whom Uvarov had commented in sorrow to Stein that 'the tsar could not be aware of so much foolishness in his capital' was now painted as a crusader and a leader of kings: modest, principled and devoted to Russia. The young man who would be a patriot even attempted to patch up the tsar's record where it was beginning to wear thin: on the matter of spending too much time abroad and showing un-Christian vengeance. Above all he declared the world should realize Alexander was a Saviour, the restorer of legitimacy to Europe, a servant of Providence and an ennobler of men. The tsar became the apotheosis of Uvarov's ideals. He was the man of guiding moral taste, the man of the *ancien régime*, the man of God, and lastly, to bring him into the nineteenth century, the man of History.

All Uvarov's negative feeling about the irrationality of the war years was transformed in the idea of a triumphant Christian Russia giving a new lead to Europe. Alexander, as Uvarov painted him, embodied the highest marriage of political design and romantic feeling, thus implicitly reconciling principles strained in conflict within himself:

> No sovereign in history has achieved a comparable triumph; raison d'etat has never been so admirably reconciled with the most noble sentiments of the heart; to win battles, burn cities, sow discord, propagate civil war,

force the signature of a treaty, is the role of ordinary conquerors; but to deliver nations, bring down an odious tyrant, restore everywhere legitimate authority, to act like a king after having fought like a knight, to remain a man on the most absolute throne in the universe and at the height of grandeur to bow before Providence, modestly and simply to push aside homages, to flee his own glory, this is what the Emperor Alexander has done.[15]

Uvarov was excited about an idea which seemed genuinely capable of uniting the diverse breeds of patriotism advanced by Shishkov and Karamzin, Speransky and Uvarov, Zhukovsky and the Turgenev brothers, Alexei Razumovsky and even the lone Maistre. It was the idea of a benevolent, progressive, Russian monarch who presided over international peace. France was no longer in Revolutionary chains because Russia had achieved the restoration – that heroic deed Catherine had promised when Uvarov was a child.

France is free, and the most enormous revolution which has ever taken place has been executed with admirable concert. It is the dawn of a new state of affairs; the reign of disorder has now ended; everything will return to within its natural limits … God has shown Himself clearly, He has no desire for the order of royal generations to be interrupted … the patrimony of the centuries will no longer be the price of one day of audacity or happiness.[16]

On 19 June 1814, he wrote to Maistre:

All men's minds strive now towards a common centre, though many do not realize it; they do so more or less at the same pace, despite taking different and sometimes opposite paths. A baptism of blood, of which the other baptism is only a forerunner, has pacified the human race.[17]

Alexander's triumph seen as restoration would shortly lead him to propose the Holy Alliance. Uvarov rightly perceived, however, that the restoration had two faces, and if it meant Christianity abroad, it also meant official recognition of the force of 'the people' at home. And so he did bow to the transformation in sensibility of which Zhukovsky and de Stael made him aware. He wanted Alexander to know that the restored world would not simply continue the old, because the common people had become aware of their power:

If on the one hand the cause of the king has been won by 20 years of revolution, on the other the peoples have learned to know their strength; they will remember having been the last bastion of humanity; they have a right to the recognition of the sovereigns they so valliantly defended. Filled with reciprocal esteem, and better enlightened as to their own interests, kings and nations will make on the tomb of Bonaparte the joint sacrifice of despotism and popular anarchy. ... Never has Europe presented a more imposing spectacle nor given rise to such great hopes.[18]

The people had demonstrated their strength in the Peninsular War, and Uvarov urged 'men of power' to study the new phenomenon Bonaparte had not reckoned with:

Religion, love of the fatherland and national honour [my emphasis] upraised the whole Peninsula. These powerful motive forces, which too great a curiosity had not in the slightest weakened in that land of enthusiasm, became the triple good which united all the Spaniards.[19]

Religion, honour and patriotism were the three virtues which had enabled Spain to resist the undermining effects of the godless Enlightenment. They could also be extracted from the Russian experience at Smolensk, Napoleon's last conquest before Moscow:

That was the signal for a new war, a national war, in which one saw renew themselves the prodigies of Spain.[20]

'The people' for Uvarov was a wholly academic concept, but out of his intellectual distance and his desire for more general Enlightenment within firm political order, and urged on by the promptings of German Romantic philosophy, he now drew this concept of the people as a useful national force.[21] Twenty years on, he would devise a political philosophy of 'the people' in which exactly these three terms, religion, love of the fatherland and national honour, would be cornerstones. Uvarov's was the system the critic Pypin afterwards called Official Nationality[22] and it began to take shape in Uvarov's mind, and heart, finally as the solution to his mixed feeling about patriotism and *patrie*.

Religion, honour and patriotism were close to what official propaganda had distilled from the 1812 campaign as the essence of Russia: resignation (to the will of God), devotion (to the tsar), and loyalty (to the honour of Russia), and they grounded him in his own country and among his own people. He recognized the political value of the burning of Moscow, which had produced an extraordinary collective strength and given Russia nationality as something tangible and heartfelt. As Karamzin did indeed write to him, it had been 'a time when we Moscow refugees who had lost everything we owned to the enemy and the flames only saved ourselves by our love for the fatherland and by finding friends amongst complete strangers'.[23]

Yet privately, given the divisions in himself, we have to conclude that 'nationality' was also – and simultaneously – just another way for Uvarov to long for the lemon trees. What he really wanted was international peace and a cosmopolitan freedom which would allow the disinterested pursuit of learning within a stable political order. He set the German humanist ideal of *Bildung* above autocracy. He wanted peace, like a man in his study trying to work; and like the scholarly Hegel he found political disorder a nuisance.

6

The republic of letters

After 20 years of misfortune and bad fate, Europe has just been liberated. The republic of letters is ready to emerge from the depth of its ruins; it will plant flowers on the debris of the most odious tyranny which has ever been, and it will without doubt take up once again its ancient rights of which the finest is that fraternity of sentiments and thoughts which draws together, around a single centre, so many men scattered across the surface of the globe.

(UVAROV, PREFACE TO THE 1816 EDITION OF 'ELEUSIS')

Uvarov's spirits soared to their greatest height from the day his thoughts appeared to coincide with those of the tsar, would-be leader of a Europe reunited under the Holy Alliance and restorer of cosmopolitan freedom. He joined in the celebration of Alexander's victorious return in August from Paris by translating Graefe's Greek verses for the occasion into French and enjoyed following the Congress of Vienna. Stein was in Vienna, advising the tsar, as was Humboldt for Prussia. Andrei Razumovsky and, until his death in December 1814, de Ligne were senior diplomatic figures. When the tsar returned home he made a number of enlightened appointments and ordered out the Jesuits: Maistre's power was at last eclipsed. Everything conspired, not least the return on stage of familiar faces, to encourage Uvarov's liberal conservative hopes.

The pleasing state of public affairs allowed Uvarov to feel freer than he had done for many months and to enjoy his private life as he approached his thirtieth year. He now had two daughters, Alexandra and Elizabeth, named after the tsar and the tsarina, and the family lived in comfort in the capital, dividing their time between their town residence and the residence they had in the country. They saw a lot of Sergei's 'upright and courageous' brother Fyodor, who had survived injury in the war and was now a lieutenant-colonel in the cavalry, and of his beautiful and gifted wife Catherine Lunin. Fyodor and Catherine married in 1814 and had their first child the following year. Ivan Davydov, one of Uvarov's nineteenth-century biographers, noted that Sergei and Fyodor had always been close since their fatherless upbringing together, though Fyodor was not drawn to public life.[1]

No one quite replaced Stein in Uvarov's affections in these years and in the neoclassical fashion of the day he built a summerhouse in his garden to commemorate their friendship. But the apparent return of an age freed from war-necessitated chauvinism and which revitalized Russian intellectual life was great compensation. Uvarov played a prominent role in the literary restoration when he helped found a dining club of like-minded friends called Arzamas. In that jokey, disorganized club which brought together men of his own gentry background, he found friendship and the chance to share his literary interests and antipathies. The original group in October 1815 included Alexander Turgenev, Vigel', Dmitry Dashkov, Dmitry Bludov, the writer and poet Peter Vyazemsky, Zhukovsky, and another fine poet, Konstantin Batyushkov. Later Pushkin was introduced while still a schoolboy. The members met weekly at the house of either Uvarov or Bludov, the two married participants.

Arzamas, with a discriminating generosity and impartiality reminiscent of the German humanist ideal of *Bildung*, demanded of its members only intelligence and talent. Dashkov, like Uvarov, had been a brilliant young recruit to the then College of Foreign Affairs and was now employed in the Justice Ministry. His leisure time was given to literature and he translated Herder, offering passages to Arzamas for discussion and scrutiny. Bludov's career followed a similar pattern. He served in Sweden for two years with the foreign Ministry and brought back excellent French and the fruits of a close friendship with de Stael. But generally the members could not have been more heterogeneous. Vigel' was something of a loner, convinced of his disadvantages, which included lack of a university degree, which blocked his promotion in the government service, and his homosexuality. He only slowly found his métier as a satirical chronicler of contemporary society. Alexander Turgenev spent a lifetime considering Romantic ideas in conjunction with the future of Russia, but indolence was the other side of his marvellous capacity to be a sounding-board of his times. He was a close friend of the more active and public-spirited Vyazemsky, who was a poet, journalist and diplomat. The range of interests and personalities in the society allowed for subdivisions and cellular friendships. In and beyond Arzamas the three poets, Zhukovsky, Vyazemsky and Batyushkov, enjoyed ties of friendship among themselves and with Turgenev, and they were close to Karamzin (an honorary Arzamasian) and later to Pushkin. Batyushkov was accomplished in the elegant classical tradition of Russian verse perfected by Pushkin, and might have achieved world renown had he not suffered irreversible mental breakdown in 1821, aged thirty-four. His Latinist, neoclassical talent complemented that of Zhukovsky, Russia's only Romantic poet of merit in the sentimental German vein.[2]

The Arzamasians met to discuss their intellectual and artistic interests, mainly classical and eighteenth century, but also to eat, drink, sing and be foolish. The atmosphere resembled an undergraduate society, devoted to the destruction of pompous opponents. The members wore costumes and ceremonial hats for their meetings which were acted as much as held, and all had nicknames taken from Zhukovsky's ballads. Uvarov, for the fussiness and effeminacy which were now prominent aspects of his character, was fondly known as 'Starushka', the old woman. Vigel', dubbed 'Crane of Ibykus' after Schiller's poem and 'permanent rogue at the Ministry of Foreign Affairs' after his substitute for a profession was given the title of the now ridiculed *Conservateur impartial* as another name. The element of theatre drew a playful line of defence between the Arzamasians and the real establishment world they attacked. The butts of their antipathy were any remaining ultra-conservative institutions, such as the Bible Society, the St Petersburg Public Library and the Colloquium of Lovers of Russian Literature. In lengthy speeches and mock Masonic rituals the Arzamasians disposed of members of the old guard. Uvarov called on his friends expressly to debunk the extremists in the Bible Society and received unexpected support in so doing from the emperor.[3]

The most serious side of Arzamas was perhaps the companionship it afforded. Zhukovsky, permanent secretary of the group, wrote in one his reports that Arzamas brought its members 'the friendship of loyal comrades for life, roast goose once a week, a resilient spirit in exile, the red hood and the sweet enmity of the Colloquium'. It was finally an answer to Uvarov's prayers for intellectual fellowship. Vyazemsky likewise saw it as a return from a kind of exile: 'Our Russian life is death. I shall come and refresh myself in Arzamas and recover from death.'[4]

Like Pushkin and like Uvarov in a memoir forty years later, Vyazemsky spoke of Arzamas as a brotherhood, embracing men of similar temperament. Vyazemsky later also called it a republic which valued intellectual breadth and liveliness and respected art and personality: 'We were often reproached, you must have heard./We met within the walls of Arzamas,/ And behaved ourselves like oligarchs:/ In a republic of letters/ We conferred.' Arzamas's simultaneously cosmopolitan and patriotic members saw it as the ideal fatherland, a far cry from that frenzied creation and focus of jingoistic imagination which was Russia in 1813, but a distinctive Russia all the same, imbued equally with self-respect and wise consciousness of its place in Europe.[5]

In an imagined dialogue between Kantemir, Russian ambassador in mid-eighteenth-century Paris, and Montesquieu, known for his negative view of Russia, Batyushkov argued that Russia was not so much backward as special. 'I make bold to disagree with the great creator of a book on the spirit of the laws ... Russia has awoken from a deep sleep... . The dawn illuminating our land promises a beautiful morning, a magnificent midday and a clear evening.' 'Maybe in two or three centuries, maybe sooner, the favourable heavens will give us a genius who will wholly realize the great idea of Peter – and the most extensive land on earth, measured by its creative voice, will find its place in the treasury of laws, and the freedom based upon them, giving continuity to those laws, in a word will take its place in the treasury of enlightenment.'

The Russian poet and staunch Arzamazian concluded that although Montesquieu was a very clever man, he knew nothing about Russia, which could not be judged by Western standards.[6]

Uvarov later dwelt on a more straightforward patriotism by recalling the presence of Karamzin at some Arzamas meetings. Yet what mattered to him above all was that Arzamas was not a political group. Linking it with his beloved salon culture he wrote that Arzamas belonged to an epoch when politics had not yet seized hold of literature:

> It was a society of young people (some of whom later achieved high office in government service), linked together only by their vital love for their native language, literature and history, and gathering around Karamzin, whom they regarded as their leader and the man to show them the way. The tendency of this society, or rather of these friendly meetings, was primarily critical. Those who took part occupied themselves with the strict analysis of literary works, the application to Russian language and literature of classical and foreign literature from every source, and with the search for principles which might serve as the basis of a solid, independent theory of language, and so on. The more varied the society's aims were the less consistent its activities became.[7]

Yet Arzamas did, indirectly, have a political significance, because of the value it attached to personal freedom. That was a quality which Uvarov admired in his youth but wished to forget in his old age. Arzamas was to be recollected in his life like an indiscreet early love affair.

Much Arzamas time was spent laughing. One meeting was recorded as being held in a cart. Zhukovsky, the most playful member, wrote up some of the minutes in hexameters and dodged the responsibility thrust upon him to draw up a 'constitution'. The field of activity when it was not literature was literary sport, though among the Arzamasians was a dawning awareness of their role as literary men in society. They were in fact in many ways to provide each other with congenial company, a self-help society, the first to consider the artist and his problems in Russian society. Under that heading Vyazemsky, a true radical, proposed free print for writers. More moderately, the Arzamasians acquired a government stipend for Zhukovsky who was in need and Turgenev and Uvarov used their contacts to help Vyazemsky and Batyushkov secure posts. Vyazemsky also hoped Uvarov would also provide a way round the censorship, since his job in St Petersburg made him one of its chief administrators in the capital, and the Superintendent reciprocated. Uvarov went on cherishing the ideal of the Arzamasians helping each other to avoid red tape some years after Arzamas had disbanded.

He enjoyed the non-partisan camaraderie but would always have liked Arzamas to be more directly under his influence than it was. The first meeting was held at his house on 12 October 1815, and Vigel' wrote that he would have liked to have been elected leader and was disappointed the leadership proceeded on a rotating basis.[8] In the only address we have of Uvarov's, from a meeting on 11 November 1816, he tried to turn the mythology of Arzamas's origins to his own advantage. A third-rate dramatist, Shakhovsky, had published a play satirizing Zhukovsky which annoyed the poet's friends. Meanwhile, an unknown man had set up a school of painting in Arzamas, a provincial town famous for its roast goose. Bludov, amused, drew together the two unrelated events in a play called *The Vision in the Arzamas Tavern*, which caricatured Shakhovsky as a madman and established Arzamas as a shrine of reason and taste.

Uvarov, who evidently felt by the autumn of 1816 that Arzamas was straying from its original aim to set fresh aesthetic standards, imagined going back to the tavern some months on and hearing the message that Arzamas was larking about too much and not what it used to be. It was a characteristically self-centred account:

The main aim of my journey was the desire to bow before the tavern where our society began ... Alas! Dear Arzamasians, all my expectations were dashed. Arzamas is no more in Arzamas! An academic darkness has covered our beloved country; the tavern lies in ruins. In their deep ignorance the citizens of old Arzamas know neither of our battles or our glory, and after stubbornly consulting their address calendars, maintain that Meshkov is in charge of both the government and Parnassus.[9]

The oracle, the old man of the river at Arzamas, told Uvarov:

Geese! Geese! ...The kingdom of literature is almost in your hands. When will you stop drowning the fools of the Colloquium and the Academy in my pure waters? It was praiseworthy to show society that they were stupid, but for that their own works are sufficient ... I expect more from you; I expect the renewal of our literature; I expect a triumph for reason and taste.[10]

Uvarov thrust himself forward through performances like this. Some of his fellows were uneasy about his character. The older poet Vassily L. Pushkin, who joined the group in 1816, commented, 'What sort of a man was Uvarov? It was hard to know. He resembled a kaleidoscope, changing every minute before the eyes of his companions.'[11] Alexander Turgenev was slowly coming round to Zhukovsky's view that Uvarov was using scholarship to enhance his own prestige. Vigel' could see that while Uvarov was actually relieved to be able to share some of his interests his inner daemon drove him to affect superiority and distance:

It was curious to see Uvarov at that time. He had been lightly touched upon in Shakhovsky's comedy and seized he chance to show enormous displeasure. But I think he was rather more pleased at the chance to get together more closely with his new friends. In his mind he saw himself already as leader of a band of fighting men, amongst whom there were so many glorious warriors; it seemed that he intended for his head a shining crown, in which, like a precious diamond, he would set Zhukovsky. Experience showed him he could expect no servility from his comrades-at-arms; all the same in Petersburg society he was much better known than they were and in its eyes may have appeared the main party. The eternal calculations of this man in the interests of his vanity were often unreal, but sometimes they were successful and then helped to raise him both in the general estimation and in the sphere of government service. Friends of literature would have acted imprudently to refuse the help of the son-in-law of the Minister of Enlightenment, a man who had direct influence on censorship.[12]

Bludov's daughter Alexandra knew the Arzamasians as a child when they met in her father's house, and writing in middle age she remembered primarily a performer: 'Uvarov, with his fine looks, and spoilt by aristocratic society; witty, agile, high-spirited, with a touch of the vanity of a fop, but highly educated and truly enlightened.'[13] Her picture of Uvarov contrasted with happier recollections of Zhukovsky's kindness and humour, of Turgenev's lazy, bulky, shambling figure, his good-natured expression, and the enormous amount of food he put away; of Dashkov's swarthy good looks and the 'elevated spirit' which made him instinctively valued and loved by the children; and of Vigel's coal-black eyes and his affected gestures with his snuff box.

FIGURE 1 Portrait of Count Sergey Semyonovich Uvarov *by Orest Adamovich Kiprensky (1815–1816).*
Source: Getty / Heritage Images.

Around this time Orest Kiprensky, a leading artist of the early decades of the century, painted Uvarov. He had known his subject from the days when they both frequented the Olenins' salon and had a feeling for Uvarov's superficiality and his vanity. Kiprensky's Uvarov, fine-mannered and intelligent, is nevertheless dominated by fashion. His clothes, the position of his hands, the mildly melancholy expression on the face are all carefully composed by the sitter. Uvarov adopted a Byronic image, almost ahead of his time in Russia, and in that way had painted of himself a portrait wholly readable in Europe, where he wanted to excel. When I first visited this portrait in the Treytakov gallery in Moscow in 1979, the attendant introduced me to Uvarov as the prototype for Pushkin's Evgeny Onegin, and in spirit she was right: here was a classic superfluous man, a *lishnyi chelovek*, one who could not find a home for his talents in Russia, the refuge of Arzamas notwithstanding.

The mixture of superiority and need strained Uvarov's relations with his friends. On the side of need he particularly wanted Zhukovsky to like him, but had a hard task of it. Zhukovsky brought out in Uvarov a rare humility and softness and Uvarov claimed he was devoted to following the course of this 'superlative talent'. For one thing Zhukvovsky highlighted the different course his own life had taken – Uvarov was never now going to be a poet. But the main emotional appeal of Zhukovsky was that like Stein he reminded Uvarov of his humility. Before Zhukovsky, as before Stein, Uvarov did not feel elevated. He did not have their gifts, their stature, their moral qualities, and this awareness inspired in him a sentimental devotion, rivalled in strength only by the contempt in which he could hold lesser men. That feeling especially in the case of Zhukovsky may have been love, even erotic love, and Uvarov's worshipful attentiveness around the poet did not escape Vigel'. After his own portrait, Uvarov had Kiprensky paint a portrait of Zhukovsky, and hung it in his study where it remained for the rest of his life. He may well have claimed authorship of Arzamas too in a gallant gesture to avenge Shakhovsky's slur on Zhukovsky and gain favour.[14]

Uvarov was also fond of Batyushkov and that relationship progressed more smoothly. Batyushkov turned down the job Uvarov found for him in government service in Petersburg, but stayed in touch when he took up a preferred post in Italy. Uvarov became Batyushkov's first serious critic and gave him a unique excellent notice in his lifetime. The two men worked together translating classical poetry, and Batyushkov paid Uvarov the compliment of seeing in him the achievement of that balance between politics and poetic taste which it was his dearest wish to maintain in his first years in service. In a tribute in verse he praised Uvarov's grasp of the classical world, the charms of which he was able to convey to his friends so imaginatively. He praised him as a scholar and a most stimulating companion, able to bring Greece and Rome alive in darkest Russia.[15]

Arzamas began as an intelligent literary society with a moderate atmosphere of patriotic self-respect and a feeling for freedom. It became more political as the months went by. New members joined, chief among them Nikolai Turgenev, Mikhail Orlov, and Nikita Muraviev, and in their hands the society's hope for Russian Enlightenment was transformed into a programme of action. They gave Arzamas a constitution and rules, revived the idea of a journal and addressed the weekly meeting in a new spirit of campaign. Nikolai Turgenev criticized the cliché goal of 'reason', which to him smacked of continuing poverty and lack of liberty. The most political of the Arzamasians, and as a republican the most radical, Nikolai Turgenev seems to have suspected in what has more recently been called the moderate Enlightenment a way of perpetuating pre-revolutionary conformity.[16] In April 1817 he told the Arzamasians the cultivated life of the mind and the artistic sensitivity they cherished brought with it fundamental moral responsibilities; that Arzamas should grow up and play a more responsible, fuller and more diverse role in society. After one meeting that year agreement was reached on the need to abolish serfdom and 'all' were present according to the records. Uvarov would soon have to break rank.[17]

Under Nikolai Turgenev's influence the Arzamas programme for a journal in June 1817 was much bolder and more popular – citing the matter of public opinion – than anything Uvarov might have formulated:

> Politics: to spread the ideas of freedom, as suited to Russia in its present state, according to the degree of enlightenment, not destroying the present, but making possible the way to a better future. Examples of public opinion. These articles will consist in:
>
> **i)** discussion of political subjects of our own making, drawing on the latest books and periodicals, and on exemplary works by ancient and modern authors
>
> **ii)** a survey of current events: news, correspondence, feuilleton.

The idea was also to include foreign literature, criticism and opinion and to outline measures taken by foreign governments to aid the power and well-being of the people.[18]

Uvarov withdrew his support. His name did not appear anywhere in the minutes or documents of the June meeting, although it was held at his house, and it was absent from the next one at Orlov's. He had rejoiced in the establishment of a classical kingdom of letters in which literature and government were happy bedfellows, but stepped back when the Romantic revolution which had really taken place now began to make itself felt among his friends and colleagues.

Arzamas developed rapidly in a direction wholly foreign to him as a public man and as a literary critic. Above all it reversed his emphatic priority that aesthetic education should precede education in politics. He was an educator, not a populist campaigner, and he had to distance himself from at least some of his erstwhile brothers. In fact other members felt the same. Dashkov left literature for ever the same year, 1817, and as a writer Bludov also melted into the background. Arzamas disintegrated as a formal society, leaving intact only professional and psychological bonds between old acquaintances. The strongest friendships existed among Alexander Pushkin, Vyazemsky, Zhukovsky and Alexander Turgenev, and they lasted over the next two decades. These were the literary men. Ironically Uvarov counted as one of the politicals.

* * *

He was a writer, indeed a Russian writer, but he was almost entirely ignored as such in his own country and time because he wrote in French, and occasionally in German, but almost never in Russian. Possibly written Russian didn't come nearly as naturally to him as his elegant literary French.[19] In French and German he was an essayist and occasional poet, meanwhile in German he was an independent scholar. The Arzamas period and the five years following were when he did his best work. He wrote articles on classical subjects, continued his private Greek lessons, read and reviewed the work of his friends, and worked, finally, in six languages on scholarly and poetic material as a commentator and translator.

A poetic imagination shaped by a love of the ancient world was his chief gift as a literary critic. He described 'this immense and magic world' from Homer to Nonnos as the richest source of poetry he knew, and he compared its tangibility and epic form favourably with the modern reflective, epigrammatic, melancholy spirit.[20] At the end of 1816, in German, he produced an essay entitled 'Nonnos of Panopolis', which was an anthology of extracts from the Egyptian Hellenic poet's immense Dionysiaca, written some time before 500 AD. This was an interest which had been stimulated by Graefe, and it tallied with a wider interest he had in degeneracy, perhaps the way he mostly deeply felt his own times, in contrast to the optimism of, say, Batyushkov. Nonnos of Alexandria was a cataloguer of Greek myth in luxuriant, densely packed verse. Like other modern scholars Uvarov found the artistic achievement patchy, but this assessment did not dim his personal enjoyment. The richness, colour and sheer oddness of Nonnos's imagery, his use of the hexameter and his intense depictions of love left their mark. Uvarov selected a score of passages, including a favourite one about elephants, and used Graefe's German translations as a parallel text. He also financed publication of Graefe's work on Nonnos.[21]

In 1817 Uvarov took a contemporary French critic to task for identifying the classical hero Hercules with the sun. He published this short essay, 'A critical examination of the fable of Hercules interpreted by Dupuis', in French. In 1821 an essay he wrote in German, 'On the Prehomeric Age', commented on the latest German scholarship on Homer and Hesiod, while 'Memorandum on the Greek Tragedians', in French in 1824, praised the literary quality of the works of Aeschylus, Sophocles and Eurypides, and showed how Greek tragedy flowered suddenly, fitting no scheme of evolution.[22] These were dry works, rooted in a wide reading of secondary material, but they were immensely purposeful in their time. As brief introductions, reviews, anthologies and signposts, they acted as footnotes to a greater body of learning waiting to be explored in Russia.[23]

Uvarov's most substantial achievement as a critic though was virtually to discover Batyushkov. The two men shared their interest and joy in Greek, French, Latin and Italian poetry in the Arzamas years and in 1817 began working together on translations. It was a time when Batyushkov was brilliantly productive in his own right, having just completed one of his finest poems, 'The Dying Tasso', and the following year he recalled to Alexander Turgenev how important Uvarov's help had been:

> Give my regards to Uvarov. If everything goes well, then he of course before anyone will be pleased at my travelling [to Italy] and put in a good word. I cannot conceal from you how grateful I am to him, how much I owe him for his attention and his indulgence. He revived my spirits, as a poet and as a man. He praised me before he knew me, and once he knew me, of course he loved me. It is to him that I owe the best minutes in your Piter, and I shall keep the memory of them long in my mind and my heart.[24]

Uvarov hailed Batyushkov as a Russian poet in the Latin tradition, contrasted his talent with that of the German-leaning Zhukovsky and declared them together the two great poets of the reign of Alexander. His short essay appeared anonymously in the *Conservateur impartial* in French in October 1817, on the occasion of the appearance of the second volume of Batyushkov's works in poetry and prose:

> They have in common a subtle feeling for the beauty of language, brilliant imagination, perfect harmony; but they go different ways: Zhukovsky, nourished on the works of English and German poets, created for us a genre of Walter Scott, Lord Byron and Goethe; Batyushkov, a passionate lover of Italian and French poetry, is drawn to the molle atque facetum (supple and graceful) imitation, which distinguishes the first and the wit and aesthetic quality of the latter. Zhukovsky is more eloquent and striving, while Batyushkov is more exquisite and complete; one is bolder, the other leaves nothing to chance; the first is a poet of the North, the second a poet of the South. Zhukovsky's colours are strong and picturesque, his style sparkles with imagery, profound and vital sentiment inspires all his work. Batyushkov is more balanced and controlled, and where boldness appears with him wisdom shines through; his taste is more highly refined; he is more erotic than loving, more passionate than sentimental, and he imitates Tibullus and Parny with equal success.[25]

Uvarov informed his judgement with the popular Classical-Romantic, South–North dichotomy which from its inception with the brothers Schlegel was to dominate Russian criticism for the next quarter of a century. He did so with flair and a light touch, and the result was illuminating.[26]

From 1817 to 1820 Batyushkov and Uvarov worked together on a project introducing Russian readers to *The Greek Anthology*, an anonymously compiled collection of the Greek verse of various ages. Batyushkov translated into Russian poems from the collection by Meleager, Asklepiades, Paulos

Silentarius and others and Uvarov put them into French. Uvarov also wrote an introduction in Russian. The work was edited by Dashkov, presented as a piece of scholarship which found its way into the hands of the Arzamas brothers, and published in 1820.

Uvarov took the opportunity of the introduction to *The Greek Anthology* to stress once more the need for authentic experience of the Ancients. His aim was to provide translations through which 'we breathe with them, we live with them'. Greece was the home of that 'wonderful people, whom bounteous nature endowed with every perfection of mind and every charm of beauty and taste'. It was the same quality he found in Batyushkov's work: a cultivated sensuality. Present in abundance in Greece, it coupled there with an exuberance in living to give birth spontaneously to poetry:

> The poetry of the ancients can be explained in the sky, in the earth and in the sea of Italy and Greece. We who live in the North can receive those glorious impression which nature produces in the south by a supreme effort of mind, not by quick feeling … . But can we feel in its entirety that worship of the sun, that passionate desire for cool, for freshness, for night? That regret for the years of youth in such a blessed country, that love of pleasure, that genuine delight at the sight of beauty; that feeling which the Greeks gave to flowers and plants; in short can we feel the divine harmony among all things which exist on earth, from which soulless nature also takes its movement and its life?

Uvarov translated epigrams reflecting the pleasures of the senses, beautiful appearance, erotic attraction, the drinking of wine and sexual conquest, and which were contrasted with the passing of time and the ageing of the body. He pointed out the ancients had towards the physical world and the passing moment an utterly different mentality from his own day:

> The ancients limited themselves to external things surrounding them and neglected to bring the light of experience to the dark depths of the human soul: everything summoned them to external objects of a bountiful nature. We on the other hand, everything repels us from them, everything forces us to pay attention to ourselves. For the ancients life was everything: for us even life is only a transition to another, better existence. They directed the immeasurable strength of their genius into the transient sphere of the present; for us, perhaps against our will, our heart yearns for some invisible, though known land, where a different sun and a different heaven wait for us. The poetry of the ancients, even in its most sublime moments, could not step outside the bounds of their public life. In modern times everything which bears the stamp of poetry belongs to a higher order of

things such as this, so that poetry itself evaporates and loses itself in the realm of the infinite.[27]

The poems showed the overt nature of sexuality in the ancient Greek world, which was too direct and crude for modern taste; they celebrated 'the shameful sin to which they gave their name'. But Uvarov wanted the Greeks appreciated, not judged. To compare their passionate poetry with the modern equivalent, he wrote, was like comparing the glory and pleasure of an athlete to the whims of an exhausted sybarite.[28]

These were two of his translations:

Pourrais-tu regretter l'inconstante jeunesse?
Tes traits n'ont rien perdu de leur vive beauté.
    Crois-moi, mon aimable maitresse.
Le temps, qui detruit tout, a pourtant respecté
    Et tes appas et notre ivresse;
Une beauté novice est moins faite aux amours,
Son ardeur incertaine use de cent détours
    Don ne se sert jamais la nôtre;
Mais habile à jouir, savante en volupté,
Ton automne vaut mieux que le printemps d'une autre,
Ton hiver a des feux que n'a pas son été.
(Paulos Silentarius)

* * *

Sur le seuil de Phryne je suspends ces guirlandes:
Festons que j'ai tressés, que j'arrosai de pleurs;
Soyez de mon amour l'emblème et les offrandes,
Versez autour de vous vos suaves odeurs;
Mais si Phryne parait, rendez sur sa tête,
Ces pleurs, témoins discrets de mes longues douleurs
Qu'un spectacle si doux la suprenne et l'arrête;
Fleurs, versez vos parfums, et faites en ce jour
Boire a ses blonds cheveux les larmes de l'amour.[29]
(Asklepiades)

Uvarov, perpetually fascinated by the contrast between the Pagan and the Christian world, revived interest in the ancient world as seen through eighteenth-century German eyes and contrasted it with modern sensibility. He thus virtually single-handedly introduced German classical humanism to Russia.[30]

Meanwhile, his literary ideals were supported by translations in the same way that his desire to suffuse education with classical learning was supported by actual reforms of the curriculum. The practical ability which accompanied his intellectual enthusiasm was marvellous.

But since he didn't use Russian as his literary medium there was the rub. To have been consequently ignored as a man of letters ever since looks like a peculiar punishment for his lack of cultural patriotism, meted out by the subsequent writers of national history.

7

A good sacred task

While Classical civilization and verse, and the contemporary poetry of Batyushkov and Zhukovsky, filled Uvarov with enthusiasm for the power of literature his practical task remained the reform of Russian education. In this though he could be optimistic, after the difficult political period that followed his 1811 essay. The peace that stimulated new creativity also opened the way to measured social change. When his gymnasium reforms, held up by the war, finally went into effect in St. Petersburg at the end of 1816, they brought broader courses in history and geography, and new courses in Greek, into secondary education, as well as the necessary heavy dose of patriotic and religious instruction. He asked for these changes to be approved for general practice in the gymnasia of the empire.

Still in society, particularly among the highest privileged class, Uvarov found many barriers to reform. He conceived of gymnasium teaching to provide training for university, but the gentry did not generally approve of university attendance for their sons, which was something new. The lower, merchant class also showed no greater enthusiasm for an education which might be long and impractical, impeding the earning of money. Another problem was the quality and quantity of teaching staff. In the past, as his own experience testified, these had been mainly foreigners at the higher level. The university of Moscow, founded in 1755, and given its independence from Imperial Decree in 1804, had particularly low standards. Teaching was done for a very small wage by foreigners obliged to communicate in Latin, and who were often indifferent to their tasks and disloyal. Private 'pansions' run by foreigners, like the German school, where the German tutor and playwright Reinbeck had taught, and the Italian school, where Batyushkov was educated, offered more, but were only open to a tiny elite, like the lycée at Tsarskoe Selo. Even in basic education the gentry preferred foreign tutors at home, a habit Uvarov found hard to break even by legislation. And so began a campaign to overhaul Russian education and change attitudes nationally, a project in which Uvarov's immediate aims were to make lower school teaching more efficient and to introduce new Russian blood and competence in the higher institutions.

To improve attendance Uvarov devised an incentive scheme which gave gymnasium graduates a higher rank without examination as soon as they entered government service, and the ploy succeeded.

The number of students staying the course in St Petersburg doubled from 300 to 600, and they were undoubtedly better prepared than their predecessors.[1] Meanwhile in 1817 the Pedagogical Institute under his supervision was expanded and divided into two, one half becoming an improved Teachers' Institute to provide more and better elementary teachers, the other being elevated to a place of higher learning on a par with a university.

His critics later said that being, by virtue of his academic leanings, instinctively drawn to the upper reaches of education, Uvarov concentrated his official attention there, and neglected the other sectors. But much of his early energy was devoted to improving primary instruction for all classes to spread the basis for general enlightenment. Under Uvarov's guidance, for instance, Russian elementary schools practised the methods of the Swiss educationalist Pestalozzi, a pioneering opponent of rote learning, and tried out the revolutionary Lancaster method, under which the pupils, supervised, taught each other to read and write. A small number of Russian teachers were sent to England to familiarize themselves with the scheme, designed to educate large numbers and compensate for a lack of sufficient instructors, and in Russia when they returned the method proved so popular it was used in the Armed Forces as well as in schools. Uvarov also showed himself to be thoroughly professional in his concern for teachers and teaching standards. Facing a shortfall of funds, he tried to improve training and conditions by introducing small payments for schooling on the French and German models.[2]

Uvarov impressed the tsar with these achievements and on 12 January 1818 an Imperial ukaz named him president of the Academy of Sciences at the unprecedented age of thirty-two. Two months later, in March, the newly separated higher part of the Pedagogical Institute inaugurated a chair of Oriental Languages, which it awarded to the French scholar, who was one of Uvarov's cultivated foreign contacts, Louis Matthieu Langlès. This realized one of the dreams of *Project*. Then, the following year the Pedagogical Institute became, with the tsar's blessing, the first St Petersburg University.

Uvarov's confidence grew, and he felt free to explain his plans for the future. Speaking at the inauguration of the Oriental Department he expounded nothing less than his vision of a more liberal Russia. His confidence didn't appear misplaced, because the tsar seemed to indicate he liked what Uvarov was doing, and certainly politically the moment was well chosen, for only the week before Alexander had made one of the most significant speeches of his reign in Poland, suggesting the possibility of a constitution. In the Baltic provinces he had also freed the serfs.[3]

Uvarov spoke at length and went into great detail.[4] His 'Superintendent's Speech at the Celebratory Gathering of the Main Pedagogical Institute', delivered on 22 March 1818, drew on the full extent of his education, from Cicero to Machiavelli, Christian dogma to Herder, to deliver a message of gradual human progress, guided by God. Evidently he felt the time had come to draw public attention more closely to those ideas which he had previously half-hidden in scholarly form. So he declared that the forms of society were not immutable; that climate, religion, war, economic factors, 'the spirit of the times', and some eternal law of necessity all played their part in wringing change towards a better life. He hinted that change therefore was possible even in Russia, and not simply change either, but Providential change for the better. Progress promised men more liberty and greater closeness to God, Uvarov told his audience in the closest he ever came to using the terminology of democratic revolution, and he explained that this was in part thanks to the developing national spirit, in part the result of the exchange of mutual gains on the part of the different social 'castes' or classes making up society. The latter explanation of social momentum was a curious anticipation of Marx. Not surprisingly the address of 22 March 1818 has been called the most important document of Uvarov's early years.

Uvarov's sources were, to repeat, highly eclectic. Essentially he offered the doubled-edged Burkean view of gradual change which had absorbed him since he was a student in Germany, that change was in the hands of men, but the ways and pace of change were set by Providence. Around that basic cautionary argument he adumbrated other ideas on processes of change which would take place within continuing balance and harmony. Thus, like Schiller in *The Aesthetic Education of Man*, Uvarov said the key to right discussion of man's complex future as an individual and a political animal was to consider his development on two levels, the material and the spiritual. Any theory should cater for the parallel development of man as citizen and man as the creature of God. Uvarov's goal was more prominently the harmonious state than the harmonious personality desired by Schiller, and it was history rather than Art which became the guiding light of his argument, but to Schiller he owed much of the form of his thoughts. Aesthetic Idealism led Uvarov to formulate a philosophy of history – he argued that the modern state was moving towards ever greater political freedom in its institutions and ideals; that history was the story of the divinity, which wanted man to realize his potential as a free and rational creature; that history was gradually showing him the way. This was Russia's first positive philosophical response to the French Revolution and its growth ran parallel to the development in Germany of Hegel's philosophy of restoration.[5]

By simultaneously pressing the case for progress and conservatism, Uvarov indeed anticipated Hegel:

> History shows us, young students, how [in feudalism] these three classes of people [slaves, free men, lords] organized into three different castes in the state, strove under the influence of the Crusades to expand their spheres of power, including the monarch who then craved absolutism. Do not think that in this confusion of rights, in this battle of hostile passions, that each state caste was prompted by some grand idea of social welfare! No! Not one of them stretched their vision beyond the narrow circle of their own profit. ... Each acted for himself only and not one knew he was a blind instrument in the hands of Providence, that he acted only to lay the foundation for a balance of all political powers and that these individual, limited efforts would constitute a general thrust forward in the welfare of Europe.

Both Uvarov and Hegel were inspired by the earlier aesthetic idealism in Germany, and in Uvarov's speech there were passages which closely echoed Schiller's dualistic hopes for the integration of the political and the moral man:

> History will tell you that all great political changes ... are the slow fruit of time, the free working of the national spirit, the exchange of mutual gains on the part of all the state castes; it will tell you that the emancipation of the soul through enlightenment ought to precede the emancipation of the body through legislation; and that ... civic and political freedom [emerge in] the transition from the turbulent years of inexperience to the years of mature and real adulthood.

Uvarov added elements of Montesquieu and Herder to this hybrid German model. He stressed the modifying effect of local conditions on government and culture. Finally he arrived at a philosophy of history which most suited emergent Russia:

> Who can entertain the hope of taking in at a glance the entire immeasurable scope of history? Only infinite reason embraces the great panorama of the unfolding eras. We ought to be satisfied with the conviction that each event in history is related to its origin and enters into the composition of the moral world and that all great political changes are subject to the eternal law of necessity. ... You will want to know how a people, which has participated in none of the general changes in Europe, is now in charge of its destiny? How has this people, the youngest son in the large family of Europe, in the course of one century surpassed its brothers and, having preserved

in its institutions and in its morals the traces of the emotional state of youth, now craves enlightenment and aspires to steal from others both the laurels of military glory and the palm of civic valour? *By what remarkable combination of circumstances has the grandson of Peter the Great restored the throne of St. Louis on the banks of the Seine?* [my emphasis]

It was a theory which now welcomed the benefits of the French Revolution, for it could be argued that the upheaval was of the same historical order as the rise of nineteenth-century Russia.[6]

Uvarov had read Machiavelli, but more importantly he knew Ancient Rome through Machiavelli and Gibbon. If, as Machiavelli suggested, the Classical world could be taken as a political model for contemporary society, if Livy could be adapted to modern affairs, then, once again, Russia might be the place where that could happen in the early nineteenth century. Roman ethical concepts such as *fides* – the aristocratic obligation not to abuse one's position of power, and *auctoritas* – the setting of some men above their fellows by virtue of their wisdom, force of character, achievements and family distinction might find their Russian equivalent.[7]

Uvarov in his 1818 speech married Classical political thought to contemporary German thinking to create the promise of a stable, powerful, enlightened Russia to come. Rare men with insight into the ways of history were heroes of Romanticism. It was not difficult to refocus this idea in Russia on the superhuman powers to the tsar. The traditional rulers of Russia had a quasi-divine overview. They understood historical development and recognized when change was due. Much that Uvarov argued was a clever sleight-of-hand, giving different significance in Russia to terms that implied more radical political change in the West. Transferring Romantic interest in heroic individuals to the tsar himself was of course a way of using historicism to justify continuing despotism:

Listen to the voice of history! It will answer you; it will resolve all your doubts, all your questions; it will tell you how enviable is the fortune of a people to whom Providence has given a series of tsars who conformed to the demands of the times and fully satisfied the spirit of their century. States have their epochs of birth, infancy, youth, their actual maturity and finally old age. The observation of these changes is the primary task of a supervisory government. The wish to prolong one of these ages longer than the time appointed by nature is as vain and foolhardy as the wish to enclose a grown youth in the close confines of an infant's cradle. The theory of government in this instance resembles the theory of education and upbringing. One cannot be worthy of praise for successfully perpetuating physical or moral youth; the man of wisdom is one who mitigates the transition from one age to another, guards over inexperience, early encourages the faculties of the mind, warns of danger and delusion, and, upholding the law of necessity, matures and grows along with a people or with an individual. All these great truths are contained in history. It is the supreme judge of peoples and tsars. Woe to those who do not follow its directives! The spirit of the time, similar to the terrible Sphinx, devours those who do not understand the meaning of its prophecy![8]

But it did also whisper: change is imminent. To allege that the tsars knew the great and celebrated Germans without having read them could be seen as an artful way to get Alexander to see that Russia's future lay with a less autocratic society. It could seem as a clever and intelligible stratagem, couched in the progressive philosophical idiom of the day, and I think Uvarov intended it that way.

The 1818 speech contained a vision of restored morale and good sense. Uvarov envisaged a strong public society, with freer and better-educated citizens, and humane laws. His model was the Roman Empire, to which his Göttingen professors and Pozzo di Borgo had brought his attention:

When your attention, young pupils, turns to the enormous structure of Rome, then you will comprehend the true transition of the human mind to its age of experience and maturity. There you see for the first time the meaning of the word 'man' and even more, of the word 'citizen'. ... Ardent fantasy governed the Greeks, while strict and controlled reason ruled in Rome; there we observe the dominance of imagination, the dominance of political wisdom and perspicacity ... [and] the remarkable influence of strong will and love of glory.

The qualities Uvarov perceived to be Roman approximated to Machiavelli's idea of virtù and they informed his own burgeoning idea of national goodness. He wanted to see a culture producing public-spirited, active, forceful men, characters of 'stern reason', like Moreau, Pozzo di Borgo and Stein. Russia required just such citizens to make an active public contribution to the stability and social harmony of the state. Uvarov declared that he found Rome inferior to Christian civilization in its moral ideas, but in every other way it was his ideal.[9]

But finally and disappointingly for those who listened, Uvarov's speech sounded cautiously on serfdom. The Russian people should not expect too much change too quickly. They had to realize that, though feudal, serfdom was a Christian institution in Russia, and only the tsar, listening to history, could say when it should end. Education had to increase first. The tsar was linked metaphorically with the Crusades, to suggest the dawning of a new age of greater equality in Russia, but when his pictorial speech ran out Uvarov could only ask for patience.

Both conservatives and radicals attacked Uvarov for hedging. Nikolai Turgenev impatiently declared the speech was good, but did not go far enough. Alexander Turgenev opined, 'It cannot please our public.' Vyazemsky enjoyed more the section on Oriental languages, but was less taken with the ideas on history and questioned Uvarov's view of feudalism. Both he and Nikolai Turgenev objected to the introduction of Christ into the argument. A review by a specialist in the progressive subject of natural law, Alexander Kunitsyn, who was to become a source of inspiration for the December Insurrection of 1825, observed that there was nothing per se revolutionary about Uvarov's appeal to foreign ideas of freedom.[10]

From the political right Karamzin too was scathing. He saw Uvarov's speech as merely a reflection of the constitution mania which had gripped young men since Alexander's Warsaw speech, 'laughable and pitiable'. Russia had to have autocracy, came his riposte. No other system was possible and no experiments worthwhile. This did not stop men thinking what they liked.

Both Karamzin and Kunitsyn in fact reproached Uvarov for not treating Russia as a special case, as a letter of Karamzin's to his friend Ivan Dmitriev amplified,

To give Russia a constitution in the fashionable sense is to deck out some important person in a clown's outfit, or for the learned Linde to teach grammar by the Lancaster method. Russia is not England, nor even the Kingdom of Poland; it has its great and suprising destiny as a State and is more likely to fall than to rise higher. Autocracy is its life and soul, like republican government was the life of Rome. Experiments are inappropriate in such a case. But I don't want to stop others thinking differently … . Posterity will see what is better, or what was better for Russia. For me, an old man, it is more pleasing to go the comedy theatre than into the National Assembly or the Chamber of Deputies, although in my heart I am a republican, and will die one.[11]

Uvarov was in a powerful position but involuntarily he was at a distance from the world in which he had to act. That distance made a bad impression in an age beginning to look for commitment as a guarantee of sincerity. Indeed most of Uvarov's contemporaries saw only a haughty young man acting a part, as if he were a missionary from a more advanced civilization; which he was. Pushkin's friend, the writer and academician Peter Pletnev, had actually felt sorry for Uvarov, in the enormity of his task, when two months earlier he had given another speech, this time on his inauguration as president of the Academy of Sciences:

On January 28 1818 ... into the midst of this gathering of learned men, known to the world by their works, came a young man about 30, of fine appearance, clearly with the habits of the highest social class. An honoured seat was left empty for him amidst the Academicians, which he took without false reticence, with an awareness of his rights and a certain dignity. Turning to his gathered colleagues, he opened the meeting with a lively speech, in which above all he conveyed how flattered he was to be President of the Academy, which for many years had deservedly enjoyed a glorious reputation ....

Not surprisingly, when the President took his place among the luminaries for the first time, expecting the meeting to have about it some weight and splendour, he was greatly disconcerted to see before him only 15 people, which was all the membership the two Sections of the Academy could muster to meet him. Two Academicians were absent: Storch and Kirchhof. This accounted for the entire body. The inertia and decrepidness of the general membership had become the reason for the exhaustion of its productive capacity. Correct organization and an alert administration were now most essential for concerted activity, he said ....

Thus the President ... felt from the beginning .... that for the Academy to achieve its goal, he would have to rebuild everything in it, beginning with the economic side and working through the administrative and the academic.[12]

It was not easy to be a highly educated man in a backward country.

The Academy though was the least of Uvarov's worries because he was free to rebuild it. Moreover the tradition of appointing as many foreigners as Russians – on the Academy's very foundation Peter the Great had been advised by Leibniz – quite suited Uvarov's purposes. Within weeks of his arrival he had introduced as new members Langlès and his fellow Orientalist and compatriot Silvestre de Sacy, who had just edited the third edition of 'Eleusis' in Paris. These experts were closely followed by the Prussian naturalist and explorer, Alexander von Humboldt, brother of Wilhelm, and by the elderly Karamzin. All these appointments, though they contained a personal element, were designed to further the Russian fund of knowledge and its academic prestige.

1819 was a mixed year. In January the tsar gave his approval for the transformation of the Pedagogical Institute, and from its inception in February the new university offered Russian students courses in their own language in philosophy and history, natural science, natural law, jurisprudence, classical and Oriental languages. This was the first time they had the chance to study in Russian rather than Latin under the tuition of Russian scholars. The very same January, however, the strongly reactionary Ministry of Enlightenment, where Alexander Nikolaevich Golitsyn had succeeded Alexei Razumovsky in the summer of 1816, critically inspected the worst-run university in the empire at Kazan', about 550 miles due east of Moscow, on the Volga, and attempted to close it down. The move was a deliberate bid to limit the number of universities in the empire and also a sign of growing resistance within the Ministry to the Uvarovian reformist spirit.

Opposition to liberalization in the Ministry of Enlightenment had increased since a merger with the Ministry of Worship in October 1817. The new Minister Golitsyn was neither a seeker after power nor a cruel man, but he was weak and blind to all causes except fundamental religion, and now his schools' Board was dominated by fundamentalists, fanatics and unscrupulous careerists. One of its members, Alexander Sturdze, had drawn up for the tsar a report on recent student unrest in Germany. As across Central Europe the Austrian chancellor prince Metternich called for a tightening of the imperial reins, to keep the spirit of the newly self-aware German and Polish nations in check, conservative Russia was only too happy to oblige.

Another member of the Schools Board was Mikhail Magnitsky, a Bible Society man anxious to curry favour in the capital after a period of exile. Magnitsky had been a liberal at the same time as Speransky and been sent off to the provinces to atone for his miscalculation. Magnitsky also loathed Uvarov. Thus Uvarov – who was also automatically a member of the Central Board – was baited into a sudden showdown over the universities spinning out of control. Magnitsky recommended to the Board, after a personal inspection of the morally corrupt and godless university of Kazan', that it be terminally purged. Uvarov alone objected and the debate rapidly took on a personal colouring.

Uvarov mounted a spirited defence. He lauded the spirit of free inquiry and the freedom of academic life. He accused Magnitsky of perpetuating a travesty of justice and told the Board to exercise great caution before sending a state institution to its political death. If Magnitsky had found disorganization in an institution comprising individuals of different faiths, persuasions and origins, the Superintendent said, he would still have to prove conspiracy:

> Because the university has not fulfilled the hopes of the government, and because it has perhaps turned out to be unuseful, it does not follow that it can be called harmful and that one should search within it for a school of deism and immorality.

Uvarov was both superior in his attitude to his fellows and dismayed by a witchhunt which took him back to his worst experiences in 1812–13:

> Once again these wholesale accusations, falling on a whole mass of people! But fortunately Europe's scholars have no need of me to justify them.

But Magnitsky believed that to close Kazan' would teach a lesson about the consequences of so-called enlightenment, and pressed ahead. Whatever he believed, his witchhunt contained a strong element of personal spite, since Kazan' had newly established a course in Asiatic languages, Uvarov's pet cause, and the course was being taught by a German friend of Uvarov's, Professor Fraehn.[13]

Uvarov appealed to the Board invoking reason and moral integrity, as he had done in the letter to Stein six years earlier. He told his fellow educationalists it was not a matter of trying to persuade them to think as he did, but simply a request that they should be reasonable. Invoking 'the pure sense of the responsibilities laid upon us' he concluded proudly and stoically: 'It is enough to save one's conscience and one's own reasoning.' He won a stay of execution for Kazan' after the tsar personally intervened and took his part, but how delicately the balance of favour was poised could be seen in the fact that not long after Uvarov's Pyrrhic victory Magnitsky became educational superintendent of the Kazan' district, whereupon the cause of education for its own sake was lost. Not only did Magnitsky and the Bible Men wreak havoc in Kazan', halfway to the Urals, they also obstructed at every possible stage the growth of the new university in Petersburg. Uvarov worked feverishly from the beginning of 1819 to draw up the foreign-influenced statute giving the institution its own regulations, but his opponents made sure it was never passed in that form. An obstinate member of the Board, Filaret, archbishop of Tver, objected to the lack of provision in the statute for moral guidance. He said it smacked of being a 'dormitory republic' in which seventeen-year-olds might choose their consuls and tribunes. He was bothered by Uvarov's proposed scaling down of theology from a faculty to a chair and the idea of giving students the power to elect their own representatives. Meanwhile Magnitsky condemned the statute as a cheap imitation of a German university, and accused Uvarov of acting without consultation.

Uvarov had no support from the fundamentalist Minister for National Enlightenment and Spiritual Affairs, Golitsyn. In a letter of 9 November 1821 to the curator of Kharkov University, Golitsyn noted he first of all looked for a Christian in his colleagues at the Ministry and that talent and knowledge were nothing without belief. However, when some professors accused of teaching 'materialism' and 'atheism' were brought before him he didn't know what to do with them, except to urge continuing vigilance. Golitsyn was a pathetic figure, and no one that his St Petersburg Superintendent could turn to.[14]

That winter and spring Uvarov fell ill with worry and exhaustion. He looked to literature for support and wrote to Batyushkov. That letter has not survived, but the poet replied from Naples in May, offering Uvarov sincere encouragement to continue his 'good and sacred task':

We read [your letter] with pleasure and congratulated you heartily on such a good beginning. Those who know you respect you, but those who know you intimately love you. There are so many reasons for wishing you success in your good, sacred task. How could anyone not wish from the depths of his heart success to the cause of enlightenment in Russia, that is to half the inhabited world, which cannot long enjoy glory or good fortune without enlightenment. For happiness and glory are not to be found amid barbarism, among a few benighted minds, fabricators of phrases, and astrologers. It is not only with us, but everywhere that such blind men run free. In vain does learning feed them, clothe them, protect them from social and physical harm; they go on singing their own song, and will continue to do so; you cannot teach them, nor enlighten them, nor heal them. Thanks to God the world is not in their hands, and things run their course. A good man is able to do good, and you are an example of that. And that is why Providence sends you good fortune, for the chance to found a university in Peter's capital I call good fortune. Do you remember how many times I wanted that, and how often I spoke of it? My wish has been completely fulfilled, all the more so for having been done through you.[15]

Alas the good and sacred task was not enough to protect Uvarov in a land so rampantly conservative that the empowered majority in the Ministry of Enlightenment and the church were gleefully awaiting the day when the latest attempts at reform would collapse. At a time of substantial personal success Uvarov was failing, because, in spite of all his ambivalence, he was more liberal, more progressive and more foreign in his thinking than the always conservative Russian system could bear, except as an occasional short-lived experiment. His liberalism was not an ideal for republican government; he still respected autocracy, but the danger lay in the unacceptably pure value he attached to education.

8

'Sire, Resist the Friends of Darkness!'

In the summer of 1819 Uvarov was exhausted and dispirited. Defeat over his statute came as a shock and cause of anger. With his 'pure' responsibility and his conscience he had wanted to bring the structure of university teaching into line with the general development of knowledge; he wanted to cut back on the extent of theology; he wanted to relieve teaching staff of administrative duties to raise academic standards; and he wanted to bring in outside managers to run the institution more efficiently. His rightful concern was to give the professors more time with their books. But Uvarov's opponents only had eyes for his foreign-influenced and purist heresies. The very strengths he had used to bolster his confidence over the past decade were now turned against him. He was an academic and the way to attack academics was to allege incompetent administration and moral chaos in their establishments. A chorus of time-servers led by Magnitsky declared Uvarov unworthy of his position as St Petersburg Superintendent. One prominent cleric accused him of being a charlatan, whose reputation rested solely on 'Eleusis'.[1]

A sympathetic academic accepted that Uvarov wasn't a born administrator:

He is an academic in every respect, and it would be better for him to be a professor than a Superintendent. The pansion of the Pedagogical Institute is in a terrible state; I found in it neither organisation nor order, nor cleanliness, nor even tidiness.[2]

Ivan Davydov, a professor of philosophy, would become one of Uvarov's closest allies twenty years later. Uvarov, he said, preferred to take part in lessons at the Pansion and the St Petersburg gymnasium, to test the pupils in Latin and watch the Lancaster and Pestalozzi methods at work. But his public posturing, indeed his very theatricality in affecting a professorial manner, gave his enemies an easy target. Everyone now called Uvarov 'the professor', Pushkin noted. Cast as a pedant he was becoming disliked and risked being ridiculed.[3]

It was a vulnerable educator therefore, and one who was politically naïve, who in May 1819 absented himself for the rest of the year from the Schools Board to protest against the undoing of his statute and the manhandling of Kazan'. Meanwhile a staunch reactionary, Dmitrii Runich, took his place. A blow still worse came when the tsar himself reversed his liberal path. Metternich's determination to turn the Congress of Vienna heads of state against their peoples, for fear of nationalist uprisings, had a powerful effect on him in this respect. In Russia Alexander began to clamp down not long into 1819, despite his support for Uvarov's new university. In March 1819 a German student murdered the reactionary poet and Russian agent Kotzebue, believing the act to be in the cause of democracy. Metternich responded by calling a meeting of European heads of government in Karlsbad in August, and the anti-revolutionary Karlsbad decrees were issued in September. Metternich wanted to see no relaxation of absolute power in Russia and exerted increasing pressure on Alexander, who vacillated, then gave in.[4] Most conspicuous among his lapsed liberal plans, was his failure to implement the constitution promised to Poland.[5]

As the new spirit of fear and reaction made itself felt Vyazemsky, invoking the Arzamas spirit, asked Uvarov to help get his translation of Voltaire's letters past the censor, but Uvarov was afraid to oblige. Another censor then rejected the work as harmful to morality and religion.[6] Over the next months, as the tsar grew increasingly afraid of unrest, Metternich only encouraged him, reminding him in a secret memorandum of the dangers of the age culminating in 1789:

> The progress of the human mind has been extremely rapid in the course of the last three centuries. This progress having been accelerated more rapidly than the growth of wisdom (the only counterpoise to passions and errors), a revolution prepared by the false systems, the fatal errors into which many of the most illustrious sovereigns of the last half of the eighteenth century fell, has at last broken out in a country [France] advanced in knowledge, and enervated by pleasure, in a country inhabited by people whom one can only regard as frivolous. This evil may be described in one word – presumption; the natural effect of the rapid progression of the human mind towards the perfecting of so many things. This it is which at the present day leads so many individuals astray, for it has become an almost universal sentiment.
>
> Religion, morality, legislation, economy, politics, administration, all have become common and accessible to everyone. Knowledge seems to come

by inspiration: experience has no value for the presumptuous man; faith is nothing to him; he substitutes for it a pretended individual conviction, and to arrive at this conviction, dispenses with all inquiry and with all study; for these means appear too trivial to a mind which believes itself strong enough to embrace at one glance all questions and all facts. Laws have no value for him, because he has not contributed to make them, and it would be beneath a man of his parts to recognise the limits traced by rude and ignorant generations. Power resides in himself; why should he submit to that which was only useful for the man deprived of light and knowledge? That which, according to him, was required in an age of weakness cannot be suitable in an age of reason and vigour, amounting to universal perfection, which the German innovators designate by the idea, absurd in itself, of the emancipation of the People! Morality itself he does not attack openly, for without it he could not be sure for a single moment of his own existence; but he interprets its essence after his own fashion, and allows every other person to do so likewise provided that other person neither kills nor robs him.

In thus tracing the character of the presumptuous man, we believe we have traced that of the society of the day, composed of like elements, if the denomination of society is applicable to an order of things which only tends in principle towards individualising all the elements of which society is composed.

Presumption makes every man the guide of his own belief, the arbiter of laws according to which he is pleased to govern himself or to allow someone else to govern him and his neighbours; it makes him in short the sole judge of his own faith, his own action, and the principles according to which he guides them.[7]

The Russian answer to the presumptuous modern spirit was repression, which strengthened the hand of the church, and spawned a cluster of underground political societies conspiring to achieve future reform. Uvarov was set to suffer publicly, without shelter.

In 1820 revolutions broke out in Spain, Portugal, the Italian states and Greece, which seemed to confirm Metternich's worst presentiments. In July 1820 the fear of upheaval in Russia became intense in court and conservative circles when the tsar's bodyguard, the Semenovsky regiment, mutinied for a reason unconnected with events in Europe: the cruelty of a senior officer. The proximity of dates was enough, and Petersburg was thick with anxiety and confusion.

Magnitsky profited from the atmosphere to deal another blow at the surviving enlightened educational establishment. He attacked a book newly published by Kunitsyn, the second volume of his Natural Law. This was the same professor of law who had noted, on the occasion of Uvarov's 1818 speech, that the Russian people was undyingly devoted to the autocracy. That might otherwise have seemed a safe enough position. But for one thing Kunitsyn enjoyed great popularity with students at the university and Tsarskoe Selo Lycée; for another he believed the rights of citizens should be enshrined in laws. He had read Rousseau and the French materialists and he believed the serf economy hampered Russian development. Magnitsky was joined in the attack by Runich, the man substituting for Uvarov, and it was Runich who then led the way:

> Kunitsyn's book is nothing other than a mass of appalling and abominable pseudo-thinking which, unfortunately, the overly celebrated Rousseau brought into the world and which has agitated and still agitates the hot heads of the defenders of the rights of man and citizen. In effect, the consequences that this philosophy has had in France since the acts and constitutions of 1796 until the empire of Buonaparte, are in reality only the application to the social order of Kunitsyn's teachings. Marat is nothing other than a sincere practitioner of this doctrine. The entire book … contains definitions contrary to the doctrine of the Holy Revelations … it is a sacrilegious attack against the divinity of the Holy Revelation, an attack all the more dangerous because it disguises itself under the broad cloak of philosophy.[8]

Pushkin, a pupil of Kunitsyn's at Tsarskoe Selo, was incensed at the stupidity, dishonesty and cowardice of the attack and four years later wrote powerful verses in response:

> Oh, you fool and coward, what are you doing with us?
>> Where one ought to ponder, you stare blankly;
>> Not remembering us, you tarnish and thrash about;
>>> You call white black on whim;
>>> A satire – a libel, poetry – debauchery;
>>> The voice of truth – a revolt, Kunitsyn – Marat.

The poem also featured the couplet that stated the problem of Uvarov's educated generation mildly: 'What London needs/ Is premature in Moscow'.[9]

The proceedings against Kunitsyn were carried out behind Uvarov's back, while he was away from the Board, and when he became aware of them in February 1821 a proposal to tighten censorship was already underway. Because of what he stood for, Uvarov was pitched into the middle of the fray. He was bound to respond. He stopped attending meetings of the Board for a second time and resigned his post as Superintendent that summer.

Runich then took over his job permanently, saying of him, 'He was simply a mould from those German universities as they are these days.'[10] Runich and Magnitsky then attacked Petersburg University with renewed force, the way they had assailed Kazan'.

In the ensuing purge any incumbent professors who taught original, stimulating, in any way up-to-date courses were attacked. Alexander Galich, who had studied idealist philosophy in Germany and whose teaching inspired a chain of students culminating in the men of the Marvellous Decade of 1838–48, was a prominent victim. He and his colleagues were accused of engendering presumption as an attitude of mind; of teaching philosophy and history in a spirit contrary to Christianity. Their courses were described as instruction in 'atheism, apostasy, and the rebellious ideas which we have already seen ruin the strongholds of other governments'.[11] Runich, who briefly became immensely powerful in education, held interrogation sessions lasting hours into the night, at which he was both accuser and judge. After the first hearing one professor was so distraught that he lost his memory. Galich subsequently became an alcoholic and a recluse. The evidence against the professors consisted in the handwritten notebooks of the students, which neither the teachers nor the University Council were allowed to examine. Their books, though they had been passed previously by the censor, were also cited in evidence against them.[12]

In the sheer enormity of injustice and unreason of these events Uvarov, educational idealist, classical scholar and servant of the tsar, could hardly believe. The men on trial were like himself, devoted supporters of church and throne. His sense of outrage outdid even his feeling of the personal wrong he had had suffered in being forced out of the Ministry of National Enlightenment. He could not believe, no more than he had been able to accept in 1813, that the tsar knew of such wrongdoing in his midst, even in his name, and he wrote to him, with an innocence born of unswerving loyalty, to complain of the uncivilized, unprincipled events blackening the year 1821.

The letter was written in French:[13]

Sire,

The most natural decision of my conscience, the simplest impulse of my heart was to come and throw myself at the feet of your Imperial Majesty when I heard what had happened during my absence at the University of Petersburg. But a premature step on my part might have weakened the cause of the accused and shown my concern in a false light. My silence was the most painful sacrifice of all but the most expedient in a good cause and such as would test my confidence in the magnanimity of your Imperial Majesty.

However events have taken their course; now the business has reached a head, and I would consider myself blameworthy in the full sense of the word if I kept silent any longer.

When for very serious reasons, of which Your Majesty knows only a few of the least grave, I was forced to resign from my post as Superintendent of the University of Petersburg, little did I think I would have turned against me the very weapons which I had always employed against a group of men whose vengeance is now complete. By a stroke of fate without parallel those whom I, in the full and complete execution of my duty and with the courage of my conviction designated as the fomenters of disorder and the secret yet powerful enemies of public peace, those with whom I turned down with horror the idea of an alliance, those same men now stand before your eyes in the name of defenders of the throne and the altar against attacks which I would have, if not tolerated then at least not known about or misunderstood in their system!

This simple account says everything: it presents such a reversal of ideas and such a monstrous and bizarre displacement of people that I no longer hesitate to speak out and to recount to you, Sire, the true state of a matter which is properly speaking my own: A Board meeting of the Ministry of National Enlightenment of 19 September notes on the subject of the suspension of Professors Hermann, Raupach, Galich and Arsenev that 'their teaching consisted in a premeditated system of atheism and of principles which endangered morality and public welfare'.

Sire, it is up to the accused to plead their own cause. I will allow myself to ask only wherein lies the offence, the plotting of which has been so noisily proclaimed – in Raupach's Latin notebooks, Hermann's lessons as taken down by his pupils and two books published several years ago by Arsenev and Galich and approved by the Ministry's censor, not the University's? Of these four exhibits two have already been laid aside and since Hermann himself did not commit his lectures to paper there only remain Raupach's notebooks. It is a strange conspiracy in which the offence dissolves bit by bit even before the inquiry!

If one were to pass from there to a brief recollection of the unheard of scandals which took place when the papers were confiscated, if one were to say that in the middle of the nineteenth century, in the 20th year of Your Majesty's reign, 30 yards from your Royal residence, in the middle of the night, people dared to use such dreadful machinery to compromise the honour of an institution created by Your Majesty, dared to threaten to make soldiers of those peace-loving students who would not be roused to action, to speak of prison and Siberia, and to have derisory sermons preached; if one added that all these scandals were exceeded by those of the proceedings of the University Council , in which everything was violated, even human respect, one would doubtless have the right to ask what was the source of such a keen and fierce desire to prevent the free and legal defence of those professors from reaching Your Majesty's throne. Why have there been so many tricks, why has there been such enthusiasm to try to deprive the accused men of their legitimate right, accorded them by Your Majesty? They asked to have proved, not that the perverse doctrine revealed in their questioning was their own or that they approved of it, but that it existed in their notebooks and lectures. What did they hear in reply? 'That this very request was seditious', and that 'it was solely thanks to the magnanimity of the president that the accused were not brought into the assembly and forced to explain themselves while standing between two gendarmes holding naked swords'.

What cause, Sire, is it that needs such means in order to triumph!

But all these considerations will find their place elsewhere. The voice of truth will not be stifled; it will reach the magnanimous and generous heart of Your Majesty. You will know everything, Sire, as soon as you deign to permit everything to be said to you.

Today, pressed by the limitations of a letter and obliged to overcome the feelings which pour from my heart, I take the liberty of presenting to you a single matter for consideration.

Sire, if it is true that an irreligious and revolutionary system of instruction was established at the University of Petersburg, the responsibility cannot and should not fall on anyone other than the Minister and the Superintendent who were in charge of it. Either both of them were immersed in the conspiracy or one of them deceived the other, or both were the dupes of a group of perverse and cunning men. Logic and justice make possible only these three propositions.

I do not know how Prince Golitsyn sees the question in relation to himself as Minister. In my eyes the matter is quite clear. I will not listen to the sophisms of a timorous ego; it is up to me to justify the University of Petersburg. In itself, Sire, I regard this painful and distressing affair as an event wrought by Providence to show men and things in their true light. With this belief and in full awareness of my duty, I will not for my part accept the too easy transfer of responsibility from the Minister to the Superintendent, from the Superintendent to the rector or to the director. In your presence, Sire, I turn down the shameful amnesty that has been offered to me. Not only do I accept the part of the responsibility that must fall on me, but I would have it widely known.

Under the name of the Pedagogical Institute the University of Petersburg has for 18 years shaped a generation of educated and religious men, law-abiding and enlightened citizens, who fill honourably most of the educational establishments of the Empire, military and civil.

This university has passed muster before a number of Your Majesty's faithful servants and never has the slightest suspicion fallen upon it, yet suddenly here it is transformed into a house of atheism and sedition! Permit me to say it: it is not a question of a few imprudent ideas found by chance in notebooks taken from students, notebooks whose authenticity incidentally no one was allowed to put to the test. It is not even a question of some errors in the teaching of the political sciences, errors which it would be easy to correct were they to be proved (none of which I will allow myself to judge before I have received the documents); what was declared to Your Majesty, and to the public, was 'a premeditated system, an association of ideas which has existed for a long time among professors in league against religion and public morality and which by authorities either blind or carried away has been allowed to grow'. The indictment was couched in these terms and no one has the right to have them changed; thus this is the way the matter must be considered; if I am not wrong, it is there that the heart of the matter lies. Since my temporary successor in the post of Superintendent has declared that he has found in the university I administered for more than 10 years 'a house of perverse and seditious doctrines, an establishment of which he had some knowledge before he took over', I can ask of Your Majesty without too great a presumption to be heard in my turn. I am prepared to say that this matter is larger and more important than people want to believe; all things being equal it possesses aspects so bizarre and so mysterious that I can say it is of the highest importance for light finally to be cast on this work of darkness.

The Council of the University of Petersburg to which this matter was referred could only fulfil imperfectly in this respect the views of Your Majesty. If the details of its three memorable sessions have reached you, you may judge, Sire, the degree of audacity of those who felt that any possible justification of the accused involved the condemnation of their accusers, and that once this link was broken, the whole chain of iniquities would come to light. The Council, though it was dominated by terror, conducted itself honourably almost throughout. The soundest amongst the professors withstood the veritable moral torture exerted during three sessions, day and night; they withstood insults, threats, the most insidious questions, the most inexpressible rages. Seven professors, the flower of the university: Balugiansky, Graefe, Soloviev, Chigov, Demange, Charmoy, and Plissov, protested in writing against this procedure. In their capacity as judges they took note of the banning order with which they were threatened in the name of Your Majesty. Isolated individuals, without support, without money, without protection, these seven judges had the courage to obey only their consciences and the their signed declarations are assuredly only a pale reproduction of what they witnessed during those three memorable sessions.

Sire, such is the way things stand in this matter. Since the grudge is held against me, it is up to me to reply. I was thrown the gauntlet and I pick it up in your presence, in the belief that with the aid of God I shall succeed in uncovering where this matter is placed in the chain of events which it is time Your Majesty knew about in their entirety. Then perhaps it may be clear who the men are who threaten the established order, and which men are the friends of order. Should these not be sought among the ranks of men essentially religious and monarchist, men bound to preserve what exists by all the bonds of principle, sentiment, patriotism, national pride, education, property and family; men who know but one way and who, faithful to God without ostentation and faithful to Your Majesty without servility, are ready to shed their blood for you because they know that you are the cornerstone of the social edifice and their only rallying point? And are not the instigators of disorder rather more this group of unprincipled men who, with rancour in their hearts and charity in their mouths, are the born enemies of all positive order and consequently the friends of darkness, who dress themselves up in saintly names to seize authority and sap the foundations of the established order, these cold-blooded fanatics who in turn as exorcists, illuminists, quakers, masons, lancastrians, methodists, everything in the end except as men and as citizens, pretend to defend altar and throne against non-existent attacks and at the same time plants seeds of suspicion concerning the true supporters of altar and throne, these adept comedians who wear all masks to alarm all consciences and trouble all men's minds, who create around them chimeric dangers in order to prolong for a few moments their own ephemeral existence?

Sire, I have been induced so far to keep silent; but the time for caution has passed. I stand accused in my duties to God and to you, in my duties as a public man and as a citizen and head of a family, and I appeal openly to Your Imperial Majesty. I am not asking for your benevolence, Sire, to which I declare I have no right, so long as the University has not been vindicated, I am asking only for your admirable equity:

i) that the accused professors be given all the latitude necessary to defend themselves

ii) that all the minutes and protocols of the University Council be presented to Your Majesty's eyes not in extracts or copies, but in the original

iii) finally I dare to express the wish of being heard in my turn

Sire, if those unfortunate things which have been publicly voiced and supported by an uninterrupted sequence of violent events turn out to be well-founded, if the University under my administration was 'a school of atheism and rebellion', a huge and disastrous responsibility must fall on its top men; but if a deep and rigorous investigation of this matter throws up the truth and tumbles this construction of intrigues and impostures, if Your Majesty's wisdom can make out, as I have no doubt, the true nature of this odious fabrication, then those who have been so ignobly outraged are owed the repair of their honour and the consolation of knowing that Your Imperial Majesty has not found them beneath is trust.

Sire, I have spoken to your Majesty as I was bound to do: in the utter simplicity of my feelings and with all the abandon of absolute devotion. It is up to you, Sire, to weigh, in your wisdom, whether this loyal and unswerving appeal to your unshakeable justice warrants your attention. In throwing myself into this affair I have done my duty – God will do the rest.

I am, with the most profound respect, Sire, Your Majesty's very humble and very faithful servant and subject,

Uvarov

Petersburg November 18,1821.

Uvarov's pitiful rhetoric, his conviction that the Russian leader could not be so unjust, was lost on Alexander, who granted him no interview and did nothing to investigate the affair at the university. The former Superintendent sent another letter, two days later, to the weak Minister of Enlightenment, Alexander Golitsyn, proposing an independent inquiry, but that too had no effect. These rebuffs further wounded the pride and honour Uvarov had set out to retrieve, and the whole episode suggests that his patriotism blinded him as to how the autocracy actually worked. Nikolai Turgenev, the radical whose brief career before he was forced abroad involved him both official and dissenting circles, later wrote that the unpredictable mixture of Enlightenment and obscurantism was of the Russian essence, and needed always to be reckoned with.[14] Yet if Uvarov lacked this insight, so too did Alexander's other ministers, who commonly became confused in their policies and in themselves in their attempts to serve the changeable autocrat.[15] For himself Uvarov would have needed to be more cunning. He failed to see that without the tsar's support he would be dangerously exposed. He didn't take into account the animosity he inspired and the ambitions of others trying to win the tsar's favour. He told Golitsyn he had been worrying over the struggle in the education Ministry for over a year and that he had disdained advice from friends to keep quiet and look after his own reputation, and to be thankful that he hadn't himself been a victim of the purge. Yet when the time came he went willingly to the slaughter.

It is the conviction underlying the present study that the plight of the Western-educated, or Western-leaning, committed Russian intellectual, valuing integrity, reason and probity, but who was a Russian, living in Russia, where he could not make those values work for him, was outlined virtually for the first time in Uvarov's experience of 1821. It was a relatively new problem because it could not arise where there was no education, nor any Russian aspiration to Western ideals, on the part of the tsar or his subjects, and education had only begun in Russia in the eighteenth century. It was absolutely new because of the enormous step forward the West had taken with the French Revolution, suggesting the moral scope of the individual to think and act for himself. It rested on the issue Rousseau had championed, and after him de Stael, of conscience, the concept itself a variant of consciousness. The gulf between Russia and the West truly opened up after 1789, when the new individual-centred learning aroused unprecedented Russian antipathy, for it was then that efforts began to define Russia and Russianness in contradistinction to Western ways. On Uvarov's example, the problem for an educated Russian was not that he lost his patriotism abroad, but that when he returned he could not square his conscience with serving a country where justice and truth were routinely flouted; where they were just means to an end, and that end was the personal power of one man or another. What was he to do in the face of his colleagues, 'these adept comedians who wear all masks to alarm all consciences and trouble all men's minds, who create around them chimeric dangers in order to prolong for a few moments their own ephemeral existence?', as he had described them to Alexander. All around him Uvarov saw frightened, peevish, inexperienced men lurching from one conspiracy to the next, disregarding truth in a constant jockeying for power.[16]

At the height of his misery Uvarov was in correspondence with Speransky, by now governor of Irkutsk and writing a historic study of Siberia, and he told his friend that the question of how he might be a patriot plagued him:

How joyful, for a Russian who loves his fatherland, is the sense of general recognition of your books and your industry! Your letter to me contains the highest promise of right-thinking men. May God give you sufficient resolution of mind and physical strength to finish your great work you have begun. *In magnis et tentasse sat est* ... [In mighty enterprises it is enough to have tried].[17] This idea comforts me too in the modest, but laborious sphere of my duties. To struggle with all that surrounds him and even with himself is the watchword of a man in public and even in moral life. Of course the struggle is not always successful, but for his conscience it is always inevitable. Leisure is even sweeter after the storms of public life, leisure spent with friends from every century, alive and dead, leisure spent with you, with Cicero and Montaigne.

Allow me to say from afar: *Macte animo, sic itur ad astra!* [Draw strength from the life of the mind! That is the way to the stars.] When I was speaking recently about Siberia I happened to say that the history of Siberia divides into two epochs 1. from Ermak to Pestel 2. from Speransky to … I think and believe that.

I dare to comfort myself with the hope that I can in some way help you in your great undertaking; the founding and the spread of Oriental languages is bound to produce the spread of sound ideas about Asia and its relations with Russia. It is a huge field, not yet illuminated by the mind, a new sphere of glory, a virgin source of new national politics, which should save us from premature decrepitude and from the European infection…

Karamzin is writing but has not yet published the ninth volume of the History.

Accept this assurance of my heartfelt devotion and unshakeable respect, Uvarov.[18]

Macte animo! Draw strength from the things of the mind! The events of 1821 marked Uvarov's acceptance of the divided life which he must now lead to survive in Russia. Russian public life would be a burden to be born, and only in the private sphere would he be free to look for moral comfort and consolation.

He could have given up and gone abroad, yet he would have been penniless without the fortune which was tied up in his estates and his serfs. It was also his overwhelming belief that he was born to serve the tsar. He could have joined the new dissenters around Nikolai Turgenev, but he was not a revolutionary and did not believe in radical political ideals for Russia. Indeed, he wanted to save his country from 'the European infection', while encouraging it to become better-educated, fairer-minded and more rational, and this was his conservatism in the national spirit. But Russia, in crisis after the renewed manifestations of the revolutionary spirit in 1820, was moving rapidly out of eighteenth-century conservatism into nineteenth-century reaction. It was the way Uvarov too would go, or be dragged, into a Russian age in which the very existence of the more liberal West was regarded as an ongoing threat to established Russian order.[19]

9

Retreat into scholarship

Uvarov watched his work in education undone in a matter of months. The University of St Petersburg was put on a tight curb under Runich, and what freedom the former Petersburg Superintendent had sought for general Enlightenment by sophisticated argument was now utterly lost. The student body was purged to rid it of unacceptable moral attitudes, professors resigned or retired; in the elementary schools the Lancaster method was suppressed on the grounds that by obviating the need for textbooks it gave less control of young pupils' minds. For a year, Uvarov had only his private scholarship, the care of his family and estate, and his official duties at the Academy to pursue. Happily his private life came as a source of relief and pleasure. He had received in 1819 a fortunate blessing in the form of a large country house, with land and 6,000 serfs, at Porechie, outside Moscow, which he now enjoyed every summer. His wife had also had another child in 1820, who became his favourite daughter, Natalya.

The Academy meanwhile greatly benefited from the interruption to his main career. As a former Arzamasian, literary critic and lover of painting and poetry, enthusiast of the natural sciences, archaeologist, palaeontologist and classical historian, no better man than Uvarov could have been found to take charge in 1818, to see the Academy through the entire period bar a year of the reign of Nicholas I, the next tsar. He would fit it out to face nineteenth-century scholarly Europe with confidence. Setting about rebuilding the depleted institution, which had been leaderless for eight years before his arrival, Uvarov continued to introduce new full-time and corresponding members. Professor Parrot, a physicist who had helped him to his small initial victory over Magnitsky in Kazan' was made a corresponding and later a full member of the Academy, as was Graefe. Uvarov raised salaries and provided stipends to give academic life a chance to subsist, and altogether reorganized the Academy's finances. With substantial subventions from the tsar, he also had the library expanded and catalogued, built new buildings and patched leaking roofs. His aim, as he had explained it in his inaugural speech on 28 January 1818, was to ensure adequate material support to maintain a healthy morale in academic life. He took much the same benevolent and perceptive attitude lower down the scale to the well-being of university students and of teachers.

The thrust of the Academy's work was national, in the classical sense Uvarov had understood the word in *Project*, and it reflected the cool-headed loyalty to their country and culture in which men like Uvarov and Speransky believed. The Academy aimed to build up a national culture through accumulation of scientific knowledge about Russia and through the training of Russian scholars. Books were written and expeditions continued, opening up the Caucasus, and Siberia, the Crimea and Southern Russia and the Urals, to scientific examination for the first time. The Crimea, with its ancient sites, became a fashionable passion in society because of the amount of serious interest it had suddenly generated. Uvarov had a particular personal interest in seeing the Academy set up a special publishing committee to produce a series of *Voyages of Exploration of the Academy* to chart the exploration of the Russian Empire.

Always in the Petrine spirit of gaining knowledge and expertise from the West to enhance Russian achievement, there was a strong international flavour to the Academy's programme. It sent travellers on a voyage round the world, and in many lesser enterprises Russians and Europeans participated side by side in measuring the Empire, answering the challenge of recent expansion. The Academy fulfilled some of the functions Uvarov outlined for an Oriental Institute in 1810, including the preparation of a vast apparatus of scientific, political, social, economic and linguistic information. One of its achievements was to facilitate Russian contact with China.

Uvarov was personally devoted to the Academy's work in Classics and Oriental studies and as active as he could be in the natural sciences, where he established contacts with institutions in Europe and the United States which were invaluable in providing for the exchange of information and in boosting Russia's collections of natural history, zoological and mineralogical specimens. His sense of history and his orderliness impelled him to document the proceedings of the Academy for the first time and to publish its papers annually. In July 1818 he wrote with a passion to the former military governor of the Caucasus, General Ermolov, urging him to cooperate in local research:

You have been placed in a position where your contribution may have great consequences for the sciences. The objects which surround you are either little known or have never been described. The Caucasus conceals in its depths a thousand treasures, which could enrich and broaden the scope of the natural and the historical sciences. In addition, the lands lying at their feet, Georgia itself, the banks of the Caspian sea, and that part of Persia which your work has not yet encompassed, or at least not yet spoken upon, all these present a huge field for those who investigate nature, a field in which every stone, every flower, every wild inhabitant of the forest may serve as a new trophy for the academic world. The Academy never ceases to hope it may complement its earlier undertakings with new journeys of discovery. In anticipation of a favourable occasion when this might take place, I limit myself now to asking you most sincerely to send, as far as possible, everything that catches your attention, no matter to what kingdom of nature it belongs. Every object you send will be investigated as it should be, and I shall be particularly pleased to let you know the results.[1]

The documentation of the Academy's proceedings and of the work of its members, which Uvarov encouraged, was sent out to members annually with the specific aim of broadening knowledge, mingling disciplines and building up the kind of academic community Uvarov had most wanted when he returned to Russia from Vienna. His friend Speransky in Siberia was one of the most appreciative recipients. The Academy was thus a unique forum for Uvarov's good qualities and a personal mainstay in the troubled last years of Alexander's reign.

In terms of daily reality, through the Academy, which had the advantage of being large and official, it was possible for cosmopolitan culture and international learning and Russian politics to coexist, and for Uvarov to survive. Survival was helped by that symbolic link between the present Academy and the achievements of Peter the Great, its founder. It implied a cultural continuity through the eighteenth century and into the nineteenth, which Uvarov cherished. The symbolism and the reality were perfect.

Uvarov was never in any doubt as to the political function of the Academy, however, as his inaugural speech made clear:

We may hope that under the guiding hand of the Most August Patron of the sciences, the Academy will retain to the full its rights to the respect of the academic world and to the gratitude of the country. To this high goal we must unite as one will and together, with sobriety, unanimity and mutual trust, overcome all obstacles in our path.[2]

His fellow Academicians were expected to understand the bargain. 'Sobriety, unanimity and mutual trust' was a three-part formula, rhetoric which easily converted into policy, to help Russian culture grow. The Academy would serve a strong Russia and make its modest contribution to public order in return for tolerance of scholars' modest freedoms: travel abroad, stipends and books.[3] Undoubtedly some of the negative sides of Uvarov's character were indulged by his being president of the Academy. He loved the attention and the pomp, the chance to publicize his work, and to gain the notice and favour of the tsar. But he was a uniquely useful instrument to this highest institution of learning in his native country and passed into posterity with rare high marks for his achievement.

Outside the Academy, however, his erstwhile Arzamas colleagues noted disapprovingly that he was currying favour everywhere. From 1819 he published a series of eulogistic obituaries of the Royal family and henceforth chose his subjects strategically. He cultivated the dowager empress Marie and the empress Elizabeth and gave presents to the Minister of Finance, Dmitrii Gur'ev. But they were efforts which did not go unnoticed by the autocracy and its most faithful servants, and perhaps that was what most upset the Arzamas men. Gur'ev appointed Uvarov director of manufacturing and internal trade in his Ministry in July 1822.[4] The year 1822 altogether brought an upturn in Uvarov's luck, for it was also when his father-in-law Alexei Razumovsky died. Through his inheritance Uvarov became one of the richest men in Russia, with a total of 14,000 souls and several estates.[5]

He was not excessively enthusiastic about his new job in finance, but it provided the chance to return to government service and he did what he could in practical terms to encourage new enterprise. He set up on his own estates a textile factory staffed by serf labour, according to the most progressive methods. But the chief problem besetting the backward Russian economy was the immobility and inflexibility serfdom dictated, and as a conservative thinker and a wealthy landowner he was disinclined to seek radical change, though he did believe it would one day disappear.[6] He had called the institution Christian in his 1818 speech, which, always in his case was a way of asking for time.[7] He believed that premature liberation of the serfs could cause a right-wing revolution, or at least a crisis among the upper class that was so dependent on their labour.[8] Men like Speransky and Nikolai Turgenev, who freed his serfs, took a far greater interest in its abolition. Uvarov's liberal critics were also not impressed by his self-important implementation of political economy as a science. It was put about that he had managed to bankrupt several factories.[9] Vyazemsky, who called him fussy and characterless, declared his job in finance 'empty'. But he didn't hesitate to ask his old friend for help. In his reply Uvarov made no secret of his boredom 'amongst the piles of cotton pieces and huge ledgers' and reached out to the memory of better days. He called Vyazemsky by his Arzamas name of Asmodei and told him: 'The spirit of Arzamas secretly lives on.'[10] He was, out of political necessity, already leading a double life. When in the summer of 1823 he was made a director of the six-year-old commercial bank, he was in a stronger position to help himself and his friends develop small industries in textiles and sugar beet on their estates. But he still had ground to make up in the eyes of the tsar. This gulf in official confidence in him was underlined when, along with only one other servant of the Ministry out of fifty, he was passed over for a routine bonus award.[11]

He redoubled his determination to please. The self-abasing spectacle of Uvarov running round after Gur'ev's successor in 1823, Georg Kankrin, was too much for old Arzamas to bear. 'He's not only ingratiating himself with the Minister but with his wife and children too,' retorted Alexander Turgenev in a letter to Vyazemsky on 15 April 1824: 'Uvarov knows the names of all Kankrin's nannies and gives the children their little bowls of kasha.'[12] While others were similarly disgusted by Uvarov's fawning, Turgenev was all the more outraged to see Uvarov promoted in July to privy counsellor, number three in the downwardly ascending table of ranks, and in military terms equivalent to lieutenant-general.

Quoting general opinion in Petersburg, Alexander Turgenev declared Uvarov had now outstripped even the most ambitious and opportunist of his peers. Vyazemsky absurdly alleged that he was afraid to speak Russian. Together these two asked Zhukovsky if he was not ashamed to be seen walking with such a man down the street, and they were furious when Uvarov tried, because they were close to Pushkin and to Karamzin, to steal some of their glory by contact. Turgenev complained, 'Sergei Uvarov meddled in something of no concern to him and handed the Empress a copy of "Fontan" [Pushkin's poem, "Bakhchiseraisky Fontan"] before Karamzin did, and ruined everything.' In a letter to Vyazemsky in October 1824 Turgenev referred to Uvarov definitively as a former friend from the more casual days of the their youth. To their disgust Uvarov also tried to buy a part in Zhukovsky's success, ordering the very high figure of 100 copies of his poem 'Chernets' when it appeared in the Spring of 1825. In a deliberate put-down, Turgenev commented, he was given only ten.[13]

The personal attacks on Uvarov grew fantastically in the years after his defeat in education, when he seemed to lose pride and scruple. One 'friend' he could still cherish was Goethe, who, he believed, would always understand the depressing conflict between the public and private self. He was a poet who had borne the burden of state service, and he understood the gulf separating the mundane world from the life of the mind. In 1817 Uvarov wrote to Goethe of the consolation he drew from his example: 'The fine fruits of your mind … are always beneficial and refreshing to a man in the dreary world of business.'[14] But then on grounds of manliness even Goethe snubbed him: 'Go out into the world!', he told his occasional Russian correspondent. Uvarov was unrelenting when eight years later he sent a copy of his latest essay, 'Memoir on the Greek Tragedians', to Weimar:

Be so kind as to allow me to present the enclosed piece to you. In the midst of dry, alien administrative business I have finally managed to write this treatise, more as a note of earlier studies, which I shall always love, than as an intended contribution to the discipline itself. It would give me endless pleasure if you would run a kind eye over it; it contains only a pointer, but as it seems to me, one not without psychological and philological importance. Who anyway could judge better the course and development of the spirit of the Ancients than you, who are so closely related to it, and does a brilliant elucidation of the whole question not lie in your own personality?[15]

Goethe did not reply.

Uvarov took Germany's unique Renaissance genius born in the mid-eighteenth century and still flourishing in the third decade of the nineteenth as his model in trying to rise above the pressures of a modern Russia in the making. Not least, like Uvarov, Goethe was both literary man and scientist. Further, unlike many Russians under the sway of literary fashion, he didn't make the mistake of taking Goethe as an archetypal romantic poet. It was Goethe's lucent inner calm that was most worthy of emulation, the personal achievement of a neo-Olympian ideal. And so he took it with him to Porechie and tried to realize it, in limited Russian circumstances, in the quiet flat countryside around Moscow. The effect psychologically, however, was simply greater isolation. Uvarov escaped from a world in which had no positive place into unproductive privacy.

He fell victim to the extraordinary change which was coming over Russian society as it began the nineteenth century a quarter of a century late, and always with the irony that he himself was partly responsible for that change. Particularly between 1815 and 1825, despite political repression, Russia acquired new energy, as emphasis shifted from the state to the individual, from the showpiece to the ordinary man. The changes were first visible in literature. New forms grew up in poetry and criticism and fresh ideas circulated in philosophy and history. In this climate Russia experienced Romanticism, partly home-grown, partly foreign, and the unique figure of Pushkin, whose literary personality, unlike Uvarov's, touched both the French–Russian past and the future Russian national age.

How Arzamas disintegrated was also symptomatic of the times: an active liberal minority broke away from the established conservatives. The Turgenevs, Orlov, Vyazemsky and the young Pushkin moved into the radical camp, while Zhukovsky, Bludov and Karamzin were more moderate and less demonstrative and Uvarov opted for slow retrenchment. The divide opened widest after Nikolai Turgenev was tried in absentia as an anti-government conspirator in the Decembrist Insurrection of 1825 and accused Bludov, who was prominently involved in the subsequent official inquiry, of betraying him. The worst story was of Dmitrii Kavelin, a friend of Zhukovsky, Dashkov and Turgenev from childhood, who joined Arzamas in 1816 but turned Judas when the tsar turned reactionary. Kavelin campaigned with obscurantist vigour for the closure of the new university of St Petersburg and for a political economy founded on the Gospels. The time was ripe for such violent transformations.[16]

Arzamas contained sincere men and opportunists; men who believed in strong government control and others who favoured maximum individual liberty; men who thought one way yet believed that in the interests of the Russian state they should act quite differently. Until now it had not been the habit to divide men according to their declared ideological commitment, but to accept them, as Arzamas did, as a heterogeneous crowd. But the new spirit separated the men who believed passively in freedom and enlightenment while acting otherwise from the men who wanted to put the same beliefs into practice. Out of the latter group the nineteenth-century intelligentsia was born.

Suddenly the word 'liberal' became common currency. Vigel', who observed that the term had not been in use before 1815, said it meant that all of a sudden rich sons of the landed gentry were willing to give up everything for an idea of liberty.[17] Thus new patterns emerged in politics and political psychology. A binary pair of psychological types appeared, dividing social idealists into two camps. On the one hand stood the aesthetic man, on the other the political; the old-style literary man versus the revolutionary. The aesthetic man believed in government based on the rightness of tradition and experience, the wisdom of Burke's 'sort of middle', while his revolutionary opponent, the new man of the people, believed in government based on absolute moral standards, before which each man was equal to the next. Uvarov clearly belonged among the old-fashioned aesthetic men. That psychological fact was to cause him pain for the rest of his public career.[18]

Uvarov's subtle mind was lost to Russia in the Romantic upheaval. He never returned to literary criticism, though he retained his interest in literary and religious history throughout his life and resumed writing in his last decade and a half. He was quickly forgotten as a writer and critic, except in France, one reason being that his style was neither sufficiently open nor bold enough for a Russian age now interested in passion and commitment. He had a dry personality and esoteric learned interests. But, much more importantly, Uvarov was an elitist in an incipient democratic age. His belief in the Fall clashed with the humanitarian optimism of liberal thought after Rousseau. That vague Christian religiosity also tempered his enthusiasm for material progress as essential to the progress of humanity. Then his isolation triggered his defences. He saw his beleaguered position as confirmation of his superiority. That assumption blocked the further development of his talents. He persuaded himself that he need not search too hard nor too wide for excellence, and so fell into that complacency to which greater minds in the form of Stael and Maistre had once indicated he might succumb.

What was lost to Russia? At his best Uvarov was self-sufficient scholar who belonged to no one school of thought, but was dominated by his highly intellectualized Christian faith. One of his great delights was to trace the origin of religious ideas in the Orient as they passed through Greece and through Graeco-Roman civilization to Christianity. His fascination was with 'bizarre' and 'poetic' Neoplatonism, on which he once intended to write a book.[19] He was praised by an English critic of the day for describing 'very philosophically and beautifully' in *Eleusis* what later would be called 'The Great Chain of Being':

> The natural state of man is neither a savage state or a corrupt state; it is a simple state, better, and closer to the godhead; the savage and the corrupt man are equally far away from it. We have to accept these monuments, both of which attest to that fall of man which alone contains the key to his entire history. Hence the retrograde march of the moral world, opposed to the eternally ascendant force of the human mind; hence the present order in which the wisdom of men is only an intuition, a memory of the past, and in which virtue itself is nothing but a return towards God.
>
> This great truth of the Fall of man seems to have been glimpsed by all the religions. It is to be found in all the theologies of the world, and serves as the basis of ancient philosophy. In the mythological traditions it may be perceived now as a principal idea, now as an accessory notion: often it appears there beneath symbols of combat, or of mourning; sometimes it occurs in the image of a killed god; and sometimes it is spiritualized; and philosophy then declares the degeneration of the soul, and the necessity of its gradual return to the place it once occupied.
>
> All the moral truths of the first order which are linked to the fall of man, these primary truths either directly transmitted or developed by the divinity, could not but survive even the greatest aberrations of the human mind. The dispersion of peoples, the abuse of allegory, the personification of the attributes of God, and of the powers of nature, the confusion of ideas over immaterial substances, all these could not prevent some relics of the primordial truth from being conserved in the Orient; and these relics, by some miraculous turn ... became ... the object of the great mysteries of Eleusis.[20]

No perceivable emotion attached to Uvarov's religious views, but they civilized him. As he wrote in *Eleusis*, quoting Cicero, belief in ultimate divine mystery 'elevates man and teaches him to live agreeably and die with hope'.[21]

When he was free from political pressure Uvarov's religious faith kept him from committing himself to systems of philosophy, and he resented any encroachment of the natural sciences into the moral-aesthetic sphere:

The human spirit, accustomed to the constant, sensible order which governs the physical world, naturally seeks to apply to the moral world this law of progression which submits all beginnings to a visible and gradual development. It is certain that one can discover without difficulty, in the history of those sciences we call exact, that continual succession of ideas which enriches them with new inquiries and superior observations to those which have gone before; but it is not the case at all with the arts of the imagination and the mind.[22]

The same point was made repeatedly in *Eleusis*:

In general one cannot repeat enough that in the present state of human knowledge, the only system to follow in history, in philology, in mythology, in criticism, is to adopt no system at all.[23]

Particularly considering hypotheses about the origins of civilization, Uvarov averred,

One should not hope to link together all the difficulties in a single explanation, nor to reduce everything to a single system.[24]

The spirit of Uvarov's thinking may recall Hegel's, but there was no question he would, like Hegel, construct a system to apply that thinking universally. As a principle of development in nature he could accept the organic idea of progress he found in Herder, but any moral theory had to accommodate leaps and miracles:

Since in the universe every beginning develops according to its own laws, so man finds nothing more repugnant than apparent arbitrariness on the part of the spirit, which in its course will rob whole generations in order to endow excessively one individual, or will fragment the gifts of genius so meanly that no prominent head can stand out from the crowd. The connection between this arbitrariness and the general plan of the development of mankind is the great problem of its history.[25]

Indeed at every point Uvarov may be seen making sure there is no excess of German 'system' in his thinking. Outstandingly, he resisted making of ancient Greece a mythological ideal in itself, as happened in Classical German culture, where it became the symbol of the ideal age and the model for the civilization which modern, fallen man should strive to resurrect and integrate with Christian morality. In the history of Russian thought this is a creditable and unusual stand. Germany produced the dualistic Romantic theory that given the gulf between the classical, southern and the modern northern intellectual world a new third culture might arise to unite the two and transcend their deficiencies; and when this theory reached Russia from about 1815, it immediately prompted thoughts that the third great Western civilization would be Russia. The Third Rome argument, that Russia might be the next capital of the Christian world, had existed for several centuries but now found unusual philosophical dress. By avoiding the scheme Uvarov avoided speculation. He believed in Russia's future greatness, attached to its Eastern heritage, but there was no need to make of this a doctrine, for the historical evidence was sufficient. It was the point of view of a classicist, not an ideologist.

Uvarov put the point about the Oriental heritage in his letter of 1 December 1819 to Speransky:

> The spread of Oriental languages is bound to produce the spread of sound ideas about Asia and its relations with Russia. It is a huge field, not yet illuminated by the mind, a new sphere of glory, a virgin source of new national politics, which should save us from premature decrepitude and from the European infection.[26]

He believed simultaneously in Russia's backwardness and unique potential; and in Europe's attractive richness, present superiority and potential demoralizing future influence in Russia. In this respect Uvarov could never have been labelled exclusively a Slavophile or a Westernizer. He was both and more, for such partisan thinking was alien to him. Moreover, the complexity of his political position was a direct outgrowth of his immersion in the classical heritage, or to put it another way, in his politics his support for teaching classics found its full meaning. He idealized in all things balance and moderation.

In sum, his mind was clear and painstaking. While he often leaned towards the non-literal, sometimes symbolic interpretation of facts he checked himself against excessive speculation. His enthusiasm was tempered by scholarship and his clarity of thought was helped by fastidious attention to style. He failed to give this mind to Russia because he was not a man of his times, and did not consider their need, except negatively, later, as the tsar's chief ideologist. But in immediate practical terms to write the way he did, in French and German, without so much as an attempt at a Russian rendering, was bound to be unproductive. His potential audience at home consisted of a handful of men. In addition, Zhukovsky's criticism of *Project* held good for the later work: it was self-interested and singularly inappropriate in a country where even the educated class was backward compared with men of the same reputation and standing in Europe. Too obviously there was a kind of disloyalty, which said he was not prepared to sacrifice himself for Russia, although he was deeply interested in the Russian language, contrary to popular accusations. To affect foreign ways so pretentiously, with the gestures of false modesty to be found throughout his small oeuvre, was a deep flaw in his Russian fate. Uvarov does not seem to have realized how much political harm he inflicted upon himself through his flaunting of foreign languages and arcane scholarship. He told Goethe he used French and German because they were appropriate to subjects in which the greatest advances had been made by French and German scholars. It was an idealistic conclusion to draw from his cosmopolitan education, and Goethe was impressed, but it was unlikely to make Uvarov appear a man of the people in a popular age.[27]

I speak of Uvarov's fate as a Russian fate. Elsewhere a case could be made for disinterested study and educated exclusiveness. But in Russia it was not enough. A man had to be seen to serve his country. The element of service as writers was very strong in Uvarov's most enlightened critics, Zhukovsky and Karamzin, and in the Decembrists. In the nineteenth century the feeling took the form that a writer or poet was both bad and wrong if he did not share with the community its most pressing social and political problems. The idea was consolidated by the intelligentsia in the 1830s and 1840s, particularly by means of Vissarion Belinsky's pioneering 'civic' literary criticism. Uvarov did not appear to be sharing very much. The connection he proposed between his work and Russia, via the Eastern heritage, was too esoteric to be noticed at a time when Russia wanted pictures of national character and words of social reform.

On a valedictory note, the way the cultural mood would change might have been foretold from two symbolic events in Europe in 1814: the defeat of Napoleon, seen by his enemies from the ranks of the *ancien régime* as a highly unaesthetic object, and the death in December of de Ligne, their prince of finesse. Individual power, rebelliousness against established order and tradition, and historical greatness were what would interest literature now; Russian literature would proliferate with little Bonapartes, not little de Lignes. From Pushkin came classic studies in individual aggrandisement like Evgeny in 'The Bronze Horseman' and Hermann in 'The Queen of Spades'. In a quieter vein poetry was to explore inwardness, lyricism, and reveal the world of private emotion. Such inwardness, if it was to be authentic, was virtually inseparable from dreams of greater freedom. Thus the models of Uvarov's adolescence – cultivators of light, didactic album verse in a world of amorous convenience and a disenfranchised mass – passed away as a Russian art that would campaign for reform and liberty waited in the wings.

To repeat,

The epoch of 1789 arrived, the revolution which was so fatal to taste and to the republic of letters whose first need is peace, it robbed him of his titles and his fortune and incensed his soul, by nature gentle and sensitive; but it did not destroy his courage; he did not follow the example of a number of writers and embrace these destructive principles. To turn his eyes away from the fearful spectacle it presented by its swift progress, he sought, like a Roman orator, to still his pain in the embrace of literature and friendship.

The obituary of Delille might have been the spiritual obituary of Uvarov. He drew from his French background predominantly aesthetic values: an aesthetic of behaviour, which sanctioned social acting, an aesthetic of knowledge, which bound knowledge to order, and an aesthetic of statecraft which was benevolent dictatorship. The aesthetic of knowledge drew limits to the kind of knowledge which could be aired publicly, in the same way as neoclassical theatre proscribed the appearance of the handkerchief. The aesthetic of behaviour was the manners of the salon. Against all these Uvarov would come to contrast politics, by which he meant the legacy of the Revolution, and the business of 'sincerity'.[28]

He took his farewell from the world in which he was happy in a single remarkable essay, 'The Prince de Ligne', written in 1815, after de Ligne's death. It is his best and most original creation, owing its continuing vitality to a number of striking images and pictures built up by Uvarov from his recollections of Vienna. The effect is Watteauesque: a picture of eighteenth-century French court life, ageing and decaying behind the elegant and witty masks.

10

A doffed cap to the Tsar

Pushkin saw in the great floods which washed over St Petersburg in
November 1824 a metaphor for the question which divided Arzamas
and decided the course of Uvarov's middle life: whether it was possible to
unite belief and action and openly challenge injustice in an autocratic society.
His poem 'The Bronze Horseman' dramatized the emotional ties between
tsar and subject. But those ties were so subtle that the question remained
unanswerable. Written with several years' hindsight of the first abortive
attempt in Russian society at a political revolution, this great poem, perhaps
Pushkin's greatest work, sharply portrayed the psychological turmoil of the
crisis year, 1825. Evgeny the protagonist, was an impoverished commoner
who could not accept losing his bride-to-be in the flood. He became a beggar
and a social outcast and in a mad vision raged at the statue of Peter the Great
on the banks of the Neva. The tsar had tamed Nature, and built a city, but poor
men were his sacrifices. Evgeny's challenge failed because of his own half-
heartedness. The statue seemed to pursue him and when his rage subsided
he was ready to doff his cap and lower his eyes.

Poor, Romantic, socially oppressed, one of the anonymous urban mass,
Evgeny was the first of the downtrodden in nineteenth-century Russian
literature. Like Peter he stood as the measure of the age, but at the opposite
extreme of the vast, unjust range of human experience. Pushkin intuited what
Hegel reasoned, a world in which powerful world-historical individuals stood
at one end of the spectrum and at the other end cowered the rest. This vision,
which was the post-Napoleonic legacy in Europe, laying the foundations for
socialism, in Russia cast the rule of the tsars in a new light. The plight of
the common people gave the intelligentsia its conscience and the outsider or
the underling became its touchstone. Henceforth, the new Russian moralist
would educate his conscience by reading not Schiller's mature aesthetics,
which spoke to the ruling class, but Schiller's heartfelt youthful drama against
social injustice, *The Robbers*.

Uvarov chose not to fight after his own clash with the tsar in 1821. He considered that to survive he had to capitulate. The Decembrist Insurrection, therefore, which took place on 14 December, 1825, three weeks after the death of Alexander, appalled him. When members of the nobility, in and outside the military, challenged the institution of autocracy and demanded a greater share in political decision-making, an action which drove home the possibility of political revolution in Russia, he called it 'a damnable aberration' and spoke of 'the murderous attempts of a gang of factionists; of madmen who, despising the most cherished interests of their country, set about tearing its breast, and with their lies and murder gave themselves a foretaste of the destiny which their madness was preparing for them.'[1] The Decembrist leaders were men of Uvarov's social standing and similar education who had betrayed everything he held dear. They had massed a few hundred troops in Senate Square, not sure of their ultimate goal. It was a vague, uncoordinated and hardly violent protest in the uncertainty surrounding the accession of Alexander's second brother Nicholas, but a shot was fired by one of the rebels and a prominent general on the government side was killed. Uvarov however spoke of a rebellion against God, the new tsar was equally shocked, and the punishments were severe. Five of the Decembrists were hanged. Another 121 were sentenced to hard labour and Siberian exile, among the lesser-punished rebels being Uvarov's relatives Mikhail Lunin (his brother-in-law) and Sergei Grigorievich Repnin, and Lunin's cousins Nikita and Alexander Mikhailovich Muravyov.

Russian political life was irrevocably changed. The Decembrists were not a unified movement, but the groups they embraced held radical views which frightened the autocratic establishment. Nikita Muraviev expressly rejected the absolute authority of the tsar. He said the Russian people were not the property of any one person or family. Sovereign power belonged to the people. He declared the right of citizens to vote, to hold public office, to be tried by jury, to enjoy freedom of belief and worship, and attacked many existing social evils. He even suggested a bicameral people's assembly.[2] In response, when Muraviev and his friends were tried, the prosecution tried to have them tarred as regicides. The Decembrist uprising was perceived as bringing the events of 1789 to Russia's doorstep.[3]

Uvarov was ten years older than most of the insurrectionists and he had repeatedly declared himself against revolution as a method of change, emphasizing in his 1818 speech that 'in order to learn one's rights and obligations, it is necessary first to tear down the unbridled strength of youth'. Nevertheless he shared some of the Decembrists' aims, which included more and better education for all classes. The rebels were inspired by education and travel in Europe just as he had been ten years before, and among the injustices of daily life which appalled them had been the purge of Kazan' and St Petersburg universities.[4] They explicitly wanted improved political institutions and an end to serfdom, but overall their ideal was a more independent and wholesome culture, proud of itself as a state and a national entity. They decried one that excessively followed foreign fashions and the dictates of foreign leaders. Their consciousness was moulded in the years after the Congress of Vienna and when nothing came of Alexander's speech to the Sejm in 1818, promising a constitution, their disappointment was laid down to mature in rebellion.

It was painful and puzzling for Uvarov to be so close and yet so divided in spirit. Painted into a corner by unexpected events, and left without an argument, he responded viscerally, by calling his opponents' ideas mad. When he was calmer he insisted the only way ahead lay in redoubled loyalty to the autocracy and the church:

May Russia, protected by a paternal administration and by wise laws, see grow beneath its sceptre the sources of public prosperity so that the foreigner who comes to visit will say to himself: Here is a wise, intelligent people! Here is a powerful nation![5]

After his early, so formative years abroad, he always worried what that 'foreigner' would think of his country. How to make good Russia's poor cultural and political reputation in foreign eyes would become a major feature of his work when he finally returned to power.

But the 14 December event forced Uvarov to reformulate his ideas meanwhile, because the very existence of such literate and civilized protesters defeated his key argument for harmonious Russian social progress, namely that an education in good taste guaranteed political stability. Just a few weeks into the reign of Nicholas he switched to an argument which was unambiguously political. The way ahead lay in building up Russia's international prestige. Europe was to be an admiring spectator of Russia's rise and rise.

He had company, and not necessarily bad company, in publicly rejecting the events of December 1825. Even those committed to the idea of liberty vacillated in practice, like Pushkin's Evgeny, so strong was the idea that Russia, the parent, the autocrat, was right in the end, and the outbreak of liberal idealism had been misguided and foreign. Many of the Decembrists at their trial blamed themselves for poor organization of their aims and a failure to grasp the situation in their country; they continued to swear their loyalty to the tsar and Russia; to doff their caps. Uvarov's relinquishing of his liberal ideals has to be seen in the light cast all around him, at different times, from Speransky to Nikolai Turgenev, of other good men's defeat. He may well have feared the waste of his life and talents had he resisted the pressure of autocratic convention. The times were such that it was impossible to be too careful.[6]

Nicholas's image in the first years of his reign profited from his firm handling of a dangerous affair, coupled with a strong military campaign against Persia. Conservatives who had tired of Alexander's self-absorbed neglect of Russia were impressed. Nicholas employed the finest administrative talents in the country to account for the unrest and take action against a future recurrence. Education and censorship were overhauled at top priority by specially formed committees, and he set up of the Third Department to watch over security, lest there be a regrowth of the underground societies which, Nicholas was told, had facilitated the Decembrists' rise.

It was nevertheless unfortunate that Nicholas had to begin his reign on the defensive, events pushing him rapidly in a direction where he had every natural propensity to go, for the Insurrection of 1825 coloured his entire reign. He had been brought up unequivocally to detest the French Revolution and saw it as his redoubled and unequivocal task now to keep Russia free of the spirit of 1789: 'The Revolution is at the gates of Russia but I swear it will not penetrate as long as I have left a breath of life, as long as I am Emperor, by God's grace.' Subsequently at the slightest disruption to the order and peace of society he was wont to say, ironically in French, 'It's my friends of the fourteenth.' He made the allusion almost as a joke, convinced of the basic soundness of the existing order.[7]

Nicholas believed his authority derived from God, coupled with a natural stubbornness of character that faith made immoveable. 'I doubt that any of my citizens will dare not to go in my direction, once my precise wish has been conveyed to him,' he declared in 1826.[8] The new tsar was unshakeable and uncompromising. He was untroubled by the learning and dreams which had introduced doubt into his brother's heart and hope into the minds of his subjects. He may have wept when he found himself in power, but he quickly grew into kingship and modelled himself on Peter and on his brother's greatest foe, Napoleon, whom he admired as a foil to revolution.

Uvarov could hardly have been drawn to this man in his heart, though he swore allegiance to him as emperor. From a small social distance he had known him for ten years, the earliest occasion being when the tall, lean twenty-one-year-old prince, noted for his moroseness in public lightened with occasional jokes, spent the summer of 1817 with his new bride at Pavlovsk. The daily programme included dances, walks and readings, and Uvarov sometimes went along with Zhukovsky to participate. The young tsar was ungainly, had a wild and ungracious manner and did not value the limited formal education he had received.[9] But Uvarov would not be caught out again by letting his personal tastes obtrude. He learnt under Nicholas to wear ideas as a style, and to make sure the pattern was cut to fit the autocrat. Nicholas formed two committees to deal with education and censorship at the beginning of his reign and Uvarov served on both. By that route he found his way back into the mainstream. Nicholas made him a senator within a year of coming to the throne.

The official inquiry had condemned as the root of the December problem the education that had elevated and enlightened the revolutionary side. The familiar conclusion was drawn of the dangers of a little learning. The Education Committee, formed in May 1826, was entrusted to look into where the state was failing in the production of loyal citizens, and Uvarov worked ironically under the chairmanship of the septuagenarian Admiral Shishkov, erstwhile foe of Arzamas and Ministry of National Enlightenment since 1824.

The energetic Education Committee did good and fruitful work after five years of obvious chaos in the universities and schools of the empire. The other members included the wise and practical prince Karl Lieven; Speransky; Count Sievers, a contemporary of Uvarov's at Göttingen; and Heinrich Storch, the German free-labour economist and academician who taught the tsar political economy. The duty of these men was to coordinate the educational institutions of the empire, and they carried out their work intelligently and consistently, laying the foundations for education under Uvarov in the two decades to come. Runich's instructions in Petersburg were countermanded and in Kazan' the tables were finally turned against Magnitsky, who was exiled to Revel (Talinn) in Estonia, the other end of the empire. A breakthrough was achieved which affected academic life for the next two decades when university students were once more allowed to study abroad, and were given government support, with a view to improving the quality of Russian teaching. The Pedagogical Institute was revived and reform of the corrupted universities put high on the agenda. The committee resisted the most extreme recommendations which were being put Nicholas's way, including military control over schools to avoid the spread of the noxious 'lycée spirit'. Instead they emphasized something not new but dear to Nicholas's heart, the need for a unifying and unified national basis to learning.

Uvarov must have been gratified to see his ideas of fifteen years ago now re-acknowledged. For the general education of the empire three categories of schools were designated, more or less according to social class, just as he had envisaged as St Petersburg Superintendent. There were parish schools for serfs and peasants and factory workers, district schools for the children of merchants, lower-ranking officers and some of the nobility, and gymnasia, mainly for the sons of nobles, with a view to their entering university. The aim was to encourage the upper class, but pupils could, and did, come from either of the other schools to the gymnasium, so essentially the system was open. Attempts were made to keep children at school by not allowing their parents to remove them before the end of the course and making chancery work conditional on having a district school-leaving certificate.

All schools taught the doctrine of the Orthodox Church and Russian history. At the elementary level the parish schools taught the three r's, while the district schools performed the function of secondary technical schools, introducing pupils to the sciences, mathematics, history, geography, and Russian. Necessarily curriculum problems only arose where intellectual development was more advanced, in the gymnasium. Some committee members wanted to see Greek and Latin taught there extensively, according to Uvarov's ground plan of 1811, but Uvarov himself in the light of experience objected, saying good teaching was scarce and Greek should be restricted to just a few schools, with a corresponding increase in the amount of French and German offered. Others, including Lieven, wanted to see more mathematics. The diverse opinions were intricately bound up with colliding views of the future of Russia. One view supporting Greek said the rigours of the dead language would improve discipline and keep the heads down, whereas any contact with the spirit of France caused trouble. The committee had just worked out a compromise when Nicholas intervened to say what he had decided over their heads that French was a necessity, Greek a luxury. It was thus decreed that this unique passport to high rank on entering government service would now be taught only in the gymnasia of university towns, as Uvarov had wished, but not for his reasons. The gymnasium curriculum otherwise comprised divinity, church and religious history, Russian language and literature, logic, Latin, French, German, mathematics, geography and statistics, history, physics, orthography and drawing. Pupils could specialize in mathematics or classics in later classes.

The committee, linking the school curricula closely to the teachings of the Orthodox Church, founded an imperial education system which taught a paramount Russian truth. The schools and universities were tasked with forming political and moral views in their pupils. But the basic system was academically impressive, and did not shun difficult subjects, nor contact with abroad. The moderation of the period immediately after the Decembrist Insurrection was a distinct improvement on the manic repressions of 1821, and the moral and political emphasis was no greater than that to be found in English, French and German establishments of the day. It set Russian education on its modern path.

The Censorship Committee, on which Uvarov sat as president of the Academy, also began its work in 1826 in a moderate and positive spirit. It expressly aimed to create more 'positive censorship' than before, guiding Russian writers and journalists as to what they should undertake. Hitherto censorship had been vague in its permissions and prohibitive in all other respects. Uvarov sat on the Board alongside Lieven and the head of the new Third Department, Count Benkendorff. The effect this committee had may be seen in the flourishing few years enjoyed by the periodical press to 1831. The public passion for knowledge and liberty which burst forth in Alexander's reign was permitted to feed on a rich diet of foreign literature and ideas. A group which had been vocal in 1823–25, 'The Lovers of Wisdom', gathered around the writer and educationalist Prince Vladimir Odoevsky, created an appetite for German metaphysics and Romantic poetry which was soon catered for by two rival periodicals, Nikolai Polevoy's *Moskovsky Telegraf* and Mikhail Pogodin's *Moskovsky Vestnik*, respectively 'the Moscow Telegraph' and 'The Moscow News'.

Pogodin was a young history lecturer at Moscow University with great enthusiasm for German philosophy. He was the son of a serf, and his rise signified the relatively generous spirit of the times. Polevoy was also an historian of non-noble birth, his father being a Siberian merchant. His trademark was his extreme pro-European outlook, and one of his chief collaborators on *The Moscow Telegraph* was Vyazemsky. Compared with later decades it was not a partisan intellectual age. The new generation of educated men were united in that education and displayed an enthusiasm for European learning and Russian self-betterment which exceeded the confines of Arzamas and transcended the neoclassical era. These Russian Romantics took to heart the wholly foreign idea of 'philosophy' as an answer to how they should live as Russians.

The 'Lovers of Wisdom' met to discuss theories of beauty and read the poetry of Goethe and Byron. Stepan Shevyrev, a contributor to *The Moscow News* and lifelong friend of Pogodin, delighted readers with his critiques of German aesthetics and his reading of Goethe's *Faust*. Polevoy published among other stimulating ideas in translation August-Wilhelm Schlegel's 1808 Vienna lectures 'On Dramatic Literature'. The intelligentsia was laying the foundations for the flowering of its ideas in the next two decades, just as official education had begun to be built and would reach its apogee in the same years under Uvarov.

Censorship however was a tricky matter, and if the committee proceeded judiciously it was particularly thanks to the mature leadership of Lieven who had spent a number of years as rector of Dorpat University. This was the most relaxed in the empire because of its position on the fringes, in close touch with the German-speaking world, and Lieven in the few years he was influential in St Petersburg remarkably increased conservative tolerance.[10]

Uvarov witnessed in these few years a public passion for intellectual fruits which had already lost their sweetness for him. He watched over the democratization of such knowledge as he viewed to be too esoteric to be widely understood. He might have wished the times and his taste had not been so far apart when he had been a young enthusiast for German letters around 1810, for Russia was indeed now passing through a thinking revolution. Possibly the experience was disorienting, and he resolved privately not to be caught out twice in his life by a sudden change of the autocrat's mind. As Nicholas I's Official Russia thus took shape, he played a quietly obeisant role in education and censorship. Where he stood firm, despite some initial pressure to resign after the crisis of 1821, was at the Academy of Sciences.

There were ways in which he did not fit the mould, for most of Nicholas's advisers were military men, and many, following tradition, which included a hereditary distrust in the Russian sovereign of the Russian nobility, were foreigners of a kind, like the Baltic Germans Nesselrode and Benkendorff. Still Uvarov shared with Nicholas's early advisers, alongside devotion to political stability in Russia, an instinctive cosmopolitanism which ensured that one of the best aspects of Alexander's reign was initially carried over. Until Nicholas began to assert his domineering personality the feeling among many men, not just Uvarov, was that suddenly there were opportunities again. The officially sanctioned cultural atmosphere of national progress augured well.

The 100th anniversary of the Academy in 1826 gave Uvarov an early opportunity to emerge from a round of elaborate receptions, speech-making, textbooks, yearbooks, honorary degrees and medals for the royal family to remind Nicholas that enlightenment was essential to his reign. Peter the Great had set an example to be followed.

> In his profound reflections on the glory and well-being of Russia, Peter the First understood the place the arts and sciences occupy in the life of a powerful people. The strong hand, accustomed to ruling now by sword, now by trident, to holding the reins of government and to scattering the seeds of future greatness throughout the vast Empire, the hand which shaped each part of the machinery of state, ended by illuminating his magnificent creation with the beacon of learning and education. Peter, on his journey through Europe, saw the effects of the arts and sciences on the fate of states; concluded that without their strong influence his gigantic labour would not be perfected; realised that enlightenment, which has become part of the life of the European nations, is one of the indispensable foundations of cultivated, durable societies. He resolved to steal for us a spark of that divine flame of which the blossoming countries have long been proud, and to found on the banks of the Neva a shrine of learning, duty bound to spread to the furthest limits of Russia knowledge useful to all men, and to implant in men's minds the striving for peaceful achievements in the field of public excellence: he founded the Academy of Sciences.

Uvarov's message was that the Academy, sired by the Promethean genius of Peter and nurtured by the Russian soil, nursed the future educated generations of Russia. His speech urged Nicholas to put himself on a par with

Peter and keep it flourishing. The speech also implied Uvarov's role in the years of official national culture to come: he would be the midwife.

Not all foreign visitors to the Academy would be impressed the way Uvarov hoped. In 1829 the explorer Alexander von Humboldt, brother of Uvarov's educational mentor Wilhelm, felt greatly put upon by an excess of government supervision, and a greater emphasis on commercial gain than scientific advancement seemed to threaten the integrity of his journey across Russia. He also loathed the chauvinistic pomp that greeted his return to St Petersburg. Since the tsar financed his extraordinary trip, however, he held back from expressing any view of the backward social and political conditions he witnessed in the eight months he was away, and his experience as a naturalist in Siberia, topped by a first sighting of the Altai Mountains, dazzled him.[11] Humboldt's visit seems to us now to fall into a pattern that many official foreign visitors to Russia enjoyed in the past and would experience in the future: an emergent modern Russia, excessively keen to impress, could not always hide its coercive domestic practices, nor shelter the visitor from them. Yet the land itself had so much to offer that the host could be proud.

Uvarov wanted to be influential and instrumental in this burgeoning modern Russia that might yet impress Europe. Among the new journalists he befriended younger men who wanted publicly in their editorials to advance the cause of enlightenment by encouraging a broader education in Russia, like Shevyrev, the aesthetics and literary criticism specialist, and the historian Pogodin. Both these men had resources of nationalism and conservatism which Nicholas's reign would encourage them to develop further. Uvarov meanwhile forged closer links with Ivan Davydov, who was one of his earliest sympathizers over the difficulty of administering Russian education. Davydov had survived the censor's closure of his course on Schelling in 1826 to continue teaching philosophy and literature at the Moscow Pansion for the Nobility. This handful of men whom Uvarov chose as close colleagues came to rely on his patronage as much as he depended upon them for their company and their political support. They occupied a role in his life, depending on their age, somewhere between intellectual foster-children and Roman clients and they gradually took the place of the Arzamasians in his life under Nicholas. For the time being, however, he continued to see Zhukovsky, and Turgenev and Pushkin, whom the tsar had allowed to return from exile as a gesture of benevolence in the first year of his reign, while he adjusted his threnodic output to suit the births, marriages and deaths at the court. He cultivated Benkendorff and Lieven, his immediate superiors; he devoted a eulogy to Lieven's departed wife Marie and another to Empress Elizabeth; a third was dedicated to the dowager empress Marie Feorodovna and yet another marked the passing of his famous military relative, General Fyodor Uvarov. He was the Romanovs' servant, but he was also Russia's, in a still greater sense.

To secure his political position and serve his country's stability and prestige he would now develop his notion of an official Russian culture, as a foil to the new individualism from France.

The threat to the very idea of an official culture appeared to be the existence of individual imagination and conscience, and Uvarov's work attempting to control it set him on course to become Russia's literary Metternich. A speech to the Academy that autumn of 1829, on that occasion of his return to St Petersburg which Alexander von Humboldt found so embarrassing, provided a landmark definition. Just as Humboldt was finding Russian police controls too much for him, from his Western point of view, here was Uvarov stating the Russian case for scientific expertise harnessed to, and ultimately made to serve the end of, Russian national pride and power:

> Humboldt, having shown us the rich countries of America in a new light, has pioneered a route which no other man has taken with such striking success. From an early age he detached himself from the fame which entices vulgar men, and devoted himself entirely to advancing the natural sciences, wherein his every piece of work has signalled a new departure … and after dedicating his first investigations to regions of the New World, he has brought his rare wisdom, admirable eye and immense activity to countries which form one of the most interesting parts of the Russian Empire.
>
> If, putting aside all scientific interest, we consider this noble enterprise as a new means of acquainting ourselves, more accurately, with our vast motherland, do we not owe a double gratitude to the famous man who provides us with more reasons to be proud of the soil on which we were born, to measure its resources with greater assurance, and to deepen its standing in so many important ways? The journey that Mr Humboldt has just completed, his presence today among us, will suffice, gentlemen, as proof of this community of interests and affections, this cosmopolitanism of the sciences, which is their finest attribute and most distinctive characteristic ….
>
> Yes, gentlemen, they are everywhere, the gods of intelligence and thought, everywhere one senses the need of their presence, everywhere where they are evoked in the calm of study and meditation. Essentially cosmopolitan, the sciences are not, like the arts of the imagination, the exclusive attribute of such and such latitude or such and such people. There is not a people which can claim not to enjoy their benefits, and which does not associate itself with their triumphs.[12]

Science was objective and universal, and could therefore serve as the basis for Russian progress. Art, however, was subjective and national and problematic. In Russia even if science was free from political interference, art could not therefore expect to be. Confronting Romanticism in politics with a corresponding reactionary classicism, Uvarov hoped to retain control of intellectual growth, and in his anti-Romanticism began a tradition of political reliance on apparently incontestable 'scientific' truth. The tension between science and imagination was the tension once again between eighteenth-century Enlightenment and nineteenth-century Romanticism and he saw it as his political task to reconcile them. The fate of Russia and of Uvarov, an eighteenth-century cosmopolitan living in conditions of nineteenth-century nationalism, drew close. He was in this respect, trying to prolong a past order, and embodying its artifices himself, exactly like Metternich. Both men to a degree forged policies which would also have solved their personal dilemma at being misplaced.

Even in office Uvarov began to speak in two voices, the idealistic and the realistic, the first to set the goal, the second to acknowledge the difficulty of achieving it against the tide of the times. The optimistic voice spoke to a potential international audience of the idealized Russian state and the progress of autocracy as an enlightening institution. In this big arena the sciences vouchsafed progress and progress vouchsafed the Russian status quo. Uvarov spoke of Russia as being not at all backward, rather as having caught up by taking the fruits of Western learning and realizing them in a unique empire-state:

Is it not by means of civilisation, under the influence of enlightenment, that this Empire has been able to reproduce in one century the long infancy of the European monarchies and spread itself majestically from the shores of the Baltic to the banks of the Aras? This imperturbable moderation, this reflective calm in the midst of triumphs, this redoubling of energy in the depths of misfortune, this continuous and progressive development in all elements of the life of society, is it not a certain sign, an indubitable effect of enlightenment?[13]

But the second practical voice, intended for trustworthy domestic ears, looked at real conditions and tried to provide real, relatively small-scale solutions. Uvarov inspected the province around Nizhny Novgorod in 1829 and pondered the immense difficulty of ruling a country at once 'so young and so old, so rich and so poor, so weak and so strong, so barbaric and so civilized' except by central power.[14] His 'realistic' solution was to educate officials who could restore trust between the monarch and his subjects, and build confidence in the national future.

Yet even that idea, embodying and uniting the functions of consul and tribune from an older empire, was excessively hopeful. There seemed, as

Uvarov approached ministerial rank, to be an essential duplicity about Russia, to which he had to conform, and which in his characteristic way he would end up by embodying. What he did not and never would anticipate, however, was the sheer arbitrariness of the tsar, who was yet to show his mature colours.

The system of government under Nicholas rapidly became as whimsical as the tsar's character, and those who served them constantly feared demise.[15] Uvarov's obituary of Alexander praised as faultless the obscure, often absent, inconsistent tsar who had done Uvarov such a grave injustice, and declared him a wise genius with a common touch who had achieved a unique reconciliation of Russian royal authority and public liberty. Uvarov would deceive himself equally for the new monarch. Those who have tried to rescue him from the classification of an unquestioning reactionary have rightly drawn attention to his moderation and his gradualism. But all the while Uvarov's essential weakness was to believe in the tsar as a man equally tolerant of those virtues.

Within two years of his accession the tsar began to assert those despotic traits which made it impossible for the committees to do their work. As often as he listened to his advisers he began to overrule them and unable to trust either men or institutions he had no other way to rule except personally. He believed in the rule of law but no sooner had he conceived of it than he destroyed it; and he could not uphold education in any real sense because he could not tolerate the freedom to think.

An exemplary fate befell the Censorship Committee. In April 1828 its recommendations were made law and it was allowed to turn itself into the Chief Directorate of Censorship, a body under the Minister of National Enlightenment. But it was almost immediately undermined by the tsar's interference through Benkendorff's Third Department and once it lost its quasi-autonomy it became negative, arbitrary and repressive. A Russia formed which was a projection of Nicholas's personality, shored up by the progressive institutionalizing of traditional Russian conservative principles, and isolated from the infectious West. Karamzin, who attained new authority and posthumous eminence under Nicholas, but remained capable of sophisticated and unpredictable judgement, lived just long enough to recall sadly those 'innocent and gracious' Alexandrine days, now passed, when no one feared the secret police or Siberia.[16]

Those were also the days before Uvarov created his 'system'.

11

Orthodoxy, autocracy, nationality

I wish for the good of humanity
there could be learning but no learned men.
CLEMENS METTERNICH

Nicholas reigned in the realistic belief that the threat of revolution was never far away. When in 1830 the July revolution in France secured power for a revolutionary government and the Poles rebelled against Russian rule the following year, he was nevertheless as shocked as he had been in December 1825. He tightened controls in the northwestern part of the empire and made new appointments. In April 1832 Uvarov was named Deputy Minister of National Enlightenment under Lieven, Bludov Ministry of Internal Affairs and Dashkov Ministry of Justice. Alexander's cosmopolitan Russia passed over into Nicholas's nationalistic state with this final distribution of the Arzamas men.

Political failure brought education under close scrutiny and hardly had Uvarov arrived in office than he was plunged back into a purgatorial atmosphere such as had ruined him in 1821. The tsar closed Vilna University in the Polish-dominated western provinces in May 1832 and clamped down on the few freedoms of Polish education secured in the last decade by one of Alexander's early liberal advisers, Adam Czartoryski. This time, however, the drastic events took place further away and had no personal meaning for Uvarov. He condemned the Polish action, as did Pushkin, notoriously in a similarly chauvinist and imperialist vein.[1]

The first actions of Deputy Education Minister Uvarov were decisive and the tsar was impressed. His immediate brief was to ensure the few student disturbances at Moscow University in sympathy with the Poles did not spread, and he carried out a purposeful inspection of teachers, students and facilities in August and September 1832 to that end. Aware that Nicholas thought too much unsuitable education had caused the Decembrist Uprising, Uvarov proposed a new national system of instruction to try to turn the tsar's extreme political fears to some socially beneficial end. The inspection generated a memorable six weeks, both for the students, a number of whom were purged for unsuitable behaviour and indiscipline, and for those professors whose lectures Uvarov attended. Vissarion Belinsky, the future literary critic and socialist, was one of the students ousted because he had written a play against serfdom.

Uvarov conducted himself with confidence. He was a man in his mid-forties who knew his job. Still his public persona seemed false. The novelist Ivan Goncharov remembered how Uvarov brought Pushkin with him to a lecture by Davydov on Russian literature. What excited the student Goncharov about the occasion was the proximity of genius, and by comparison Uvarov's behaviour seemed forced:

> When he came in with Uvarov, the sun lit up the entire auditorium for me: I was at that time taken to the point of fascination with his poetry ... I and all the young men of the day who were interested in poetry felt the direct influence of his genius on our aesthetic education. ... Suddenly here was this genius, this glory and pride of Russia before my eyes, not a few yards away! I could not believe my eyes. Davydov, the professor of the history of Russian literature, was giving a lecture.
>
> 'Here you have the theory of art', said Uvarov, turning to us students and indicating Davydov, 'and here you have art itself', he added, indicating Pushkin. The sentence was delivered for effect and had evidently been rehearsed. We all fixed our eyes hungrily on Pushkin. Davydov finished his lecture.[2]

On this and other occasions Uvarov, otherwise so assured, became anxious in the presence of Pushkin. He might have felt that he had become a mere bureaucrat, when originally he too had wanted to be a poet. He wasn't happy standing next to a man who made him feel artistically inferior. Uvarov pioneered Russian Oriental studies but Pushkin wrote the lovely 'Fountain of Bakhchiserai'; Pushkin wrote 'The Bronze Horseman', using the floods in St Petersburg as one of the great extended metaphors in Russian literature. Uvarov sat on the 1824 Flood Relief Committee. The comparisons were easily made.

Vigel', in a letter to Pushkin, was fascinated by the mixture of achievement and frustration, grandiloquent insecurity and quiet conviction in the middle-aged Uvarov:

He's a man of the court, irritated by his lack of success, but not so bitter he would refuse a good post when it was offered to him; he's a clever man, who enjoys a surfeit of intellectual pleasures, but is always ready to begin a literary and academic career over again; when it comes down to it he's a good but vain, discontented man, impatient that neither of his chosen paths has achieved him the respect and the power he had reckoned on … . It's my opinion he's changed, at least I find him more likeable than he used to be. The whole trouble is that he began on the path of glory, then changed to the path of honours, moving from the one to the other in succession, and ended up by confusing the two. That was a mistake, but his old friends asked too much of him. I would say they were even unjust: they supposed in him, though goodness knows why, the firmness of a Stoic, the spirit of a Roman; when they saw they had made a mistake they cut themselves off from him, as if from a deserter or a perjurer. My respect and my indulgence for him notwithstanding, I don't find him so guilty. I have shown him politeness and friendliness and have received the same from him in return.[3]

When Uvarov toured the Moscow classrooms in the autumn of 1832 he displayed his inveterate fascination with the practical ways of education. Accompanied by a delegation of dignitaries, he would walk in on a lesson and take over the teaching himself, or join the students at their meal, and, if these actions were sincere, the sincerity was painful to critical onlookers. In his report to the tsar he claimed he evoked ubiquitous enthusiasm for Russian learning and that his homilies glorifying the autocrat were always well received. He believed Russian education was primarily a matter of winning hearts, and that he could succeed in the task. 'I often interrupted the students' lectures', he reported, 'and finished them myself with exhortations and sermons which emphasised devotion to Your Majesty, the throne and the altar. I told them these things must precede universal enlightenment.' '[I told them] it was essential to be Russian in spirit before becoming European in education.'[4] The confidence with which Uvarov delivered these exhortations, combined with an assurance that his review of Moscow intellectual life had thrown up no signs of the revolutionary germ having spread from Europe to the schools and universities, to neither teachers nor students, was however not totally believable to those who knew him well.

The Deputy Minister weighed the need for ideological security against the need for a rise in academic standards. He accepted Nicholas's general desire for rigorous extra-curricular discipline, but called for better buildings, a better library and improved salaries and conditions for staff. His loudest cry was a perennial one, for more money. He was critical of the teaching and administrative staff and recommended improvements, faulting particularly the faculties of politics and law and the unsuitable personality of the rector. On the other hand, he was generally lenient towards the students. He advised that they should be supervised to the degree that each of them be known by name, and that they should be smartly turned out, but he could not remind the tsar often enough that they were basically harmless. He was pleasantly surprised by personal meetings, he said, having been prejudiced before his inspection. The students might be arrogant, foolish, shallow, even sinful, but he had found no trace of political wickedness or criminality in their midst. Yet the tsar needed guarantees and Uvarov was searching for a way to provide them:

> [We should keep young minds] in that desirable equilibrium between ideas which are seductive for immature minds and which have, to its misfortune, taken hold of Europe, and those firm principles on which not only the present but also the future well-being of the fatherland are founded … [We should try] *to bring them almost unconsciously to that point where these ideas and principles blend and resolve one of the great problems of our time, namely a correct, fundamental education, which is essential in our century, combined with a deep conviction and a warm faith in the genuinely Russian conservative principles of Orthodoxy, Autocracy and Nationality, which comprise the ultimate anchor of our salvation and the most reliable guarantee of the strength and greatness of our fatherland* [my emphasis].

Traces of Uvarov's earlier reliance on the indirect aesthetic method of persuasion were visible in this classic formulation of his mature policy. The balance and harmony of French neoclassical art could still be adapted to meet the needs an anti-liberal political ideology. Uvarov could go on talking about 'bad taste' when he meant political indiscretion. But the effect was to bowdlerize both his repeated tributes to the age of Boileau and his own youthful ideal of *Bildung*. The German reformers of the 1810s, translating the age of Goethe and Schiller into Prussian educational policy, had projected a rich spiritual as well as knowledge-based school experience oriented to the individual's all round capacities and needs. Russian domestic stability, now Uvarov's priority, could not tolerate so much individualism.

He knew it and the slogan 'Orthodoxy, Autocracy, Nationality' expressed it as the ultimate requirement of the modern Russian citizen in the light of revolutionary threats to the tsarist regime spreading from Europe. The tripartite formula demanded absolute fidelity to Russia as the precondition for any advanced education as such and it raised Uvarov to the pinnacle of his career when Nicholas made him Minister of National Enlightenment in March 1833.[5]

The policy declared in 1832 was Uvarov's first attempt to systematize an education which would keep out undesirable Western ideas, while maintaining high standards of science and scholarship. One might see it as the moment when a learned man afraid of disorder offered his services to a militaristic disciplinarian contemptuous of learning. In Nicholas's Official Russia the academic administrator had to learn from the soldier, even as he would seek ways to keep the soldier from seizing his arms.

The real problem however was journalism, especially the literary journalism that was rapidly becoming the real source of education of the intelligentsia. 'Orthodoxy, Autocracy, Nationality' was a banner under which education could flourish but literature would struggle. Plato knew exactly the difficulty Uvarov faced:

> It is not only to the poets therefore that we must issue orders requiring them to represent good character in their poems or not write at all; we must issue similar orders to all artists and prevent them portraying bad character, ill discipline, meanness, or ugliness in painting, sculpture, architecture, or any work of art, and if they are unable to comply they must be forbidden to practise their art. We shall thus prevent our Guardians being brought up among representations of what is evil, and so, day by day and little by little, by feeding as it were in a healthy pasture, insensibly doing themselves grave psychological damage. Our artists and craftsmen must be capable of perceiving the real nature of what is beautiful, and then our young men, living as it were in a good climate, will benefit, because all the works of art they see and hear influence them for good, like the breezes from some healthy country, insensibly moulding them into sympathy and conformity with what is rational and right.[6]

For artists and craftsmen read journalists. Uvarov's Plato-inspired task was particularly to constrain the Moscow press to which he devoted a uniquely negative part of his 1832 report. He followed up with personal face-to-face warnings to editors that they should not instruct the Russian public in errant thinking.

He didn't pursue his friends and protégés Shevyrev and Pogodin, who were nationalists of a different stripe, but focused his attack on two particular scapegoats. One was the cultural theorist Nikolai Nadezhdin, very much a German Idealist in his idea of how the Russian nation should make progress by arriving at national self-awareness as 'the people'. Nadezhdin was professor of aesthetics at the university and editor since 1831 of the journals *Teleskop* and *Molva*. Uvarov's other target was Polevoy, the editor of *Moskovsky Telegraf* whom he was reputed personally to dislike.[7] Uvarov was wary of the power of these men's journalism as a source of unofficial education. He referred in his report to penniless, lonely students sitting in their rooms and being particularly vulnerable to the influence of harmful foreign ideas. Foreseeing the creation of troubled and politically troubling figures like Dostoevsky's Raskolnikov, the ex-law student protagonist of *Crime and Punishment* (1866), living in extreme poverty in St Petersburg, and who spent his time logically justifying murder, Uvarov was prescient that the challenge to official thinking in the next two decades would come from such young men who were poor, educated and independent in spirit. These men would become known as the *raznochintsy*, the 'men of mixed class', and he did his utmost to stop them coming into being.[8]

Uvarov was on the threshold of a brief time of strength. Alexander I's wish had come true and the world of Russian education lay at his feet. He had lost friends and made enemies on the ascent to high rank, but his tsar needed him. He was bound to feel a little isolated and perhaps that amplified his self-congratulatory tone. Vyazemsky went to hear him speak while he was in that mood, still in March 1833, and didn't like him at all. Uvarov had written a speech in appreciation of Goethe who had died the previous year, but it was nothing but 'a little brochure', his once partner in literary pursuits scoffed. The Minister, who really thought of himself as a writer, read it to the Academy on 22 March just ten days after his appointment was announced.

'He found ways of saying while talking about Faust that he was Minister,' complained Vyazemsky, reporting to Alexander Turgenev that the speech contained only grand words, no ideas, and was mostly trivial and superficial in its literary criticism.[9] Yet it was here that Uvarov made his debt to Plato explicit. On the flyleaf he called Goethe 'Amicus Plato', and Plato's spirit hovered over every paragraph of his address.[10] Goethe was a Platonic guardian and Uvarov had modelled himself on that heritage. No other document of the time provides so much insight into Uvarov's private state of mind. To mourn Goethe was to recall the critical distance Goethe took from the French Revolution. Uvarov spoke of the better-ordered past to which Goethe had belonged and which he had embodied. It was difficult to understand the present 'transitional' age which had succeeded it. The problem was the 'redistribution' of intelligence and what that meant for political culture and society:

Death, striking with redoubled blows at the elite of truly European men … seems to have assimilated the catastrophes of the intellectual order to the disasters of the political world; it has walked along the heights of intelligence, at the same as another power, no less fatal and no less absolute, has decimated the summits of political order, and if we need not fear for the wellbeing of civilisation in general, if the law of progress cannot cease to be the express condition of our existence, it is nevertheless evident that we are entering, everywhere, into one of those epochs of transition, which are not unknown in the annals of the human spirit, epochs at once stationary and progressive, in which the resolution of an agrarian law of intelligence seems suddenly to become the ultimate symbol and the supreme instinct of society.[11]

That 'redistribution of intelligence' was the keynote of the present age and it was what gave Uvarov his problems with the Moscow journalists. Suddenly it was clear the Plato-inspired Minister had not shifted position from when he was a young idealist facing de Maistre. He and one or two other men knew what was good for their fellows, which might, in time, mean evicting the 'artists'.

On the other hand, the Goethe speech was a renewed call to progressive men for patience. The age was 'at once stationary and progressive', with all that was aristocratic about it certainly museum-bound and yet the future unclear. In fact Uvarov's mind was blank when he looked forward. He could only look back at those aspects of intellect and faith which did not seem worth sacrificing to the passage of political fashion. Goethe, who lived at a time 'when the entire activity of the human spirit rested on the progress of intelligence, and nothing of what today absorbs opinion entered then into the passions of the multitude' represented fact over fancy, the classicism of immutable law over the Romantic spirit, providence over presumption. He belonged to a time when literature eschewed politics and concentrated only on 'universal' themes. Uvarov's point, however, was that Goethe was such an aristocrat by choice and not by birth. His political calm and disinterest could still be acquired. By implication, if one wanted greatness, still in the modern world, one should not be a political partisan. History was implacable, but one didn't have to side with this or that opinion. The same aloof wisdom was shown by Goethe in his attitude to German Idealism, which happened, with the times, but didn't need to be 'followed' politically:

> Not only did [Goethe] maintain himself an aristocrat in his principles, his taste, his sentiments, when the entire aristocracy was forced to abdicate, he also openly professed the most complete disdain for the triumphant opinions of the multitude. Thus, when the irreligious systems were introduced in Germany, when the mania for abstract formulae shook the foundations of the moral sciences, Goethe took pity on his compatriots' frenetic passion for metaphysical investigation, and followed their laborious incredulity with his sarcasms. In the middle of the fire of Kantism, which raged, he treated with little respect and declared unreadable the dark works of the Königsberg philosopher, which were then the words of an oracle, but of which hardly the titles even are known today.[12]

Uvarov exaggerated Goethe's opposition to Idealism and ignored his subtlety. He was utterly wrong about the significance of Kant, the philosopher whose Copernican revolution emphasized the autonomy of human knowledge.

He ended by three times calling Goethe a monarch, an unconstitutional monarch but one whose legitimacy lay in his genius; as if Goethe and Nicholas I were equals. No wonder Vyazensky felt nauseous. Uvarov instrumentalized Goethe's genius as another way of celebrating an elite culture and casting doubt on the new fashion for the wisdom of the people.[13]

The new Minister of Education used Goethe to tell the early representatives of the nineteenth-century intelligentsia, whose journals now abounded with the ideas which had charmed Uvarov in 1810, and whose literary lives revolved around German metaphysics, that he too had been to Germany, read *Faust*, and loved the ideals of beauty and wholeness as paradigms for cultural and spiritual experience, but his passion had not destroyed his loyalty to Russia and the tsar. What enraged Uvarov about the liberal intelligentsia was that it used German Idealism as a way to attack Russian backwardness and lack of liberty. He seemed to have had Hegel's teachings on nationality and progress in mind when he claimed they misunderstood the German thinking they used to portray Russia so negatively. Equally they were wrong to use Goethe as a Romantic figurehead or to conceive of him as an Idealist. For

the more Goethe's spirit distanced itself from all artificial syntheses, in speculation and in practice, the more he felt himself drawn towards the natural sciences in their most mysterious details; with these details he occupied himself lovingly, but there, as elsewhere, he would bow his head to no system, would let himself be the prisoner of no one theory; he conducted himself as an observer; he advances alone and is free.[14]

It served Uvarov to press the case for Goethe as a scientist free from the metaphysical theorizing that Burke had associated with the revolution, because science was neutral; not a matter of partisan opinion.

Literary-historical reminiscence, a justification of the transitional nature of the age in Russia, and a sketchy apologia for his own life to date were all contained in Uvarov's polyvalent Goethe speech. When a Western critic in the 1970s, taking that line of criticism begun by Vyazemsky, dubbed it no more than an apology for the age of Nicholas, he only echoed the classic Soviet view that this was 'a political speech about the autocracy of Nicholas 1 and its advantages'.[15] But to judge the speech in these terms is to miss the biographical and the sociological content of an essay which establishes an ideological bulkhead against Russia's 'Marvellous Decade', 1838–48, already establishing its foundations. Uvarov, as he took office at the Education Ministry in 1833, was obsessed with the growing phenomenon of *knizhnost'*, the spectacle of a new generation of semi-educated men living their lives in Russia according to foreign books imperfectly understood. Of course, on the one hand, Uvarov was a Platonist out of his time, believing that everything originally good and pure was corrupted during its passage through common life. Yet as is amply testified by his journalistic writings, Dostoevsky too was enraged by this 'bookishness', which made young people contemptuous of society and impotent. The 'Underground Man' was a classic victim of *knizhnost'*.[16] What drove Dostoevsky into religious reaction in Uvarov simply confirmed his sense of his own superiority as a European-educated Russian and his isolation. He had remarked in his essay on 'The Mysteries of Eleusis' that to protect the integrity of the Mysteries the Greeks had a higher and a lower truth, one version suitable for all men and one for only the few.[17] Once Uvarov accepted the esoteric Greek solution as a model he needed Plato and Goethe as his friends, because he had no Russian contemporaries who qualified. It was precisely this isolated position which Maistre and his agreement with Plato had criticized, in passing, because he felt it made Uvarov, despite himself, 'a Romantic'.

Ascent to the Olympus of high office gave Uvarov a personal refuge, where in pale imitation of Goethe he kept his own distance from opinion and legislated for the providential well-being of Russia. His diverse views on gradualism in history, on ancient wisdom, his hatred of the French Revolution and its social and political consequences, and Plato on keeping education 'pure' did indeed become a systematic apology for the age of Nicholas. But I have wanted to amplify his personal involvement and the historical significance of his written utterances here, to stress the degree of the problem Uvarov wrestled with, namely control over the free acquisition of knowledge, which has still not departed from Russian political reality in the twenty-first century. As a quasi-European himself he can perhaps help Europeans understand that strange, persistently illiberal heritage.

As Uvarov did everything he could to retard the arrival of modern democratic and egalitarian theories in Russia, his keyword 'Nationality' fought an ideological battle with liberal Europe, while 'Orthodoxy' tapped a ready supply of national loyalty and conformity among the Russian people 'Autocracy' embraced the magnetism of tsar and of the Russian semi-mystical tradition of authority. Uvarov reworked the three ideas of wartime national resistance he had expressed in Alexander's time of need, the exigencies of the year 1812, religion, love of the native land, and national honour, into an abstract, doctrinal formula for peacetime stability. The 1818 speech equated government with a form of education and extolled an education in history which would teach Russians 'to love their fatherland, their faith, their Tsar'.[18] He hoped to perpetuate that loyalty in new generation. And yet by 1832 Uvarov's slogan no longer contained any reference to the person of the ruler. Uvarov had transformed the instinctive conservatism of the response to war into an impersonal and timeless ideology of reaction. It was a defence of autocracy distinct in its intellectual ancestry from Karamzin's, but equal in effect. It helped to barricade Russia in.

Through Uvarov it was classical Rome that gave tsarist Petersburg a model of imperial power, domestic order and international stature. It had as the foundation of public life its own trinity of religion, tradition and authority. Roman religion was formal and formalistic, a matter of correctness and scruple rather than emotion or faith, and of the punctual performance of obligations. Tradition was upheld in the notion of government by an elite, chosen by virtue of its wisdom, social position and personal and family achievements. Authority derived from this and from the tradition of filial obedience and piety which began in the family and ended with Caesar.[19] In 1818 Uvarov praised this civilization as ' the true transition of the human mind to its age of experience and maturity ... a time of political wisdom and perspicacity ... demonstrating ... the remarkable influence of strong will and constant love of glory.'

The Augustan political tradition was inherited by the *ancien régime*, and it was to this stability Catherine wished to claim further inheritance when she declared after the French Revolution that it was Russia's task to recreate the old monarchy.[20] Uvarov's 'Orthodoxy, Autocracy, Nationality' self-consciously answered the revolution's appeal to 'Liberté, égalité, fraternité'. It supplied Russia's equal and opposite answer to the claims of the new Western age.[21] It answered the philosophies' anticlerical feeling with Orthodoxy, their cosmopolitanism with nationality and their move towards democracy with autocracy. Meanwhile in its Russian aspect, Uvarov's trinity synthesized the Russian myths, with Orthodoxy serving as the bridge between pious tsar and pious people, and that gave his doctrine a measure of popular appeal.[22] Thus, what the Slavophile intelligentsia and other nationalists like Nadezhdin tried to do by transplanting German Romantic ideas to Russia, namely to give the country a new sense of identity from the below, Uvarov did in competition with them, and with authority on his side.

Uvarov's 'Official Nationality'[23] directly challenged the Romantic idea of nationality. It created a mirror image, and even a potential source of confusion among half-educated minds that the Russian government could exploit.[24] Romantic nationalism was a compound of the organic ideal of national cultural growth and the Rousseauan notion that there was a general will of the people. The Romantic national ideal which made the people 'the source and the locus of all power [and] the origin of all laws as well'[25] posed enormous problems for the Hapsburgs under Metternich, just as Nicholas was threatened in Poland, because Romantic nationalism justified political rebellion against an alien occupying power. But in Russia it was worth co-opting, cloning, as we might say now, because it potentially rallied mass support. An in-some-ways truer Russian variant of the Romantic ideal of nationality was espoused by the emerging Slavophiles who claimed the Russian people as an active force whose ways and traditions would guide Russia towards a grand future. Uvarov's sometime friend the historian Pogodin held such views. Many so-called Westernizers also believed in nationality in this Romantic sense, among them Belinsky, and they encouraged the discovery of the national imagination and the unofficial national memory. But all the while Official Nationality was something else. Official Nationality simply taught Roman-style piety, which meant loyalty to the state and its interests. It didn't matter how much or how little a Russian valued his country so long as the monarchist principle was strengthened, the empire Russified and dissent muffled under its influence.[26]

Uvarov called his system 'political religion':

Political religion, just as Christian religion, has its inviolable dogmas: in our case they are autocracy and serfdom.[27]

This 'religion' presupposed a unique organization of the people as its church. We may not want to equate this directly with the formation of the Communist Party after 1917 but certainly the Soviet term *partiinost'* was until a quarter of a century ago the only existing equivalent, meaning overriding fidelity to the Communist Party, is the only existing equivalent to Uvarov's idea of national fidelity.[28] Thus his mentality, by which his private life was hidden and his public life yielded to a network of regulations and formulae, should not seem any more strange or distant to us than the mentality that officially organized Russian life through most of the twentieth century; moreover one of the uses of his life is to help us understand the future to which he helped to give birth; Russian conservatism in the guise of revolutionary internationalism. But to return to the man himself, of whose life we still have much to tell: Uvarov was prepared to sacrifice his private self to the requirements of official authority over the whole of Russian society and expected others to follow. He saw no harm in making public life impossible for those writers, journalists, teachers and publishers who did not.

12

'Knowing that he is only feigning Russomania...'

Uvarov's aim, 'to adapt general universal education to our Russian way of life and to our Russian way of thinking', was sufficiently loosely defined to raise immediate hope for an improvement in national instruction. It was a balancing act, to 'save' and 'preserve' the national heritage at the same time as advancing learning, and I have suggested he never fully believed that balance was possible and that Vigel' liked him more for his secret doubts. Others, on the other hand, were struck by his confidence, and if they were critical, by the personal vanity that encouraged a prolonged act of self- and therefore national-self-deception. Vyazemsky was one of those old friends and lifelong observers for whom Uvarov could do no good. When on a visit early in the summer of 1833 to the University of Dorpat the students welcomed the Minister with a colourful parade and festivities, Vyazemsky reported scathingly to Alexander Turgenev:

> Yesterday's letter from Dorpat talks about Uvarov's reception by the students with full' varsity and chivalresque honours: with deputations of pashas on horseback, torches and vivats. Andrei Karamzin [son of the historian] was the spokesman for the Russian side. They say Uvarov was very pleased and very moved by this welcome.[1]

But Vigel' once again saw a case of self-sacrifice that he admired. Referring to himself in the third person, the diarist noted:

> Vigel' has every reason to hate Uvarov, but an assiduous son of the fatherland is almost always content with the actions of the Minister of National Enlightenment. I don't believe anything, knowing that he is only

feigning Russomania, but even for that he deserves thanks, other people believe him, he gives young people a good path to follow and unintentionally does a great deal of good.[2]

Their personal relations were chequered in the early 1830s, because Uvarov was responsible for legislation which allowed only graduates to advance to the highest bureaucratic grades and Vigel' had not been to university. But the diarist overcame his potential personal hostility. Others, possibly even including the young Belinsky, took the same positive view, placing Uvarov in the midst of a new climate of optimism regarding the progress of education.[3] What one feels is that his sincerity didn't matter; it was the public role he was prepared to carry out that counted; and that in turn was a value, a preference for public life over private, that Uvarov had learnt from his immersion in the European eighteenth century.[4]

Sometime during his Ministry Uvarov told a new recruit: 'Remember the Tsar is Minister of Education, not I.' He never lost sight of the fact that every move he made was politically sensitive and that ultimately his hands were tied. He had to please a sovereign whose entire mentality was defensive and who had little respect for legality. Nicholas was so whimsical he was seen as being served by adjutants, not Ministers; moreover by Ministers who had to act the part, although they were not necessarily feigning it.[5] Uvarov was all the more an odd choice for Nicholas because the tsar did not like foreign-educated officials. But he was a clever servant, given to constant displays of zeal, and to his good fortune he came up with a slogan that perfectly expressed the tsar's own wishes.[6]

Nicholas set him an immense task, to forge 'necessary uniformity' in pupils and establishments, continuing where the Education Committee left off in 1832.[7] The tsar complained, 'The education of the upper classes is handled by foreigners; there exists no set system in organising the various levels of public instruction; the new generation ignore everything Russian.'[8] Uvarov responded with systematic legislation to improve the academic equality and the Russian content of schooling at all levels. In November 1833 he told the tsar:

[Our system will] show to be an opponent of [the Ministry] everything which still bears the stamp of liberal and mystical ideas. Things liberal are inimical because the Ministry, in proclaiming Autocracy, has revealed its firm wish to return directly to the Russian monarchist principle in its full compass; mystical things are inimical, because the expression Orthodoxy has shown sufficiently clearly the Ministry's attachment to all that is positive with respect to the objects of the Christian faith and its distance from all those mystical fantasms which too often besmirch the purity of the Holy traditions of the Church. Finally the word Nationality has aroused in our opponents a feeling of hostility as a result of our bold declaration that the Ministry considers Russia has come of age and is worthy to proceed not behind but at least abreast of other European nations.[9]

The plans which circulated round the Ministry within weeks of his arrival were irritatingly embroidered with the tripartite slogan, but the living impression he left was of an eminently practical and committed educator.

Long after the Moscow inspection of 1832 Uvarov continued to go round the classrooms, putting anxious students and teachers through their paces. Mikhail Longinov, a university student in the early 1840s, who became a significant chronicler and bibliographer of the period, as well as an occasional pornographic poet, remembered the moment positively:

We students felt the beneficial influence of his administration, not only because we were able to enrich ourselves with his knowledge, but because we had personal contact with him, He did not despise our youth and poor knowledge; he loved this youth and inspired it with love of learning and the desire to work. Whoever benefited from his conversations will always recall with joy his lucid thoughts, lightened by his eloquent turns of phrase and full of warm affection for the goodness and learning and humanity.[10]

Alexander Herzen from the lecture hall was also pleasantly surprised and impressed, though he had a writer's eye for the foibles of a man who could not resist posturing in public.[11]

Uvarov and his staff began from the moment of his appointment by touring and reporting on all the institutions and areas under the Ministry's jurisdiction. They redrew boundaries to ease administration and concentrated on what the tsar had asked for: to repeat, the creation of a unified education system for the empire, a reduction in foreign influence in education, and the encouragement of a love and knowledge of things Russian. Their activity culminated in a major education bill in 1835 and by 1838, with various legislative additions, Uvarov regarded his work as complete.

The nature of the balancing act was a constant negotiation of how the educator and the military man that Nicholas was might be constrained to work together. Uvarov's first use of his power was to create a new university in Kiev for the western provinces to replace the one the tsar had closed in Vilna in the wake of the Polish uprising. Not to provoke anxiety, the new institution opened gradually, with a single philosophical–historical, philological faculty functioning in 1833. It was known as the University of St Vladimir, and was designed to be the heart of Russian-centred education in an area where Polish nationalist claims were fierce and where the majority of the students and teachers were Catholic Poles or Ukrainians. Uvarov told the tsar Kiev was chosen because the city was the first capital of Russia; the name St Vladimir invoked the tenth-century grand prince who had brought Christianity to Kiev Rus'. He ventured that the new university would remind Poles and Lithuanians of their common heritage with the Russians and urge them to rediscover their roots by learning the Russian language and studying Russian literature. Other men observed more cynically that the First Army was stationed close by.[12]

Since the Polish spirit posed a continual threat to political stability and ideological unity in the western part of the empires, where Poles refused to accept the Russians as having absorbed them into a great Slav whole, Uvarov chose men as professors and administrators who held the desired Russian view. At the same time he allowed non-Russian students to remain in the majority and to study, except in the sensitive juridical faculty, without hindrance.[13]

To deal as tactfully with the problem of increasing Russian loyalty among Russians, however, proved difficult. The matter of foreign tutors, whom Nicholas regarded as undesirable, required delicate handling, especially since the distinguished one-time pupil of the abbé Mauguin was not himself convinced. The influential, sometimes loveable, almost always peculiar figure of the foreign tutor was part and parcel of well-born Russian lives. As Uvarov became Minister, Leo Tolstoy, aged five, was enjoying the services of an elderly Baltic German, Fyodor Ivanovich Roessel, who taught all the Tolstoy children 'the language of Goethe'. In 1837 Roessel was succeeded by a stiff, capable Frenchman, Prosper de St Thomas, who headed a squad of eleven teachers in the Tolstoys' Moscow home, not counting the dancing-masters.[14] Foreign governesses would go on teaching young children in the Russian nursery until the Revolution. Yet Nicholas's point was not unfounded. Two men who would cause an outcry with their critical essays within the next few years, Alexander Herzen and Peter Chaadaev, had greatly benefited from private teaching by German academics. If Russia wanted to keep out foreign ideas, the stimulating presence of French and German preceptors had to be curtailed.

In 1834 Uvarov produced much paperwork on the subject, culminating in sixty-nine articles of advice to help parents select responsible teachers. The effort was a clear sign of his ambivalence. He also created career incentives for Russians who might be induced to take up this 'obscure and modest occupation'. Measures in 1834–35 called for 90 per cent of newly certified home teachers to be Russian, and imposed controls on the intellectual qualifications and moral and political fitness of all tutors.[15] This, however, did not eradicate the related and larger problem of foreign schools, which, to refer again to Uvarov's own experience, had catered to his generation in the absence of good Russian schools. Uvarov limited the opportunities that existed to open new establishments and insisted that all teaching in existing foreign schools should be in Russian and would be subject to Russian government inspection. But the foreign schools continued to function up to the Revolution.

The controls of Nicholas's reign in education were not watertight in part because that is the way of all paper systems imposed on living beings. But the flexibility was also due to Uvarov's own tact. He was well attuned to what the public wanted at different levels and in different regions of the empire. A case in point, when he had been Deputy Minister, had been the recently created Moscow gymnasium open to all classes. The nobility boycotted it. Used to privilege, this class wanted its sons educated separately and Uvarov, seeing the production of educated well-born young Russian males threatened if this demand was not conceded, urged Nicholas to restore the old exclusive establishment. One of his most popular innovations henceforth was to encourage the building of exclusive pansions alongside the gymnasia. By this route the nobility shared a state education but resided and was tutored in finishing-school subjects in the separate establishment. The number of private schools, including pansions, therefore increased dramatically through Nicholas's reign, reflecting the priority Uvarov gave to actual education rather than its justification or whereabouts.[16]

His Ministry made possible an education system which had a life of its own; it transcended in practice its own regulations in theory. In the gymnasia, which since 1828 had acquired a seven-year curriculum, he worked a miracle of improvement. This curriculum was solid and substantial without appearing to be politically inflammatory. The cosmopolitan Minister balanced the chauvinistic tsar's demand for more Russian studies with his own desire that the students should not lose contact with the Western world. Classics were taught, and foreign languages, alongside Orthodox religion, Russian literature and Karamzin's Russian history. Teachers were encouraged to keep up with the latest work in their subjects abroad and the Ministry also began publishing a periodical to guide them in their work. By this route gymnasia quickly came to equal the best in Europe.[17]

The district schools were also greatly improved and expanded with vocational courses. With the provision of new textbooks the academic level of these schools was high enough for the children of families from merchants to peasants to use them as a stepping-stone to the gymnasium and some schools secured permission from Uvarov expressly to teach foreign languages with that aim. Both the district and the lower schools, which taught reading, writing and divinity, were improved by two fundamental innovations of Uvarov's Ministry: inspection and the central provision of information. This was the positive function of the new *Journal of the Ministry of National Enlightenment*. Checks were also kept on pupils' health, and on the plight of the poor. Uvarov took care to cater individually for the needs of the different provinces of the empire and made special provision for the children of bureaucrats working in far-flung places, including reserved university places.

Above all the universities benefited from Uvarov's reforms. For the first time in their history they acquired a mission to advance learning for its own sake, replacing the old emphasis on training government employees. Uvarov cleared the way for academic staff to concentrate on academic work in good conditions and in exchange for a good salary, and offered staff and doctoral students every encouragement to study abroad, at Dorpat, which was German-speaking, and in Berlin and Paris. Here was an exception to the anti-foreign policy, made in the name of science, and the effect was miraculous. From the return from abroad in 1832 to the first batch of new teachers to take advantage of reforms begun by the education committee, the teaching staff at the Russian universities rose in quality to an unprecedented high level in the 1840s. Most of the young men who went abroad on such scholarships were deeply affected by the European ideas and way of life they encountered, and came back to enrich Russian literary and academic life. The novelist Ivan Turgenev, whose initial desire was to become a professor of philosophy, benefited from three years' residence in Berlin, where he attended the university and wrote a thesis on German pantheism. He was preceded by Nikolai Stankevich, the philosophical idealist, Idealism and German scholar who did much to spread idealism among the intelligentsia of the 1830s and 1840s. Another Berlin student was the philosophy student and later anarchist Mikhail Bakunin, and there was also Timofei Granovsky, a Hegelian who was Moscow University's best-known historian in the 1840s. Even those who did not go abroad themselves grew rich on the embarrassment of foreign ideas reaching home. Belinsky, who stayed in Russia, a captive of his poverty and his overt dissidence, corresponded furiously with these Berlin scholars, and helped bring the spirit of the European intellectual world to his immediate circle, and to his many more readers. As Uvarov had always implied, many freedoms could be wrought in exchange for keeping the universities in apparent ideological good order and tolerating the superficial disciplines that were imposed. His libertarian opponents went from strength to strength thanks to his political far-sightedness.

At all educational levels Uvarov encouraged entry into the state bureaucracy. He always believed a good academic education need not undermine national loyalty. He encouraged for all men, on the old noble pattern, entry into government service after school and from 1834 made this possible not only at graduate level, but also by examination after leaving the gymnasium and district schools. Participatory bureaucracy was his practical answer to democracy and a real aspect of the policy behind his slogan.[18]

As regards the professors, meanwhile, to give them more time with their research and relieve them of the tedious job of overseeing local schools he brought the universities and the gymnasia under the direct control of the state, as he had proposed in 1819. The 1835 statute proportionally strengthened the position of the Superintendent, directly responsible to the Minister, by making it his job to live in the university town and watch over the competence and morals of the teaching staff and the student body. He had the power of dismissal and a squad of assistants and an inspector chosen from the military or the civil service. These inspectors were a new breed, the first being trained in Moscow in 1834.

But then perhaps it was politically naïve, or personally myopic, with Uvarov idealizing his own time as St Petersburg Superintendent, to imagine such good moral coordination between state and high functionary: good also in the sense that the pairing would lead to genuine improvement in the content and administration of education. It has been found curious that Uvarov's reform actually resembled Magnitsky's, the actions of his sworn reactionary enemy in Kazan' a decade and a half previously, and that he failed to see the state was potentially just as harmful with a good man in charge as with a bad. It was not the first or last time he would slip unwittingly into being more the unworldly scholar than the wily politician.

But the practical desire to keep house for scholarship remained. As he had done with the Academy Uvarov overhauled the finances of all his educational institutions, encouraged higher spending and secured a more generous budget from the tsar. Most happily he encouraged the development of the Central Pedagogical Institute, resurrected in 1828 after Runich's death kiss. Among his incentives to encourage a competent teaching profession he offered a hundred training stipends and imposed competitions with special advancements as a reward. He remained an enthusiast, however much that spirit might annoy and embarrass his colleagues and employees. Herzen called him 'a genuine shop salesman for enlightenment':

He surprised us with his many languages and the detailed range of his knowledge about all kinds of things ... he committed to memory little examples of every science and its necessary conclusions, or, better still, its principles ... . When he became Minister he began discussing Slavonic poetry of the fourteenth century, whereupon Kachenovsky said to him that at the time our ancestors were fighting bears, not singing the praises of the gods of Samothrace and autocratic mercy. As a kind of certificate that he was the genuine article he carried in his pocket a letter from Goethe, in which Goethe paid him the most curious compliment, saying: 'You have no need to apologize for your language; you have achieved what I have failed to do – you have forgotten German grammar.'

This in reality secret Pico della Mirandola introduced a new kind of experiment. He ordered the best students to be selected in order that each should lecture on one of his subjects instead of the teacher. These lectures went on for a whole week. The students had to prepare all the topics of their course, then the Dean would draw a ticket and a name ... I had to talk about minerology in front of Lovetsky ... . When the Dean called me ... I went up to the rostrum. Lovetsky was sitting nearby, motionless and afraid, with his hands on his legs, like Memnon or Osiris. I whispered to him: 'I'm glad they chose me to lecture to you, I won't let you down.'

'Don't swagger on the way to communion,' mouthed the worthy professor, hardly moving his lips and looking at me.

I almost burst out laughing, but when I looked around me I was dazzled. I felt myself going pale and a dryness seizing my tongue. I had never spoken in public before. The auditorium was full of students – they were relying on me. Beneath the rostrum seated at the table were 'the powerful of this world' and all the professors in our department. I took the question and began in a voice not my own: 'On the Conditions, Rules and Forms of Crystallization'.

While I was thinking how to begin a happy thought occurred to me: if I make a mistake maybe some of the teachers will notice but won't say anything, while the others won't understand a word, and the students, so long as I don't cut my throat half-way through, will be pleased because I'm doing them a favour. So, in the name of H... Werner and Mitcherlich, I gave my lecture and ended it with a few philosophical thoughts, turned towards and speaking all the time towards the students, not to the Minister. The students and the professors shook my hand and thanked me. Uvarov brought over Prince Golitsyn to introduce him and he said something to some city councillors so that I couldn't hear. Uvarov promised me a book as a souvenir and never sent it.[19]

Despite Herzen it can still be said with confidence that Uvarov loved education as much as he loved his own role in furthering it. He was not the great Italian humanist Mirandola, but he was an immensely significant figure in a Russia which was struggling to catch up with the West in learning and expertise.

So that it truly went against the grain to try to fulfil Nicholas's crucial requirement to limit education according to class, to keep out the *raznochintsy* from the gymnasia and the university and to prevent the education of the serfs. This was one of the largest tasks of Uvarov's Ministry and one in which despite his protests to the contrary, he failed. Or perhaps he was pretending to protest. Nicholas was trying to push Russia in a direction few men, even among the nobility, thought it natural to go. To limit education according to social origin wasted talent, discouraged loyalty in the unprivileged classes and overestimated the loyalty and educability of the nobility. It ran counter to Peter the Great's meritocracy. Herzen who was never Uvarov's admirer nevertheless conceded that there was something essentially egalitarian about the Russian universities, which he contrasted with the social differences cultivated by the English:

> Until 1848 the organization of our universities was purely democratic. Their doors were open to all those who passed the examination and were not serfs or peasants or obligated men who had been freed from their community… . Social differences did not elicit pride with us in the way we find it doing in English schools and military colleges. Not to speak of the English universities which exist exclusively for the rich and for the aristocracy. With us a student who took it into his head to boast of his blue blood or his wealth would have been sent to Coventry, he would have been tormented by his colleagues.[20]

The half-heartedness of Uvarov's efforts to exclude the lower classes suggested he felt the same as Herzen. Things would change under duress, but in the first years of his Ministry he went out of his way to have foreign languages taught in the district schools, as it were as a stepping-stone for bright children to move on to the gymnasium. He did this by deeming these schools 'special cases'. After the 1835 statute he was obliged to tack on extra measures almost every year to try to keep the lower classes from enjoying a full liberal education. These included raising fees, demanding certificates from students guaranteeing they could support themselves, abolishing for the lower classes the automatic gift of the twelfth rank on graduation and banning the members of these classes from applying for grants. Uvarov kept these revisions quiet. Meanwhile, the lower classes kept squeezing past. No single will, neither Uvarov's nor the tsar's, could ensure the direction of progress.

At all levels the numbers of those enjoying some form of education improved. There was a slow increase in the total of number of university students at the six establishments of the empire – Moscow, Vilna/Kiev, Dorpat, Kazan', Kharkov and St Petersburg. The number rose from 3,317 in 1830 to 4,006 in 1848. At the secondary level the number of gymnasium students jumped from 16,506 in 1837 to 19,428 in 1848, while the number of gymnasiums rose from 63 in 1830 to 75 in 1848; the number of secondary technical schools greatly increased. Overall the number of students in higher and middle education rose from 19,406 in 1837 to 23,963 in 1848.[21]

Serfs evaded control by attending private gymnasiums. In 1849 559 or 25 per cent of educational institutions known to the Ministry were private. According to figures for 1853, for the St Petersburg district alone, 6,153 pupils were studying at private schools, of whom only 2,960 were nobles. Another loophole which was exploited by the lower classes was the existence of technical secondary schools under the aegis of various authorities outside the Ministry of National Enlightenment. The Ministry of Mines had 194 schools with over 6,000 pupils in 1841, the sons of peasants and serfs who were given an elementary education. The number of non-noble graduates from the universities grew steadily, since, exclusive entrance qualifications notwithstanding, it was possible for students to attend university privately. By trying to maintain a class distinction in middle education, Uvarov also improved provisions at the district schools, which then taught nobles and lower-class pupils alike to a high standard. To please Nicholas Uvarov presented his achievements in the first ten years of his Ministry as the creation of a complete, ideologically secure system. But the effect of his deeds was in fact ethically far more promising.

> To eliminate the conflict between so called European education and our needs: to point the young generation away from their blind, unthinking passion for the superficial and the foreign by opening their ears to the idea that they might take pleasure and respect in what is their own, and to the wholehearted conviction that only by applying general, universal enlightenment to our national way of life and our national spirit is it possible to bring true benefits to each and every man; then to take an honest look at the vast field which lies ahead of our beloved country, to evaluate accurately all the conflicting elements of our citizens' education, all the historical factors which relate to the vast constitution of the Empire, to bring these developing elements and awakened forces, as far as possible, under a common denominator; and finally to seek that denominator in the triple concept of Orthodoxy, Autocracy and Nationality – that was the goal, which the Ministry of Public Enlightenment has been approaching over 10 years; that was the plan which I have followed in all my endeavours.[22]

Uvarov's report of his decade's work as Minister of National Enlightenment, of which this passage was the culmination, contained many instances of 'saving' and 'preserving' the national heritage at the same time as ensuring the progress of learning. From his point of view it enshrined his balancing act and testified to his success, for the tsar replied that he was satisfied.

The national education system had an all-important international element, which allowed for the exchange of information abroad and visits by foreign scholars.[23] This in turn ensured a quality of instruction that was comparable with similar institutions abroad and sometimes greater. The Russian universities were subject to no more state control, class restriction and state expectation of conformity than their equivalent in Britain, and they enjoyed greater academic freedom than universities in Prussia. Unprecedented high standards in the arts and sciences resulted, and it was Sergei Uvarov's doing.[24]

13

'The Minister of Darkness and the Extinction of Enlightenment'

The true conservative is not at home in social struggle … .
He knows that a stable social structure survives not on
triumph but on reconciliations.

HENRY KISSINGER, *A WORLD RESTORED*

Since it was impossible to keep foreign ideas out of Russia at the same time as encourage the pursuit of Enlightenment Uvarov was nevertheless pitched into a conflict that distorted his personality and would eventually destroy his career. A gradualist who believed in liberal education, he became with the constant threat of civil disorder in Russia a fanatic who feared the free play of critical thought as practised by the new men in literature and journalism. 'On every level intellectual perfection without moral perfection is a dream, a fatal dream,' he had declared in 1828. To Uvarov it was realistic and a sign of wakefulness to be prepared to live within an intellectual fortress. But another way of seeing his achievement is to note how he has been seen as the man who did most under Nicholas to make 'irresponsible' lives a misery.[1]

The 'age of transition' in which he consciously lived took on a harder character when in autumn 1833 Austria, Russia and Prussia signed an agreement at Muenchengraz undertaking to defend Europe against further revolutionary attack. Uvarov's system was part of the ensuing fortification. None of the other rulers was as rigid or as vigilant in looking for signs of revolution as Nicholas.[2] Yet, because the allies depended on Nicholas for their military strength, through their cooperation their agreement actually increased Russian domestic pressures to modernize. Uvarov was living in a time also of confusion of aims.

The task to strengthen Russia at a time when civil and religious values were collapsing in Europe pushed him to take an extreme position in November 1833:

[Our system will] show to be an opponent of [the Ministry] everything which still bears the stamp of liberal and mystical ideas. Things liberal are inimical because the Ministry, in proclaiming Autocracy, has revealed its firm wish to return directly to the Russian monarchist principle in its full compass; mystical things are inimical, because the expression Orthodoxy has shown sufficiently clearly the Ministry's attachment to all that is positive with respect to the objects of the Christian faith and its distance from all those mystical fantasms which too often besmirch the purity of the Holy traditions of the Church. Finally the word Nationality has aroused in our opponents a feeling of hostility as a result of our bold declaration that the Ministry considers Russia has come of age and is worthy to proceed not behind but at least abreast of other European nations.[3]

The masterly tripartite slogan, part of that coming of age, did indeed strengthen Russia, at least as an idea. Coming of age was a matter of confident self-definition on the part of the Russian state, which declared revolution against the Russian national character. In one move the slogan absorbed the European idiom of political Romanticism into the substance of Russian conservatism. Still it left Uvarov fighting in the name of an abstraction, while all around him men were pursuing warm and living causes. He was forced, like Burke and like Metternich, as a conservative in a revolutionary period, to organize himself politically, which was not his natural behaviour, and which estranged him from the times by forcing him into reaction. His obligation to narrow Russia's intellectual scope destroyed his balance as a statesman and undid his reputation as a social reformer. What he had observed of himself in 1813 proved to be doubly true in middle age. Adversity eroded his moral fabric and brought to the surface the petty vanities and the anxieties which had been with him since childhood.

He wanted to play a policeman's role in the reign of the 'gendarme of Europe'. With the creation of the Third Department the overall control of books, theatre and journalism had been wrested away from the Ministry of Enlightenment's local censors, but Uvarov played the largest police role he could alongside it. By joining the world of internal conspiracy, competition and denunciation of the secret police, he encouraged the worst aspects of his character, such that in competition with Benckendorff, the absent-minded, dangerously simple head of the Third Department, and with the tsar himself, the cases in which he involved himself became instances of scandalous fanaticism and personal vendetta. His greatest enemy was the periodical press, which was otherwise the bulwark of the first great age of Russian literature. Uvarov set himself up as its adversary and even as its torturer. Thinking of Nikolai Grech, the editor of *Syn Otechestva* (Son of the Fatherland) he told the censor Alexander Nikitenko: 'I have an order from the tsar with which at any moment I could turn him into nothing. In general these gentlemen do not realize, I think, in whose clutches they find themselves, and that I have already softened a great deal what they consider cruel.' Nikitenko had already made a note in his diary: Uvarov was despotic.[4]

An outstanding instance of that vice was Uvarov's treatment of Polevoy's *Moscow Telegraph*. This periodical had acquired the second biggest circulation in the country and was a rallying point and a source of information for the liberal intelligentsia. The literary historian and critic Igor Panaev remembered the happy days in 1827, when aged fifteen he sat around reading it with his friends. Belinsky recalled its great influence. Having denounced it in his 1832 report to the tsar, Uvarov became fixated on destroying *The Moscow Telegraph*. In September 1833 he tried to have it banned on the grounds that Polevoy had published material unworthy of the honour of the Russian people. The offending article was a review of Walter Scott's biography of Napoleon, which suggested Russia had mustered little energy or outrage to resist the invader. Uvarov took offence – Russian courage in 1812 lay at the heart of his Official Nationalism. But even the tsar decided that Polevoy's article had not intended harm and the *Telegraph* should continue. The angry and ambitious Minister then ordered his deputy to keep a dossier of all work published by Polevoy, for it was well-known he held pro-French, anti-Russian views and was sooner or later bound to take a wrong step.[5]

Sure enough the following spring, Polevoy read a new play on a patriotic theme and was displeased by it. He wrote a deservedly negative notice. But in the meantime the play was staged and won the tsar's acclaim. Polevoy tried to get his article dropped but was away from Moscow and failed to get his message through in time. Despite Benckendorff's attempts to dissuade him, Uvarov moved in for the kill with a file of cuttings proving the editor's work was seditious. No further editions of *The Moscow Telegraph* were published and Polevoy spent the rest of his life in financial difficulty. Uvarov's action appeared fanatical and partisan. Polevoy was sure he was mainly irritated at the *Telegraph's* having derided certain Academy publications. But there may also have been tensions between the Minister and the Third Department head, Benckendorff, who supported the journal. Uvarov wanted to assert his newly won authority. In any event it was Uvarov's careful building up of negative evidence which led to the first forced closure of a periodical under Nicholas.

At the same time censorship was a frightening, precarious and saddening task for the best of men in its employ, and Uvarov was sensitive to their plight. In 1835 he begged his contemporaries to observe an unwritten social contract, which gave privileges in return for certainty that nothing irresponsible would see the light of day. A year later this strategy didn't seem to be working, so more general constraints were introduced. No more requests for new publications were allowed. The shaky possibility of a contract for a new journal was made all the more impossible because it was never clear which way the tsar would opine, and public opinion was also often divided, as it was in Polevoy's case,[6] when some blamed the censorship for being misleading. The tsar was both easy to read and disingenuous. For those who did read his character he was hardly a man whose behaviour matched his own proclaimed ideals of probity and disinterest. In short the style of public behaviour in Nicholas's reign mirrored the sovereign's own arbitrariness, distrust of others, and fear of talent. It combined grand posturing with essential mediocrity.[7]

Nikitenko, a censor almost heroic in his fair-mindedness, and whose meticulous daily journal of events saved his soul in these gloomy years, several times tried to resign.[8] He noted, when the axe fell on the *Telegraph* on 5 April 1834:

The Moscow Telegraph has been banned on Uvarov's orders. The Tsar at first wanted to deal very severely with Polevoy. 'But', he said to the Minister afterwards, 'it is our fault that we have put up with this disorderliness for so long.' Everyone everywhere has strong opinions about The Telegraph. Some say bitterly that 'the only good journal we had no longer exists'.

Others say, 'Quite right. He [Polevoy] took the liberty of attacking Karamzin. He did not even spare my novel. He's a liberal, a Jacobin, we know all about his kind, etc. etc.'

The case bothered Uvarov and he discussed it at some length with Nikitenko:

'He [Polevoy] is a harbinger of revolution,' Uvarov said. 'For several years he has been systematically spreading destructive advice. He does not love Russia. I have been watching him for a long time. But I didn't want to take decisive measures suddenly. I warned him personally in Moscow to tone things down, arguing that our aristocracy is not as stupid as he thinks. After that he was officially censured. That didn't help. I first thought of bringing him to trial; that would have destroyed him. We had to remove from him the right to speak to the public – the government always has the right to do that, and what is more on thoroughly legal foundations, for amongst the rights of the Russian citizen there is no right to address to the public in writing. That is a privilege the government can give and take away where it wishes. Moreover, said the Minister, it is well known that we have a party which desires revolution. The Decembrists have not been exhausted.

Polevoy wanted to be their organ. Of course they know that they will always find firm measures taken against them in the office of the Tsar and his Ministers ... . But that Polevoy, I know him: he's a fanatic. He's prepared to put up with anything for an idea. He needs firm handling. The Moscow censorship was unforgivably lax.'[9]

Uvarov's defence was tailored to counter criticism of the way he and Benckendorff had handled the case. But it was rooted in a larger vision, which on another occasion Nikitenko explained further:

August 8, 1835. Minister Uvarov was burning to speak today. I quote the monologue he delivered in its entirety: 'We, that is men of the nineteenth century, are in a difficult position; we live amid times of political storms and upheavals. Nations have their own ways of life, they renew themselves, agitate, move forward. No one here can prescribe his own laws. But Russia is still young, virginal, and should not sample, at least not yet, these bloody cares. We must prolong her youth and in that time educate her. That is my political system. I know what our liberals, our journalists and our slanderers want ... . But they will not succeed in casting their seeds in the field which I sow and watch over, – no, they will not succeed. My task is not only to watch over education, but also to watch over the spirit of the age. *If I succeed in holding Russia back 50 years from what the theories are preparing for her, then I will have done my duty and will die peacefully* [my emphasis].[10] For that I have a willing heart and the political means. I know that people shout against me: I don't listen to these shouts. Let them call me an obscurantist: a man of State ought to stand above the crowd.'[11]

Uvarov, we note, 'burned' to explain himself. He burnt to justify his actions against the liberal press, as Russian literature flourished despite and because of the erratically administered censorship.[12]

It's important to note that many of Uvarov's contemporaries, among them Pushkin, saw the necessity for some control. The grudge against Uvarov's involvement was more that while citing objective standards, he allowed his personal judgement to intervene. In that respect his persecution of Pushkin became notorious. Pushkin himself was no moral hero. He had joined in the chorus of dislike against the 'Jacobin' Polevoy out of sheer personal dislike.[13] But he was, as Uvarov had admitted back in 1832, 'literature', a cause all of its own, while Uvarov was 'administration'.

Pushkin's relations with Uvarov in the 1830s were marked by the unique confusion his unfettered spirit caused Uvarov, a mixture of fear, envy, spite and regard for genius. When the poet returned to the capital from exile in 1826 he at first tried in the Arzamas spirit to make use of his well-placed old friend. Uvarov, quite possibly flattered, responded by encouraging Pushkin's election to the Russian Academy, the literary wing of the Academy of Sciences, and also eagerly took up the cause of his petitioning to publish (five years before the 1836 ban) a new periodical, *Dnevnik*.[14] Vigel', who was now employed in the Ministry of National Enlightenment, enjoyed liaising between them. He wrote to Pushkin in August 1831:

> The project for a literary-political journal is exciting, and I am very busy with it; I have been looking for, and I think I have found, a reliable and at the same time honest way of realizing it. You know Uvarov, who used to be a member of Arzamas. Although he does not have particularly good relations with my superiors, he is well disposed to me and gets on very well with Benckendorff. He has been told about your project, he is happy with it, taken with it, and if you want he will speak to Benckendorff about it. ... He took up the project with enthusiasm, I might even say with the passion of a young man. He promises he will bow and scrape to help it see light of day; from the moment he knew your (political) views were good, he was ready to worship your talent, which until then he had only marvelled at.[15]

Yet, even in relatively harmonious times Pushkin and Uvarov were not comfortable together. They were wary, fundamentally and instinctively. Around 1830 Uvarov had found out that Pushkin's grandfather was an African slave brought to Russia by Peter the Great and, assuming Pushkin as vulnerable as himself in matters of the family heritage, he put word about that the poet was of dubious breeding. His loud musings gave the court scribbler Faddei Bulgarin the idea of writing a satire against Pushkin, which appeared in an official periodical. It accused Pushkin of being a bourgeois, but pretending otherwise. The poet recovered his dignity with a riposte, not published in his lifetime, in which he referred to the ennobled Musin-Pushkin branch of his family:

> I am Pushkin simply, not Musin
> I am not a rich man, not a courtier
> I am my own master: I am a bourgeois.[16]

This was Pushkin the writer speaking in a 'Marriage of Figaro' moment for Russian literature. Not by coincidence Beaumarchais was one of his heroes, for the quality, but also for the spirit of his writing. Pushkin, presumably informed by Vigel', meanwhile also dug up the story of Uvarov's father, 'Senka the bandore player' and published it in a collection of anecdotes entitled, in English, 'Table-talk'.[17]

Neither Pushkin nor Uvarov wanted their enmity to become public, but it pressed itself upon them. The poet had a public attractiveness the very opposite of that which Uvarov inspired. He was lively and outspoken, and had loyal friends and a commitment to poetry which of itself advocated liberty and decency. He was ever in and out of trouble with the authorities over the cause of free speech, but cleverly so, he managed to charm the tsar and even to turn him into his special protector against the bypassed Third Department. This unlikely alliance only heightened Uvarov's dislike and frustration.

They dined together and made use of each other's relative prestige. Uvarov praised Pushkin for work which was 'fine' and 'of the people', but was irritated when Pushkin did not always rely on him, as a former Arzamas friend, to exert some influence at court. For his part Pushkin was greatly angered when Uvarov travestied his poem condemning the Polish Insurrection with verses of his own. Pushkin wrote to the Minister:

> Prince Dundukov brought me your fine, truly inspired verses, which you were modest enough to call an imitation. My verses served you as a simple theme from which to develop a brilliant fantasy. It only remains for me to thank you sincerely for the attention you have shown me, and for the strength and fullness of the ideas you have generously attributed to me.[18]

Eventually in 1834 their bad relations did emerge in public. The poet had dinner with the Minister at his house on 10 April and complained of 'deadly boredom'. That same month Uvarov, having persuaded Nicholas to revoke Pushkin's special status, ordered the censorship of Pushkin's works 'on a general basis' and had several stanzas cut out of his poem 'Andzhelo'. The move followed on directly from his suppression of the *Moscow Telegraph*.[19]

Pushkin's patience finally deserted him nine months later, when he had just completed his *History of the Pugachev Rebellion*, recounting one of the great events in Russian history. Uvarov called it 'a work of incitement' and refused to let it pass. Hatred and contempt erupted in a diary entry for February 1835:

> Uvarov is a great villain. He's shouting about my book, calling it a work of incitement. His minion Dundukov (a fool and a poetaster) is persecuting me with his censorship committee. He won't agree to let me publish my works simply with the permission of the Tsar. The Judge likes them, but the Drudge doesn't. Incidentally on Uvarov: he's a good-for-nothing and a big charlatan. His corruption is well-known. He stooped so low that he was running errands for Kankrin's children. About him they say that he began as a b...*, then became a nanny, then found himself promoted to President of the Academy of Sciences. ... He stole firewood which belonged to the authorities and still hasn't paid the bill (he has 11,000 souls), he used the Academy's carpenters to do his own work, etc. etc. Dashkov, who used to be a friend of his, when he met Zhukovsky arm in arm with Uvarov, led him to one side and said 'Surely you are ashamed to be seen walking in public with a man like that!'

Pushkin went on to complain to Benckendorff whom he believed was Uvarov's victim. He saw his work hindered by a corrupt man who was abusing his official power and was unsparing when the chance came in the autumn of 1835 finally to have his revenge.[20]

In August that year one of Catherine Uvarov's uncles on her mother's side, Dmitri Sheremetyev, though still a young man, fell dangerously ill and the Minister was known to be fussing over the terms of a will from which he stood to benefit copiously. Public anger reached a climax when one Count Litt accused Uvarov publicly, in the Council of Ministers, of being anxious to get his hands on the money. Someone said the sick man had 'scarlet fever' to which Litt, turning to the Minister of Enlightenment, added bitterly, 'Yes. And you have the fever of possession.'[21]

When Sheremetyev began to get better Pushkin could not contain his glee:

On the Recovery of Lucullus
Imitation from the Latin

You were dying, rich young man!
You heard your sad friends crying.
Death appeared to you
at the door of your crystal canopies.
With the morning she slipped in,
like a patient creditor,
looming silently in the hall,
not moving from the rug.

In your gloomy room
Sullen doctors whispered.
The faces of Cercean men,
your hangers-on, darkened in confusion;
while loyal serfs sighed
and entreated gods for you,
afraid of what for them the secretive fates
had judged, and not knowing.

Meanwhile your heir,
Like a crow eying flesh,
Went pale and shivered at your bed,
Trembled with the fever of possession.
Already his miser's wax
stained the locks of your office;
and he dreamt he pocketed heaps of gold
from the dust of paper stacks.

He dreamt: 'no longer shall I wait
on the children of a lord;
I shall be a lord myself;
bounty, my cellars overflow.
Now I have honour – hooray, hoorah!
No more will I cheat my wife,
Or remember how I stole firewood.'

But you rose from the dead.
Your friends clap hands and rejoice.
Serfs, like a good family,
kiss each other with joy;
The doctor's spirits rise, he takes off his glasses,
The gravedigger bows his eyes;
Together he and the bailiff
drive out the heir with a shove.

Thus life was given back to you,
with all its charms;
Look: it's an invaluable gift;
Use it well;
Make it fine; the years fly, it's time:
Bring a beautiful wife into your house,
And the gods will bless your marriage.[22]

Sheremetyev did die, but Uvarov had his money at a high price thanks to Pushkin's efforts. By April 1836 Petersburg was awash with malicious gossip. On the orders of the tsar Benckendorff reprimanded the poet, but nothing could appease Uvarov's hatred. He began to put a thousand objections in the way of Pushkin's works at a time when Pushkin, needing money and having recently succeeded in publishing his own journal *Sovremennik* ('The Contemporary') for the first time, was all the more vulnerable. Zhukovsky, who recognized in Pushkin's fury the seeds of his downfall, tried to mediate by persuading Pushkin Uvarov had been turned against him by Benckendorff. He feared the consequences of the war between the headstrong poet and the powerful arbitrary Minister. But the conflict was already well advanced, with Uvarov feeding slanderous gossip into society against the proud and penurious poet. The censorship agreed that to the best of their ability *Sovremennik* should not continue into the next year.[23]

1836 was when Glinka wrote his merry overture 'A Life for the Tsar', but the time grew tense to the point of frenzy for Uvarov. Too many men had personal scores to settle with him, because they felt the force of his personality obtruding through his office, and enough pressed for a showdown. One, in the shadow of Pushkin, was a Belgian, Alphonse Jean Jobard, who had wilfully translated 'On the Death of Lucullus' into French, with Pushkin's knowledge, and sent it to the Minister of Enlightenment with a note accusing Uvarov of plagiarizing the professor's own work.[24] That act itself, aimed at a man who had spent a lifetime working in French, seemed like vituperative parody. Jobard came to Russia as a prisoner of war and began teaching French in the Riga gymnasium. Eventually he made his way to Kazan' university where he became a favourite of Magnitsky who appointed him to the chair of Latin and Greek. Yet he had no academic qualifications and still fewer personal ones and after two years of violent behaviour and abuse of his position Magnitsky as university rector sacked him. Jobard's long campaign against his dismissal was what brought him into indirect contact with Uvarov. Jobard went on wearing the uniform of a professor and insisted on the title. The Minister had him examined for insanity and imprisoned for two months for contempt of court. Jobard believed Uvarov bore him a personal grudge and accused him of setting himself above the law, but he was powerless to help himself. After another eight months in prison he was deported.[25]

The story of Jobard, whose professional history was indefensible, would perhaps be a trifle if it did not reflect on Uvarov's manner of dealing ruthlessly with other men who infringed upon rules he believed in. But Uvarov often set himself up as an enforcer of the quasi-arbitrary law. Polevoy said after the suppression of *The Moscow Telegraph* that the Minister had behaved more like the policeman whereas Benckendorff's behaviour had been positively ministerial.[26] The same shadow fell over his role in the scandal over Peter Chaadaev's 'Philosophical Letter', published in Nadezhdin's *Telescope* in September 1836.

Chaadaev was an intellectual immersed in foreign ideas who dared to suggest that Russia was an inferior civilization and that its better future lay in growing closer to Europe, moreover that since the cause of this inferiority was the Orthodox faith, Russia should look to what benefits might accrue by drawing closer to the Roman church. Not surprisingly, this essay, one of an intended series, brought the full wrath of the higher censorship down on Chaadaev's head. He was declared 'mad' in the fashion of the day and confined for a year under medical supervision, while Nadezhdin received two years' exile. Uvarov devoted much energy to seeing these punishments meted out and Nadezhdin's journal destroyed. As he did in his indictment of Polevoy, he also strove to link the event in the tsar's mind with the Decembrist Insurrection, using both crises to press for firmer controls on the intellectual life of Moscow.[27]

Hard on the heels of the Chaadaev affair Vyazemsky spoke of Uvarov as 'a man who abases everything' and Pushkin, voicing deep frustration and hatred, wrote another poisonous squib linking Uvarov and his friend and lover Prince Mikhail Dondukov-Korsakov. Not only had this man recently been made vice-president of the Academy, he was also in charge of censoring Pushkin's works:

In the Academy of Sciences
sits Dunduk.
They say he's not earned the luck.
Why then is he sitting there?
Because he's got something to fuck.

Pushkin put to good use his penchant for obscenity. As for being 'a man who abases everything', it was true that Uvarov was now one of the richest men in Russia, yet the story went he stole government property in the form of firewood. He was righteous, yet well-known for his preferment of those who fawned before him. He held high public office but made no secret of his pursuit of sexual favours in exchange for influence. The year passed into 1837 with the fifty-year-old Minister much hated.[28]

The historian Mikhail Lemke in his essay 'Torments of a Great Poet' strove seventy years later to implicate Uvarov in the final tragedy of Pushkin, but the proof is missing. The slighted Minister was only the author of one of several critical sketches in circulation in the capital welcoming Pushkin to the order of cuckolds after his wife's alleged adultery with Captain D'Anthes Heeckeren.[29] This matter was well-known, for Pushkin had complained to Benckendorff in November 1836 of the rumours against him. The authorities, however, including the tsar, were uneasy at the possibility of a duel and Uvarov must have known he was pouring oil on the fire. Certainly by the evening of 26 January when D'Anthes designated a society ball as the rendezvous for final arrangements, all Petersburg knew the poet was about to risk his life. One account of his last evening says Uvarov tried to intercede with Benckendorff to have gendarmes sent to stop the duel, but that Benckendorff refused, arguing the government would be well rid of a troublemaker.[30] On the other hand it was Uvarov who invited Pushkin to that last ball at the 'Countess Razumovsky's', as if to make him publicly accessible and to provide the setting for a showdown. Uvarov it seems was playing two parts, one of the nervous official and the other of the back-seat conspirator, knowing that in both he looked well. It might be fairly assumed that he sympathized, as the tsar did, and feared the loss of a distinguished, if aberrant, subject; others might be reassured that Uvarov harboured no bitterness over 'Lucullus'; others again might well have assumed he was one who would be pleased to see a government opponent removed. Uvarov stood, as he customarily liked to arrange his life, in indirect relation to the central incriminating event. When Pushkin and D'Anthes faced each other on 27 January 1837 and Pushkin was fatally wounded, Uvarov's hands were therefore clean.

There is no direct evidence of Uvarov's complicity, yet his behaviour at Pushkin's funeral was remarkable. He looked ashen and not himself, and people avoided him. It was said he felt the nervous excitement which came from cold resentment mingled with the shared fears of the entire Third Department that the occasion meant upheaval. Afterwards he persecuted the dead poet with redoubled energy and meanness of sentiment. Who was this man who was not an official, he asked, who held no position in government service, who had no career? What justification could there be for so many impassioned tributes? The funeral aroused a fervent degree of public support, but Uvarov expressly forbade students to attend.[31] Afterwards, either personally or through his censorship committee, he oversaw everything that was written about the funeral.

On 31 January 1837 Nikitenko noted, 'He is very busy trying to curb the loud wailing caused by the death of P. He is unhappy with the lavish praise of him.'[32]

It was a rare occasion when Uvarov's zeal outdid that of the tsar, but this was one, for Nicholas throughout his reign had made Pushkin an exception and treated him almost tenderly. Nikitenko predicted Uvarov's fury when he discovered that the tsar had ordered all the works of Pushkin already published should continue in print, without alteration. It was as if Pushkin himself were dealing Uvarov a final slight.[33]

Mikhail Lermontov, Russia's surviving great poet, believed it was the society that killed Pushkin, a society of Uvarov's making. His lines rang with the accusation that orthodoxy, autocracy and nationality had annihilated virtue:

Oh you descendants of illustrious ancestors,
Proud of a base deed.
Your fathers begrudged the high play of happiness
and you made good their loss by crawling on your knees.
You are the hungry mob gathered round the throne,
the executioners of Glory, Freedom and Genius.[34]

Through such suspicions and allusions Uvarov earned the title Belinsky gave him, the Minister of Darkness and the Extinction of Enlightenment.[35]

14

A life for the Tsar

Love of the fatherland is certainly a very beautiful thing,
but there is something better.

PETER CHAADAEV

To adapt a famous remark Belinsky would make to Gogol, Belinsky's Russia could forgive an untalented man but not an evil one. To the men of the 'marvellous decade'[1] Uvarov seemed uniquely tainted.[2] At the Academy and in the press he had acquired a hungry clientele of administrators, historians and mediocre theorists of literature ready to teach the official line, and in his private life he associated with the same men, some of the most disagreeable of the day. When Shevyrev and Pogodin received permission to publish articles and edit journals, and Belinsky and Polevoy were left out in the cold, the division of values seemed clear cut. Belinsky considered Shevyrev as a personal enemy and Uvarov an enemy of good literature, and he accused Pogodin of pimping for a corrupt Minister. Many of Belinsky's contemporaries suspected that behind Uvarov's asserted principles there were no fixed principles at all. On the conservative, Slavophile side, devotion to the Orthodox Church surely had nothing to do with such a man. However, it was from the Westernizing camp that Uvarov's trinity of principles came under most consistent intellectual fire, for everything from fatuousness to wishful thinking and wilful deceit, and his academic associates like Shevyrev were tarred with the same brush.[3] The Westernizers even found they had to defend the veteran nationalist historian Karamzin against Uvarov.

An instance which particularly angered Vyazemsky, Pushkin and Alexander Turgenev in the mid-1830s was the Minister's cavalier treatment of Karamzin's authority. Treated now as Alexander's historian, Karamzin had already incurred criticism from the new generation of romantic historians, including Polevoy and Pogodin. Both said he ignored the greatness of the Russian people and underplayed the achievements of Peter the Great. The Arzamas friends were most angered when Uvarov as Minister of Enlightenment arranged a competition in 1836 for a history book to replace Karamzin's as the standard school text, and allowed the contest to be won by a favourite of his, Nikolai Ustryalov. As with Uvarov's hostility to Pushkin, the issue seemed once again to be a matter of a corrupt bureaucrat trying to ruin the cultural legacy of a great writer. Vyazemsky instantly deemed Ustryalov an unqualified nobody.

In fact the winning dissertation, *On a System of Pragmatic Russian History*, indicated only a very slight move away from Karamzin. Uvarov exaggerated it, in order to create the need for the competition at all.[4] It was embroidered with the Romantic notion of organic growth, and it sang the praises of the present tsar where Karamzin, who had died in 1826, could not, and lauded Peter the Great, Nicholas's personal hero. Like Karamzin Ustryalov continued to see Russia as a power whose strength depended on autocracy and orthodoxy. But Ustryalov's history was useful to Uvarov because it supported the official view of the Russianness of the Western Provinces against the claims of Polish and Lithuanian nationalism, and 'when it is written up, the history of our country will advance in many ways and stand on a par with the monuments of other European states'.[5] That Russia should come into contention as a leading European cultural power was perhaps Uvarov's greatest wish, while Karamzin too much stressed Russia's difference, which tended to amount to its continuing backwardness.[6]

Still Vyazemsky was outraged at the slight to the glory of Karamzin, and the elevation of Ustryalov, whom Uvarov rewarded with frequent appearances at his lectures and gave privileged access to the Foreign Ministry Archives to complete his research on Peter the Great.[7] The Arzamas friends were dealt another blow when Uvarov thwarted their desire to publish materials relating to Karamzin for what seemed to be spurious, unspelt-out political reasons, namely that the time was not right. In retaliation they accused him of fornication, vainglory and avarice.[8]

The foundational tsarist era for the police state that Russia would remain, with varying degrees of intensity, for the next century and a half and indefinitely thereafter,[9] saw a battle for the moral high ground, between officialdom and dissenting intellectuals which was only once openly repeated, only once again played out in such high moral terms, namely in the magnificent era of Soviet dissent of the 1960s and 1970s. But our relative proximity to that struggle is yet another reason why we need to understand Uvarov's career, and the ethical compromises he made. Back in the mid-1830s, against the poor moral reputation that official church and government administrators enjoyed under the official religion of tsarism,[10] Uvarov's vehement moral opponents virtually defined the ethical scope of a more liberal modern Russia that might develop in the aftermath of the French Revolution. Part of that heritage was, indirectly, the influence of Rousseau, founder of the European dream of reborn moral innocence. Among the great alternative intellectual leaders of the 'marvellous decade' of 1838–48 were Stankevich and Herzen who aimed rather to be 'beautiful souls' in the manner of Rousseau's German disciple Schiller, than grand public men in the style of Voltaire. And so times of great courage, and vision, were born, both their style and their ethical quality nurtured in defiance of *ancien régime* inequality and despotism.[11]

Had Uvarov been their sole opponent, the independent spirits of the 1830s, the men of the 'Marvellous Decade', would still have become known for their intellectual heroism. Indeed one might argue that they needed such a figure, representative of the old style and entirely negatively portrayed,[12] to define themselves as new. Using literary comment as a vehicle for moral exhortation, and aesthetics as a bridge to politics, the new intelligentsia defied every one of Uvarov's cherished beliefs about the sanctity of art and its appropriateness as a channel for social criticism. They represented their thoughts with direct actions and made it their lives to think more widely and freely than the authorities who tried to curb them. Moreover, they were a social stratum drawn together solely by intellectual principles and interests, a phenomenon which challenged the principle Uvarov had grown up with, of class cohesion by birth. This revolution in sensibility necessarily came later to Russia than to Britain and France, and conservatives everywhere were unhappy with it. Burke, arguing the case in the British parliament, observed the fundamental change which came over public style after the French Revolution, and opposed to it the earlier breed of 'wise and sober statesmen'. Burke said the new men in politics were 'warm and inexperienced enthusiasts' who preached as from a pulpit. They exploited extremes, believed in the validity of opinions, and their markedly personal and emotional style did not augur well for noble order and the guarantee of civil rights. By contrast the classical politician was prudent, cautious and respectful of the deficiencies of human nature; he was subtle, sceptical and professional, compared with the excited, ruthless amateurs who had moved onto the stage.[13]

In Russia Uvarov was an exaggerated representative of the old art, and his ambition was evidently to use his capacity to play the conservative part in order slowly to introduce post-revolutionary changes to society. So much was evident in his educational reforms of the mid-1830s. In his case both his contemporaries and subsequent historians have been confused by his public actions and private intentions over which to believe to be the essence of the man. Uvarov was 'not without ideals ... and trying very hard to improve the outlook of the Ministry to which he belonged', wrote, a century and a half later, an outstanding historian of tsarist Russia in its final crisis in 1917.[14]

The new generation alternately laughed at Uvarov and feared him when he imposed his false and fussy manners and his 'enlightened' apology for autocracy on their lives. Tense, he redoubled his zeal to serve correctly. The eighteenth-century *punctilio* which guided his behaviour directly reflected the legitimism which shaped his political outlook.

There was a European parallel for Uvarov's conservatism and it belonged to the Austrian chancellor Clemens Metternich, for thirty years continental Europe's most powerful leader who did everything he could to halt the advance of French revolutionary influence. A portrait drawn of Metternich almost three quarters of a century ago, by the most distinguished Western political conservative, and historian, of the era, might almost describe Uvarov in the same mixture of physiological, psychological and political terms:

> His face was delicate but without depth, his conversation brilliant but without ultimate seriousness. Equally at home in the salon and the Cabinet, graceful and facile, he was the *beau-ideal* of the eighteenth-century aristocracy which justified itself not by its truth but by its existence. And if he never came to terms with the new age it was not because he failed to understand its seriousness but because he disdained it. Therein too his fate was the fate of Austria.
>
> Opposed to revolution, Metternich fought it in the name of outdated ideals, preferring the subtle manoeuvre to the frontal attack. He saw himself as the supreme realist and 'visionaries' as his chief enemies. Cosmopolitan and rationalist, he was always more at home in French than German.

The perceptive portrait-artist in question was sometime US Secretary of State Henry Kissinger.[15]

Like Uvarov Metternich invited sneering from his contemporaries for his facile philosophizing, his polished epigrams and his misplaced 'rational certainty'. For both men revolution was so foreign to their temperament that neither was willing to probe into the existence and nature of the conflict that followed it. They refused to see as inevitable the transformative consequences of the disempowered classes and nations of the nineteenth century coming to self-awareness. Neither was a publicist or a pamphleteer, but both were masters of a rhetoric by which they also deceived themselves. Uvarov's linguistic slipperiness was well demonstrated in his speech 'Alexandre' wherein a well-turned paragraph he slipped over the excruciating dilemma of the age: how the Russian monarchy could accommodate the increased political demands of the people.

Stankevich and Herzen were great examples of the alternative ethics of a would-be liberal age in Russia. But the one man whose life best highlighted the outmoded moral quality of Uvarov's style was Belinsky, the man to whom the chronicler Pavel Annenkov attributed the entire character of the anti-official culture of the 1830s. Belinsky's exhortation to his countrymen in his first published essay, *Literary Reveries* (1834), was typically spirited and formless: 'Write, speak, shout! That is what I say to every man who has the slightest disinterested love of his country, of goodness and truth.' This unofficial nationality was not ashamed to stare native cultural poverty in the face. Belinsky wanted to see Russia develop as an organic culture, which would arise out of a conscious appreciation of what it was to be Russian. Thanks to his foreshortened time at Moscow University he was steeped in German Idealism, and his breathless romantic style relayed the originality and vitality he dearly wished to see informing Russian art and society. He worried that Russia did not have a national literature, though it had fine beginnings in Karamzin, Zhukovsky, Batyushkov and Pushkin. His criticism would create the first national literary map. By 1835 he was devoting a whole essay to 'realism' in Gogol, his pioneering essay appeared on Lermontov in 1840, and he went on to write eleven essays on Pushkin which became a fundament of nineteenth-century criticism. Indeed Belinsky was virtually creating Russian literature single-handedly. He was poor man, the son of a village priest, who suffered periodic unemployment and ill health and never married. He lifted these biographical facts above the level of gossip by demonstrating that his literary life was inseparable from the rest of his turbulent existence. He nourished a passion for a literature enriched by the uneven texture of simple, everyday life, and everything he wrote, even the number of times he changed his mind, reflected the intellectual excitement and confusion of the foreign-oriented philosophical 'circles' of the day. The foreign ideas he tested on behalf of Russia were restlessly and self-consciously lived through. Schiller's cherubic moral idealism, excessively literally understood, Belinsky finally overcame with a visit to a brothel. Belinsky's every essay, review and private letter continued the search for quality of experience in art and in life. He was poorly served by his scant, untutored knowledge of any language except Russian and his spontaneous, sprawling style, vigorous, repetitive, urgent and exclamatory, could not have been further removed from the carefully wrought, delicately nuanced ideal of the eighteenth century in France. But in his passion for calling a spade a spade, love love and liberty liberty, he recalled the publicist in Victor Hugo, the man who overthrew the old France in art. His literary mission led him deep into European literature, into Shakespeare and Calderón, Byron and Goethe, into the German Romantic philosophy of Schelling and Hegel, upon which he pronounced warm and enthusiastic judgements. He was translating foreign literature to Russia as Uvarov had done, but doing it in Russian and on a level which had far wider appeal.[16]

Uvarov had nothing in common with Belinsky's age.

Let us then restate his fundamental position, which was an honest one, genuinely held.

He believed in that version of the social contract that had governed the nobility's relations to the autocrat since the eighteenth century.[17] That accounted for much of the personal offence he took at the Chaadaev affair. In Nadezhdin's offences Uvarov perceived a breach of trust. In particular they violated the positive censorship 'agreement' not to undermine the government which had been drawn up at Uvarov's own instigation the previous year. Uvarov refused to accept the publisher Nadezhdin's protestations of innocence and had little sympathy either for the luckless censor who passed the article.[18]

Second, fundamentally in the *ancien régime* mode, he believed restrained political behaviour was a matter of good taste. He still spoke of taste, in that eighteenth-century fashion which presumed it coincided with moral goodness and truth. Indeed in 1833 he made taste the censor's point of departure:

> I wish not only that the content and spirit of these publications [books and periodicals] contain in themselves nothing contrary to censorship rules, but also that their tone and exposition be in accord, as far as possible, with the demands of propriety and decorum, in order to raise and ennoble this branch of literature.[19]

Uvarov believed he could still call the political subservience he sought good taste. He meant not causing offence.

Thirdly, in adhering to his idea of Official Nationality, he believed that the activity of propaganda was not 'politics' but positive instruction in 'the Russian principle'. When over a decade later the tsar asked him to define the difference between his Official Nationality, Slavophilism and Panslavism, three current ideologies which all had loyalty to Slav roots at their core, he replied that Official Nationality was a didactic principle, whereas the other two were manifestly political. He applied his term to teachers, 'whose place it is to arouse a social consciousness not on the basis of Slavdom, a creation of the play of imagination, but on the basis of the Russian principle, within the confines of science, without any trace of contemporary political ideas'.[20] It was a distinction that singled out a Russian domestic need for nationally oriented ideological coherence, and kept that need essentially separate from any politics, any realpolitik, one might say, that Russia pursued abroad.

Autocracy was acceptable to him. Ultimately benevolent, it was compatible with the spread of education to a wider and wider constituency of the people, provided educational reforms proceeded gradually. In the light of his unswerving acceptance of the tsar as the ultimate arbiter of progress's direction and pace his own task was clear: to produce an ever more educated populace which would still accept the Russian state as the supreme source of social, moral and intellectual value. Official Nationality was a device to spread the necessary knowledge and skills across a wider section of the population without stimulating political unrest. He told a French interviewer in the early 1840s it was the only way to ensure Russia continued along the Westernizing path pioneered by Peter the Great.[21]

The subtlety of Uvarov's plight, as a progressive European but a Russian conservative, was not understood in his time and has been rarely understood since. Savagely echoing the tripartite slogan when he dubbed him the Minister of Darkness and the Extinction of Enlightenment, Belinsky called his three principles the Whip, the Knout and Reaction.[22] To his critics, the men of the Marvellous Decade, to encourage repression as he did, in the face of blatant human injustice, was simply immoral. Still it seemed to him that given Russian conditions, and despite the progress of democracy in the West, he had to create a service imperative to bind the non-noble classes to the state and limit public intellectual activity. Creative energies could not be allowed to run free in an immature country. By the end of his life he rightly perceived the times had moved on too far to understand him.[23]

In bureaucratic form, suitable for the activities of a government Minister, he created much that was positive for Russian culture. He focused all his positive cultural energies on the Academy, where his efforts reached their apogee in 1838.[24] With government money he saw a new building erected to house one of his great dreams, an Asiatic Museum, and this was enriched with the purchase of hundreds of rare volumes and manuscripts. An important collection related to the ancient languages was also purchased for the main library. Uvarov saw through a new constitution for the Academy, increasing its budget and its autonomy, established plans for a central observatory and guaranteed the salaries and pensions of the academicians. Scientific work was proceeding successfully and expeditions to investigate the languages and topography of further flung parts of the empire had taken teams of experts to the Caucasus and the areas around the Black and Caspian Seas. It was a moment of high personal satisfaction for the president when the tsar inspected some of the fruits of this expanded, flourishing research institute in March 1838.

But nothing of this institutionalized flowering at the hand of a man who had effectively made himself Minister of Culture helped art. Nothing of it helped responsible journalism and social criticism. When facts were potent politically they were subordinate to the needs of the state. Uvarov excelled in building a culture comprising museums, research institutes and schools. But that was the final extent of his idea of nationality: a museum culture and a handful of good universities.[25] He was no more concerned with the will of the people or the organic principle than the tsar himself. And this was another reason why instinctively he made enemies among the intelligentsia. Though steeped in the classical world, the Renaissance and eighteenth-century France, he had only an archaeologist's idea of Russian culture. He believed it was, and would be, a cultivation of Russian history and letters, enlightened by the West, but not Western, and which would not interfere with the course of the tsar's politics. His scholarly idea was accurate in the name of science, but by dispensing with imagination it lacked any sense of the people, and seemed cold, distant and unsympathetic to the joys and hardships of humble life. That was why his critics said, wrongly in a literal sense but rightly in spirit, that Uvarov was afraid to speak Russian and had never read a Russian book in his life.

Efforts have been made to pinpoint Uvarov's position in the great historical and cultural debate which gripped Russia in the 1830s and 1840s, but he has remained an ambiguous figure. It was left to other men to advance definitions of Russian history according to which the present was justified or decried, the censorship accepted or castigated, and social backwardness vis-à-vis the West viewed as an advantage or a disadvantage. Uvarov has only very recently entered authoritative considerations of the thought of the day. Essentially he viewed the Petrine era as monumentally positive and a touchstone for a modern Russia which would borrow from the West to achieve unique greatness. But that was too general a gloss in a sectarian age to be accepted as a committed position.[26]

The quality of debate came instead from the 'Westernizers' and the 'Slavophiles'. The first advocated a critical assimilation of Western institutions and ideas, much as Uvarov did, but without the restrictions he imposed in the form of slavish worship of tsar, nationality and church; the second found an ideal of community in the allegedly uncontaminated pre-Petrine era. To critical outsiders it didn't pass without comment that both attitudes were formed under the influence of German philosophy. Indeed Herzen called them two heads on the same banner. The Slavophiles stood out by virtue of their negative view of tsar Peter as a destroyer of the ways of the people, but both tendencies were patriotic at heart and literary in character, and both were the work of creative minds trying to formulate an original Russian future as prompted by new developments in Western philosophy. Slavophilism was steeped in imaginative thinking and myth, while the foremost Westernizers were literary critics and speculative historians, given to thinking in images. The Slavophiles were at their most spiritual through the thinking of Alexei Khomiakov, and the Westernizers at their most intelligent and energetic in the young Herzen. Uvarov in his official political and cultural views, on the other hand, was confined to the servile restatement of a dead formula. The contrast between orginality and servility is one distinction which can be made to help pinpoint his position.

Another distinction about Uvarov's position is the distance he kept between himself and the various other 'nationalists' airing their views in the 1830s. Into this group fell his associates Pogodin and Shevyrev, both former Romantics, and ironically often labelled Official Nationalists because of their association with Uvarov. They shared with the Minister an admiration of Peter the Great, and an interest in defining where Russia's worldly strength lay. But their style, bordering on the fanatical, and their Romantic thoughts, sometimes put them at a great distance from Uvarov. Pogodin had a deep interest in ancient Russia, which he supported with detailed palaeographic research. It was he who stressed for the first time that Russian history and the Russian principle were distinct in the world and unique, and who hailed as a great Russian cause the Orthodox Church which had always submitted to the state. But he also sang the praises of the 'national personality' and 'the people' and on occasion drew close to the dangerously imaginative Slavophiles, so Uvarov was both with him and not.[27]

Shevyrev championed a strong and unique Russia by examining literary and artistic history. In the early 1830s he tailored Romantic aesthetics to serve a projected culturally supreme Russia, and it was only gradually that he allowed himself to be overtaken by a mania for Orthodoxy, Autocracy and Nationality. In his prime he argued that the passion for German theory had diverted Russia from discovering a vital cultural tradition of her own, but that this same intellectual passion would finally drive Russia back to its own resources. It would discover its own national poetry and at the same time take up the leading cultural position in the West, uniting those principles which had been taken to an isolated extreme by the succession of cultural ages in Europe. Shevyrev predicted Russia would synthesize the Ancient and the Modern world and the divergent traditions of speculative and empirical thought in a new whole.[28]

The views of these men were at once too systematic and too speculative for Uvarov's personal classical taste. The Minister promoted their academic careers, so that his name became readily associated with them. Pogodin's textbook was used in Uvarov's schools. But a great distance remained between Uvarov and these worthy academics too often seen as his henchmen.

Ideologically Uvarov was closer, though it was not to his intellectual credit, to the so-called dynastic nationalists. The dynasts were an infamous triumvirate of popularizers, Nikolai Grech, Faddei Bulgarin and the Pole Osip Senkowski, who curried favour with the tsar and spread calumnious gossip in the widely read columns of their magazines, *Severnaya Pchela* ('The Northern Bee') and *Biblioteka dlya Chtenya* ('A Reading Library'). Like the tsar they gloried in the Russian autocratic principle and expected non-Russians to submit to it. For their popularizing they were greatly loathed by the privately fastidious Uvarov, though the Minister of Enlightenment could hardly differentiate between his loyalty to the tsar and what they professed. Such was the crudity of association from time to time which Uvarov's public position and his private personality imposed upon him.

But in the end all any nationalist group meant to Uvarov was the degree to which he could make use of them politically. Any advocacy of autocracy and Orthodoxy might on occasion advance his realpolitik. In that respect his legitimism and relative lack of concern for either 'organic' nationality or Official Nationality as presented by the scribblers accorded with the tsar's.[29]

Ironically, but in line with his consistent denial of politics in Russia all through his life, and just as he denied Russian censorship was a political act, Uvarov refused to call his nationality policy political. Its fideistic nature made it rather 'didactic'. He told the tsar that Official Nationality differed from Slavophilism and Panslavism because it alone was not hostile to Russia. A philosophy was 'political' if it presented an alternative view to the government's. Politics, therefore, was a matter for the West, not Russia, where there existed only one Russian truth. Official Nationality existed instead of politics and was intended as a guideline for teachers, 'whose place it is to arouse a social consciousness not on the basis of Slavdom, a creation of the play of imagination, but on the basis of the Russian principle, within the confines of science, without any trace of contemporary political ideas'. Official Nationality thus enshrined that fear of Western-style politics which caused Nicholaevan Russia to barricade itself in.[30]

Yet ultimately, in a way which has mystified commentators on the period, Uvarov stood alone, and in its own way the public notion of Official Nationality helped protect his private self from scrutiny. His aesthetic taste remained what it had been in his Arzamas days, often far removed from his country and century, and culturally he was in no sense a nationalist. His public pronouncements could be misleading. He was 'delighted' with Gogol's hilarious and pitiful satire on the Russian bureaucracy in *The Government Inspector* which appeared in 1836, but only because the tsar was. Uvarov remained both suspicious of and unattracted by a great deal of modern literature, both Russian and European. In public he avowed that the poetry of Pushkin and Lermontov were dangerous. Apparently in private too he was undyingly distrustful of the now ubiquitous Romantic spirit. He could tolerate Victor Hugo without approving of him as a novelist for mass Russian consumption, but he was less sure about the value of Voltaire, and Byron, the Decembrists' favourite poet, and George Sand, though he took the time to read them.[31]

Such was his anxiety at the nature of the contemporary that he wrote an essay in 1840, entitled 'Some General Views on the Philosophy of Literature,' read to the Academy, in which he once again set out his ideas in favour of classical literature. He dismissed as a relative trifle the growth of national literatures such as were affecting the whole of continental Europe, and Russia.

He also wished to see literature remain the pursuit of the elite and opposed lower forms of reading matter such as penny magazines. He wished literature to express authority and what he held against Voltaire, Byron and Sand was their encouragement of scepticism. His position was at once anti-democratic and anti-national. He is on record as saying he wished Russian literature would cease to exist.[32]

To stand beyond the reach of the culture of his day was a huge loss. Out of the Western and Slavophile roots emerged in Russia a love of 'philosophy', combined with an instinctive sympathy for the humble Russian life and people which set Russian literature on course for a century. To this rich young substance Belinsky as a Westernizer brought literary criticism which was 'social' and 'civic' in character, and in literary practice Gogol's short stories began to glorify Russian and Ukrainian ordinary life. In philosophy the high-minded, metaphysical Slavophile Alexei Khomiakov defined a Russian spirituality which naturally bridged the gap between church and society and individual and community. On the Westernizing side Stankevich represented in himself and in the German idealism he absorbed a highly appealing call for individual moral idealism. These two initial directions of nineteenth-century Russia brought true nationality alive.

Dostoevsky was later to satirize their extremes as *knizhnost'* and *pochvennost'*, love of foreign ideas and love of the soil, but it was within their bounds that Herzen too was able to sketch an ideal Russian originality. As a young man he described fearless, unscholastic adventures of the mind which would embrace both the 'objective' science and the 'subjective' imagination to be found in the Western tradition and produce a Russian synthesis. The novelist Ivan Turgenev also took up a unique position between the poles of national sentiment and Western-inspired criticism with the short stories he began to publish in the 1840s.

Yet Uvarov's position outside all these developments was not governed only by political choice. Even if he had wanted it, Uvarov's Platonic pessimism on behalf of an imperfect world would not have fitted. His very character was out of tune. He ignored the humble life and disdained 'philosophy'. His self-defined task was to fight the very philosophizing which was the lifeblood of both the Slavophile and Westernizer circles, as he told Davydov:

> Those of us who are concerned with ideas, frequently a fickle element, have a constant struggle ahead of us; against this elusive element we have one defence – national education, based on respect for Orthodoxy devotion to the Throne and love of the Fatherland.[33]

To the loyal tsarist Minister in the end *any* Western ideas were anathema because they threatened Russia with premature stimulation.

Yet, to be accurate about the position he occupied rather than the one he avowed, it must be said that those writers who were open to the West had a diversity and a weight which otherwise would have attracted him. He was to say a few years later that the two periodicals where the Westernizers published their work, *Otechestvennye Zapiski* ('Notes from the Fatherland') and *Sovremennik* ('The Contemporary') contained the highest journalism of the day. The Westernizers were also not a unified ideological camp, but rather individuals brought together in a wide-ranging, passionate search for cultural quality. They had something substantial in common with Arzamas, wherein at the time Uvarov had found a natural place. The diverse present generation of progressive literary men included Mikhail Bakunin who was an anarchist and a political activist, and Belinsky who was a most individual literary terrorist. The Hegelian Granovsky, a lecturer in history, actually became a close personal friend of Uvarov's. Most self-conscious about present-day intellectual activity was Ivan Turgenev. His poetic fiction took the pathos of daily life as its subject with the whirlwind of contemporary intellectual passions as its background. The slow-moving Russian provinces poignantly framed lives alternately stimulated and frustrated by so many infectious ideals which turned out to be impossible to fulfil. Uvarov's mind also bore the stamp of such poetic pessimism, but unlike Turgenev, who viewed the Russia that lost his heart, and was lost to him in his self-imposed European exile, Uvarov's distance from his time was that gained by the perspective of pre-revolutionary France.

Ambivalent and elusive ideologically, Uvarov was always practical, almost in spite of himself. He was able to play a positive role in a growing culture because he truly had an eye for materials, talent and men who would serve the Russian nation day-to-day. He promoted able, popular teachers. In the department of literary history at Moscow University Shevyrev laid the foundations for a new Russian academic discipline concerned with the circumstances and nature of the production of works of art. A generation of students benefited greatly from his wide-ranging general surveys. Pogodin as a teacher was reputed to be chaotic in his methods, but he was a good researcher. Moreover, no one was more influential as a teacher of the Slavophiles of the next decade. In 1835 Uvarov helped Pogodin get abroad for the first time in his career, after an earlier thwarted attempt. The young history lecturer went to Western Europe and also to Prague, where he met leading exponents of the Slav movement and later became an important catalyst in the creation of the Pan-Slav movement.[34]

A third academic protégé was Davydov, who had survived his 1826 dismissal from academia and become professor of Russian literature at Moscow University when Uvarov became Minister. Davydov was another former Romantic, also a medical student, who, like Uvarov, saw in his time of crisis that he was either going to have to fit in or lose the career he wanted.

Few could later believe that in maturity he was the same man who once got into trouble administering an overdose of German Idealism. But what he learnt, like Uvarov, was to manipulate the Romantic idea of the people. When he turned from philosophy to literature in 1829 he put forward a fashionable view of art as the supreme expression of the people and it was welcomed. He anticipated a notion made famous by Belinsky when he called literature 'the depiction of the thinking of a people, its inner life, not its outer garments'.[35]

Not everyone admired Uvarov's academic choices as men, but he found efficient candidates for his schools and universities. On one well-known occasion he even tried, under the pressure of Pushkin and Zhukovsky, to accommodate Nikolai Gogol, who wanted to be a history lecturer as well as a writer of short stories. The penniless, barely known Ukrainian was given a job at St Petersburg University in 1836. The exception proved the rule of Uvarov's better judgement. Gogol's students quickly laughed their lazy, uninformed instructor out of class.[36]

From a longer perspective, however, the landmark which most nearly pinpoints Uvarov's position in the intellectual and political life of the mid-decade is Chaadaev's 'Philosophical Letter'. This brilliant essay doubted the principles upon which Uvarov had founded his political life. It constituted the ultimate challenge to a man who was European in education but Russian in politics.

In his essay Chaadaev openly equated Orthodoxy with backwardness and declared Russian national consciousness a fiction. This is how his accusers described his heresy, in words which were partly Uvarov's:

> Such a virtually open attack, for the first time, on the Graeco-Russian Church, the life of which is so closely bound up with the life of the state, gives this work a new feature which makes it stand out from other liberal lampoons, a feature which betrays an echo, some kind of tie with the latest catholicism, which has recently raised its head in France under the leadership of Lammenais and his school, at the same time as O'Connell in England, and Potner among the Belgians, and some extremely radical sects in Germany and Switzerland, like Lammenais not separating themselves from the Roman Church but which are together with him looking for a point at which its teaching will unite with the revolutionary principles which have seized most of Europe.[37]

Chaadaev had read European literature and thought and travelled widely abroad. What was extraordinary from Uvarov's point of view was that with the same knowledge as Uvarov in 'Project' and 'Eleusis' Chaadaev now implicitly opposed the arguments contained in those essays, drawing opposite conclusions from the same facts. He spoke of 'miserable Byzantium' and declared, 'Though we were Christian, the fruit of Christianity did not mature for us.'[38] With a devilish suggestion which may have stirred in Uvarov a memory of another opponent of genius, namely the Jesuit Maistre, Chaadaev also argued that the Western world, because it had been cradled by Roman Catholicism, had advanced further along the road to moral perfection than Russia and Russia therefore should heed the example, and align itself with the Catholic church before it was too late.[39]

What Chaadaev wrote was implicitly a devastating attack on Official Nationality. The nub of it concerned history. Other men had dared to say it, even recently, but Chaadaev repeated with a terrible boldness that Russia lacked a history. He did not regard himself as unpatriotic and he did not attack the autocracy, but he believed his country would only be redeemed if it set itself immediately on a course of re-education, in which connection he proposed its spiritual re-marriage with the West.[40]

Glance over all the centuries through which we have lived, all the land which we cover, you will find not one venerable monument which might evoke powerfully bygone eras and might vividly and picturesquely depict them again for you. We live only in the most narrow kind of present without a past and without a future in the midst of a shallow calm. And if we stir sometimes, it is neither with hope nor desire for some common good, but with the puerile frivolity of the child who raises himself up and lifts his hand towards the rattle which the nurse shows to him ... .

Our early years, spent in immobile brutishness, have left no trace in our minds, and we do not have any individuality on which to base our thoughts; but, isolated by a strange destiny from the universal movement of humanity, we have absorbed nothing ... . If we wish to take up a position similar to that of other civilized people, we must, in a certain sense, repeat the whole education of mankind.

... We are one of those nations which does not seem to form an integral part of humanity ... Europeans have a common physiognomy, a family resemblance. Despite the general division of these people into Latin and Teutonic branches, into the southern and the northern, there is a common bond which unites them in one whole, evident to anyone who has profoundly studied their history ... .

In Europe each individual enjoys his share of the heritage; without strain or work during his lifetime each collects and utilizes notions disseminated in society. Draw the comparison yourself and see what elementary ideas we can acquire in this way during our daily lives, in order to use them, for better or worse, in molding our lives. And note that this is not a question of study or reading, nor has it anything to do with literature or science; it is simply the contact of intellects; in the crib the child is seized by these ideas which surround him amid his games and are communicated to him by his mother's caresses; these ideas ... have formed his moral being even before he is sent out into the world and society ... duty, justice, law, and order ... they are the integral elements in the social world of these countries. This is the atmosphere of the West; it is more than history, more than psychology; it is the physiology of the European. What have you to substitute for that in our country?

... This sphere in which the Europeans live – the only one in which humanity can find its final destiny – is the result of the influence which religion exercised among them ... it is clear that impetus must be given to us, for it is Christianity which has produced everything over there. That is what I meant when I said that we have to begin the education of humanity all over again in our country.

These were bold ideas, which while they did not destroy Chaadaev's faith in autocracy, invited intelligent, objective debate by virtue of being one of the most accurate analyses of the spiritual ailments of Russian society ever written by a Russian. But Uvarov expressely forebade intellectual discussion of Chaadaev's letter.[41]

The Chaadaev affair once more highlighted the attachment of dissenting voices to disinterested standards of morality and truth, which could not be found within the autocracy. Chaadaev himself suffered the classic fate of a dissident, and struggled to defend himself against accusations of madness. His re-iteration of his position in his 'Apology of a Madman' was ethically impressive:

Love of the fatherland is certainly a very beautiful thing, but there is something better than that; it is the love of truth. Love of one's fatherland makes heroes, love of truth makes wise men, the benefactors of humanity; it is love of the fatherland which divides peoples, which feeds national hatreds, which sometimes covers the earth with mourning; it is love of the truth which spreads light, which creates the joys of the spirit, which brings men close to the Divinity. It is not by way of the fatherland, it is by way of the truth that one mounts to heaven. It is true that, as for us Russians, we have few men in love with the truth; we lack examples, so one must not expect too much from a nation which has always been so little concerned with what is true and what is not, if it was so affected by a slightly virulent address directed at its infirmities. Moreover I have no rancour, I assure you, against this dear public which cajoled me for such a long time; it is with composure, without any irritation, that I am trying to explain to myself my strange situation! Must I not try to explain to myself where one upon whom insanity has been imposed stands vis-à-vis his confrères, vis-à-vis his fellowcitizens, vis-à-vis his God? … More than anyone at all, believe me, I love my country dearly, I am ambitious for its glory, I know how to esteem the eminent qualities of my nation, but it is true that the patriotic sentiment which animates me is not formed exactly like those of the men whose cries upset my obscure existence … . It is true I have not learned to love my fatherland with my eyes closed, forehead bowed, mouth closed. I find that one can be useful to one's country only on the condition that one sees things clearly; I believe that the times of blind loves are over, that fanaticisms of any kind are no longer in season … .

It is in the gentle belief of felicities to come for mankind that I take refuge whenever, besieged by the frustrating reality which surrounds me, I feel the need to breathe a purer air, and to look upon a more serene sky.

These last italics are mine. I believe Chaadaev was eloquent and truthful and spoke at last what Uvarov had long harboured in his heart.[42]

It is possible that for the Minister the whole Chaadaev experience cut too close to the bone. He had had his own occasions to crave a purer foreign air and to complain that his love for his country had been misunderstood. Indeed he was already on record as fearing the fate of an outsider:

If mankind needs to emancipate itself from the vulgar shades of ignorance and set itself in motion continually and without end towards the light of knowledge, it is necessary for peoples that the government assumes for them a protective and directive role. In effect the government alone possesses the means of knowing simultaneously what progress has been achieved by universal civilization and what are the real needs of the country … . To safeguard the real needs of the people and heal their moral and political injuries should be the aim of its activity. These injuries, just as physical injuries, may not be unuseful in the general plan of Providence, but love of one's fatherland as well as simple common sense tells us that we should try to avoid them and not accept the sad, hardly enviable fate of one who suffers to provide a lesson to others.[43]

Once again (as with Pushkin, in creative talent, so here with Chaadaev in addressing Russia's place in world history) the comparison must have been deeply painful. Chaadaev wrote in the French Uvarov also delighted in[44] and expressed the sentiments of a man of Uvarov's own class, moreover one who was only eight years his junior. His text confronted Uvarov with his suppressed past.

Unequal to the psychological challenge, Uvarov reacted by making petty, facetious remarks in the margin of the papers for the case.[45] The occasion recalls his involvement with de Stael, without which comparison one might wonder how a clever man could be so small-minded as to use his power for petty destructions, such as the exile of Nadezhdin and the sacking of the censor. Always there was that weak, vain personality seeking to come into play. Both when he was young and now in middle age Uvarov seems to have been confused, both attracted and repelled by what he was bound to reject. It was his willed opposition to political Westernization, in fact his emotional allegiance to nothing but the depersonalized autocrat and the irrecoverable world of antiquity, which forced him into negativity.

15

Politics devours everything

Where Official Nationality was extended into a policy for the empire, the strain on Uvarov became enormous. The goal was to contain and unify diverse peoples of increasingly divergent educated views within one Russian state. He argued characteristically that the aim could be achieved gradually, accompanied by gently persuasive policies, but the obvious adverse evidence of reality undermined his position.

He was also in theory on infirm ground. It was a seminal piece of political sleight-of-hand to use the word 'nationality' in the imperial context. Purged of its Romantic content 'Nationality' meant autocracy. In fact Uvarov's entire slogan could be reduced to a tautology and the sheer starkness of the imperial policy it summarized was clearest in the parts of the empire where appeals to the Russian church and Russian history held no magic. Nationality was the principle intended to compel the Poles and the Baltic Germans to recognize a force majeur rather than investigate and revive their own roots. Its repressive potential was magnified particularly in Poland, where the imposed system was deeply alien.

> Paradoxically ... the Tsarist system called for a greater degree of conformity and submissiveness from its wayward Polish subjects than from its submissive Russian core. And it called not merely for blind obedience but for what in a later age was to be called 'internal censorship'. The good citizen ... was taught to discipline his thoughts actively, to cleanse from his mind all trace of personal will. Politics were reduced to the point at which the subject strove to divine the will of his superiors in advance, as a form of spiritual exercise. The Tsar-Otets, the 'Little Father', was to be trusted implicitly. ... People were encouraged to think communally, denouncing and expelling all wilful elements form their midst.[1]

Uvarov passed into Polish history as an entirely negative figure.[2] And yet his own career was fraught with its own paradoxes, not least that he tried to convey to the 'subject' peoples that political conformity would bring its own relative emancipation, as long as the authority of the tsar was not undermined.[3]

The moderate in him was always apparent, and it pained him to betray that moderation, even to himself. Where, as in the western provinces with a population mainly either Polish or Ukrainian, he found himself promoting Russification in the schools and universities where it was not wanted, he believed he was doing his best to tread softly. As he put it in 1835, he was doing this in the case of the western provinces:

> in order not to frighten from the outset minds blinded by continuing and recent mistakes, and above all to win the trust of the region in maintaining these institutions, according to a firm plan, [the idea is] to come first of all to meet those local demands which are not openly opposed to that plan, and in the meantime to introduce without compromise in the spirit and the form of the teaching the main conditions which relate directly to the aims we have in mind.[4]

The non-Russian provinces made Uvarov alternately cringe and blush at the political necessity of which he was the chief executive. Yet his indirect approach made others, particularly the Poles and the Jews, doubly suspicious. Nikolaevan Russia's 'stagnant and oppressive self-image', as Uvarov had formulated it, 'crept in everywhere, marking even the most unpolitical literature with a stamp of alarmist jingoism. Not surprisingly, it was to resurface a century later, under Stalin, as a foil against "rootless cosmopolitanism" in art.'[5] These words, written by a Polish historian of the presentday, underline just that continuity, between Uvarov's policy for the tsar, and Soviet communist practice in its Cold War empire, that this study of Uvarov's life has sought to spell out, in passing, through revisiting his life and work. Echoes of a similar chauvinism in its border regions continue today.

The Polish people presented an insoluble problem to the Russian authorities. In their resistance to Russian cultural domination and with that instinctive sympathy for the French Revolution which helped inspire their rebelliousness they appeared to embody the Romantic imagination as a political force.[6] In 1835 the tsar, stung by the insurrection four years earlier, and observing the recent uprising in the Republic of Cracow against his Austrian ally, threatened to annihilate Warsaw if the citizens of the Kingdom of Poland did not give up their dreams of re-establishing a Polish republic:

> I declare to you that in the event of the slightest disturbance I will order the destruction of your city; I shall demolish Warsaw and, of course, I will not rebuild it. Believe me, gentlemen, to belong to Russia and to be under her patronage is true happiness. If you will conduct yourselves properly, if you will fulfil all your obligations, then my fatherly solicitousness will extend

to all and, in spite of everything that has happened, my government will always be concerned about your welfare.[7]

Both the western provinces, where a Russian past could be argued, and the Kingdom of Poland, where Polishness was indisputable, called for frequent official visits from St Petersburg to enforce the authority of local Russian governors. As Uvarov said in 1838 after returning from the latest of a number of trips himself: 'In the sphere of the eternal struggle against the Polish spirit the government is now giving general battle.'[8] The tsar had ordered Russification as the only way to solve the age-old conflict. However, against this violence Uvarov stressed the essentially religious and eternal nature of the Polish–Russian conflict, between Catholicism and Orthodoxy, between Western and Eastern Christianity. He rejected excessive and speedy measures because he recognized the Polish problem as greater than the politics of the day. In their place he offered gradual re-education.[9]

The University of Kiev was a cornerstone of the gradual plan, slowly to reduce the historic cultural gap between Russia and Poland:

The new university was meant as far as possible to smooth over the characteristic sharp differences dividing the young Poles from the Russians, and particularly to crush in them the idea of separate nationality, to bring them closer and closer to Russian ideas and values, to transmit to them the general spirit of the Russian people.[10]

The plan failed because Polish education was superior and more widespread than Russian. But it was a noble failure in terms of Uvarov's rendering service to his government. All his efforts in the non-Russian parts of the empire can be seen in a similar light.

In 1835 he had drawn up a new statute for primary and secondary education in the western provinces, suggesting a system of instruction in the Russian spirit, but preserving as far as possible the outward appearance of the old Polish system, including names. Attempts were made to root out Catholic priests from education and to minimize the use of Polish as the language of instruction. In all establishments non-Russians who wanted to enter the local administrative service had to do well in Russian language and literature and in Polish private schools the campaign was particularly fierce.[11] Uvarov here was campaigning on his favourite indirect front. In place of direct coercion again he encouraged a re-assessment of Slav history to support the tsar's cause in the western provinces. This was the prize competition for a new history book won by Ustryalov. It was precisely why Ustryalov merited a prize – that he sidestepped completely the issue of possible Polish sovereignty. His work became the most important tool of Uvarov's Ministry abroad.

There [in the western provinces] particularly, because of local circumstances, it acquired a special value and helped to bring minds closer and to spread amongst young people the basic facts about Russia and its history, revealing on an uncontrovertable basis of facts, that Western Russia, particularly Lithuania, comprised an intrinsic part of the Russian state.[12]

Uvarov was committed to the cause of absorbing the Poles into Russian culture. He had to believe he was succeeding.

But the evidence grew every year to the contrary. In 1836 and 1837 he visited Kiev, where he reported to the tsar that the still palpable Polish national spirit would surely die away in coming generations when the 'illegitimate' and 'irregular' element of Polish professors would disappear. In reality few Poles thought all blessings and high standards flow from St Petersburg. Moreover, Uvarov was mistaken in thinking that the empire of Nicholas I was Imperial Rome. Still an incident when Uvarov was in Vil'na the following year shows how ready he was to deceive himself and how vulnerable he remained to public flattery:

When on the day of my departure I ordered that all the students of the institutions in Vilna under my authority, some one thousand persons in number, be gathered in the palace courtyard, a pupil of the boarding school for the gentry, Bronski, stepped forward from the ranks and in the name of his comrades greeted me with a brief address. After saying, in excellent Russian, that they thanked me for my visit and my fatherly treatment of them, he concluded: 'Be also and always our protector before the Most Gracious Monarch. Tell Him that we remember Him, that we love Him, that we shall be worthy of Him, that we too are His good children.' Here this thirteen-year-old youth dissolved in tears and rushed to embrace me. Of course not a single spectator remained unaffected by this expression of sentiment which was undoubtedly unfeigned and flowed straight from the heart.

Uvarov, Machiavellian in Russia, was naïve in Poland. He did not reckon with what happened to Bronski back in the classroom.[13]

Uvarov's work in the non-Russian provinces in the end exhausted him and pleased no one. And finally the system began to turn against him. His optimistic reports to the tsar, that the Russian government had the upper hand in the western provinces, were soon proved wrong. In 1838, only weeks after Uvarov's visit, Kiev University was declared to be riddled with revolutionary propaganda and imbued with 'false nationality' and 'false patriotism'. Simon Konarski, a hero of the 1831 Insurrection, was seized as one of the chief conspirators and executed for allegedly trying throughout Russia to foment a new revolution. The tsar reacted by acting over Uvarov's head, dismissing the moderate, highly effective German Egor von Bradke as Superintendent of the Kiev educational district. He also replaced the governor-general with a more militant man. Uvarov meekly agreed that the disturbances confirmed the need for extreme precautions in Poland.[14]

In a painful experience which must have recalled the years in which the new St Petersburg University fell victim to the anti-scientific purges of Dmitry Runich, Uvarov witnessed the closing for the rest of 1839 of the latest university of his creation. Patiently he worked for its reopening, but when the institution was restored to life the next year, all the Polish teachers, that was one half of the academic staff, had been replaced by Russians and among the students Orthodox believers outnumbered Catholics. Kiev had undergone a thorough transfusion.

The Kingdom of Poland, which since 1832, in the wake of the anti-Russian insurrection had been reduced from semi-autonomy to an imperial province under the control of the hostile general Paskevich, presented even greater social and political problems and embarrassment. In his first years at the Ministry Uvarov called the Russian education system in the area around Warsaw slipshod, and blamed it on Jesuit influence, freethinking and revolutionary nationalism. From 1840 he increased pressure on this region, the heart of Poland, to conform with the rest of the Russian Empire, and school curricula in the capital's gymnasia were confined to vocational subjects. But Polish Enlightenment there remained passionately Western-oriented. Uvarov was prepared to concede the point, and avowed the need to proceed delicately, but his gradual suppression of their language seemed all the more menacing to observant Poles. Meanwhile, few in Russian ruling circles were prepared to agree with Uvarov on the need for a gradual policy as long as Warsaw remained a hotbed of anti-Russian conspiracy. He quickly became isolated. He further weakened his position by allowing exceptions to his own rules. He permitted a quota of Polish students from the kingdom and the western provinces, because of local restrictions, to train as Polish gymnasium teachers in Russian universities, believing that they would absorb and propagate a spirit of loyalty to the autocracy. His sentimental loyalty to the tsar made him politically myopic.[15]

In a third problem region, the Baltic territories, where a Lutheran and advanced German intellectual culture flourished, even Uvarov's patriotic optimism failed him. He had to reckon with superior local education taught in a foreign language and a complex society with its own aristocratic traditions which considered itself of a higher quality than Russian. After his visit in 1833 he had proposed minor changes at Dorpat University, such as more discipline, more Russian and more Divinity, but he accepted the historical evidence that for many years Russia had looked to the Baltics for superior technical and academic expertise. Since the time of Peter this Protestant civilization had acted as a bridge to the West and furnished the Russian state with ideas and personnel.

In 1836 Uvarov introduced new plans to russify the Dorpat Education district, but was forced to admit hopes of their full realization were 'premature'. It was the same word with which he staved off political change for Poland and for Russia in 1818.[16] For their part local society and institutions were unintimidated by the efforts of Russian officialdom to control them and either circumvented or ignored instructions. Uvarov introduced measures to curb student life after-hours, leading temporarily to a reduction in the number of taverns around Dorpat University, but the academic establishment continued to steer things its own way, impressive, as Uvarov could not but admit, in its traditional and continuing excellence. Dorpat University in fact attained its Golden Age under Uvarov, as Kiev did in the next decade, and both were allowed to continue to organize themselves on the German model. Uvarov was reduced to delivering his reports to the tsar in secret on the unsuccessful Russification of the Baltics. He had to claim that Russia had come of age under Nicholas, therefore the debt to the Baltic Germans was reversed. But the local aristocracy, fiercely opposed to Russian changes, and the Lutheran church, problematic because of its inwardness, were factors outside his control. 'Every man judges according to his conscience on the matters of his faith,' Uvarov complained of this Protestantism:

> In this strange situation it is difficult for the government to find support for its views. An orthodox protestant faith does not in truth exist anywhere. The obligation of the government to protect the prevailing church can only take effect where the church protects itself. Here on the other hand ...[17]

The Baltic Provinces came away relatively untouched by Russification and it was a graceful admission of failure under Uvarov that he sent the most promising Russian students to Dorpat University as part of their 'foreign' years, to return the better teachers to Moscow and St Petersburg. It was also the university where he chose to submit his own doctoral thesis as an old man.[18]

In fact all non-Russian groups presented difficulties for expanding Russian culture and Uvarov's combined aggressive and defensive tasks never eased. With regard to one group, the Jews, he became known for his sympathy, but there too the final outcome was disappointing. Uvarov envisaged the creation of special secular schools to teach Jews national and Russian subjects alongside their religious education and give them 'the opportunity of amalgamating themselves with European civilization'. He had the model of Jewish schools which had recently been successfully established in

Austria and Prussia and the enthusiastic cooperation of a young German rabbi based in Riga, Max Liliental. But once again he was caught between extremes and in his emphasis on moderation and gradual progress he seemed ready to betray both sides. To Liliental he suggested that broader culture would emancipate the Jews of the empire, whereas in camera to the tsar's Jewish Commission he envisaged conversion. Of the Jews, as of the Poles, he believed they would be more accessible to his Ministry's propaganda in Russian state schools and would accept it in exchange for greater academic and worldly prospects. Liliental felt personally betrayed, and the state schools for Jews when they finally opened in 1847 met with little success.[19]

Thus although the cultural conquest was spelt out on paper by Uvarov, that was where much of it remained. He encountered fewest problems in the Caucasus and Siberia, where local national consciousness was less political, and where it was imperial policy and also his personal preference to further the local languages rather than repress them.[20] By 1840 people were beginning to say that the Minister of Enlightenment was failing and the tsar didn't like him. At home censorship wasn't working as well as the emperor required; in education the lower classes were rising; and abroad the Polish spirit presented an undiminished threat. After the student conspiracy in Kiev, Uvarov never recovered his full credibility with the tsar and his anxiety was expressed in almost annual visits to the West. Some of his policies, moreover, had the reverse effect of what was intended. A classic example was the official encouragement of Slavic studies. These were furthered for political loyalty's sake, but in the event they awakened sympathy for the very Slav peoples Russia was trying to subordinate. Uvarov operated in the climate of Romantic Nationalism despite himself, and despite himself he accelerated the growth of small nations' self-awareness.[21]

He deserves some sympathy around the year 1840, when he was in his early fifties, and deeply embroiled in the timeless contradictions of the Russian government, for out of loyalty to that government's false claims, he was allowing the contradictions to destroy him. Some of those closest to him pitied his failings and his impossible task. These 'friends', who played that role somewhere between clients and adopted children in Uvarov's life, included Pogodin and Davydov, and they were left guessing at a concealed element of self-awareness which would prove this functionary still had a conscience. 'And can a man who has dedicated his whole life to truth, happiness and beauty not have a good heart?' asked Davydov, his staunchest supporter. But Uvarov expressed in himself the indifference towards truth, honour and moral conscience which seemed, for instance to the visiting, by no means insensitive or blindly anti-Russian Marquis de Custine, to be the essence of Russia in 1839.[22]

With Pogodin, the ambitious, thwarted son of a serf, Uvarov was in correspondence throughout 1840. The historian showed there considerable curiosity about Uvarov's values. In the letters between them Uvarov sometimes almost confided in the fanatical historian, but only to withdraw again into his official position and speak only through his authority. Pogodin had a reputation for indelicate behaviour and blatant favour-seeking from anyone in a position to help him, so no wonder Uvarov withdrew, you might say, but still Uvarov, with his unfailing bad taste in companions, chose this man in whom partly to confide. The impression left on Uvarov's side by the short correspondence with Pogodin is one of personal confusion. At the beginning of March 1840 Uvarov spoke of the difficulties of doing his job, and how selflessness was not always the way to success. He determined not to yield, to stick to his chosen path, and complained of being surrounded by men who did not think.[23]

In August he continued to write to Pogodin from Poland, where he paid an official visit to mark a new plan for elementary and secondary schooling in the Warsaw district being put into practice. This included keeping the university closed. He had to prepare a report on the effects of a decree passed by the tsar, despite the Minister's objections, that Church Slavonic should replace half the Latin taught in Polish schools. Having argued that Latin was too important to the Polish Church to replace it with Slavonic, Uvarov went obediently to ensure the top three classes of the gymnasium and the top two in the district schools amended their curricula.[24]

It was a difficult visit, but in September Uvarov wrote saying he had been able to present Polish youth to the tsar in a new light and inspire new hopes.[25] However, others saw him as rapidly losing ground.

> You know his pure Russian soul, his fine ideas about the well-being of our society. If he has succeeded in nothing, then he is not so much to blame himself as are people and circumstances. I think the tsar won't leave him without a job.

This comment came from one of his own employees at the Ministry.[26]

It was perhaps the degree of pressure he was under that made Uvarov so enjoy his leisure time in Saxony on this trip. He reported to Pogodin that in between official duties he had been staying 'on the banks of the Elbe' in Dresden. His allusions to these moments read like fairy tales. They have the same quality as his youthful dreams that he would one day escape the confinement of a politically fanatical Russia to stay with Stein in his German castle. One morning he was admiring Raphael's Sistine Madonna in the Royal Gallery, the next he was out walking, enjoying the natural beauty of Saxony, while in the evenings the German dramatist and Shakespeare scholar Ludwig

Tieck read to him from the Bard. From Dresden Uvarov went to Leipzig to see the classical scholar Hermann. His youth came vividly to meet him, for this was the same Hermann with whom he had been involved in an appreciative learned dispute in 'On the Prehomeric Age' more than twenty years previously. One of the Leipzig highlights was a visit to the opera to hear Mrs Devrient sing Mayerbeer. This was the kind of Western cultural experience which he had not had since Vienna, and, softening him, it brought to the surface many suppressed and forgotten hopes. He looked at schools in Saxony before returning East to Warsaw and from there journeyed to Kiev to inspect the reopened university. An easy prey, he fell ill there with haemorrhoids, rheumatism and nervous exhaustion.

On 12 November 1840 he was still indisposed, and his office declared the malady to be the result of too much travelling, too fast. He needed rest. In a letter to Pogodin at the end of that month Uvarov referred to having been seriously ill and said he was recovering, though still sitting at home. He was grateful for the concern people had shown for his health.

At home, however, he restlessly plunged himself into the journalistic whirl. Despite censorship the debate over Russia's past and future was now a large-scale public event which had encouraged the consolidation of ideological camps pitched around the most prolific journals. The tsar himself had allowed the showcase for Belinsky's writing, *Otechestvennye Zapiski* (Notes from the Fatherland) to come into being in 1839, and *Sovremennik* under a new editor, Peter Pletnev, was also thriving as a forum for Westernizing views and the best new literature. Uvarov renewed its mandate year after year because he considered it beneficial to literature.[27]

The passion for philosophy meanwhile took new directions. Belinsky abandoned the mysticism of Schelling for the 'realism' of Hegel and Feuerbach and was now for the first time approaching socialism. Conservative opinion, also embroiled with Hegel, became more polarized. The Slavophile Konstantin Aksakov was so immersed in Russian peasant ways that he now wore a beard and dressed in a smock, to the hilarity of his friends. Pogodin and Shevyrev, however, were noted for their espousal of the apparently traditional Russian virtue of *smirenie* or graceful submission to authority. Encouraged by Uvarov they brought out a new periodical, *Moskvitanin* (The Muscovite), which published both Romantic nationalist and Slavophile views.[28]

'The Muscovite' was conceived by Uvarov as a foil to the Westernizers' publications and the ever-popular output of Bulgarin and Senkowski. Uvarov was in the position of encouraging the open debate at the same time as not wanting to be associated with any one position himself. When he felt strongly on a particular subject Davydov acted as his mouthpiece. He felt the precariousness of his position, and the more so as Russian intellectual life grew up.[29]

In their correspondence of 1841 Pogodin tried to get Uvarov to discuss his hidebound position by venturing some theories of his own:

> You often get carried away by the heat of your character and the speed of your understanding; some of your important and celebrated plans sometimes seem to you to have been put into practice from the first moment of their conception, and you are quick to talk about them as you see them in your mind, though not in reality; this undermines your real achievement and tempts mediocre minds who find it painful to concede honour where it has been earned and are always ready to latch onto trivia about people in high station. Your actions are such that they speak for themselves, louder than anyone can speak about them, and sooner or later they will silence all envy and all calumny.

Uvarov had achieved so much for education and the academic life in Russia. Why then, Pogodin implicitly asked, did he let himself down by courting trivial and dishonest praise? Why did he allow himself to be so susceptible to negative public opinion?

> When I read in the newspapers a nasty account of your trip to Belorussia [the Warsaw–Kiev visit], written by some schoolmaster, I am bound to consider it crude flattery which your ill-wishers use to condemn you. As your director [Pogodin was premature here] and a guardian of your reputation, I will not permit crude praise; though because of that heat of character I mentioned above you sometimes allow it to touch you. You see it only as an honest tribute in recognition of your services and your efforts, something which is always pleasant for a man of action and a citizen who has devoted himself to the service of his compatriots.[30]

Pogodin was perceptive about Uvarov's weaknesses: his vanity, his sentimentality and his susceptibility to his own arguments, and he was bold. In exchange for this intimate advice he asked for a post which was not vacant, as head of the Archeographic Commission, the centre of the country's historical archives, and Uvarov turned him down, both as head of the Commission, and as a nursemaid. Pogodin who had gone too far was made to realize it with a reply of Olympian brevity and condescension. 'I always know how to value a pure outburst of independent thinking,' Uvarov wrote. He told the historian he was used to reading good and bad of himself in the press and had become indifferent now to what was said. Thereafter he split his behaviour towards Pogodin cleanly in two, making clear that his private and official selves were not equally available for friendship. When the March issue of The Muscovite generated a small scandal because of two cartoons, Uvarov was stern in exemplary fashion. This time, he told Pogodin, he would quieten the noise but he would not take responsibility in the future. He withdrew his offer to Pogodin of the chancellery job, while assuring him of his personal friendship and interest at all times. By the end of 1842 he was asking Pogodin, an officially right-thinking man, to ensure their names did not appear together in print, and to take great care when they met in the presence of others.[31]

One man Uvarov did admire and was close to in the early 1840s was Granovsky, who was lecturing with great popularity in Moscow[32], but because he was an avowed Hegelian and greatly popular with students Uvarov found it politic to refrain from open association. Granovsky had studied in Berlin where he was a friend and contemporary of Ivan Turgenev. Occupying a position neither wholly Westernizing nor Slavophile nor in subservience to the court, he had no high-flown illusions about the quality of the Russian simple life but believed improvement could come about from above through education and the beneficial influence of Western Enlightenment. He was loyal to Russia's potential at the same time as he believed it was possible to be both Russian and European. Most outstandingly, however, he had a Western belief in the central position of the individual in the march of progress.[33]

Uvarov approved of Granovsky in silence. Bound by his peculiar etiquette of eighteenth-century evasiveness and nineteenth-century service to the autocracy, he did not feel free to contribute publicly to the sum of ideas on literature and history except under the aegis of the Academy. Granovsky was a private friend in an intellectual life otherwise now almost entirely given over to nostalgia. Significantly, in his correspondence with Pogodin over the difficulties he had had to face even over his support for The Muscovite, Uvarov had summed up his reaction with the Latin words of encouragement he had once sent to Speransky in exile: *Macte animo*! For the sake of things of the mind! To him his position, fighting for the cause of pure Enlightenment against the multifarious factions and tendencies of the day, had not changed in twenty years. He longed to be above politics, but he had learnt to tread carefully.

Nostalgia permeated the revealing, though unsatisfactory, essay 'On the Philosophy of Literature' that Uvarov wrote in 1840 while he was convalescing. In what was a habit and a foreign orientation from earlier years he dedicated his endeavours to the French ambassador, the Baron de Barante, a man known for his wit and gastronomy. (One presumes he was not a very original kind of Frenchman.) Uvarov's piece was carefully written in French with a mortifying stylishness, and he had sketched, as had always been Uvarov's practice, the most general outline of an encyclopaedic work he would never write. The subject matter took him back to the distinction between the classical and the Romantic worlds which had also preoccupied him as a younger man. Uvarov presented the classical spirit as materialistic, by which he meant that it delighted in the present moment and lacked what he guessed the modern world would call both a religious and a moral sense. By contrast modern literature was unified by its Christian heritage and moral vision.

The essay was in reality another defence of the pre-revolutionary order and rehearsed the same ideas Uvarov toyed with in 'Eleusis'. It was hugely flawed for what it did not say twenty-five years on. It only indirectly took on the German Romantic school of literary history, and assiduously avoided its grand scheme for the development of the human spirit, which the Schlegels had explored, and which was the dominant preoccupation of contemporary Russian literary criticism. Modern literature received a single paragraph. Uvarov displayed a rather sarcastic and superior wit, employing to describe the Ancient world such contemporary trigger words as 'democratic' and 'materialistic', knowing that for liberals these signalled the best themes in progressive philosophy. He delighted in making them signify time past. It was a way of accusing such writers of having no historical sense. He identified with the modern Christian order, as he had always done, speaking of 'the certitude of the divine principle, such as we possess it', but he believed modern literature had taken a wrong path, which would lead it into self-destruction and have an adverse effect on society.

The single paragraph on modern literature, however, included the following prophetic words:

> When literature wishes to shake off the providential yoke, it will destroy itself with its own hands; the mocking disbelief of Voltaire and the passionate disbelief of George Sand will not remove it from the influence of those ideas without which society as we know it would not exist for a moment. Does not the scepticism of the nineteenth century itself take umbrage at the shameless cynicism of more than one modern writer?[34]

Uvarov foresaw Western literature 'shaking off the providential yoke'. What he could not begin to imagine was that socialism, on the far side of eighteenth-century revolutionary scepticism, would now join with and now replace Christianity as the bolster of a new literature in Russia. Yet socialism was where Belinsky, the most representative mind of his day, had arrived at in his thinking. Uvarov's politics thus excluded him from further literary debate and circumscribed his existence as much as his public life.

16

A Russia within Russia

The Empire of the intelligence should be, like the Elysium of the Ancients, separated from the real world by the river of oblivion.

SERGEI UVAROV

By a reversal of the normal order of things Uvarov would occasionally discuss politics in a literary environment. He would talk more freely of serfdom when he felt the political consequences of his thoughts were somehow suspended by his surroundings. In St Petersburg he visited two literary circles in the early 1840s, one around Princess Dolgorukov, and the other around Grand Duchess Elena Pavlovna.[1]

The first of these was an invitation to immerse himself in a more comfortable past, itself an oblique comment on the insufficiencies of the present. The aged princess Dolgorukov had been in Vienna in 1806, when Madame Rombecq and others in Uvarov's circle had become friends of her illustrious family. According to a French observer in St Petersburg from 1843–44, Charles de St Julien, the star attraction of the princess's drawing room until his death in 1844 was Prince Alexander Golitsyn. This was the same man who as Tsar Alexander's credulous and pietistic minister of Enlightenment had allowed Magnitsky and Runich virtually to destroy two universities, but who under Nicholas served in various responsible posts and came to be regarded as highly dependable.

At the age of seventy Golitsyn was a gifted and prodigious raconteur. He would resurrect his days as a page at the court of Catherine, to which Princess Dolgorukov and Count G. A. Stronganov would respond with their own memories. The princess's guests were mostly elderly and all socially distinguished, the Russians coming from aristocratic families whose service heritage went back to Ivan the Terrible and who in the eighteenth century had cultivated strong, fond connections with France. Members of the Stroganovs and the Golitisyns had been pillars of the Russian aristocratic colony in Paris before 1789. The princess also invited into her salon a sprinkling of aristocratic Frenchmen domiciled in the Russian capital, like St Julien, who was lecturing on literature at the university. Uvarov stood out among the Russians by being almost a generation younger, but he contributed a rich fund of anecdotes, mostly based on the society tales and personalities he recalled from his youth.

The most fitting words to encapsulate the strange charm of the Dolgorukov salon were to be found in Uvarov's description of de Ligne's circle in Napoleonic Vienna, St Julien, who was a keen observer, suggested. He quoted Uvarov's own words: 'It was a conversation among the dead, but these dead men and women were full of life and grew younger in each other's company.' Uvarov, with his memories stirred anew, now decided to publish for the first time that essay of 1815, possibly with St Julien's encouragement.[2]

Uvarov's other standing social engagement in the early 1840s was the salon of Grand Duchess Elena Pavlovna, which gave high government officials, mingled with the inevitable Frenchmen, a chance to converse in a relaxed atmosphere under the protection of a member of the royal family. The grand duchess's position allowed for a freer than usual discussion of social questions. The business of social and economic reforms was frequently raised and the grand duchess's salon contributed most positively towards creating the right intellectual climate for the abolition of serfdom twenty years later. It was particularly effective in gently persuading the conservative aristocracy to adapt its views. St Julien reported that Uvarov became known in this forum for his good sense, clarity and enlightened liberalism.[3] Yet, around this time Pogodin noted Uvarov arguing for the retention of serfdom on fifteen different counts, in such a way as to suggest serfdom was the true third term of his tripartite political faith. At the salon of the grand duchess then he probably continued to act the required part, rather than to speak out of conviction; he clung to the privilege of disinterest.[4]

St Julien rightly drew attention to the escape the salons provided for this enigmatic Russian public figure who, seeming more French than Russian, was a foreigner in his own country:

Uvarov enjoyed these intimate, talkative occasions because where he was sure of being appreciated his personality was at ease and he could indulge in the full extent of his lively imagination without constraint. At such times the learned man, the Minister and the man of state disappeared, leaving visible only a worldly wit and an attractive conversationalist. And yet Uvarov's conversation did not immediately attract attention; to begin it was slow and abrupt; he seemed to have difficulty finding his words and needed time to choose and formulate his sentences; but after the first moments his speech became relaxed, fluent and picturesque. We are speaking here only of his conversation in private, when he excelled in a spectacular display of his talents. Also we are inclined to attribute to this kind of success he enjoyed the thousands of little jealousies he aroused in society. People exist everywhere who begrudge others the wit they lack.

Not surprisingly Uvarov's salon life did nothing to improve his public image among the new men. These French-speaking salons maintaining a last-gasp connection with the *ancien régime* aroused hostility, particularly among the more extreme Slavophiles and nationalists. They were perceived as a slight against Russian cultural self-sufficiency. St Julien reported that no one less than Alexei Uvarov, Uvarov's only son, now a university student, was among the most fervent opponents of such manifestations of Western influence. He was apparently rejecting some of the blessings his father had showered upon him. But the salons gave Uvarov comfort and he persisted.

It is curious and telling that a visiting French professor and author of stage comedies such as St Julien should understand Uvarov's dilemma more readily in a few months than most of his compatriots over years. This man later published, in France, an interview with Uvarov, in which he sought to explain this unusual personality whom he found modest, accessible and as French as himself. The interview framed Uvarov as he wanted to be seen, as a Russian statesman and European man of letters, and in response he allowed himself to be drawn out extraordinarily on his dilemma as a servant of Nicholas. His defence of serfdom to Pogodin had spoken of a frightening domestic political experience which began with the murder of Paul I and now Uvarov positively declared his eternal fear of revolution whether from below or above. He would not cease to aver that for the sake of the well-being of Russia there had to be a class or a caste which would accept service to the autocrat, and accept to serve autocracy, unconditionally. It was that unconditional acceptance which he embodied in himself, though his obedience did not mean he always agreed with the tsar's policies. To St Julien he prided himself on his skilled handling of the tsar when there were differences between them:

Uvarov [St Julien wrote], when he spoke of the business of his ministry, took pleasure in his capacity as a Russian dignitary, in often putting the Emperor first, which did not in the slightest detract from what was true and intelligent in his words. One day someone congratulated him for not having been afraid to touch the heart of the matter of public instruction, which until his time had been so weak, so incomplete, and of so little use in the country.

'We had to impose it,' said the minister. 'It was the only way to complete education. We had above all to give it roots in the native soil, so that it might produce useful fruits.'

St Julien found the Minister confident in his own powers and popularity, and professing to have a unique qualification for ensuring the loyalty of his subordinates:

The university teachers like a minister who can judge them and who has the knowledge to appreciate them. They find in me two men – alongside the minister there is always the man of letters, who enjoys them as a colleagues and as equals, [he said].

The Frenchman mentioned rumours that Uvarov's power was waning, but the minister's sense of his strength seemed to be redoubled:

I have only one idea and that is to do good, the Emperor knows that, he has confidence in me and allows me to take action, despite the fact that I sometimes contradict him in his personal views. It's true the Emperor is suspicious of intellect and of the power of the imagination … . But what does that matter if one knows how to contain and direct those faculties? … The Emperor knows for certain that I work only in the interest of Russia, which is his own interest, and he lets me do it. What would he gain in contradicting me? He would get a replacement who would destroy the good that I've done, while I would retire to Paris where I would read in the *Journal des Débats* what the newspapers had to say about my fall from power. The point is I am independent, I have 15,000 serfs, and I am not entirely unknown.

Uvarov indeed believed much of his political strength derived from his exceptional position in society. He told St Julien his country and the tsar both had confidence in him in that respect, especially Russian young people: 'I have a name in –ov, I am rich, and I have no other interest than justice and my country. People know that, they see it and they grant me the measure of it.' Yet he admitted he was tired and forecast accurately what would happen when he did leave office:

'Doubtless there would be a reaction and things would return to the point where I found them; but that would only be for a time, for if in the end we want to stay on the European paths which Peter the Great opened to Russia, national, public instruction is our only resort.'

St Julien went away impressed by Uvarov's sense of patriotic mission and his fine perception of the needs of Russia. He noted that the Minister spoke of the revolutionary threat throughout Europe and of his private vision that it might be nipped in the bud by a transnational education system on a classical model which would teach a united anti-revolutionary morality. The interview took place at Uvarov's Porechie estate, where St Julien was a guest in the summer of 1843, and that geographical fact is as important as any in our understanding of why Uvarov should speak more frankly of himself than usual. Porechie was Uvarov's own salon, the place where he could show his colleagues and subordinates he was a man of letters as well as a man with state responsibility. Able to relax and be more himself away from ministerial pressures, he gave a truer account at Porechie of his politics and of personal aspirations than at any other time or occasion of his life. The estate was 'an oasis in my busy life', he told Pogodin, and one might say it was also home to his better, younger self. To Graefe he had described one of his first summers there, in 1822, as 'life as it was lived by Lorenzo [di Medici] and Poliziano in the Middle Ages: bookish, restful and based on sound historical principles'. Having come to him through his wife's family, Porechie was an elaborate form of escape. Uvarov had created his own renaissance idyll, where he and his family and guests were free from the pressures of politics to devote themselves to learning and the liberal arts.[5]

The neoclassical mansion which was repaired annually fulfilled the function of hotel, gallery, museum and garden; a culture farm where guests, both Russian and foreign, were invited months in advance to spend the summer, deepening and broadening their interests in nature and art at leisure. Davydov, a frequent guest and unqualified admirer, described the 33,000-acre estate with 2,500 souls and including a rich timber forest as being strikingly wealthy compared with the poverty of the nearby town of Mozhaisk. His account of it, which began: '35 versts Southwest of Mozhaisk, not far from the glorious Borodino, at the confluence of the Inoch' and the Moscow river, lies the village of P...' echoed the fairy-tale quality of Uvarov's dreams. The little church and the winged mansion built on a raised piece of ground were reflected in proud splendour in the sparkling Inoch.' In the grounds stood some huge stone buildings housing the cloth factory which was one of Uvarov's progressive economic experiments, and pavilions which overlooked the English park. Davydov suggested it was an attractively laid-out estate, where the casual visitor might meet happy peasants wearing neat clothes. The vast ancient forest round-about also 'reconciled the traveller to Northern nature'.[6]

The house itself was a large two-storied stone building, flanked by two wings, and enclosed by Ionic pillars, with an attractive belvedere commanding a view over the entire surrounding area of villages, hamlets and groves, with parkland to the right and left and the whole bounded by the blue ribbon of the Inoch'. It was built towards the end of the eighteenth century by an Italian architect popular with the Russian aristocracy, Domenico Ghilardi, and was one of the finest country-houses or *usad'by* owned by the great families, on a par with Arkhangel'skoe and Kuntsovo for its picturesque position. It was a typical example of the *usad'ba* culture which, beginning in the reign of Catherine and lasting through that of Alexander, created lasting monuments to Russia's assimilation of European and especially French standards.[7] While in comfort it rivalled the finest town houses in Moscow, in essence, with its characteristic French and English gardens, its church, and its interior simplicity, it expressed the peculiarity of civilized Russian country living. Yet Porechie's particular merit was its scope for being called a second Academe, a Russian Athens. Shaped with the erudite life in mind, Porechie did not contain a ballroom, but was arranged around rooms of learning. The reception rooms, the drawing rooms and dining rooms on both floors were admirable, but the most important room was the study, in the middle of the house, at the top of the stairs, under the light belevedere. The study was linked to three other library rooms arranged in a cross-shape. These were 'Professor' Uvarov's *Kunstkammer* and in them he built up some of the finest pre-revolutionary collections.[8]

The books in the library ranged over all branches of learning,[9] with much history, and literature in Greek, Latin, English, German, French and Italian, and all the works on the Classical world by European scholars from the seventeenth century on. Among them were bibliophilic treasures, such as the first Florentine editions of the Iliad and the Odyssey, early editions of Pindar, and a rare seventeenth-century Dutch edition of Virgil. There were encyclopaedias, and rows of volumes from the learned societies. In his study Uvarov also kept favourite works of art, including groups of female figures by Razumovsky's favourite, the neoclassicist Canova. Another contemporary sculptor Uvarov collected was Finelli. He sat at his desk surrounded by busts of Raphael, Michelangelo, Dante, Machiavelli, Ariosto, Tasso and looking up at Kiprensky's portrait of Zhukovsky, and a famous portrait of Goethe by Hermann. He sought to add to his collection portraits of all the men who had mattered in his youth, and only Silvestre de Sacy and Humboldt were wanting. Uvarov and his house spoke of the cultural and artistic achievement of centuries, but he also managed to speak for himself and those he had known. The whole experience was found liberating and instructive by Uvarov's visitors:

Sometimes the guests talked in the garden over tea, surrounded by camellias, eucalyptus, … and other tropical trees. Here Uvarov, not in his official capacity, but as first among friends, allowed us to speak to him openly and sincerely. Sometimes his excited guests would contradict him; but all of them were sure that he would hear them out individually with the generosity, goodness and courtesy which were characteristic of him. He indulgently treated young and old equally, gave his full consent to friendly conversation, and himself enlivened everyone, so that the atmosphere amongst the guests was always merry.

> With his wide range of knowledge and his beautiful, fluent speech, he had everyone listening to him attentively. Thus the time passed in the lively exchange of ideas about the sciences. literature and art. Modern intellectual phenomena, learned reminiscences and literary impressions of Italy, ineradicably fixed in Uvarov's memory, his relations with the distinguished academics of Germany and France gave an inexhaustible content to these discussions, which were far from the trifles of daily living and personalities. Our titled patron at home always seemed the most genial Russian host, unimposing and indulgent.

Porechie embodied myriad allusions to foreign life and letters. Uvarov spoke to his guests who were generally 'educated lovers of art' of how nature in Greece and Italy stirred the imagination and how the gentleness of the climate there developed delicacy of feeling, making possible the education of artists of genius. He hoped by his own provision of gentle manners and circumstances in a different latitude to foster similar blessings. Porechie was his 'Tusculum' (an old town in Latium near Frascati), where he married all that he had loved at the Olenins and at Razumovsky's palace in Vienna with the inspiration of Lorenzo di Medici and his enduring hopes for himself. Davydov suggested Porechie could also be compared with the palace of an English lord whose estate reflected the thoughts and the principal activity of its owner. It was cultivated, spacious and free.[10]

Uvarov preferred Porechie to all his other estates, the one in Penza on the Insar, the one in Saratov on the banks of the Volga, and the Muromsky estate on the river Oko in Belorussia, because it was the realization of a dream, a place to study art and nature and rediscover the natural balance and integrity of life. 'Where can we bury ourselves, to study ourselves and the people around us, where can we bring our inner lives into harmony with nature around us?' Davydov heard him ask. 'Only where nature becomes more real for us.' Ultimately Uvarov wanted to die in its very special Russian atmosphere which he had drawn and shaped out of himself.

Uvarov's guests stayed in fine, clean, well-equipped rooms with wonderful views. They were prestigious men of their day, though none of them great enough to be remembered today, with the exception, in Russia, of Granovsky. The day would start with tea or coffee in their rooms, and an hour's work from 10to 11, or they might take a book into the garden. Davydov remembered reading, writing, walking, conversing and in later years, when Uvarov must have procured a serf orchestra, listening to music. One year Shevyrev addressed the friends on the subject of Peter the Great and Lomonosov, while Professor Perevoshchikov talked about the solar system and Professor Spassky discussed aspects of physiology. Various visitors set to classifying the library holdings and the statuary. But whatever events were arranged Porechie contained 'everything that an enlightened mind and beautiful taste could think of: it is the estate of a rich man of letters ... as always we cultivate in ourselves a feeling for all that is true and good and beautiful and it triumphs over the rottenness of the material world'. Uvarov seemed to be incarnate Enlightenment to Pogodin, Davydov and Shevyrev, his most frequent visitors. They said he had the talent and generosity to make each day stimulating and harmonious. He was also a source of continuity and stability in a world in which, as state employees and academics, they were all highly vulnerable to political change.

Uvarov encouraged, and delighted in, the adulation of these men. They in response gave him company, made him feel superior and helped compensate for his poor public reputation at large. In Porechie he had the power of a man who had made his dream come true. He had made a move not uncommon in those of high intellect and imagination but unable to reproduce their full worth and aesthetic vision on paper: he had shaped his life until it spoke eloquently for that ideal. The result was a miracle in Russian literary life of the 1840s, if not also a mirage. Uvarov was like Andrei Razumovsky, the foreign connoisseur and patron of the arts, except that he had returned to Russia. He was like the Napoleonic exiles in Vienna who carried their lost culture with them. He brought paintings, sculpture and books from enlightened Europe to the plains and woodlands around Mozhaisk. He wanted with his wealth and expertise to be a medium to transmit the Classical and Renaissance worlds to Russia. His friends and clients understood the necessity behind the Porechie enterprise, that Uvarov's views, taste and gifts fitted no existing cultural niche in Russia, and they understood the reaction to it, that Uvarov's oddness predisposed him to be a victim of other men's envy and misunderstanding.

Davydov stressed Uvarov's commanding presence in middle age, with a regular and handsome face, medium build, expressive, sparkling eyes, a sharp, powerful voice, and fluent speech. He believed, like St Julien, and Pogodin, that Uvarov's qualities in every sphere worked to his detriment in public, because they were so abundant: 'All excellence bears the burden of the mediocrity of the majority. It is not rare for the talent to create good to be accompanied by the talent to be disliked.'[11] He declared it was essential to see Uvarov relaxed and in private to have a true idea of the man:

Despite the gentleness of his character and a kind heart, in society he appeared inaccessible, because of from his earliest years being accustomed to command. But at home he was affectionate and hospitable. During his entire administration of the Ministry there were no complaints about him;

all those he employed were rewarded and promoted; no one who went to see him in his office emerged without having been comforted or calmed. Despite his wealth and the trappings of luxury which surrounded him, he led a simple life, ate and drank moderately, worked incessantly; he was only inspired by changing from one subject to another. His character, which was too pliable in social relations, was essentially firm and constant; he loved those close to him, and unfailingly remembered every servant.

Porechie was the key to a complex, misunderstood personality:

> When you enter the house, with its rich furnishings and exquisite taste, and look around you at the pictures, and the sculptures, and the library, you know that the owner is an educated, titled man. This is where Uvarov used to come with his family in the summer, to rest from official duties. There were usually academicians and professors staying with the hospitable owner of the house; he did not leave off his academic pursuits even during his holiday. It is good, he used to say, to contemplate oneself in solitude, to think through one's intimate thoughts, and to order the thoughts which often fly about in one's heads when one is engaged in society, and which quickly pass, giving way to other thoughts, born of other feelings and impressions. When the inner life is concentrated the sweetest impulses are awakened towards everything that is beautiful, good and true; the man who buries himself in nature, purging himself, enjoys contentment; lucid thoughts come down to him there from above. In that rural retreat, in the library, or in the museum, but more often in Uvarov's study, classical dialogues would take place, commemorating the dialogues in the ancient Platonic Academy.

The acolyte went into rich detail over the contents of this extraordinary asylum of culture in the hope it would speak for the quality of Uvarov's inner life.

Yet viewed in an unfriendly light Porechie was a consummate cultural 'Potemkin village', a facade for a Russian renaissance which did not exist, and one which exposed Uvarov's fantastic vulnerability as its builder.[12] In office he was as insecure and as anxious to cover himself in the tsar's glory as ever, Nikitenko observed. The conscience-stricken censor told the story of what happened when Uvarov, revelling in his enthusiasm for Davydov, arranged for him to read a special lecture on Russian literature, to the expected glory of them both:

> Recently he had Davydov give a single lecture at the Ekaterininskaya Institute at the Smolny Monastery, having told the girls at this school in advance that they were going to hear 'the Russian Villemain'. Davydov performed

and didn't produce the expected effect. He seemed in particular bad taste in the Smolny Monastery. Giving an outline of Russian literature, he denied Derzhavin any poetic gift and didn't even mention Pushkin, wanting, of course, to please Uvarov who cannot forget Lukull. In conclusion Davydov said that everything in Russia took its life and its direction from the Minister of Public Enlightenment. And he said all this in the presence of Uvarov, who did not even blush when Davydov triumphantly proclaimed that 'if he had said anything of value, then he owed it not to himself but to the presence of his worthiness: himself he was only the statue of Memnon, animated by the rays of the sun'. After the lecture Uvarov went to the headmistress, Mrs Leontiev, and said to her: 'You will of course write to the tsar about my visit?' Then he left, taking the orator with him. Both of them nevertheless pass for intelligent men.[13]

It was common knowledge that the Porechie 'party' consisted of some rather shabby personalities boasting of their exalted summers in pursuit of a goodness, beauty and truth which they never manifested in their lives. Of Davydov it was said he was 'petty and vengeful' and one who made censorship decisions for personal reasons. Sergei Aksakov described Pogodin as a man 'whose nature was coarse, callous and clumsy and lacking in every feeling of delicacy, tact and tenderness'. Shevyrev was remembered as being petty, vain and underhand, always in search of honours. Granovsky was one of the nicer visitors.

When one of Davydov's several adoring accounts of Porechie appeared in The Moscovite, Belinsky's response was virulent:

Is it not true, after all, that Pogodin how shall we say takes boys to Uvarov out there, lads distinguished by the sharpness of their minds and the bluntness of their ****? This matter was written about indistinctly in the *Journal of the Ministry of National Enlightenment* and proposed to Pogodin as something he might do to serve Russian education in the spirit of Orthodoxy, Autocracy and Nationality, and it's surely why Pogodin was nominated for an annual pension, as a reward. This rumour seems to me all the more likely to be true now that Dunduk has grown old and grown fungus, and Uvarov can only use him when he needs to delegate work and farm out jobs, that is, now he only needs make use of his head, not his ***.[14]

The judicious Nikitenko commented,

Professor Davydov is very much in Uvarov's good books. He achieved this by crude flattery, which the Minister always receives with the simplemindedness of a child, over which it is impossible not to be surprised, for one has to grant him, if not a profound mind, at least a sharp one. Davydov won his heart particularly with his article 'Porechie', Uvarov's country estate, an article that was so flattering that in Petersburg , where manners are not as naïve as in Moscow, it made everyone laugh. Now Uvarov welcomes Davydov here with wide-open arms.[15]

By the 1840s Porechie was well-known in Moscow and St Petersburg as a court of fantasy, where Uvarov gathered around him the Russian academics and officials who became his 'party'. Belinsky, following Pushkin's example, attacked Uvarov for his homosexuality, but it was not the sin of fornication which bothered either critic or poet. Rather, Belinsky was accusing Uvarov of leading a shallow and exploitative existence. Belinsky knew Uvarov as a classical scholar after recently reviewing Russian translations of his early essays. If casual homoeroticism was a cheap way to reanimate the Greek legacy in Moscow, it was also a way of accusing Uvarov generally, for all his erudition, of selling his morality cheaply.[16]

Uvarov lacked a kind of self-awareness: the self-awareness that makes possible conscience, as opposed to fear of authority. He lacked the self-awareness which brings a sense of moral duty. The lapse particularly jarred in an intelligent, educated man. Nikitenko was at pains to spell it out:

Yesterday [diary entry for 20 May 1843] the Minister was at the Russian literature examination held by Pletnev. He spoke a lot. No one could have failed to recognize in him a genuine minister of public enlightenment. All his comments were intelligent, true, full of knowledge and very well put. *What a pity this man lacks just one strength – the strength of moral will!* [my italics] Achieving influence and favour at court, he bound himself hand and foot and deprived himself simultaneously of the respect of court and society. He wanted to sacrifice the latter to the former, and made a cruel mistake …[passage missing in original]. Undoubtedly the court knows his worth. The French are right when they say there is nothing more contrived than impeccable behaviour … Uvarov is always losing himself in the subtleties of his mind. He thinks he has caught a fly in his web … but fails to notice that he has simply shown his enemies the way to his nest.[17]

Uvarov was not truthful, neither to himself nor to others. All his relations were dictated by flattery, which when exercised inwardly became self-deceit. He had this dishonesty and showiness as facets of his character, demonstrated in his youth in his treatment of Germaine de Stael. His personal life in this rare respect merged with his public life. The ability to uphold falsehood, and to ignore contradiction, however solid and factual, made it seem as if he were blinkering himself deliberately. It was a negative skill which brought him rewards insofar as it corresponded to an inveterate servility and corruption in the manner of Russian government. But it left him vulnerable because he was just too much that government's man. He did not seem to have any other spiritual resource, or moral authority, to fall back on, having deliberately relegated art and personal integrity to the second league. Service to Nicholas took Uvarov far into self-deception. Nevertheless the causes of his adherence to the old order make both the intensity and the obstinacy credible. Even if he was the ultimate hypocrite Uvarov was not a cynic.

17

To eliminate the conflict

There was a coherent political philosophy behind Uvarov's actions. He wanted Russia to modernize gradually, taking expertise and even liberal ideas of political reform from the West, but only at a pace which would allow social order to be retained. Yet Nikitenko by the early 1840s judged Uvarov to understand neither the ways of the court nor of Russian society; and now the former had turned against him. In the vexed matter of censorship he was at once sidelined and used as a scapegoat. After Uvarov's death, Pogodin, another voice critical of the Minister's handling of the censorship, claimed he had always refused to face reality.[1] He failed to acknowledge both the degree of ultra-conservativism at the court and the extent of dissent in the rising intelligentsia and its audience. In his lifetime two parallel societies came into being, a fact that pushed back hard against Uvarov's belief that education would produce a unified people.

In 1843 when he produced for the tsar the report on his ten years work in education, he stressed his unwavering commitment to this ideal, and concluded,

To eliminate the conflict between so-called European education and our needs: to point the young generations away from their blind, unthinking passion for the superficial and the foreign by opening their ears to the idea that they might take pleasure in and respect in their own, and to the wholehearted conviction that only by applying general, universal enlightenment to our national way of life and our national spirit is it possible to bring true benefits to each and every man; then to take an honest look at our beloved country, to evaluate accurately all the conflicting elements of our citizens' education, all the historical factors which relate to the vast constitution of the Empire, to bring these developing elements and awakened forces, as far as possible, under a common denominator; and finally to seek that denominator in the triple concept of Orthodoxy,

Autocracy and Nationality – that was the goal, which the Ministry of Enlightenment has been aiming at for ten years; that was the plan that I have followed in all my endeavours.[2]

The tsar read it, and, pleased with Uvarov's systematic approach, declared himself satisfied. Yet in reality Uvarov had managed neither to increase the percentage of gentry receiving university education nor to halt the ascending rate at which the lower classes were entering the faculty. He had to resort to increasingly severe measures under pressure from the tsar to keep Enlightenment within class bounds. A bill in 1844 banned the lower classes from teaching, and raised fees for secondary and higher education to try and keep out the lower classes, especially the *raznochintsy*, those between classes, often the sons of priests. The bill included the right to ban entry to university on the grounds of insufficient progress at school. The Minister suggested the new measures be implemented secretly.[3] Still the lower orders kept on coming. More and more came to the university as private students, including serfs, and Uvarov was forced to cast about for ideas on how to limit them with a qualification of 'relevant activity' or 'appropriate intellectual level'. Merchants' sons and petit bourgeois had to present certificates of permission to leave their community in order to go to university, and by 1846 students were asked to prove with legal documents their social origin. In the schools, though fees were raised, they could not be made too high or they would encourage resort to home tuition again; and in any case a large number of private schools persisted.[4]

Outside Russia attempts to control education and thought were all the more humiliating. Even in the year of his report there was open antagonism between the Orthodox and Lutheran churches in the Baltic provinces and Nicholas wondered why Uvarov was not doing more to keep the Imperial house in order. A sympathizer with the population in her native lands, Madame Nesselrode, wrote to her husband in 1845 that Uvarov and the Interior Ministry were subjugating innocent victims.[5]

For Poland Uvarov's 1843 report set out new proposals on how to steer a course between the extremes of Russification and Polish nationalism. Kiev, always special case among the Russian universities, needed tighter government supervision in all non-academic matters. In schools Polish children were pressed to learn Russian and offered less Polish, with suitable rewards for those who did well. Private and home education was cut to a minimum. From January 1841 and 1842, respectively, teachers in Polish gymnasia and secondary schools were required to have Church Slavonic; students wanting to attend university had to get high marks in Russian and Slavonic.[6] But all these measures were taken against the odds.

What Uvarov did fulfil in his ten years at the ministry ironically had little to do with his national propaganda aims. What came out on top was that commitment to 'pure education' which still allows him his reputation today as the originator of modern Russian education. The rise in the quality and quantity of secondary and higher education during his Ministry were unprecedented.

In the humiliating matter of censorship, however, he was like a teacher having the rules flouted to his face. Nikitenko once recorded the absurdity of a day's work:

> I was with the Minister. I reported to him on some novels translated from the French.
>
> He ordered Victor Hugo's *Notre-Dame de Paris* not to be passed. However he expressed high praise for the work. The Minister thinks it is too early for us to read such works, while forgetting that people read Victor Hugo anyway in the original and find there all the things for which he thinks these books dangerous. There is not a single censored foreign book which cannot be bought here in a secondhand bookshop.[7]

By 1842 the state of affairs was so chaotic, which is to say petty, unjust and inaccurate, it was a matter of open complaint. Nikitenko was desperate in December 1842, when he found himself along with another censor suddenly under arrest after some members of the military took objection to an article in Grech's *Son of the Fatherland*. He appealed to Benckendorff:

> Your Excellency, speak to the Sovereign for us. Tell His Majesty how difficult it is to be a censor. We really do not know what is required of us ... . We are never safe, and can never fulfil our obligations.

News of Nikitenko's plight quickly spread and as he was a figure commanding some sympathy when he arrived to give a lecture at the university after a night in the guardhouse the students cheered loudly. The tsar heard of the 'incident' and irritated, demanded to know why Uvarov had not told him of the 'disturbance'. Nikitenko recorded on 12 December that Uvarov considered the chain of events a black mark against himself. He urged the tsar to tighten the rules, particularly concerning periodicals and translations from French, so that all those concerned might be clear what was the tsar's wish. As things stood, no one could be sure, and writers, journalists and bureaucrats of every stripe were enraged and fearful at the confusion.[8]

An individual victim was Gogol. In 1836 criticism of *The Government Inspector*, his classic satire against corrupt provincial bureaucracy, had enraged him; when a Moscow audience in 1839 decided to like the play, however, this time he fled in anger from the tumultuous applause. Gogol's own changeability, which caused him to destroy manuscripts and embark periodically on courses of 'spiritual education', replicated the whims of the very bureaucracy he satirized, and caused him much pain. At the end of 1841 the first part of his novel *Dead Souls* was rejected, suspected of being an attack on the censorship, or God, or both. In need of money Gogol sent the manuscript to St Petersburg instead, using Belinsky as an intermediary, at which point the fate of *Dead Souls* came close to being determined by Uvarov.[9]

Belinsky, more than most, blamed Uvarov for what he called 'the censorship terror'. Most recently a short story by an otherwise well-known patriotic writer called Kukol'nik had brought cries of indignation from the Minster of the Fleet in the Senate because it featured a serf beating a landowner with a stick. Uvarov had ordered the censor to be more careful not to pass stories which concentrated on 'moral ugliness and weaknesses' or any such descriptions taken from national and peasant life. He also banned stories in which the portrait of an individual, or of social conditions, was too satirical. When at the end of all this Uvarov turned a reproachful eye to Belinsky's own work, the critic was exasperated:

> To crown everything Uvarov turned his attention to my article in No 1 [On Griboyedov's play *Woe from Wit* in the first issue for 1842 of *Notes from the Fatherland*], and said to the censors that although he himself would have passed it, the tone was not right (i.e. hey, you, *canailles*, if you let something through like this I'll thrash you.).

Belinsky feared what would happen if Gogol's manuscript fell into the hands of 'the Minister of Darkness and the Extinction of Enlightenment' and proceeded to attack Uvarov, together with Shevyrev and Pogodin. Together they constituted a dangerous anti-literary mafia:

> Shevvers published a denunciation of Kukol'nik's tale in *The Muscovite*... well, make up your own mind: what could we do? ...You have no idea of what goes on in Piter [Petersburg]. And then there was Odoevsky [one of the censors] handing the [Gogol] manuscript to Velegorsky [another censor], who wanted to give it to Uvarov; but he was getting ready for a ball at the Grand Duchess's , and his highness had no time to think about such trivia as Gogol's manuscript. Then luckily he thought of giving it to Nikitenko to read privately. He began to read it as a censor, but fell into reading it as a reader, and had to start again. When he had done he told Velegorsky he would have to show some of it to Uvarov. Fortunately the manuscript did not fall into the hands of *The Minister of Darkness and the Extinction of Enlightenment in Russia* [my italics]. In Piter the weather changes like this a

hundred times, and Nikitenko decided not to let through only a few phrases and the episode about Captain Kopeikin. But here's the rub: the manuscript was sent on March 7, in the name of Pogodin, to No. 109, but Gogol didn't receive it. I think Pogodin stole it, to exchange it on the secondhand market for old trousers and skirts; or to keep it to himself for a while and then to wheedle out of Gogol (who is naïve and deceives himself about this swindler) something else for his servile journal.[10]

Six days later Belinsky wrote to the 'naïve' Gogol to warn him:

Notes from the Fatherland is now the only journal in Russia in which honourable, honest and – dare I say it – intelligent opinion can find a place and a refuge in Russia, and *Notes from the Fatherland* must not in any circumstance be confused with the serfs of the well-known estate of Porechie.[11]

From Moscow, however, Gogol continued to worry about the fate of his novel and sent a begging letter to Uvarov, pointing out that to ban it would ruin him financially. The Minister of Enlightenment and president of the Academy of Sciences took no action. Another anxious letter was despatched to the chairman of the board of censors. Nikitenko finally saved the day by imposing an alternative title on Gogol's work and removing a chapter.[12]

Uvarov protested that during his Ministry more books had been published than ever before. In fact that was true, but mainly because the Academy published more. This was no substitute for a broader national culture. One glance at the Academy's output in 1843, which included Uvarov's own *Études de philosophie et de critique*, edited under the aegis of Graefe and the grovelling secretary of the Academy Pavel Fuss, was enough to show that it was devoted to producing work of a small academic circulation and appeal.[13]

In the 1843 report Uvarov defined the aim of his Academic policy:

While preserving all the advantages of European learning which have helped Russian intellectual life reach a level equal to that of other countries, it [the Ministry] wanted to give it national independence, to base its work on native principles and have it respond equally to the requirements of the people and the state.

The Academy, a repository of solid Russian feeling, not xenophobic, nor excessive, but devoted to Russian achievements of excellence, undertook a project to reprint the Russian Slavonic Bible. Slavonic dictionaries were published, and the first substantial studies of the Russian language were produced. It spread its conscience wider in the new empire and appointed a member to represent the languages and literatures of Armenia and Georgia. But these were building blocks towards what we have already identified as a museum culture, while a living culture was being stifled.[14]

Was he aware his influence was diminishing? Uvarov laboured under three outstanding pieces of self-deception in the early 1840s: that Russia had 'caught up' in relation to Europe from the backwardness he had diagnosed in 1818, this supposition therefore justifying the active Russification of the (once) superior cultures of Poland and the Baltic States; that counter-propaganda worked; and that he personally was of outstanding importance to Russia. The evidence against the first two beliefs was before his eyes. Russia had made very little industrial progress; its institutions, thanks to the will and interference of Nicholas, had grown every more distant from anything resembling democracy, equality and legality, though there had been an apparent step forward in the codification of the law. In the meantime independent intellectual life flourished, bringing with it the first Russian socialism and the first Russian school of Hegelian history; and Moscow and St Petersburg were awash with foreign liberal ideas. What he did know was that the tsar had recently overridden his wish to keep the Russian Academy, the official institution and patron of literature, and the Academy of Sciences apart. They had recently merged.

When in 1843 Uvarov marked twenty-five years as president of the Academy of Sciences and ten as Minister, with celebrations in January and March, respectively, Nikitenko found that he quickly 'lost himself in self-praise'.

Enumerating his achievements he mentioned incidentally very cautiously 'the freedom of thought, the movement of minds'. He spoke also of 'the firm foundations he had created, of the truth of these foundations, and of the fact that all this was not a momentary desire of the tsar but a lasting and stable system.' A couple of times he expressed himself unfortunately, saying 'the tsar and I' or 'I and the tsar'. 'Even the enemies of the Ministry acknowledge that we know our business,' he declared. He mentioned the possibility that he might leave the Ministry.

All this ceremony was in reality, as they say, aimed at drawing to himself the well-imposed attention of the court, which for several months now has shown Uvarov so little good will that this manoeuvre can hardly help him. By calling the opinion of society to his defence he is more likely to damage his case.

How can he not understand that Russia doesn't want state benefactors, only state functionaries, or, more to the point, functionaries of the tsar, and that to offer up one's work for judgement by the many means to go against the egoism of the all-devouring will of the one. I'm sorry for Uvarov: he has spoilt things for himself. At the same time he's the best Minister ever to have directed our Ministry. Enumerating his services, he didn't or couldn't mention the most important, that in the ten years prior to him, there hadn't been a man, according to him, capable of realizing an idea. Even the limited Prince Lieven, even he managed to kick our education in the shins ... . Uvarov is not guilty in that respect and in the present time that means a lot. Whatever one says about him, if we lose him, God knows what soldier we'll have to take command of our minds and run the education of our citizens and our thinking.[15]

One unexpected event in 1843 forced Uvarov to admit to having been defeated by the world: his favourite daughter Natalya Sergeevna died on 13 January, aged twenty-two. Pletnev described her as 'a fine creature, happy, and seemingly brought into life to enjoy its highest pleasures', adding that 'this was ... a terrible blow, and it burst like a storm over the head of a man used to counting his days only in terms of seductive successes and alluring expectations'.[16]

Uvarov's biographer used the family bereavement to hint also at the beginnings of his political downfall. It seemed as if by Natalya's death a spell had been broken, and Uvarov's will to live, enshrined in hard work for worldly achievement, had suddenly been challenged by disintegration and decay.

Uvarov was wretched at both losses, but strange creature that he was he did not hesitate to confound them and play them off one against the other. Indeed Nikitenko observed him trying to make political capital out the sympathy and attention he received from the tsar's family over the death of Natalya. The occasion was the evening of 21 March, after the celebration of Uvarov's decade at the Ministry:

> In the evening there was a concert at the university. Fräulein Freigang sang beautifully. She has an astonishingly pure and fresh voice. It is the true voice of a little bird. Afterwards I went to Pletnev's. Our [educational] superintendents were there, Prince Volkonsky, Prince Odoevsky, Arsenev. They were talking about Uvarov ... [and] telling the following story about him. The Grand Duchess Elena Pavlovna, when his daughter died, sent him a letter of condolence. Instead of a reply all he did was send her a copy of the volume of his works which had just been published in French.

Uvarov alluded in the Ministry anniversary speech to the fact that he might leave the Ministry because of his daughter's death, but Pletnev said the tsar dissuaded him from premature retirement. A personalized word from the emperor, interpreted flatteringly as care and concern for himself, convinced him he was still needed.[17]

Instead of retiring in 1843 therefore he took a holiday. He was suffering from nervous strain, which always wrought havoc with his physical health, and for the first time since he was a student he travelled out of Eastern Europe and the Russian Empire. In the early autumn he went south to Italy.

Saint-Julian reported that his departure was surrounded by a thousand rumours: that he was charged with a secret mission to the Vatican, that his trip was of political and religious significance, and that the fate of the Catholic Church in Russia depended upon it, but that others were prepared to accept it was a personal trip. The truth was he was going as a tourist and a poet to a fashionable destination. Shevyrev, Pogodin and Gogol had all recently spent holidays in Italy and Gogol had published his sketch 'Rome' in The Muscovite. Uvarov travelled to catch up with his friends and also to recapture some of the emotions he had felt as a young man on first crossing the Alps. Yet it was clear he was allowing Natalya's death to mark a full stop in the text of his worldly progress, giving him a chance to look in from outside and reminisce.

Crossing the Alps in Switzerland he descended upon Lake Como and made his way south to Rome; the return journey took him to Florence, Bologna, Ferrara and finally Treviso, where he re-crossed the mountains into Austria. The round trip inspired three essays, one on Rome, one on Venice and one on Napoleon's campaign in Italy, which included material from an interview with the elderly Tuscan statesman Fossombroni. Uvarov also wrote a poem, or perhaps several, one of which was published for the first and only time by Saint-Julien. He travelled as a sad, elderly man, bereaved and yet conscious of some daring at the freedom he had taken to roam large in Europe. He was in the land where the lemon trees grew at last.

Rome and Venice were drawn with the same painterly skills he brought to 'De Ligne' and mirrored a heavy heart. Uvarov found in both cities a melancholy and a sense of lost greatness, which helped him bear his own loss. The Rome essay ends with one of the most effective passages of his published writing, with the death of Natalya allowing him to recall an idealism sadly passed:

Rome est un doux asile sans cesse ouvert aux grandeurs dechues comme aux intelligences désabusées, aux plus éclatantes comme aux plus obscures douleurs; on n'oublie pas ses maux, mais on en porte le poids avec plus de courage; la tristesse a sa pudeur sur cette terre trempée de sang et de larmes. Là ou tant d'hommes ont souffert, ou tant de generations ont succombé, on ne se livre qu'avec une sorte de retenue à des impressions purement personnelles. L'homme pensant et sensible, l'homme preparé par ses etudes et ses goûts à ce grand spectacle, s'identifie promptement avec lui. Avoir été à Rome est un souvenir honorable; en sortir sans un profond regret, c'est chose impossible. Bien qu'on n'y laisse aucune affection, bien qu'on n'en emporte aucune, le coeur se serre quand on repasse par La Porta del Popolo pour retourner dans ses foyers lointains. En cette instant suprême, Rome entière apparait à vos yeux comme une personne tendrement aimée, vers laquelle on tend les bras, et qui semble de loin jêter un regard d'adieu au pelerin étranger qu'elle a acceuilli dans ses murs et couvert de son ombre.[18]

Rome is a gentle resting-place always open to lost visions and disappointed minds, and likewise to the most vivid and most obscure sufferings; a man doesn't forget his troubles, but he carries the burden with greater courage; sadness has its own modesty on this soil saturated in blood and tears. Where so many men have suffered, where so many generations have succumbed, one is somehow reluctant to give in to purely personal impressions. The thoughtful, sensitive man, prepared by his studies and his taste to confront this great spectacle, immediately identifies with it. To have been in Rome is an honorable memory; to leave without some profound regret is something impossible. Although one leaves no affection there, and takes none away, one's heart shudders when one passes through the Porta del Popolo to return to one's faraway homeland. In this supreme moment Rome itself appears like someone one loves dearly, to whom one holds out a hand, and which seems to throw from afar a glance at the foreign pilgrim which she has accommodated within her walls and covered in her shade.

Uvarov visited the sights, of which the most memorable was a torchlight procession at the Vatican, aesthetically splendid and, for a man in a state of delicate melancholy, triumphantly cathartic. He remembered well the day he made an excursion outside the city to Tivoli, site of the finest ancient villas. He visited the engineering works just completed at the instigation of Pope Gregory XVI to divert the Aniene, a tributary of the Tiber which threatened to flood the valley. The river went through a tunnel where it emerged in a spectacular display, in a park with smaller cascades and grottoes. A Russian Prufrock, repressed by years in office in a secretive country, following a code of public performance and strict personal privacy, Uvarov toured the waterfalls on a donkey. He noted the ruins of a Renaissance palace which had been recently turned into a factory, and decried industrialism as one of the plagues of modern society.

Among his most characteristic reflections in Rome were those on the villa Albani, where for a time in the mid-eighteenth century the German classicist Johann Joachim Winckelmann had been librarian to the cardinal. The story of Winckelmann, who with his essays on the Ancients shaped the European classical ideal for decades to come, and deeply inspired Goethe, was well-known to Uvarov. He read and remembered now the essays which conveyed their author's outstanding sense of the Greek ideal of male beauty, and a hint of Winckelmann's homosexuality:

> As I walked through the palace and the gardens, I seemed to see the Cardinal surrounded by his party of travellers, ancient historians and artists, leaning familiarly on the arm of his friend Winckelmann and abandoning himself to animated discussions which today would be instructive and learned, but which then created a new branch of learning.[19]

But for a general impression of the south Uvarov remembered what Goethe, 'the truest painter of this beautiful country', had written.

For Uvarov Italy was the country, at last, where he breathed a purer air, the air he longed for locked up in official, fanatical Russia, and after thirty years of self-denial he managed to write a poem again:

Rome

Au coeur de l'Italie est la Ville immortelle;
Et lorsqu'au voyageur, de loin, on dit: 'C'est elle!'
À peine s'il saisit le sens de ces deux mots.
L'éternel mouvement et l'éternel repos
Semblent planer sur Rome, et de cette urne immense
Verser incessamment le bruit et le silence.
Je voyageur surpris mesure d'un coup d'oeil
Des peuples et des rois ce colossal cerceuil;
Il craindrait de troubler dans leurs tombes celebres
Tous les vieux habitants de ces rives funèbres,
Où le marbre respire, où tout prend une voix,
Où les destins du monde ont abouti deux fois.
Grandeur inexprimable, étrange destinée!
Deux fois reine du monde et deux fois detronée!
Que pourraient t'apporter les siecles à venir,
Qui ne fut pale et froid devant ce souvenir?
À moins que l'on ne vit un jour au bord du Tibre,
Au pied du Vatican, les flôts d'un peuple libre
Recevant à genoux, de tes augustes mains,
Le labarum sacré des ses nouveaux destins,
Et l'Italie entière, autour de toi pressée,
S'unir par l'action comme par la pensée,
Pour la dernière fois sortir de son tombeau.
O Rome! quel triomphe et quel destin plus beau![20]

Uvarov's verses looked forward to a unified Italy. They alluded to the idea of the Third Rome, an idea which the Russian Slavophiles applied to the future greatness of Moscow as the seat of Eastern Christianity. Characteristically the cosmopolitan Uvarov hoped only for the renewal of Italy.

In middle age he had retained some talent as a poet. Some of his lines well conveyed a sense of eternal flux: 'À peine ... le silence', and of ebb and flow. The sonority of the two lines in which he confronts the judgement of history: 'Grandeur inexprimable ... deux fois detronée' suggest the strength of human understanding as well as its wide-eyed intelligent amazement at what the passing of time can wreak. Uvarov was particularly gifted metrically in French. As he implied, for a Russian to leave Rome was a wrench. It meant leaving a rich, civilized land for a poor and semi-barbarous one. The 'foyers lointains' of his poem opened in the opposite direction from the phrase he once used in a poem when he was young and optimistic and free to travel: 'J'ai quitte pour longtemps les foyers de mes pères'.[21]

But it didn't seem right to dwell on personal unhappiness in a place that had seen such historic events, and so, less intense than the poem, the Rome essay reflected lightly on art, on scholarship, on erudite passions and on the waxing and waning of political power. Art, he quoted Lucretius, had a continuity which carried its power beyond nations and generations: *et vitae lampada tradunt*. Art carried the torch of life from nation to nation, from generation to generation, as one runner passed it to the next. Furthermore, 'Is not the life of a people made up half of art, half of political might? Whenever one of these elements has been lacking, social life has been incomplete; peoples who have lacked both elements at the same time have no place in history.'[22] Yet Russia, Uvarov implies, has only political power, and that is why his heart aches when he has to leave Italy, which has art.

In Venice, already on the northern path home, the air seems less pure, the sky less blue. Nevertheless the unique city astonishes him with its history of beauty, power and tyranny. He admires the traces of a past magnificent empire; enjoys the juxtapositions of cruelty and luxury, worldly riches and a rich and powerful church. The sense of the demise of a once great empire is strongest now that Venice had spent forty-six years under first French and now Austrian rule. It is an occupied city, half its life extinguished. The phenomenon of occupation was something he had not appreciated when he first experienced the impact of the French in Italy in 1805.

There is nothing more sad than the first sight of this modern Pompeii which is called Venice. Imagine a city struck by a recent calamity which respected its walls but killed its inhabitants, and you will be able to imagine the feeling which seizes the heart; not the vivifying feeling which the Roman ruins give, but that vague sadness, that profound trouble which takes hold of you at the sight of a splendid, deserted house, whose inhabitants seem to have only just left, or a half-lit theatre, empty of its audience, or a ballroom the day after the celebration.[23]

Venice, though it furnished thoughts on the then apparently inevitable fading of the great frescoes, and on the great meeting it embodied between Eastern and Western Christian art, turned Uvarov's attention ultimately to the idea of imperial power, and its passing. Magnificence has a value in itself, and its loss is an absolute loss.

'Venise' is a curious essay, a mixture of sound, if unoriginal historical generalizations, with a scattering of telling moral judgements. Uvarov objects to the fate of the political prisoners who died horrible deaths in the damp dungeons of the Doge's Palace. From an agrarian society still, he is damning about the rich pickings modern industrial society in the West was discovering, mining the treasures of Venice's glorious past: 'The spirit of industrialism is applying itself to the dying body of Venice, like a greedy heir calculating what he expects to inherit while standing at the bed of a dying man.' But what a strange moral faculty he had! In the second instance here he was describing himself as portrayed in Lucullus! It was as if Pushkin had taught him one moral value he could be sure of: when he had felt society's condemnation of his own avarice. Even his other display of moral certainty may also have been derivative. The Marquis de Custine had just published in France, to the anger of the Russian government, a description of his horror at being given a tour of the damp dungeons of the Peter and Paul fortress in Petersburg. Uvarov as a censor would have read the banned book and surely knew the passage.[24]

The third essay to come out of Uvarov's Italian journey, 'Napoleon's Views on Italy', was not published until the Leduc Paris edition of Uvarov's essays in 1848, but was probably written during or soon after his Italian trip. It combined the same mixture of travel, political observation and moral judgement, again taking up the theme of Italian unity. It started promisingly with the idea of what Napoleon did for Italy:

Crossing the rich plains of Lombardy, making my way along the coast of the admirable gulf from Genoa to Florence, the seat of medieval Italy, and above all in Rome, which summarizes all one has seen, I often found myself thinking about this question, which seems to have been the last chance of greatness for Italy. I approached all the sources in Italy which could satisfy my curiosity; most considerable authorities came to my assistance, and yet so intense a curiosity could not be completely satisfied. It was in combining the diverse opinions that I came to formulate my own.[25]

Napoleon took Uvarov back to early manhood, but this time to a key political experience, his fascination with the power of Bonaparte. Uvarov had expressed in *Alexander* thirty years earlier his intense curiosity at setting a prophet alongside a conqueror; now he asked what the plan of the half-French, half-Italian conqueror was for Italy and why it was so inconsistent. He visited surviving members of the Bonaparte family, from whom he learnt that 'the Italians were incapable of governing themselves and needed to be taught the art of government'. That Napoleon had such a considered plan Uvarov doubted, however. He went to Florence to discuss the matter with Vittorio Fossombroni who had served under Napoleon, and later became foreign affairs Minister and a cabinet Minister in the Duchy of Tuscany. Fossombroni was not far off death when Uvarov reached him. According to the essay he extended the Russian visitor a warm welcome and immediately offered words which confirmed Uvarov had touched the heart of the matter. The theory was that Napoleon had been an Italian who wanted to make Italy great, and that the exigencies of French politics had set up an irresolvable conflict within himself. 'But Napoleon had never been to Rome', cried Uvarov, 'no one could truly understand Italy without that.' Interrupting him suddenly, Fossobroni cried: 'But how can you, a man of the North, have guessed this intimate secret of our history? Do you know that it is Rome which is at the heart and in the eyes of an Italian? Mark well too, that everything was done to keep the Emperor from going there … Napoleon himself, as unbelieving and superstitious as any true Italian, could not make up his mind to go to Rome.'[26] Uvarov concluded that Napoleon, though briefly he offered the possibility of unity, did nothing for Italy. He may even have retarded its political regeneration.

Napoleon was a stimulating essay which could have been better had it not descended into characteristic self-praise. But just as with the example of the dungeons and the grasping heir at the bedside in Venice struck a false note, so here praise for an independent Italian nation, free from Austrian rule, sounded odd coming from a Russian whose job it was to destroy the Polish and Baltic nations. Uvarov's unquestioned acceptance of Russia's unique case was again in evidence, but it would not marry with essays supposed to exemplify some objective pursuit of truth.

When he indulged in that pursuit it showed up his weaknesses and his compromises. In Fossombroni he visited a man who might have been a political hero in Uvarov's more liberal days, a man who had made of Tuscany a model of enlightened paternalistic government. But in the Italian trip there was no true purchase of redemption by means of intellectual rebirth. Uvarov went back to the origins of his thinking, about art, about politics, about the beauty of the south and came away with an urn, which illustrated with a marble carving of the life of Bacchus and Ariadne his old thesis about the

Orphic mysteries. Winckelmann had described it and now Uvarov was able to buy it and make it his own.

Uvarov thus took his last look at European civilization. The oval sarcophagus from the Villa Altemps, along with a leaf from the cypress tree shading Virgil's grave in Naples, he took back with him to Russia, where they went on display in his Porechie study, as souvenirs. He was putting his affairs in relation to Europe in order. Over the next five years he would decide which of the essays scattered over a lifetime would be available to posterity. But when he turned to face Russia again he felt defeated. Translations into Russian of his classical essays began to appear, duly noticed by Belinsky, but at heart Uvarov knew he had little to offer. Italy had been only a temporary respite from facing the truth of his superfluity.

18

Decline and fall

Une fatalité attachée aux chose humaines.

UVAROV *ELEUSIS*

Uvarov was hastened towards his demise by ill health, personal quarrels and the increasing resort to secrecy in his political life. The growing disparity between the wishes of the tsar and the independent activity of the intelligentsia weakened him in a way of which he was only too aware when he returned from Italy early in 1844:

> After breathing freely under the beneficent sky of Italy, surrounded by every intellectual pleasure, I have returned with renewed strength; but I fear I will soon use up this small store; I wish that God should lead me next summer to Porechie, where the Museum will be enhanced with several excellent ancient and modern works of art.[1]

For Nikitenko the Minister's vulnerability was thrown into high relief in October, when, having been granted the happiness of that summer, he returned to St Petersburg:

> This morning I was with the Minister. I think the flattering welcome laid on for him by the Moscovites [Pogodin, Shevyrev and Davydov] had its effect on him; he is only just back from Moscow. The weak nerves of this vital, but not firm mind will not stand that kind of tickling. He is terribly armed against Notes from the Fatherland, and says it is heading in the wrong direction – socialism, communism and so on. Evidently this idea has been fanned by the Moscovite patriots, who now want to be leaders of their time at any cost. The Minister will spare no mercy for Notes from the Fatherland.[2]

The war between the promoters and destroyers of Russian literature was never so fierce. A year later Uvarov was still 'tightening up fearfully' on the periodicals, though unable to avoid contradicting himself. Notes from the Fatherland espoused socialism and left Hegelianism, but it was also the centre of Russian intellectual life, with a list of distinguished contributors from Belinsky to Herzen. Uvarov pilloried it but stopped short of pressing to have it closed. He also attacked others for denouncing it. Such discrepancies in one man helped to make the censorship ineffective.

The high quality of emergent Russian national culture was Uvarov's Achilles heel. It embroiled him in a furious quarrel with a prominent and popular figure in the world of academic administration, Grigory Petrovich Volkonsky. The story of their relations reveals graphically the corner into which the Minister of Enlightenment had painted himself. At the age of thirty-five, of noble birth, well-connected, and liberal in his outlook, Volkonsky was appointed Petersburg educational superintendent in May 1842. He became chairman of the Censorship Committee while holding the belief that censorship should not inhibit Russian literature, because good literature would promote nationality. He was appalled at the bungled handling of *Dead Souls* and in public implied that Uvarov was to blame.[3] Knowing that the tsar worried about the influence of foreign literature on Russian readers, Volkonsky argued that this was all the more reason to encourage Russian literature as an alternative. He added that censors should be clear in their minds as to the spirit of their task if they wanted to have moral weight. The irony was Uvarov might himself have argued this wholly Russian, but in that rather moderate, reasonable line against the threat of extremism; yet, since he did not, Volkonsky became an immediate enemy. Volkonsky was also more radical in his statement of the Gogol case in private. '*Uvarov said ... [he] wants once and for all to see the end of Russian literature* [my italics]. Then at least there will be something definite. But the main thing is [he] will be able to sleep peacefully,' Volkonsky quoted. Uvarov under pressure was becoming a caricature of his worst self.[4]

Uvarov took the chance to hurt when as St Petersburg Superintendent Volkonsky asked for an assistant. Volkonsky's wife, Princess Maria Alekseevna Benckendorff, daughter of the head of the Third Department, was ill and needed to go away to a milder climate. To make that possible her husband needed a locum. Hoping to put pressure on Volkonsky to retire, Uvarov managed to delay the arrival of such a man for two years, whereupon the tsar intervened and told Volkonsky to choose his own assistant. Volkonsky deliberated while his wife's illness became more acute. He toyed with asking for a transfer to Odessa. A close friend, who wanted him to move, mentioned the idea to Uvarov, who then made it all the more difficult for Volkonsky to get an assistant, forcing him to ask for the transfer. Tempers frayed: Volkonsky's father, Count Peter Mikhailovich, a Minister at court, was furious his advice had not been sought; the doctor said the climate of Odessa would not be at all good for his patient and she should go to Germany; while Volkonsky himself failed to take adequate advice and in the meantime resigned his job as Petersburg Superintendent, and blamed Uvarov for tricking him.

It was a messy, unsatisfying case in which to be victorious. Volkonsky was a man much loved by his friends and colleagues, respected professionally for his fine education and humanity, and welcomed in the highest social circles for his family background, breeding and generosity. Nikitenko said he was indispensable in matters concerning the university and censorship, and often saved them from bad ends. A mediocre administrator, he had an artistic nature and great personal presence. Among those he attracted was the tsar himself. His quarrel with Uvarov became well-known, and containing a large element of envy, showed Uvarov in a shabby personal light. Almost immediately upon his resignation in February 1845 he was elected an honorary member of Petersburg University. He remained a member of the Chief Directorate for Schools, within Uvarov's Ministry, for the next two years, until he moved to the Foreign Affairs Ministry. From there he was posted to Rome, where he led the Russian Archaeological Commission and became Superintendent to the resident community of Russian artists.

Another open and scandalous quarrel involved Uvarov and Count G. S. Stroganov, rector of Moscow University. Stroganov had objected at the beginning of the decade to Uvarov's policy of secrecy in implementing measures to restrict education on a class basis. A version of their dispute was recounted by the future historian Sergei Mikhailovich Soloviev, who as a student at Moscow University became a close friend of Stroganov's but was highly critical of Uvarov:

> [Stroganov] … knew Uvarov as he was, despised him as a dirty man, and, as was his character, did not hide his contempt. I was told there was an even stronger reason for his hatred: Uvarov had a relationship with Stroganov's stepmother, which evoked such hatred between the Minister and the Superintendent, hatred which did so much harm to Moscow University and to education in the region and led to such a sad outcome for them.[5]

Soloviev compared Stroganov's 'aristocracy of spirit' to Uvarov's meanness and poverty of character. He heaped similar insults of vanity and servility and hypocrisy on Uvarov's supporters in the Ministry and the university. Davydov was unprincipled and self-seeking, and godless; Shevyrev was hard-working and well-meaning, but petty, proud, envious and easily flattered, not to mention given to drinking too much. For Pogodin Soloviev reserved his worst judgements. The rival historian was ugly, emotional, rough-mannered, cynical and covetous.

Stroganov was not a paragon of virtue in Soloviev's eyes but he had an essential dignity Soloviev found lacking in Uvarov and his circle. A poor and muddled thinker, easily confused, said Soloviev, he was nevertheless upright, hard-working, dutiful, and valued honesty and learning equally highly. He was neither a 'beautiful soul' nor a liberal: he could be proud and aloof, and cold. He believed the answer to Russia's problems lay with the aristocracy and a strong state, and he seemed to want to purify and better other people. But Soloviev judged he had moral weight on his side.

An influential and distinguished historian of the mid-century, Soloviev raised the quarrel of Uvarov and Stronganov to the level where it became typical of a recurring conflict in Russian society and set a pattern for Russian social thought. What mattered to him was what has mattered to generations of Russian opponents ever since: the sincerity with which men worked for Russia and for the cause of true learning, and the quality of heart revealed in their day-to-day actions. Since official Russia was so snobbish about the quality of the aristocracy compared with the classes below, the spiritual opposition to it, which grew up among idealistic men of different persuasions, professional writers, historians and religious philosophers, involuntarily created a category of spiritual aristocracy to counter it. It embraced the kind of civilized behaviour and ease, the quality of leadership and the sense of social duty which Russia ideally had always associated with the nobility; but it added new defining elements: moral integrity and spiritual grace, so that aristocracy became an ideal of personality and of education, a virtue utterly separate from social class. In this way Russian thought, across the spectrum from economic conditions to religious devotion, created for itself the same kind of moral touchstone that literary criticism did through Belinsky. The need was to oppose moral corruption, and among the earliest uses I have found of this way of thinking in both the literary and the personal sphere are those attached to criticism of Uvarov.

There seemed no depth to which Uvarov would not stoop. It was not his talent, as his flattering biographers said, but sheer dishonesty and unscrupulousness which were now ensuring his negative reputation, alongside an obsessive desire to thwart the growth of Russian literature. Hard on the heels of the Chaadaev affair Vyazemsky had called him 'the man who abases everything'.[6] Now Nikitenko was despairing,

On Sunday I was with the Minister. He spoke a lot about 'the bad, dirty, and commercial' direction of our literature. He recalled former days when the name man of letters, according to him, was considered something estimable.

'For example', he went on, 'take just our own literary society, comprising Dashkov, Bludov, Karamzin, Zhukovsky, Batyushkov and me. Karamzin read us his history. We were still young, but sufficiently educated for him to listen to our comments and profit from them. One day the late tsar began with Karamzin a discussion about academies. This is what our historian said to him on that matter. "You know, Your Majesty, that the most useful academy for us would be one consisting of these clowns and young people who amid their laughter tell me many useful and true things and give me honest opinions." Now it is not so. The name of the man of letters inspires no respect.'[7]

In the spring of 1845, shortly before his brother's death dealt him another keen blow, Uvarov again crossed paths with Gogol, attracted by his ultra-conservatism and his wrestling with his literary talent. Shevyrev and Pogodin ran Gogol's affairs for him, and gave him loans, but the writer was again short of money. He needed immediate help if he was to finish the second part of *Dead Souls*. Zhukovsky approached the tsar on Gogol's behalf in March 1845 while Uvarov wrote on his own initiative promising Nikolai Vasilievich protection. Uvarov hastened to pass on his enthusiasm for Goethe in a casual way, and spoke in a personal tone, as if from one man of letters to another, to invite confidence. When an official grant was secured, Gogol, pressed by Uvarov's patriotic exhortations, replied with a tormented analysis of his inability to fulfil them and an account of his new resolutions:

> All I can tell you is that your letter saddened me. I am sad, first, because everything I have written until now is not worthy of attention. Though I meant well, I expressed everything unnaturally, badly, contemptibly ... so that is no wonder that the majority of people attach a bad rather than a good meaning to my works, and my countrymen do not derive any spiritual benefit from them. Secondly I am sad because I have still not repaid the Emperor the debt I owe him for his former favours to me. I swear I never intended to ask him for anything now; I have only been quietly preparing a work which I am sure will be of much greater use to my countrymen than my former scribblings, for which you too will thank me, if only I should be successful in finishing it conscientiously, for its subject is not alien to your own convictions.[8]

Uvarov was delighted with this outpouring of gratitude and self-deprecation and immediately made Gogol's letter public. Nikitenko was amazed at the Minister's political exploitation of a troubled, masochistic soul:

> Uvarov wanted to show me a letter to him from Gogol, but could not find it amongst his papers. He told me its contents, vouching for the sincerity of Gogol's words. Gogol thanked him for receiving financial help from the tsar, and said amongst other things: 'I am sad when I look at what I wrote which

prompted this kindness. Everything I have written until now is so weak and empty that I don't know how I can make up to the tsar for not fulfilling his expectations. But perhaps God will help me do something which will satisfy him.' What sad self-denigration on Gogol's part! This is after all a man, who took upon himself the role of exposing our social ills, and really did so, not only accurately and truly, but with the feeling and sensitivity of an artist of genius! It's a pity, a terrible pity! It's just playing into Uvarov's and someone else's hands.[9]

The 'someone else' was the tsar. The tangential role Uvarov played in Gogol's tragedy has become significant in the history of Russian literature because a critical observer, this time Belinsky, once again perceived it as typical of his unseemly behaviour. In 1845 Gogol began writing his *Selected Passages from a Correspondence with Friends*, a work in which the artist in him almost entirely made way for the reactionary preacher. Gogol hoped to spark a spiritual revolution in Russia and among bizarre passages on illness, the devil, and the dreadfulness of Pogodin he called the church essential to Russia and expounded on the duties by God of landowners and serfs. Alongside lucid passages on literature he offered fanatical praise of Orthodoxy and the Throne, subjects which in his letter he had called 'not alien' to Uvarov's convictions.

When the *Selected Passages* were published in 1847 the majority of Gogol's readers were disappointed and Belinsky was sufficiently incensed by it to write one of the most famous documents of his career, the 1847 'Letter to Gogol'. In it he attacked Gogol for taking his artistic standards from Uvarov and the tsar. He told him how much his compromise with the authorities lowered him as a writer and as a man. True Russia, he said, could forgive a bad book, but not an immoral one. The document has gone down in Russian literary history as an open letter declaring the obligatory moral engagement of Russian writers, because of the very existence of slippery officials like Uvarov. The irony remained, however, that Gogol as writer transcended Gogol as preacher, and laughed at his other self, and Uvarov's. The small-minded, sycophantic officials of his fiction and his plays did not have Uvarov's intellectual complexity, but they had his servility and deviousness. Even Uvarov's most sympathetic modern biographer has observed that the men around him at the Academy and Porechie, who also lacked his intellectual gifts, acted and sounded just like Gogolian creations.[10] It was this country, which could only be adequately described by Gogol's pen, which made Uvarov a hereditary count in 1846, with the tripartite slogan emblazoned on his shield.

But Uvarov had achieved what he set out to do. After a life of striving he had assured his place among the aristocracy. Some said he was rewarded for his apparently successful introduction of Russian to schools in the Kingdom of Poland, though everyone knew his influence in education and censorship was diminishing and the tsar was displeased.[11] In fact only a tiny distance separated success from failure. The same year as he was ennobled even Pogodin accused Uvarov of neglecting censorship. By 1847, after the Stroganov affair had further eroded his standing, Uvarov was under investigation for incompetence. The same train of political events in Europe which would also bring about Metternich's downfall hastened Uvarov's end. His holding on was only a matter of time.[12]

During 1845 new signs of unrest against the three imperial occupying powers, Austria, Prussia and Russia, arose in the Polish lands. The free city of Cracow, always troublesome to those powers who watched over it, was the main point of contact between Poles under occupation and exiled Poles in Paris. In February 1846, albeit briefly, open revolution broke out on its streets. The unrest was quickly quelled, but Nicholas and Metternich were nervous. The tsar, doubting the loyalty of Polish students, closed the three upper classes of the Warsaw gymnasiums and terminated all law courses for Poles. Uvarov countered that these moves destroyed the basis on which gymnasium education was founded and managed to get the tsar to modify his plan in July.[13] In Europe, however, revolutionary events spoke louder than the Russian education Minister's familiar calls for patience. Cracow was annexed by Austria with the help of Prussian and Russian troops in November 1846. At home and abroad the perceived enemy was nationalism. Vienna's particular fear of Panslavism rapidly spread to St Petersburg. In self-defence Uvarov became obsessed with his protective tripartite policy.[14]

In 1847 Nicholas received a note from Metternich alleging that young Russian students were travelling through Slav countries campaigning for Slav unification. The same year a student at Kiev University denounced to the authorities the existence of two groups apparently dangerous to the government, the Society of St Kiril and St Methodius and the Ukrainian–Slavonic Society. The distinguished Ukrainian poet Shevchenko, later to become a national bard and hero, belonged to the second group. Uvarov was pressed by the tsar to issue a circular, appealing to all educational superintendents to watch for signs of the Panslavonic germ spreading. He explained the reasoning behind the circular in an official letter to Stroganov dated 30 May–29 June 1847. Meanwhile, a private memorandum in French added that the rector should call a meeting of the university council, where Uvarov's argument should be read out and prophylactic measures taken before it became too late, to avoid wounding 'the paternal feelings of the Tsar'.[15]

Uvarov delivered a historian's account of Panslavism to help his officials understand. Panslavism had begun in Bohemia at the end of the eighteenth century, and was now widespread. Unfortunately, enthusiasm for the Slavonic heritage had strayed beyond the peaceful limits of science, had become inflamed and distorted by political ideas, and by religion, and was subject to division and misunderstanding even within the Slavonic movement itself. It was in fact a Western concept of Panslavism which had spread abroad and in Russia this was unacceptable. The Slav principle had to be national. Anything else brought the familiar perils of 'dreams':

> Russian Slavonicism at its most pure should express unconditional adherence to Orthodoxy and Autocracy; but everything which goes beyond these bounds is a mixture of foreign ideas, the play of fantasy or a mask beneath which malevolent elements try to seize on inexperience and lead dreamers astray.

In his official letter to Stroganov Uvarov recalled what had been done by his Ministry to secure the Russian national principle. Young people were taught the language of the Orthodox Church and read the the Orthodox Bible; the factual foundations of Russian national history had been laid with the ordering of documents. The Minister spoke of the individual nation-personality, the old Herderian concept which in an adulterated form he found so useful to argue Russia's separateness and her unique case. Russia was different, Uvarov said, because she had been able to develop her independence despite encroachment from within and without. Other Slavonic nations had been extinguished, and absorbed into other countries, for instance Germanized, such that now all they had to turn to was their common Slavonic heritage; but Russia had its own Russian heritage; it needed no support from the Slavonic cause.

Uvarov's Russia was Petrine Russia. He ignored the medieval Russia to which both the Slavophiles and the Panslavs turned, Kiev Rus', where the foundations of the Christian Russian state had been laid in the far west of the empire. He believed in the Russia Peter had created, a nation equal to Europe in learning but which maintained the heart and the spirit of Russianness. Russia owed nothing to the Slavs and shared nothing with those peoples, who held out their hands not in love but in search of profit, he said. The only way to achieve a single Slavonic family, with one idea, and one will, would be for everyone to learn Russian, which was the essence of his policy of Official Nationality in the non-Russian provinces. Teachers had to understand the policy which was guiding their work. What they taught could not be confined to what was Russian, but how they taught could be. If these recommendations were not followed, the threat would hang over all Russian education that more forceful measures might be introduced to create right attitudes. The tsar had to be reassured.

Uvarov's 1847 plan was in fact as liberal as any he had ever proposed. It included abolishing gymnasium and university entrance examinations, maintaining a twice-yearly entry of students to the universities, and offering a free choice of course. He reckoned such freedoms would be tolerated if educational institutions could only be seen to be tightening up on national propaganda. The Minister was trying to carry out one more balancing act to save the cause of pure education in a political emergency. Stroganov wilfully chose to disagree with every point in Uvarov's proposals, however, and wrote to the tsar to elaborate. Belinsky said he had been asked secretly to keep an eye on the Slavophiles at the university, and had refused because the secrecy went against his conscience. But he was also one of those who wanted Uvarov's removal from office. Another huge quarrel ensued. Stroganov, in a private letter to Uvarov on 16 July, accused the Minister of deliberate ambiguity and referred him to a Ministry brief of 1842 which declared the question of Slavonic propaganda far outside Uvarov's jurisdiction. He said he would carry on as before, including providing lists of suspect people, but that he feared paper instructions were powerless to direct public opinion. The tsar asked A.F. Orlov, who had become head of the Third Department after Benckendorff's death, to try to make peace between the two men, but Uvarov was insulted and remained so. He publicized the affair as an open rebellion by one of his top officials and Stroganov resigned as rector of Moscow University on 3 November 1847. As Uvarov had ruefully predicted some years earlier of his own eventual departure from power, Stroganov's principled stand had a negative effect. He was replaced by D.P. Golokhvastov, a man Belinsky called a brute.[16]

The witch-hunt for Uvarov meanwhile gathered pace. He was under attack in education and in censorship, where since the death of Benckendorff he was without support. In January 1848 an anonymous commentator denounced him to the Third Department for being no better than any other fashionable young author with his interest in literature and his French essays. 'Venice' had appeared in translation in the Senkowski's *Biblioteka dlya chtenya* (The Readers' Library) in 1845, *Eleusis* in *The Contemporary* and 'Stein' in *Sanktpeterburgskie vedemosti* (The St Petersburg News) in 1847.

'Napoleon' had just been published in the short-lived *Severnoe Obozrenie* (Northern Survey). Uvarov's 1840 essay on literature was also cited. Uvarov's critic complained that reading these articles he always expected something important, and yet the essays never came to anything. Lots of foreign words were used and the meaning was often unclear. Uvarov might just as well have been a contributor to Notes from the Fatherland. The ambiguity which had sheltered Uvarov as a European man of letters and Russian official since his youth was now underlined and used against him. His critic said it was a pity young people did not have a better example of reliable, clear writing in the work of their Minister of national Enlightenment. The same dossier, dated 11 February 1848 contained attacks on other periodicals, one of which blamed

Belinsky and his acolytes for 'something close to communism'. Belinsky, who faced arrest any day, perhaps fortunately, died on 26 May.[17]

It was a wholly anti-intellectual age which attacked Belinsky and Uvarov in the same breath, but it became only more oppressive with a new wave of political violence in Europe. The February Revolution in Paris seemed to crown all suspicions on the side of the beleaguered imperial monarchies and all aspirations on the part of their liberal and nationalist opponents. News of the erection of the barricades sent rebellious reverberations throughout the continent. Demonstrations occurred in Berlin, from where the mood, and the news of the fall of the French monarchy, spread quickly to Poland, the Baltic States and Hungary. The news of Louis Phillipe's abdication reached Russia on 21 February, early March in Europe, and was greeted with horror. The year 1789 had been relived. 'Saddle your horses, gentlemen! A republic has been declared in France!' Nicholas is supposed to have said. In Vienna the revolutionary phoenix rose from the ashes, and Metternich resigned and fled. A fine opportunity presented itself to the men who hated Uvarov, among them Bulgarin and Stroganov, to secure their revenge.[18]

Uvarov's job for the past thirty-seven years had been to build a system of education in the Russian Empire to make revolution there impossible. If the revolution spread to Russia his entire work would be undone. His bulwark had been the tripartite slogan. Bulgarin now told the tsar this was nothing but empty words! It was a cover for writing 'little brochures and articles' on subjects which took a dilettante's fancy.[19] The three men who wanted Uvarov's job, Stroganov, Baron Korf and Dmitri Buturlin, took up the theme, complaining to the tsarevich that Uvarov was neglecting censorship and education. The tsar appointed the 'February' or 'Menshikov Committee' to investigate. The committee comprised the strictest advocates of censorship and included Buturlin and Korf themselves, as well as Stroganov's brother, alongside General Dubelt from the Third Department and a reluctant figurehead in Prince Menshikov. The express task of this committee was to watch over the Minister of National Enlightenment and take censorship out of his hands. It passed a measure banning anonymous literary contributions and demanding of editors that they keep from their readers ideas harmful to Russian morality and social order. A mere mention of revolution even in a private letter could now bring exile.

On 24 March Uvarov defended his record on censorship in a written report, but in so doing aligned himself with the periodicals under suspicion. The charges against him had been framed in such a way that any move he made would make them come true. He argued, even as Nikitenko became editor of The Contemporary, that allowing censors to be editors was not harmful, but the committee had no patience with his cautious and circuitous conservatism in a time of ardent reaction. The February committee yielded two months later to a permanent watch-dog committee, comprising Korf, Buturlin and a lawyer named Pavel Degai. This committee, chaired by Buturlin and operating almost entirely in secret, drew up an explicit list of unsatisfactory teachers and books. The net was cast very wide in accordance with Buturlin's zeal to uncover anything remotely suspicious in the periodical press. This '2nd April committee' most effectively usurped Uvarov's authority and caused horror in liberal circles. Nikitenko observed,

> The aim and the significance of this committee was shrouded in secrecy and for that reason seemed all the more terrifying. In the end, it gradually emerged that the committee was formed to investigate the current direction of Russian literature, the periodicals above all, and to draw up measures to curb it in future. Panic fear seized people's minds. Rumours went about that the committee was there especially to hunt out the noxious ideas of communism, socialism, and all forms of liberalism, to interpret them and to dream up cruel punishments for those who expounded them in print or those who knowingly allowed them to reach the public. People say Notes from the Fatherland and The Contemporary were at the head of the list of those accused of spreading these ideas. The Minister of National Enlightenment was not invited to the committee meetings, they asked no one for explanations, told no one what they were accused of, while all the time there were grave accusations. All thinkers and writers were filled with terror. Secret denunciations and spying complicated the matter still further. One began to fear every day, thinking that it might turn out to be the last one spent amongst one's family and friends.[20]

Uvarov was not informed of the committee's activities, but a list of complaints was later humiliatingly issued to him by the chief of Police in St Petersburg, after which he was reported to be in a pitiful state, 'trembling like a little government servant'. He was also saddened to have his privileged access to the tsar's family cut. Professor Vladimirsky-Budanov likened him to Agamemnon, propitiating the highest power with the sacrifice of his own creation, in order to save something which appeared to be greater. He also compared him to a sailor throwing valuable cargo overboard to try to save the ship. Granovsky was heard to say that Uvarov was 'having to step aside to make way for a ferocious Beast' in his Ministry.[21] Meanwhile minor figures came out of the woodwork to file their complaints. Grand Duchess Elena Pavlovna advised Uvarov that the tsar was still angry, partly because a woman called Van-der-Fur had complained about the distribution of jobs in the Ministry to her relatives. The grand duchess, a rare friend and ally, counselled Uvarov to resign.[22]

Uvarov however hung on, and on 8 May 1848, in the wake of overt manifestations of republican and anti-tsarist feeling in the provinces, where hundreds of thousands of Russian troops had been drafted, he set off on an inspection of educational facilities in Dorpat. Before he went his attention had been drawn once again to the general lack of knowledge in the Baltics of Russian, even by some of those who were supposed to teach it. He made his visit and was bound to lie. On 3 June he reported to the tsar that he was satisfied everything possible was being done. Permanent teachers of Orthodox theology had been appointed at the university, gymnasiums and other schools to make up for what the Minister admitted was a slackness in divinity. Uvarov did not believe repression could go any further.[23] He responded similarly when the tsar pressed him to ensure the loyalty of students in Poland. Uvarov argued no new measures were necessary. But this time he was overridden by Nicholas's military advisers, who began policing the school system.[24]

To the constant pressure on him to tighten the ideological net over institutions of learning at home Uvarov responded by enacting as few new disciplinary measures as he guessed would be tolerated. He saw nothing but loyalty among students, he reported.[25] Yet Ministry officials and teachers were now barred from travelling abroad. Vigorous attempts were made to keep out lower-class students with higher fees and legal barriers, and entrance examinations, the very opposite of what he had proposed in 1847, were made more difficult in order generally to cut numbers.

> We must prepare a brief for the Moscow Superintendent, bringing to his attention the fact that in what concerns the entrance and the leaving examinations all the regulations must be followed strictly, without the slightest deviation, and no concessions made to the idea of increasing student numbers; quite the contrary, he should make sure only that the students are worthy of their knowledge and reliable.

Uvarov briefed Prince Gregory Shcherbatov, an official in the Moscow Superintendent's office, on 14 May. On 13 September he told Golokhvastov that relations between students and professors, and students and university authorities had to be improved. Insofar as they were disrespectful on the one hand, and hostile on the other, they encouraged the students to band together and think of themselves as a distinct body. The professors had to be good, truly educated, rounded men and their influence on the students was meant to extend far wider than the lecture room. The authorities were instructed to keep an eye on the teaching staff, and watch the content of their lectures, but not automatically to take the part of the students against their teachers.

In that case there would arise the greatest evil of all: the students would begin to think of themselves as comprising a separate social class, a social class with its own views, its own voice and its own rights. That would be a harmful dream.[26]

Uvarov put up a powerful and impressive fight against his removal from office. In censorship with what little power remained to him he defiantly passed books and articles his colleagues thought impermissible.[27] Yet, as ever, he allowed his personal pettiness to undermine his strength. That September the chance arose to avenge himself against Stroganov by arbitrarily taking an extreme line of intolerance in a matter of censorship and Uvarov quickly availed himself of it. Ultimately, it seemed, he did not care which books were published and which suppressed, so long as they suited his political ends. But then he had never been a man of principle. The Imperial Society of Russian History and Antiquities at Moscow University had published a translation of a sixteenth-century English essay on Russia, Giles Fletcher's *Of the Russe Commonwealth* (1591). Thanks to a well-wisher Uvarov was the first to receive a copy off the press. Everyone accused Shevyrev and Pogodin of being the troublemaking messengers. Whoever it was, within an hour Uvarov had notified Nicholas of the essay's harmful content and retribution followed almost as swiftly. Publication was suspended, Stroganov was personally reprimanded by the tsar, and the innocent secretary of the Society was deprived of his professorship in Moscow and sent to Kazan'.[28]

All this violence and deceit and pettiness presented a terrible spectacle to a sensitive man. Nikitenko saw the feud between Uvarov and Stroganov, the dirty tricks played on each other by two government men, as a sign of the general immorality of the times. Russia, in ceasing to care for education and scientific truth, was receding from an age of superficial progress into primeval barbarity:

> If learning cannot exist without some trace of independence of mind and self-respect, we will kill learning – that is the basic idea of the obscurantists who have grown so strong that they think they can destroy the achievement of Peter for ever.

If a new darkness descended even the few moral people who had begun to act would be silenced, Nikitenko believed. The effect of the emergence of an intelligentsia would be nullified.[29]

Uvarov's concern was not as profound as Nikitenko's, though he continued absurdly to wish to protect two things: 'pure' education and his reputation. Never in his career was he able to see the nature and consequences of his unprincipled behaviour in a true light. And so a new campaign in self-defence began. If he was to be moved on posterity should know what he had achieved and what risked being wasted. Davydov was enlisted to help. As a rumour spread that the Russian universities were on the verge of being severely purged or closed altogether, Uvarov and Davydov worked together on the case for Uvarov's defence.

'On the Aim of Russian Universities and Their Part in the Education of Society' appeared in Nikitenko's The Contemporary in March 1849 under Davydov's name alone, and was essentially a catalogue of Uvarov's achievements. The two men later said their aim was to allay fears among staff and students that the rumours of closure would come true. Standards had risen and university education was valuable, Davydov told enemies of higher education and sceptics. Uvarov as Minister had increased numbers in all types of schools, furthered academic research, and tried to introduce Russian culture to the absorbed lands on the fringes of the empire, and to the Jews. Education had brought Russia such benefits over the past 100 years: could there really be people who now thought it could be done away with, without harm?

As Nicholas appeared to be turning the universities into military barracks with a curriculum of parade drill, Davydov and Uvarov declared that Russia needed more than its military academies and specialized institutes. Indeed these could not exist without the general educational support provided by the universities. Uvarov proceeded to spell out the Classical ideal which he had tried to preserve intact for almost forty years. Some people, believing the protagonists of the French Revolution Latinists, he said, objected to the teaching of Classics in the Russian higher schools. But such a view was ignorant, for all kinds of learned men were involved in the upheavals in Europe in the late eighteenth century. Political events were no reason to condemn learning as such. A true education in the ways of the Western world depended on understanding the close links between the ancient and the modern world, and Classics was the surest foundation for the study of man. As well as to develop individually Russia and Russian men had to learn to think and feel on a common basis of civilization, otherwise they would never be part of the great human family. They needed Classics to understand the common heritage. Classical education also taught a higher value than materialism and instructed men in the value of self-sacrifice for the common good. It was concentrated in the universities.

Speaking for Uvarov, and with his words, Davydov said all the Ministry's establishments were designed to provide a general education suitable for all men, according to their social position. But there were no grounds for saying the universities were mere imitations of German institutions, for they had their specific Russian ideological controls. Orthodoxy and Russian law were taught in all faculties; the students were under the control of inspectors, could only move course by examination, and wore uniforms; and the professors were answerable for the content of their lectures. Men's ideas were always in a state of flux, by their very nature, but the universities radiated loyalty to Uvarov's three principles, which kept them stable. The article untruthfully alleged that majority of students were anyway sons of the nobility.

'The Russian Universities' restated Uvarov's philosophy of a true Enlightenment. Indeed, but for the absence of advocacy that Russia should join Europe through membership of the Roman Catholic Church it brought him close to Chaadaev. He pointed out the need for general instruction as broadly as possible in the humanities, so that Russia, while retaining her uniqueness, could become part of the civilized world family. Yet the Russian note was strong. Uvarov in fact advanced in response to 1848 the same conservative case for Russia as Catherine did in reaction to 1789. Russia would safeguard an alternative, anti-revolutionary and anti-libertarian path:

> In the West the passion for reform, class unrest and contempt for tradition are the common ailment of men without a past or a future, who live only for the present. Neither faith nor law, nor rights nor duties exist for such people: they exploit disturbances in a daze of megalomania and self-interest. But in Orthodox and God-favoured Russia worship of Providence, devotion to the Tsar, love of Russia, these holy feelings have never ceased to nourish one and all; we were saved by them in years of misery; and we have been raised by them to the level of a great power, such as there has never been in the history of the world.[30]

But it was too late for eloquence. Uvarov's self-defence, never so well argued, was more than ignored; it was itself censured. Henceforth it was forbidden to write about the universities.

The man who had made himself the supreme instrument of Russian enlightenment found himself, as he had done in 1813 and 1821, pitted against fanaticism. Buturlin wrote to him on 17 March complaining about the article, which he said showed an 'inadmissible personal involvement in matters of state'. It was a perceptive comment. Uvarov genuinely wished to spread learning, but this personal passion, the only area where he was sincere, was his greatest political weakness.[31] Four days later Uvarov, taking up the complaint, replied directly to the tsar, as he did over the Magnitsky affair twenty-eight years previously, and for the second crucial time in his life he was snubbed. His letter contained a dramatic revelation of his authorship of the article halfway through, to no avail. The Censorship Committee summoned him in person on 2 April 1849, when he rehearsed the contents of his letter. He accepted full responsibility for the piece, and asked for all responsibility for censorship to be removed from his Ministry. Nicholas called the The Contemporary article 'indecent' and refused even that request. He told Uvarov to 'do as he was told' and 'keep his thoughts to himself'.[32]

On 22 April 1849, forty of the writers and thinkers whom Nikitenko had described as fearing for the safety of the next day were arrested, including the young Dostoevsky. Known as the Petrashevtsy, after their host, they had spent the last four years discussing revolutionary social ideas. They were atheists who believed in the communism of Fourier. They wanted among other things to see freedom of the press in Russia, but their ambitions never went beyond discussion. Twenty-three were put on trial after the group was denounced by a government spy, and all but two of them were sentenced to death. The terms were commuted to hard labour in Siberia, where Dostoevsky acquired the material for his pain-wracked novella, *From the House of the Dead*.

The authorities overreacted, not only in the arrest of the Petrashevtsy, but also in the retaliatory blows they rained on education and the printed word. All printed material was now to come under scrutiny, nearly all foreign works were censored, including those needed by academics, and bookshops were searched for forbidden Russian books. New inefficiencies were uncovered, such as the freedom under which postal book subscriptions had been operating, and rectified. Nicholas, on his way to Warsaw towards the end of May, 1849, signed an edict reducing university numbers to a mere 300 at each institution, an overall reduction of just under 40 per cent for the six institutions of the empire. Moscow alone had had 820 students in 1824. The bill, whose other provisions effectively ushered in the militarization of the universities until the end of Nicholas's reign, was handed to Uvarov without consultation to carry out. The act banned all academic trips abroad, demanded of professors that they deposit signed copies of all their lectures in the public library, and trimmed Classical languages from the curriculum of all but specialized students. The universities lost their autonomy and any trace of academic freedom.

It seemed a new dark age had descended on Russia. Granovsky reflected,

Even the most stout-hearted give way to despair and contemplate with indifference the sad sight that meets their eyes. The dead are the lucky ones. If only one could wipe out this intolerable state of things ... Russia is nothing but a living pyramid of crimes, frauds and abuses, full of spies, policemen, rascally governors, drunken magistrates and cowardly aristocrats, all united in their desire for theft and pillage and supported by six hundred thousand automata with bayonets.[33]

Uvarov was crushed. He put the edict into effect as slowly and as loosely as he could. On top of the blow of professional humiliation followed the death of his wife on 14 July, and he spent the summer of 1849, according to Pletnev, 'in a most disturbed state of mind' in the dacha outside Petersburg on the Karpovka river, where he had built the little summerhouse in the memory of Stein. He was alone, in an empty house, and saw almost no one. With the coming of autumn, and a new bureaucratic year, he had no sooner returned to work when on 6 September he suffered a stroke. For twenty-four hours his right arm and leg were paralysed; his speech became forever slightly slurred. He acquired a resident doctor, who prescribed rest, and was judged better by 16 September. Nevertheless the tsar officially released him from his duties as Minister on the 20th. Davydov noted how suddenly and unexpectedly the illness had struck.[34]

Pletnev says Uvarov was released by the tsar on his own request, and with the most flattering words, but his account of the events and feelings surrounding Uvarov's fall is conspicuously incomplete. Shcherbatov said Uvarov was the victim of an intrigue which had long tried to defeat him, and that he fell victim to 'envy, obscurantism and the pseudo-political wisdom of parasites'. Though his acolytes feared for the loss of their protector, Pogodin was genuinely upset and noted in his diary entry on 13 September: 'Uvarov has been dismissed and is ill. I feel sorry for him. Protasov [Uvarov's deputy] is Minister.' The next day Pogodin's spirits sank still lower: 'I read the newspapers and thought about our times. What a dead land. I need consolation.' On the 28th, as he took stock of Nicholas's draconian new measures Pogodin wrote with a frankness belying his years of Official Nationality: 'In the 150 years since Peter we have not persuaded ourselves that the sciences are useful. What striking proof of our barbarity.'

Grand Duchess Elena Pavlovna was among the invalid's visitors. Pogodin meant to come from Moscow to join them, but did not manage it. In the meantime he wrote to a friend: 'I want to comfort him. He is a good and clever man, although there is much you can say against him.' Davydov noted on 29 October: 'There is no perfection on earth; but if for academics the most important thing is to have their achievements understood, then the Count [Uvarov] was a perfect head, despite all the shortcomings of his administration.'[35]

The professor found Uvarov struggling with himself, justifying the course of events, saying all had turned out for the best, but he added that those who knew Uvarov knew better. Nikitenko, as ever, was compassionate:

Uvarov suffered a great deal in the last years of his Ministry. When his position was in jeopardy much became clear to him and more than once I was a witness to his grief. Then I grew to know this man better for what he was and was able to appreciate his good aspects – his undoubted intellect, which during his time of strength was often pushed into the background by his vanity and petty self-love. Unfortunately he ... did not have the strengths a man needs in stormy and dangerous times. Rostovtsev was right when he said to me the other day: 'No man who thinks deeply and to the heart of the matter, would agree now to take the name of Minister of National Enlightenment. For that he would need the kind of colossal strength none of us have.'[36]

19

From the house of the dead

What shall I say to Ye;

Since my defence must be your

condemnation?

You are at once offenders and accusers,

Judges and executioners! Proceed

Upon your power!

BYRON, COPIED OUT BY UVAROV

As the obscurantists took over, with the good, devout, but weak Prince Shirinsky-Shikhmatov a puppet minister, the university students were drilled on the parade-ground, and two cannons were mounted outside Moscow university. Pogodin said he smelt the graveyard in Russia, 'physically and morally', which was a devastating, quasi-Chaadaevan comment from an Official Nationalist and honorary Slavophile.[1]

Uvarov stayed in St Petersburg until the next summer, on medical advice keeping busy and seeing old friends and colleagues. But in June he abandoned Peter's capital for Porechie, and this time decided not to leave. He spent most of the next six years there, putting his papers in order and writing isolated chapters of his memoirs, some of which were published in the periodical press. His health, though not good, gave him the time for private reflection he had not enjoyed since he was a young man abroad. He dusted off the Rousseau, Voltaire and Byron he had proscribed for other men and marshalled his thoughts. The Academy where he continued as president heard a number of the new papers he wrote and at the age of sixty-seven he finished his doctoral thesis and submitted it to the prestigious University of

Dorpat. It was in Latin on the origins of the Bulgarians.[2] Other publications were a book on ancient history and an article on the affinity between Marlowe and Shakespeare.[3] Yet, he suggested, public office would have continued to lure him, had he been in full health. In 1850, after he received a medal from the tsar, the Order of the Holy Apostle Andrew, in recognition of his past services, he had even contemplated returning to St Petersburg. He remained ever capable of self-deception.

But retirement meant at last official dispensation to live in the past, which suited Uvarov's nature. As an intellectual he had always found history his greatest consolation. Granovsky had been with him in the summer of 1848, and their friendship first eased the pain of public defeat, then the death of Catherine Uvarov. Fittingly, Uvarov's first Academy paper, written during the summer of 1850, discussed the impossibility of historical certainty. When he read 'Is Historical Certainty Progressing?' to his fellow academicians in French on 25 October, he attached this note to the permanent secretary, Fuss:

> During my stay in the country, amongst the relaxations essential in my collapsed state of health, I looked for pleasure to the diversions of the mind. As a result I wrote a short essay on a question which concerns everyone. I ask you to present this essay to a general meeting as a feeble token of my eternal attachment to the Academy and my unchanging devotion to intellectual pursuits, which have sometimes delighted me and sometimes consoled me in the different circumstances of life, and have never lost anything of their salutary effect.[4]

Uvarov doubted whether historians possessed greater certainty as time went on. The amount of material available to the modern historian was so vast he could not take it all into account. Moreover scepticism, increasingly present in all branches of human inquiry, undermined the very quest for certainty. Modern history, assisted by the invention of printing, was no nearer establishing certainty than ancient history, and had now forfeited the chance to pretend that fixed truths existed, something Uvarov believed was necessary to console the mass of people, because modern impartiality and scepticism left a gap which was filled by unstable and dangerous popular opinion. In the cases of the French Revolution and Napoleon, popular interpretation of how history should unfold had led further and further from the truth, because opinion was constantly mutable. In his lifetime Uvarov had seen the idea of the world conqueror and the significance of the revolution transformed from curse to godsend. The ancient world, by contrast, offered a single, gospel interpretation of the past. This ancient history was not necessarily more true, but it was more certain. Uvarov took the case of Homer. Centuries of faith had established him as one man and even now, despite undermining new discoveries, people went on believing in a man called Homer, and that was good. Uvarov objected to popular minds performing the task of myth-making instead of high priests and poets. He found it politically dangerous. The example of how the image of Bonaparte had become transformed in fifty years from a tyrant to a liberal caused him to comment,

> Out of this powerful genius, bitter, and half-wild, out of this declared enemy of the Revolution, out of this solid, muscular figure, this positive and absolute spirit, a propagator of liberal ideas has been constructed, an apostle of democracy, a symbolic personality, in short a myth suited above all to take its place amongst the misty phantoms of Ossian.

He who remembered Napoleon would have nothing of his Romantic image 'fabricated by common usage, with the verses of Béranger and the stories of Marc St.-Hilaire'. Uvarov believed in the man 'of great qualities and great errors' who survived in the memory of his contemporaries, or Napoleon he was perceived by serious men. Serious men were those 'familiar with the calm study of men and things'. Modern historians seemed to lack this seriousness, which also entailed political responsibility. Voltaire was amusing, but cavalier with the truth. His was the form of history which corresponded most nearly to modern religious doubt:

> Either all positive appreciation is lacking, or the writer's conviction is stifled by the fear of enunciating a moral principle; it is a historical form all the more dangerous for leading more or less directly to the negation of good and evil, for exiling Providence from history, and substituting for the great laws of social order some artificial mechanism or other, created by chance, and which vilifies the dignity of man in depriving him of his best hopes.

The passion of Uvarov's time for analysis had removed from history its capacity to offer spiritual support:

> The passion of the century for dissolvent analysis, the hatred of all the syntheses, whether they be religious or historical and moral, the absolute lack of faith carried over into the realm of a reality more or less mysterious, present difficulties unknown to the Ancients.[5]

Uvarov attacked the idea that fact had value in itself, without any necessary moral, social or religious context; he attacked the spread of information for its own sake, without form and without commitment. The modern intellectual world seemed anarchic, irresponsible and ugly to Uvarov, because it did not help people find truth and peace. 'Is Historical Certainty Progressing?' fought old battles with the young Uvarov's conviction that the world – or Russia, at least – needed a firm moral and social order, rooted in Providence. It also explained the role of religion in his tripartite view of government. Religion was the repository of national wisdom and the basis for national history; it existed for the very purpose of creating mass certainty. Uvarov believed above all in the social and political value of religion. In his lifetime the effects of its unchallenged reign over the common man had been regrettably undone.

Sergei Soloviev charged Uvarov with atheism, but the accusation was both wrong and irrelevant. It was religion Uvarov believed in, as a force for social and political cohesion, and he believed in it with the same strength of moral and aesthetic conviction with which other men believed in God. He did not make clear the sophistication of his position to the people, but that was hypocrisy or prudence, not atheism. Uvarov's essay omitted any reference to the German philosophy of history which was shaping contemporary understanding in Europe and Russia. But the fact remained that his ideas, dictated by the desire for social stability and moral certainty, had developed along lines parallel to Hegel's, and that new imaginative certainties were emerging. In 1851 the spiritual lacunae of the modern world had already been filled by the omnipresence of the Weltgeist, and Hegel had inspired Marx. Uvarov was deliberately ignoring the nature and challenge of modern history, and the emergence of historicist ideology, though he himself had been part of its creation, or fabrication, in Russia. Had he lived another fifty years he ought, logically, to have welcomed the certainty of historical materialism that brought Soviet Russia new certainty after the demise of the old Providence that had underpinned tsarism. He was always caught, between Russian political need and German intellectual speculation; between what was really new in European thought and what Russia could bear to implement, in what adulterated form; between his conservativism on behalf of Russia and the greater freedoms he allowed his European-educated mind, in the privacy of his own study.

The autumn of 1850 and the winter of 1851 were meanwhile a time for personal reminiscence as much as intellectual self-collection. He remembered Germaine de Stael among the literary figures of his youth, and obliquely through her he rekindled his erotic fascination with Madame Rombecq. These notes towards an essay were found among his posthumous papers:

I had been warned that a visit from Madame de Stael was expected, who had just arrived the day before in Vienna. And indeed, about eight in the evening her arrival was announced, and she entered the drawing room, where Count Kobentzl, Madame Rombecq and I were at the time. To show how exactly I have retained my memories I will describe first of all her external appearance and her dress. Of medium height, quite plump, she was dressed that day in a green dress with big gold stars upon it. On her head she wore a brown turban, holding back her hair, which was black, like a crow's wing. On her breast she wore a large miniature – a portrait of [her father] Monsieur Necker; a shawl was carelessly thrown about her shoulders; she had in her hands her favourite toy, a fan, which when she was caught without it, she would replace with a small piece of paper; and thus was completed her rather loud outfit. The Empire-line dress shortened her figure greatly, and made her look somehow dumpy and heavy, hardly reminiscent of the image of Corinne ... . After we exchanged the initial pleasantries usual in such situations, the conversation took on a light and agreeable character, thanks to the tact of Madame Rombecq, to the exclusively obliging nature of Count Kobentzl, and above all to the exquisite self-confidence of Madame de Stael, which enhanced her attractiveness. To complete the description of her appearance, I must mention her indisputably beautiful, very lively eyes and her very white, pleasingly plump hands, while the rest of her was vulgar and almost ugly. What struck people above all about her was her genuinely unforced conversation and the simplicity of her expressions; there was nothing contrived, nothing artificial to give away the lady writer. She approached the most diverse subjects with the same freedom, and in the manners of speech characteristic of good society was without any doubtful addition of neologisms. She even tried to change the direction of the conversation if some little-informed party happened to reveal he intended to converse with her on the subject of her literary fame. She paid a great deal of attention to the tiniest details of society life and to the countless trifles so characteristic of salon intercourse. This was how I saw Madame de Stael at our first meeting, and this was how I always saw her afterwards. Drawn as it were into another sphere of ideas, she only showed all the variety of resource of her magnificent eloquence when the conversation touched on the most abstract themes or discussed the earth-shattering questions of the day.

Uvarov's memoir devoted four distant lines to Kobentzl, but drew a fond picture of Madame Rombecq:

She was one of the most original women, and for those who did not know her personally it is difficult to render her likeness: an inexhaustible goodness of heart, sincere sensitivity, an elevated mind, a lively imagination – all this combined in her with a gay, playful character, close to joking, but which never exceeded the limits of femininity. At the time about which I am speaking Countess Rombecq was carrying out the duties of hostess at the house of Count Kobentzl and performed them with her characteristic absolute charm and tact. Russians always found a warm welcome there, and I adopted by them like a son: with Madame Rombecq I felt calm, as if I were under my parents' roof.

These notes were never worked into anything publishable, however. Having already done justice to French eighteenth-century society in exile in de Ligne, Uvarov put together in his last years only a collection of idiosyncratic impressions.[6]

More successful, in terms of publication, were his literary reminiscences the same winter on the subject of Arzamas. Dashkov and Alexander Turgenev were dead, and Zhukovsky was abroad and ill, but Vyazemsky, Bludov and Uvarov were still in touch. The Contemporary published a short account by Uvarov of a private gathering to celebrate Bludov's fifty years in government service, and the choice of publication was an act of mild defiance. Uvarov was not yet defeated. He described the anniversary party, which took the form of a literary pantomime. It was an occasion to forget the harshness of political vicissitude and put on the costumes of a past culture, and to glory in the memory of Karamzin:

The evening began with a drawing-room play. The stage depicted a room in which the players were gathered, in costumes as if they were about to rehearse various plays, preparing for a performance at home. Between conversations and preparations they rehearsed several scenes one after the other. Scenes were played from the old opera of Boiledieu, *Ma tante Aurore*, with its famous couplets; the three first scenes from Fonvizin's *The Brigadier*, several scenes from the comedy *Werther* and finally the scene from *Dmitri Donskoy* [an opera by Anton Rubinstein] in which a Russian warrior tells Ksenia about the battle against [the fourteenth-century Tatar leader] Mamay. The resonant verse of Ozerov, splendidly spoken, made a strong impression, as did the actors themselves. Taking advantage of the fact that they were only supposed to be rehearsing for a real performance, they asked the warrior to recite the words of Dmitri Donskoy which end the tragedy: 'The heart's first duty to you tsar of tsars ...'

When the performance ended a young man appeared on the stage and handed over a letter, saying: 'I have come straight from Arzamas, that is from [Uvarov's dacha on the river] Karpovka.' The letter was read out: 'From the ruins of Arzamas, from an ailing, despondent Starushka, regards and a warm welcome to his old friend Cassandra Priamovna, sitting not among the ruins of Troy, but in the midst of a loving family and friends. Starushka would like to include in this letter all the memories of youth, all the dreams of bygone days, in short an echo of those attractive and amusing debates which the silent banks of the Karpovka have forgotten ... . The one who used to sit in front went by the name of Svetlana [Zhukovsky] ... poor Starushka will have to struggle with wielding a steel, foreign pen, for they say that you cannot find a single Arzamas quill in the market these days ... . How everything has changed!'[7]

Uvarov painted a fuller picture of Arzamas in The Contemporary in another longer article that summer, again stressing its apolitical devotion to literature and its closeness to Karamzin. He recalled the great controversy of the day between the Arzamasians and the Shishkovites, and compared it to the war between the Romanticists and the Classicists in France and Germany. Aware of evoking a lost world, when the arts were private, apolitical and familial, Uvarov envisaged a history of Russian literature which would acknowledge the importance of the early century, before the birth of the socially committed and politically active intelligentsia.[8]

The Russian neoclassical age lived on in Uvarov's memory, and he continued to look to the Classical world for inspiration. In a paper written over the summer of 1851, read to the Academy on 10 October, he described the urn he had acquired during his trip to Rome in 1843, whose frieze seemed to confirm his speculations in *Eleusis*. In passing he noted the doors of Porechie were always open to those who came to visit in the name of science and art.[9]

His last paper to the Academy, read on 6 February 1852, spoke of Friedrich Graefe, his old teacher of Greek who used to be one of his Porechie visitors and had died before Christmas. On their last meeting in July 1850, when they had walked in the park at Porechie on a magnificent morning, Graefe had lamented Uvarov's career in the Ministry. 'It's just that you could have been such an excellent Hellenist,' he said. Uvarov, anxious to extract glory for himself even from the dead, hastened to record this judgement for posterity.[10]

But now everywhere death was snatching his friends away, removing his last comforts. In April 1852 Zhukovsky, almost blind, expired in a hotel room in Baden-Baden. His body was brought back to Russia, where he was buried in Moscow alongside Karamzin in the Alexander Nevsky Monastery. Uvarov had last been in touch with him in 1847 when the poet wrote from Frankfurt am Main to say he had translated the Odyssey. He recalled Russia's debt to Uvarov as a pioneer of the use of the hexameter in Russian versions of the classics and thanked him for organizing a jubilee celebration in his honour earlier that year. Uvarov wrote briefly in reply. The occasion of the poet's death brought forth old affections, which Uvarov marked with a monument at Porechie. The little summerhouse, recalling the one dedicated to Stein at the dacha near St Petersburg, was designed by the painter A.P. Bryulov, who was staying in the country with Uvarov when news of the death arrived. It was built in Moscow, by men considered among the best craftsmen of the day, and erected in Porechie the next spring. Uvarov, who had in his study Kiprensky's 1818 portrait of Zhukovsky, also invited Bryulov to make a print from it. He wanted his love of Zhukovsky to be known, in which respect the monument was a brilliant idea, for it still stands today, and contemporary guidebooks connect Uvarov's name indelibly with the gentle poet.[11]

Yet death was too much present, even for Uvarov's vainglory to hide. By 1853 he had ceased to write, except an annual request to the tsar, on 1 January, to be permitted to reside in Moscow. The letter of 1852 told Nicholas he was a steadfast and enlightened ruler at a time when everything around him in Europe was crumbling as a result of years of wrong-headed idealism. Uvarov's own fifty-year jubilee came in March 1853 when he received tributes from the tsar and the Academy. He tried to shrug off the occasion as unimportant. On 5 July 1854 he wrote asking to be relieved of his post as president because of illness. The job was offered to Stroganov, who declined it.

Pogodin saw Uvarov at the beginning of 1855 in Moscow, where he had rented accommodation to be close to a doctor. He was sliding towards death. Every day of life was a struggle.

> It was sad and painful to see him an invalid, hardly able to move his legs or articulate his barely audible words, and to remember his former vitality, brilliance and allure. He often expressed a desire to set eyes on his beloved Porechie just once more, but at the same time he was afraid to set off on the journey for fear of dying on the road.[12]

Uvarov quoted from Cicero in his *Eleusis* that the best religion is one which elevates a man and teaches him to live agreeably and die with hope. He wished to depart with patience and dignity. Scattered through his writing are two thoughts on death: that it holds no fear for those who depart, and should cause them no regret; that the greatest human pain is suffered by those who remain. At the age of twenty he had been shocked by the insensitivity of the Viennese, as he saw it, towards death. The empress of Austria had died, and her subjects continued to live merrily as if nothing had happened. This belief that men should pause to consider and respect death was one of Uvarov's most attractive convictions and one of the few which he did not, observing it in himself, inflate with vanity. In turn in the 1820s, he observed the deaths of Alexander, Alexander's wife Elizabeth, the dowager empress Maria Feodrovna and Princess Charlotte Lieven. He became an official threnodist, claiming among his models Tacitus and Bossuet, and it was the closest he came to writing the kind of history he idealized, which was responsible myth. In the obituary for Elizabeth he noted the emotions evoked by death, of pain and hope in infinity, as being beyond the reach of human wisdom, however eloquent, however sincere.[13]

Pogodin recounted Uvarov's final months in the summer of 1855:

The penultimate stroke afflicted him at the beginning of August. When he recovered consciousness he asked to take the sacraments. (He had previously postponed for Porechie the carrying out of this Christian obligation.) It was midnight. He lost consciousness again. In the morning he woke and immediately asked where the priest was. He was told the priest had been summoned. In anticipation he had his nurse read out the Lord's Prayer and followed in his thoughts the words of the prayer, crossing himself. The priest came, heard his confession and administered the sacraments. He became a little better, but it was clear his whole organism had been struck.[14]

The arrival of his son Alexei from Petersburg and his daughter Princess Alexandra Urusova from Nizhny Novgorod raised his spirits, and Pogodin remarked will and habit taking over occasionally in the living corpse. Uvarov would ask for news of events in science, literature and politics and try to hide his sickness as a matter of decorum. On his birthday, 25 August, he appeared briefly at the meal table wearing a white tie. Alexei and Alexandra had come to bury him, and he was not quite dead. Around this time, in a parting gesture, he freed his domestic serfs. The Uvarov children left before 2 September, when their father suffered a final stroke. He was unconscious for thirty-six hours, breathing hard and irregularly, until his life ended peacefully at four minutes to eleven on the evening of 4 September. On his death bed Uvarov was surrounded by strangers, mainly men of rank, making the occasion suitably impersonal: a couple of professors, a couple of artists, a couple of university doctors, were present, noted Pogodin, and a couple of the servants he had freed. Uvarov departed life as distantly as he had lived it, under a canopy of prestigious names and representative men. The artist Nikolai Ramazanov made a death mask and the anatomy professor Sokolov embalmed the body. The scull, he said, was unusually correctly formed. The university posted six students to take turns watching over the coffin day and night, and masses were said before it twice a day, supported by a city choir. Professors, students, civil servants, ministers and Moscow citizens from all walks of life came to pay their last respects, crowding into the small suite of rented rooms until there was no more place to stand.

On 9 September, a Friday, the coffin was carried out by professors and borne by students in procession to the university church. Stroganov's son was observed among the bearers. Deacons of the university followed with Uvarov's medals, with Shevyrev carrying the Order of St Andrew. Pupils from various academic institutions walked in orderly pairs in front and a huge crowd assembled filling the surrounding streets of the Arbat, Vzdvizhenka and

Mokhovaya. Some of Uvarov's peasants and serfs from Porechie came and begged to carry the coffin. The body lay in state overnight. The funeral service was held on 10 September, and according to Pogodin was attended by all those who were obliged to the former minister of Public Instruction for their professional start in life. Metropolitan Filaret officiated and among the huge crowd of dignitaries, government figures and schoolchildren Grand Duchess Elena Pavlovna came to pay her last respects. The two Uvarov children were back in Moscow in time to attend.

At the end of the service several professors wanted to say a few words in praise of Uvarov. Professor Menshikov had written some Greek poetry; Professor Leontiev wanted to say a few words in Latin about Uvarov's acquaintance with the Latin classics and his knowledge of archaeology; Shevyrev wanted to draw attention to his relations with Russian literature, his membership of Arzamas, his connections with Zhukovsky, Bludov, Dashkov and Batyushkov and on his work for Greek translation into Russian. Pogodin intended to say something about the unseen efforts Uvarov made in times of 'contrary European circumstances' to protect the university and its academic business. But 'some misunderstanding' led to these tributes never being paid. They were, Pogodin, noted, thought to be out of place. The ex-minister and president of the Academy was not to be praised in public. When Bludov succeeded him at the Academy after his death he did not once mention Uvarov.

The coffin of an officially not disgraced, but certainly disregarded, man was now taken in slow procession along Dorogomilovskaya to the Smolensk road. Longinov says the students, who had their own response to his passing, insisted on carrying it,

> feeling that they had lost one of the chief architects of the university in its brilliant contemporary state, a man who by his labours and concerns had prepared from them the fruits of enlightenment which they were now enjoying.[15]

The body, at last lowered onto a carriage as it left the city, was taken to Porechie, where it was met by serfs from the estate and carried into the church there at Kholm, where after another requiem mass Uvarov was buried alongside his brother.

Uvarov's work in education was temporarily undone by the censorship terror of 1848–55, but he had created the foundations, in the universities and the Academy, on which a more liberal and better-educated Russia might build. At the Education Ministry Shirinsky-Shikhmatov reigned only four years before he died in May 1853. During that period the teaching of logic and psychology was entrusted to the professors of theology, the teaching of philosophy abolished, and all contacts with abroad remained suspended. The universities lost their academic freedom completely, with Nicholas insisting personally that morality was more important than education, and that the key to morality was faith. The tsar said Russia was practically alone in the modern world in that it still possessed a majority of active believers, united in their religious outlook. His intervention in education marked a return to the obscurantism of the early 1820s, just as Uvarov had predicted would happen when he left office.[16]

Shirinsky-Shikhmatov was replaced by A.S. Norov, a man Vyazemsky and Nikitenko both found sympathetic and honest in his devotion to education. Vyazemsky noted that he was not Uvarov's equal intellectually, but had a much warmer and more loving heart, was a purer and nobler man, who stood more firmly on one leg than Uvarov had done on two.[17]

Uvarov's personal legacy was concentrated in his son and his estate. Alexei graduated from St Petersburg University, where he studied in the philological-historical department of the philosophy faculty, in 1845. Heavily under his father's influence and benefiting from the paternal privileges, Alexei Uvarov went on to study in Berlin and Heidelberg (despite his Russophile tendency), and initially entered the Foreign Ministry. But his real passion was archaeology, an interest equally nurtured by Uvarov, and he began in the 1850s the excavations on Russian territory that quickly made him the country's leading authority. Combining archaeological research with a diplomatic career he travelled widely in the empire, and stayed for long periods in Greece and Italy studying Byzantine art. In 1864 he became one of the founders of the Moscow Archaeological Society and its first chairman. At the Academy of Sciences he created a prize in his father's memory. The woman Alexei married, Praskovya Shcherbatov, shared his love for archaeology, and together they carried out their research and brought back tokens of their finds to Porechie. They had the library catalogued[18] and new trees planted in the grounds.

Alexei Uvarov was indeed a fervent Russophile. He disliked French fashions in food, language and manners in Russian society. But he seemed to have had no interest whatsoever in politics, and only a very marginal one in education in the few years he served as a superintendent in Moscow.[19] When he died of a brain haemorrhage at the age of fifty-nine his wife continued their substantial archaeological work, much appreciated by posterity. Porechie became the first Moscow Archaeological Museum under her direction. Later its contents were transferred to the Historical Museum on Red Square, in Moscow,[20] where, high up under the roof, around a vast single table reserved for the collective use of archivists, the present author, began her study of Uvarov in Soviet times which she found kindred to Uvarov's own. For over the now almost 230 years since the French Revolution, and a century since Russia's own revolution, it has remained hard to overcome the instinctive conservatism and reaction inspired by Western liberalism.

20

Afterword

The struggle for a modern Russia

A hundred and twenty-eight years after events in France so shocked Catherine the Great and her court, among them the parents of a young boy called Sergei Uvarov, the Revolution finally befell Russia. Uvarov, who when he died in 1855 had wanted to hold his country back fifty years, did so exactly, if Russia's twentieth-century upheaval is dated from 1905.

From the first years of Uvarov's maturity a more open, more modern Russia was on the march, destined to force out the Uvarovs and their long privileged kind. Uvarov's son Alexei did not live to see the storming of the Winter Palace in St Petersburg on the night of 26 October 1917. But Praskovya Uvarova, his widow, nee Princess Shcherbatova, encountered the force of the Revolution directly.[1] A member of the wrong social class for the coming Communist era, she had her property, which was mainly Porechie and its contents, confiscated. In 1918 she fled abroad, aged seventy-eight, and died six years later in Yugoslavia.[2] There were no children from the marriage, but she left a memoir entitled: *The Past: Happy Days Long Ago*, published by a repentant State Historical Museum in 2005.

In 1914 Baedecker recommended Porechie as a tourist attraction, but its value as a positive testament to Russian aristocratic life was short-lived. After 1917 it became a state museum. It was damaged severely when Nazi German forces reached as far as Mozhaisk in 1941. After the Great Patriotic War it was partially restored as a holiday retreat for a branch of the armed services. Yet the gardens and surrounding forests survived and since the change of 1991 the buildings have been partially restored by private subscription, thanks to the new moral-political orthodoxy in post-Soviet Russia to welcome back the tsarist past.

Uvarov himself remains a controversial and neglected figure. No Soviet historian wrote a biography or a monograph, and post-Soviet historians are astonished to discover him now, coupled with the fact that their countrymen and countrywomen have never heard of this friend of Stein and Pozzo di Borgo and de Stael. After not quite equal neglect in the West during the same period – the great exceptions are Alexandre Koyré in his 1929 study of *Philosophy and the national problem in early nineteenth-century Russia*' and Cynthia H. Whittaker in a career devoted to Uvarov's achievements in Russian education – he has, finally, resurfaced as an important thinker in the West's understanding of Russia, but only with negative connotations. A history of Russian thought published in 2010 understands his significance principally in relation to the twenty-first-century Russia of alternating Prime Minister and President Vladimir Putin. Uvarov's slogan 'in many ways applies just as well to Putin's Russia' and 'The spirit of Count Uvarov's trilogy remains a force to be reckoned with in twenty-first century Russia', the study's editors conclude.[3] Missing from their account in the view of the present author is analysis of how Uvarov's slogan came into being, with particular reference to the French Revolution, and of consideration of his many critically unexamined writings, where his political views are to be found expressed in more detail and with far greater subtlety than an official slogan can convey. On the other hand, the continuity between Uvarov's conservatism and the conservatism of present-day official Russia is evident. Indeed, in the last almost two centuries of Russian history his kind of thinking has rarely gone away. Putin himself seems to be aware of the difficult issue of this continuity in finding the revolution of October 1917 difficult to classify. In 2016, ahead of the pending centenary, he gave orders that it should not be celebrated officially, but, using words that Uvarov himself might have spoken, left 'to experts to discuss'.[4] Those experts might well contend that, beneath the surface of officially progressive Marxist–Leninist state philosophy, 'Orthodoxy, Autocracy, Official Nationality' also guided Soviet domestic politics over the greater part of the duration of Soviet power, from 1917 to 1991. As I suggested above, the three terms of Uvarov's slogan, taken together found their counterpart in Lenin's term *'partiinost'*. Party-Mindedness required loyalty to the Party line, to the twentieth-century equivalent of the autocracy, before all else and unthinkingly.[5] In the words of a slogan that used to be displayed in Moscow streets, 'The Party is the mind, the honour and the conscience of our epoch'.[6] Party loyalty was officially owed to international proletarianism, but as many genuinely internationally minded admirers of the ideal found to their sadness, it bolstered an old Russian Great Power agenda. The converse of that observation is that 'Official Nationality' continues to tell us a great deal about modern, and contemporary, Russia and the tensions in its relations with the liberal world. Uvarov's life, concentrated in his experience of a radical division between his Western-educated longings and his political loyalty to official Russia, provides a model by which we can better understand the continuing paradoxes of the Russian political scene.

Bearing in mind Uvarov's life and work, and in particular his love–hate relationship with the West, his fear of the European-style liberalization of his country in tandem with his longing for European civilization and scholarship, it's possible to suppose that Russia's leaders, and its leading non-dissident cultural figures, and its compliant businessmen, differ little today from their nineteenth-century counterpart, in the quiet division they make, internally, and for themselves, between the free ways of the West, and all that can be gained from those ways for the sake of Russian prestige. They are likely to be just as aware as Uvarov was of the degree of internal political control necessary for Russia to maintain itself as a nation and a power at all. Such a duality, such hypocrisy even, is hardly intelligible to Western liberals whose politics long ago cast aside the possible distinction between the public and private and came to rest on the value of political sincerity, or, at least, the appearance of sincerity. It is a duality which entails strange discordances in public behaviour on the Russian side. A sort of miming of political obeisance is required, but it doesn't have to be believable or emotionally convincing.

I have argued that the discordances in the officially required style of behaviour on the part of high government officials began exactly at that moment when nineteenth-century Russia decided to preserve as its own mission the ways of French *ancien régime*. A unified modern Russia, an artificial construct because the aristocracy were never part of the same country as the common people, took with it, into public office, old forms of French aristocratic behaviour unconstrained by popular checks and balances. The most prominent aspects of Nicholaevan political life, the desire to forestall popular revolution at all costs, and the aim of a man like Uvarov to present himself as representative of a public order he didn't really believe in, to uphold order in a Russia he didn't really like, seemed to me live on in Soviet Russia, a country I knew first-hand, a hundred and twenty years after his death, and may well now replicate themselves in the post-Soviet country. The outstanding need, as I have argued elsewhere, has always been to preserve domestic order and a degree of national intellectual coherence in a polity otherwise desperately prone to schism.[7]

Richard Sennet in *The Fall of Public Man* studied examples of the old-style behaviour in the Western context. It can be only conjecture in the present study, but any reader of those examples of boastfulness, fantastic and grotesque appearances, and confidence in falsehood for the sake of falsehood, would recognize a sister culture across time if such a reader also knew Soviet Russia. He or she can make independent assumptions about Russia in the present day. The reader interested in comparing the pre-1789 eighteenth-century West with Russian history ever since might also recognize in Burke's description of the new actors in revolutionary politics, breathing a religious spirit on the one hand, and needing men of 'litigious' nature to do their public work for them, a picture of the style of Russian dissent which was also born of the spirit of 1789. For there were always two sides to the coin, with those who rejected the imposition of an authoritarian and unequal patrimony becoming ever more vocal as time went on.

It is possible that the Russian literature of conscience grew up as an antidote to the pervasive play-acting of conventional Russian public life. In its tsarist incarnation the false tradition demanded an anarchist (Tolstoy) and a metaphysician (Dostoevsky) justly to expose it. In Soviet times the novelist, historian and religious figure of Alexander Solzhenitsyn was in the same mould. Meanwhile, I have mentioned many times in this study the courageous critic Belinsky. Belinsky was, specific to their decades in common, Uvarov's moral opposite. He was the man who called Uvarov 'The Minister of Darkness': an exaggeration, but a mark of their times. Belinsky seemed to create out of himself that chiaroscuro moral world of striving and self-abnegation which later foreign readers, through Tolstoy and Dostoevsky, loved and admired as Russian literature as the spirit of Russian literature. Belinsky was the critic for whom, in spirit, what Henry James called the 'loose and baggy' nineteenth-century novels were written. Those novels were huge testaments of spiritual conflict, closer in shape and form to the unpredictable, erratic, infinite inner life than to the classical ideal of a finished work of art. They passionately opposed themselves to Uvarov's neoclassical idea of a conservative, but also deadened, Russia in which the most appropriate art form was tightly controlled, formal and self-censoring.

Equally in 'the Marvellous Decade' of 1838–48 that set itself against Uvarov, and in Soviet times, from the 'Thaw' in the early 1960s, a minority, dissident culture, opposed itself to officialdom. It was appalled by the hypocrisy, and the hidden use of force, and the deadness, and the lack of concern for individual integrity, and the murder of the individual creative spark, embodied in the autocracy. Uvarov's life shows how officials of his kind hardly admired the Russia they were employed to oppress. The censor Alexander Nikitenko rightly observed the existential misery of his position and has been seen as a tragic figure. Uvarov was less likeable. He corresponded with Goethe and was honoured as a great public man in France, whereas writers like Pushkin and Gogol suffered directly because of his doings. His distant descendants in pursuit of Official Nationality by another name were dead-eyed officials who discreetly imported luxury Western consumer goods and lived in a moral nowhere. He lived in a notionally continuing eighteenth-century France, and in his study of ancient world.

Part of Uvarov's extraordinary, neglected story is how instrumental he was in repressing moral dissent. In fact by doing his best to thwart everything we hold dear about Russia's first literary golden age he fomented the revolt which made it happen.

To recap a final time, his idea of nationality began from Russia's fear of infection by the freer West. He bolstered that fear with Russian pride, and stoked the desire for Russian culture to hold its own. What resulted was perversely a great culture which could both glorify *and* laugh at Russian difference. Uvarov and his officials could never quite control the self-expression of the modern nation of whom they were the clumsy midwives. In Soviet times the official life of the nation was much more heavily overwhelmed by ideological theory. The technological means were on hand to reinforce it. The result therefore was something less. From a museum culture which hailed artistic greatness but was afraid to live with it occasionally a great manuscript was smuggled out, like Boris Pasternak's *Doctor Zhivago* or Solzhenitsyn's *The First Circle* and *Cancer Ward*. We love the passionate voices of Russian civic literature which have taught us over the decades and the centuries so much about Russian dissent. But we know a lot less about those who chose obedience to Russian convention; who chose and still choose, in fact, the national way; so Uvarov serves us, after his fashion.

What his life shows, to my mind, is a national style of politics that has demanded huge personal sacrifice for Russia, by people of intelligence and influence, in the past, in order that that country project power and self-sufficiency, bolstered by mass popular loyalty. It seems to a liberal Western mindset of the twenty-first century a quite wrong-headed concept of a nation, and quite wrong to require of any morally intelligent person a life led in two quite different ethical registers, because it must lead to dishonesty and hypocrisy, and corruption of the soul. But there is always the native conservative Russian point of view, which, I think, can at least understand the contradictions of an Uvarov, insofar as he would have liked, also, to be at home in, and even to be admired in, the West.

Appendix I
A possible source for Joseph Conrad

The Polish-born English novelist Joseph Conrad had a suppressed obsession with the ruthless revolutionaries and iron-fisted conservatives who clashed through nineteenth-century Russian history. They were the driving force of his 1911 novel *Under Western Eyes*, perhaps not surprisingly because their continuous conflict formed the backdrop to his childhood, when his father, a Polish revolutionary, was imprisoned by the tsarist government. The dire family situation that ensued underlay the teenaged Joseph's decision to go to sea.

Born Teodor Korzeniowski, the future writer never wanted to talk about Russia in later life and denied all special knowledge, but it was surely too much to forget the consequences of Apollo Korzeniowski's's part in the Warsaw Uprising of 1863, when, after nine months in the wretched Russian fortress in Warsaw he was exiled with his family to Vologda in Northern Russia. Conditions were sufficiently severe to kill Conrad's mother Evelina within the year, and Apollo's own health was broken. Once free Apollo moved himself and his son back to Poland, to live with Evelina's relatives in Cracow, but died in 1869, leaving Conrad an orphan at twelve.

The full name the Korzeniowskis gave their son, Teodor Josef Konrad, born in 1858, bound him to revolution and the Polish national cause. He was named Konrad after the great Polish/Lithuanian poet Adam Mickiewicz's fictional hero Konrad Wallenrod. But it was the problem of the political morality of revolution, and its opposite, conservatism, that the writer Joseph inherited.

To get away from belonging to any nation and from fighting any government, he went to sea when he was seventeen. In 1876 he joined a ship in Marseilles and embarked on a career as a sailor which lasted intermittently for fifteen years. When at last he settled on dry land and began his second life as a novelist, he began by writing 'sea stories', working through all the dramatic material he had acquired during a life of action. Many of them focused on the problematic relation of good men to perceived right causes or to their capacity to go morally astray.

Under Western Eyes gave the topic a new complexity in a Russian setting. As the novel opened a top tsarist minister, Mr de P ..., had just been murdered in an anarchist bomb attack in the street. Conrad borrowed the scene from the real-life assassination of Tsar Alexander II in 1881 and evidently what especially appealed was the fact that the terrorists had needed two attempts before succeeding. First they blew up the coachman and his horse, attracting a gawping crowd to the spectacle. 'The Minister-President, getting out unhurt into the deep snow, stood near the groaning coachman and addressed the people repeatedly in his weak, colourless voice: "I beg of you to keep off. For the love of God, I beg of you good people to keep off."' The terrorists finished off the Minister, even as he was speaking, with a second bomb. What was remarkable was the way Conrad used the interval between the two bombs, as it had happened in the case of the People's Will attack, to present his fictional reactionary minister in a sympathetic light. In his last moments, unaware that they were his last, the reactionary minister recognized the moral horror of life and spoke kindly to his fellow men. When Conrad heard of the assassination of Tsar Alexander II, he may have noted how difficult that event itself was to evaluate in moral terms. Tsarism as a system was brutal and unjust. Yet although the extremists were right to be disappointed with Alexander's much vaunted but effectively half-hearted liberation of the serfs twenty years earlier, the tsar-liberator was widely loved. The parents of the future revolutionary Vladimir Lenin were greatly distressed at the bloodshed, and took their ten-year-old son with them to a memorial service.

Almost immediately, in the very next scene in the novel, the assassin Haldin appears, also to demand our moral solidarity and practical help. In a third bid for our moral sympathy, we are then instantly thrust into the shoes of the man Haldin forces to rescue him, the frightened, orphaned student Razumov, who, with no one to help him through life, has no alternative but to cling to the imperial establishment and its values. Razumov, who doesn't dare associate with Haldin as a revolutionary, finds himself sheltering him as a man.

There was probably another 'real' ingredient that Conrad drew on in to these opening scenes. It derived from a story that Conrad's friend in England, who became his literary adviser and agent, Edward Garnett, told him just a few years after it happened. Garnett knew many Russian revolutionary exiles in London, among them the congenial figure of Sergei Stepniak. Steppy, as George Bernard Shaw anglicized his name, was so charming that indeed both Garnett's wife Constance and his sister Olive fell in love with him. His personal aura was enhanced by his tireless underground work to end social injustice in tsarist Russia. His socialist politics brought him into close contact with British reformers of the day, from William Morris to Keir Hardie. But Stepniak had a secret, and that was that in Russia he had killed a man. The man was a general, and responsible for the horrifically cruel treatment of prisoners in the Peter and Paul fortress in St Petersburg. The young revolutionary knifed the general in the street and was lucky to get out of Russia before he was caught.

In autumn 1893, as it seems, the Russian government began to put about London political society the true story of Steppy's past, knowing it would discredit him in the Fabian world where he had found a new home. Steppy had acquired a fondness for gradual change, at least in a non-Russian context. Whether or not the cause was the revelation of his violent past, albeit in a minor journal, or not, we will never know, but quite suddenly, one morning in December, Stepniak died beneath the wheels of a suburban train in West London. At the inquest the testimony of the driver and the stoker made it difficult to believe the collision was an accident, but no one knew enough to put forward a plausible reason for suicide. A connection with the offending article was never made publicly. Yet Edward Garnett had read it, and, who knows, when he recounted Stepniak's fate to Conrad he may have speculated on a link. What is more certain is that he told Conrad of his wife's and sister's theory that Steppy had been deep in his thoughts and not heard the train, having learnt to make himself deaf at will after a stint in a Turkish prison.

Conrad removed the romantic voluntarism from the Garnett family picture of plausible death of a Russian hero. The version he used of Stepniak's fate to wrap up Razumov's story in *Under Western Eyes* entailed Razumov's deafness, but it was a real deafness inflicted on him as a punishment for being a double agent. What was more, the accident didn't kill him, only confined him to a wheelchair and the lifelong care of a dedicated woman. Conrad punished Razumov for moral vacillation, according to his own scheme of things. In the case of the revolutionary Haldin, hanged by the Russian authorities for murder, he didn't need to intervene. The moral issue was simpler. But overall what seems to have happened in the writing of *Under Western Eyes* is that Conrad distributed the element of retribution between the revolutionary and the reactionary, rather than punish one of them alone.

One can imagine that Stepniak's story made such an impact on Conrad because it suddenly suggested how a single, continuous moral narrative could be made out of the revolutionary/reactionary narrative that shaped nineteenth-century Russian history. In the novel he created a situation where the revolutionary in the mould of Apollo Korzeniowski would have to turn for help to a young man who worked for the government. This young man because of an insecure and displaced childhood was easy prey for officialdom, but retained a conscience. In the light of the Stepniak case Conrad could see himself as something like the son of a Russian-style revolutionary settling for a conservative life in England, determined to forget the past, but not succeeding.

Under Western Eyes deals with the great mistake Apollo Korzeniowski made in his life, the problem of devotion to the revolutionary cause, and how others found him lovable because of it; but how his family suffered.

Haldin the revolutionary is not a well-developed character, but his role is important in Conrad's self-education. He wants us to understand that the student assassin, author of a mortal crime, is otherwise a virtuous man, and for that reason introduces Haldin's undoubtedly virtuous sister, who believes in and loves her brother. It is Haldin's sister with whom Razumov can then fall in love and, for her sake, take up the revolutionary cause he doesn't believe in. The only real moral life is that impelled by love.

Just after *Under Western Eyes* appeared, to not a very enthusiastic press, Conrad told Constance Garnett, the distinguished translator and Edward's wife:

> The fact is that I know extremely little of Russians. Practically nothing. In Poland we have nothing to do with them. One knows they are there. And that's disagreeable enough. In exile the contact is even slighter if possible, if more unavoidable. I crossed the Russian frontier at the age of ten. Not having been to school there I never knew Russian – I could not tell a Little Russian from a Great Russian to save my life. In the book I have just written, as you have seen, I am exclusively concerned with ideas.

But one has to take this statement sceptically. In Vologda, where he spent four crucial years of his boyhood were exiled some of the most ardent revolutionaries of the day. The making of those men fascinated the future novelist.

In *Under Western Eyes* the view that Russia is 'an oppressed society where the noblest aspirations of humanity, the desire of freedom, an ardent patriotism, the love of justice, the sense of pity, and even the fidelity of simple minds are prostituted to the lusts of hate and fear, the inseparable companions of an easy despotism' actually belongs to the bien-pensant narrator, while Conrad's task is to probe how 'the lusts of hate and fear' are served by virtuous men. The novel is replete with disgust for tsarist Russia, but it devotes its best energies to understanding how people from both sides, conservative and revolutionary, get sucked in to the vortex. It's remarkable how Conrad fills out the idea of reaction by distributing it among four separate characters, so we can feel what kind of life is entailed. The four are Mr de P..., the assassinated minister-president, Councillor Mikulin, who recruits Razumov as a government agent, the senator Prince K., and his friend the general.

Haldin justifies murder by declaring that the Minister is 'a dangerous man – a convinced man. Three more years of his work would have put us back fifty years into bondage – and look at all the lives wasted, at all the souls lost in that time.' The minister's record was such that he 'served the monarchy by imprisoning, exiling or sending to the gallows men and women, young and old, with an equable, unwearied industry. In his mystic acceptance of the principle of autocracy he was bent on extirpating from the land every vestige of anything that resembled freedom in public institutions; and in his ruthless persecution of the rising generation he seemed to aim at the destruction of the very hope of liberty itself.'

Prince K., who had once pressed Razumov's hand 'as no other man had pressed it' is in fact the illegitimate father of Razumov. He is a 'man of showy missions, experienced in nothing but the arts of gallant intrigue and worldly success' with 'the mobile, superficial mind of the ex-Guards officer'. He is an art lover. Together he and Razumov go to visit the general.

The general's impressive house is adorned with classical statuary and an English coal fire, but to Razumov, he is 'a goggle-eyed imbecile', 'a grotesque man in a tight uniform' who bursts out: 'I detest rebels! These subversive minds! These intellectual debauches! My existence has been built on fidelity. It's a feeling. To defend it I am ready to lay down my life – and even my honour – if that were needed. But pray tell me what honour can there be as against rebels – against people that deny God Himself – perfect unbelievers! Brutes. It is horrible to think of.' This military functionary, who embodies

'the whole power of autocracy because he is its guardian ... [who is] the incarnate suspicion, the incarnate anger, the incarnate ruthlessness of a political and social regime on its defence' is self-evidently despicable, but it is his school friend, the much more refined Councillor Mikulin, who entraps Razumov. A weary intellectual descendent of the Inquisition and redolent of Dostoevsky's Grand Inquisitor, and of Maistre, Councillor Mikulin is a thinker who says of himself: 'I happen to have been born a Russian with patriotic instincts. Whether inherited or not I am not in a position to say.'

At the height of his career Mikulin directs 'general police supervision over Europe'. But we learn most about him when he too is defeated by the whim of the Russian autocrat. Conrad's understanding of this figure comes in a long and remarkable passage:

> Councillor Mikulin was one of those powerful officials who, in a position not obscure, not occult, but simply inconspicuous, exercise a great influence over the methods rather than over the conduct of affairs. A devotion to Church and Throne is not in itself a criminal sentiment; to prefer the will of one to the will of many does not argue the possession of a black heart or prove congenital idiocy. Councillor Mikulin was not only a clever but also a faithful official. Privately he was a bachelor with a love of comfort, living alone in an apartment of five rooms luxuriously furnished; and was known by his intimates to be an enlightened patron of the art of female dancing.

Later on the larger world first heard of him in the very hour of his downfall, during one of those State trials which astonish and puzzle the average plain man who reads the newspapers, by a glimpse of unsuspected intrigues. And in the stir of vaguely seen monstrosities, in that momentary, mysterious disturbance of muddy waters, Councillor Mikulin went under, dignified, with only a calm, emphatic protest of his innocence – nothing more. No disclosures damaging to a harassed autocracy, complete fidelity to the secrets of the miserable arcana imperii deposited in his patriotic breast, a display of bureaucratic stoicism in a Russian official's ineradicable, almost sublime contempt for truth; stoicism of silence understood only by the very few of the initiated, and not without a certain cynical grandeur of self-sacrifice on the part of a sybarite. For the terribly heavy sentence turned Councillor Mikulin civilly into a corpse, and actually into something very much like a common convict.

What Conrad's sources for Mikulin might have been, given that, as he maintained, he 'knew very little about Russians' has never been satisfactorily answered. According to Jocelyn Baines the model was 'a relatively liberal figure', Alexei Lopukhin, chief of police in St Petersburg 1902–05. But given the complexity of Conrad's family history, and the powerful shadows it throws over *Under Western Eyes,* I am inclined to think of Uvarov. Just like Conrad's Mikulin, Uvarov 'happened to have been born Russian with patriotic instincts'. Meanwhile his Ministry was responsible for the Russification of Polish education, press and publishing, those assaults on national pride which Korzeniowski senior effectively sacrificed his life to fight.

Apollo, born in 1820, surely knew the name of Uvarov and what he stood for in Poland. This seems all the more possible, given that Apollo's father, Conrad's paternal grandfather, had fought in the November Uprising against Russia of 1830–31. In the two years that followed the defeat of that rebellion Uvarov rose to the top of the Ministry on the strength of his capacity to contain the Polish element and impose ideological consistency throughout the Empire. The most striking parallel between the Minister of Darkness and Mr de P is that professed desire to hold Russia (and self-evidently the nations seeking to escape its control) back fifty years. Meanwhile the autocratic whim that removes the dignified Mikulin from power resembles nothing so much as Uvarov's fall from grace in 1849.

To understand the play of psychological forces at work in this great but awkward novel is to appreciate how important it was to Conrad himself to map where his knowledge of revolution and reaction as moral motives in the Russian context led. It seems to me to have led in the end to the only real moral question, integrity. In the character of Razumov (whose name in both Polish and Russian indicates reason or understanding) *Under Western Eyes* asks how an individual unsure of himself, without family, without protection himself from corrupting political forces can survive as a moral agent. To justify the protection the state offers him Razumov sets about learning to be a good conservative. He writes out his principles:

History not Theory
Patriotism not Internationalism
Evolution not Revolution
Direction not Destruction
Unity not Disruption

But his intended moral existence is hollowed-out from under him by the political circumstances in which he lives. Both his goodwill and his weakness are abused, until 'the feeling that his moral personality was at the mercy of these lawless forces was so strong that he asked himself seriously if it were worthwhile to go on accomplishing the mental functions of that existence which seemed no longer his own'. Conrad for reasons of his own examines the predicament of the reactionary, but clearly the paradigm could apply equally to the revolutionary.

The point about Conrad, in Martin Seymour Smith's brilliant phrase, is that he had no truck with 'non-intuitive moral judgement (the prerogative of establishments and the systems they perpetuate)'. This was the lesson he learnt by trying to understand his father's clash with the Russian Leviathan. And, in his artistic way, he wanted us to sympathize with them both.

Notes

Introduction

1 S.Ya. Karp, 'Razmyshleniya o revolyutsii vo Frantsii Edmunda Berka: russkie otkliky 90-y gg. XVIII v.', in Zaitsev et al., eds, *Kniga v Rossii v epokhu prosveshcheniya* (Leningrad, 1988), pp. 79–95, p. 86.

2 Ibid., p. 85.

3 Conor Cruise O'Brien, ed., Edmund Burke, *Reflections on the Revolution in France* (Harmondsworth, 1982), p. 151.

4 Marc Raeff, *Understanding Imperial Russia: State and Society in the Old Regime* (New York, 1984), pp. 43–66.

5 Richard Pipes, *Karamzin's Memoir on Ancient and Modern Russia: A Translation and Analysis*, new edn (Ann Arbor, MI, 2005), p. 200.

6 Jonathan Israel, *Radical Enlightenment* (Oxford, 2001), p. 115.

7 Zaitsev et al., eds, *Kniga v Rossii*, p. 91.

8 D. M. Lang, *The First Russian Radical: Alexander Radishchev* (Westport, MA, 1977), pp. 90–1.

9 Hugh Ragsdale, ed., *Paul I: A Reassessment of His Life and Reign* (Pittsburgh, PA, 1979), p. 140.

10 Ibid., p. 163; *Russky arkhiv* (1886), pp. 305–33.

11 Many members of these families had become reform-minded by the time of the Bolshevik Revolution, but Bolshevism persecuted them because of their class. See Douglas Smith, *Former People: The Final Days of the Russian Aristocracy* (London, 2012).

12 *A Journey from Saint Petersburg to Moscow*, tr. Leo Wiener, ed. Roderick Page Thaler (Cambridge, MA, 1958).

13 Ibid., p. 249.

14 The exception is R. Pipes, *Russian Conservatism and Its Critics: A Study in Political Culture*, 1st edn (New Haven, CT, 2005), p. 64.

15 *A Journey*, p. 11.

16 She behaved similarly over a French text critical of Russia. See Pipes, *Russian Conservatism and Its Critics*, p. 65.

17 Léonce Pingaud, *Les Francais en Russie et les Russes en France* (Paris, 1886), p. 236.

18 See Bernard Crick, 'A Defence of Politics against Ideology', *In Defence of Politics*, 4th edn (Chicago, IL, 1993), pp. 34–56.

19 David Mclellan, *Ideology (Concepts in Social Thought)*, 2nd revised edn (Minneapolis, MN, 1995), p. 5.

Chapter 1

1 On the circumstances of his birth, he wrote the following for a French encyclopedia: 'His father was a vice-colonel in the cavalry and an adjutant of the Empress Catherine II. Her majesty was present as his godmother when he was baptized in the court church.' *Russkii Arkhiv* 9, No. 12 (1871): 2104.

2 F. F. Vigel', *Zapiski*, 3 vols. (Moscow, 1891–3), II: 58. Many but not all the references to Vigel' used in this book can be found in the abridged *Zapiski*, ed. S. Ya. Shtraikh, 2 vols. (Moscow, 1928, reprinted 2001).

3 A. S. Pushkin, Table Talk.

4 Jacques Ferran, *Les famillies princieres de l'ancien empire de russie* (Paris, 1997). For Russian genealogy, see also the excellent website www.vgd.ru

5 Catherine Alekseevna Golovin (b. 1735) before her marriage had been Princess Ekaterina Alekseevna Golitsyn and almost by reciprocal arrangement a Golovin cousin, Varvara Petrovna, recently appointed a lady-in-waiting to Catherine, would soon marry back into the Golitsyns. The Golovin/Golitsyn social base proved a fine one when Varvara Petrovna later wrote her memoirs of Catherine's court.

6 On the marriage of Uvarov's parents, see *Vosem'nadtsatyi vek*, I: 62, 107, 112, 115, 161.

7 *Sankt Peterburgskie Vedemosti*, 10 February 2001.

8 Semyon Uvarov's body was never found. But nominally he fell in the third month of the Russo–Swedish War of 1788–90, in conscientious service to the rapidly expanding empire.

9 In fact she was able to sell it to the state for the full outstanding sum a year later. Situated on the corner of the Lviny Bridge, with its four-column portico and a classical white frieze, it can still be seen today, much as it was when it was built. It became the headquarters of a new medical college, then a school, then again a private home. It survived the Revolution and the whole of the Soviet period intact.

10 *Vosem'nadtsatyi vek*, I: 145, 192; II: 177, 494.

11 N. V. Riasanovsky, *A Parting of Ways Government and the Educated Public in Russia 1801-1855* (Oxford, 1976), p. 268.

12 Part of the gentry obligation in local service was to look after the welfare of widows, orphans and illegitimate children.

13 Cynthia H. Whittaker, *The Origins of Modern Russian Education An Intellectual Biography of Count Sergei Uvarov, 1786-1855* (DeKalb, IL, 1984), p. 13.

14 Pipes, *Russian Conservatism and Its Critics*, p. 73, called N. I. Panin 'Russia's earliest liberal in the Western sense of the word'. Before he died in 1783 Panin drafted with his brother Peter a project for a constitutional government in Russia, later presented to his protégé Paul when he assumed the throne.

15 Pingaud, *Les Français en Russie*, p. 233. On the general influence of French tutors, see E. Dupré de Saint-Maure, *Petersbourg, Moscou et les provinces ou Observations sur les moeurs et les usages russes au commencement du XIXe siècle*, 3 vols. (Paris, 1830), I: 59ff. A critical evaluation of Uvarov's social class is Marc Raeff, 'Home, School and Service in the Life of an Eighteenth-Century Russian Nobleman', *Slavonic and East European Review* XL, No. 95 (June 1962): 295–307. Dupré de Saint-Maure, *Petersbourg*, II: 33–6.

16 Vigel', *Zapiski*, I: 162.

17 The Cadet School offered a two-year course from a minimum age of sixteen years and eight months and resulted in the rank of Kammerjunker, which Uvarov received in 1804, aged eighteen. See N. S. Martynov, 'Iz Bumag Nikolaya Solomonovicha Martynova', *Russkii Arkhiv* 31, No. 8 (1893): 590–1.

18 *Vosem'nadtsatyi Vek*, I: 306.

19 M. Aronson and S. Reiser, *Literaturnye kruzhki i salony* (Leningrad, 1929), pp. 145ff. This was the culture that was so memorably depicted as socializing its way to a complete unsuspected end in Alexander Sokurov's film *Russian Ark* (2002).

20 Madame de Stael, *Dix Annees d'Exil,* texte établi par Paul Gautier, introduction et notes par Simone Balayé (Paris, 1966).

21 *Vosem'nadtsatyi Vek*, I: 346.

22 Uvarov, 'Literaturnye Vospominaniya', *Sovremmenik* 27, No. 6 (1851): 37–42. Whittaker, *The Origins*, p. 15 describes the Olenins as 'surrogate parents'. Comparable hosts were the Muravyovs, where the poet Batyushkov was a *vospitannik*. See also Marinus Antony Wes, *Classics in Russia 1700-1855: Between Two Bronze Horsemen* (Leiden, 1992), pp. 131ff.

23 Georg Reinbeck, *Cursory Remarks on a Journey from St Petersburgh, through Moscow, Grodno, Warsaw, Breslaw etc., to Germany, in the year 1805: In a Series of Letters* (London, 1807), Letter XXIII, pp. 67ff. For a commentary, see Alexander M. Martin, *Enlightened Metropolis: Constructing Imperial Moscow 1762-1855* (Oxford, 2013), pp. 105ff. de Stael, *Dix Années*, Ch. XVI shared Reinbeck's view of the superficiality of the Russian upper class and linked it to the constant threat of punishment and exile by the tsar.

24 Its German inventor August Ludwig von Rochau wrote: 'To bring down the walls of Jericho, the Realpolitiker knows the simple pickaxe is more useful than the mightiest trumpet.' He wrote *Grundsätze der Realpolitik angewendet auf die staatlichen Zustände Deutschlands* (Stuttgart, 1853) to try to explain why the Enlightenment which had shown coercion was unjust was defenceless against the rising power interests of nineteenth-century national states.

25 Whittaker, *The Origins*, p. 3, notes that Uvarov was 'appalled by Paul … whose recidivism threatened Russia's progress' and believed his assassination was providential.

26 Hugh Ragsdale, *Tsar Paul and the Question of Madness An Essay in History and Psychology* (Westport, CT, 1988), p. 203 and *passim*, and Ragsdale, ed., *Paul I.*

27 *Brokgauz i Evron Entsyklopedichesky Slovar*, p. 3.

28 John L. H. Keep, 'Paul I and the Militarization of Government', in Ragsdale, ed., *Paul I*, p. 100.

29 Ibid., 'Introduction', p. xi.

30 James J. Kenney, Jr, 'The Politics of Assassination', in Ragsdale, ed., *Paul I*, p. 135.

31 La Harpe, *Correspondance*, III: 540.

32 Ibid., III: 539.

33 A. I. Herzen, *Istorichesky Sbornik 1859*, cited in M. M. Safonov, 'Frantsuskie istochniki publiktaskii o smerti Pavla I v "Istoricheskom Sbornike" A. I. Gertsena I N. P. Ogaryova', in Zaitsev et al., ed., *Kniga v Rossii*.

34 David L. Ransel, 'An Ambivalent Legacy: The Education of GrandDuke Paul', in Ragsdale, ed., *Paul I*, pp. 1–16.

35 Kenney, 'The Politics of Assassination', pp. 135–6.

36 Norman E. Saul, 'The Objectives of Paul's Foreign Policy', in Ragsdale, ed., *Paul I*, pp. 31–43.

37 La Harpe, *Correspondance*, III: 545; 'Nikita Pavlovich Panin', www.mir.imen (downloaded 1 November 2006).

38 Burke, *Reflections*, p. 152.

39 The German term came into being when a political scientist, Robert von Mohl, who had been critical of reaction in the Duchy of Wurttemberg prior to 1848, contrasted a *Polizeistaat* to a *Rechtstaat*, or constitutional state. The usage passed into English in 1851, according to the *OED*.

40 Whittaker, *The Origins*, p. 1.

Chapter 2

1 P. A. Pletnev, *Perepiska Ia. K. Grota s P.A. Pletnevym*, 3 vols. (St Petersburg, 1896), II: 15.

2 Cf. Whittaker, *The Origins*, p. 13.

3 On Russian attendance at Göttingen see M. Wischnitzer, *Die Universität Göttingen und die Entwicklung der liberalen Ideen in Russland* (Berlin, 1907) and for the teaching staff the same author's 'Gettingenskie gody N. I. Turgeneva', *Minuvshie gody* IV (April 1908). See also E. Amburger, *Beiträge zur Geschichte der deutsch-russischen kulturellen Beziehungen* (Giessen, 1961).

4 Cynthia H. Whittaker, 'Count S.S. Uvarov: Conservatism and National Enlightenment in Pre-Reform Russia', unpublished doctoral thesis, Indiana University, 1971, discusses the Hanoverian school, p. 83.

5 J. W. Goethe, 'Gespräche mit Eckermann', *Gedenkausgabe der Werke, Briefe und Gespräche*, 24 vols. (Zurich, 1949–54), 24: 405–6.

6 For Schloezer, see E. J. Winter, *August Ludwig von Schloezer und Russland* (Berlin, 1961). The best-known Russian student of the day was Alexander Turgenev, a fellow cadet of Uvarov's at the Foreign Ministry, who arrived some time in 1802 and left in the summer of 1804. The two men don't appear to have met in Goettingen.

7 For Uvarov as a Classical scholar, see Wes, *Classics in Russia*. 'For the classical tradition in Russia it was Uvarov whose activities ultimately brought the highest returns.' (p. 180) J. J. Winckelmann would feature in Uvarov's essay. See Chapter 4.

8 Friedrich Bouterwek, whose *Aesthetik* (Leipzig, 1806) incorporated many references to Plato, and to Kant and Schiller, also taught at Göttingen.

9 For Uvarov's attitude to Rousseau, see 'Pensées sur ce qu'une Grand Puissance unié à une Grande modération peut effectuer pour la Bonheur de l'Humanité (1813) (Thoughts on What a Great Power united to a Great moderation can bring about for the Happiness of Humanity) first attributed to Uvarov in 1976 and analysed in M. L. Maiofis, *Vozzvanie ke Evrope Literaturnoe obshchestvo 'Arzamas' in rossiiskii modernizatsionnyi proekt 1815–18 godov* (Moscow, 2008).

10 From the German 'Kammerjunker', 'Gentleman of the Bedchamber.' See Jan Hennings, *Russia and Courtly Europe* (Cambridge, 2016), p. 214.

11 V. F. Bogolyubov, 'Pis'ma V.F. Bogolyubova k knyazyu Alexandru Borisovichu Kurakinu', *Russkii Arkhiv* 31, Nos. 10 and 11 (1893): 233–46 (257–315).

12 This was Andrei Razumovsky's judgement quoted in S. N. Durylin, 'G-zha de Stal' i ee russkie otnosheniya', *Literaturnoe Nasledstvo* 33–4 (1939): 215–330 (225). Durylin's is the fullest published material on Uvarov's stay in Vienna and draws on his 'Tablettes d'un voyageur russe' and a late sketch, 'De Stal'. See also Charles de Saint-Julien, 'Hommes publiques russes, Le Comte Ouvaroff', *Revue de Paris* XIII (1856): 481–512. That he had never met so many interesting people was expressed in 'Stein et Pozzo di Borgo', reprinted in *Esquisses politiques et litteraires*, pp. 93–115 (pp. 109–10). 'Pis'ma V.F. Bogolyubova' (see note 11) also describes the Russian colony and the social round.

13 Durylin, 'de Stal'', p. 227.

14 Ibid., p. 248.

15 For Andrei Kirillovich Razumovsky (1752–1836), see Durylin, 'de Stal'', p. 216, and A. Vasil'chikov, *Semeistvo Razumovskikh*, 6 vols. (St Petersburg, 1859–1900), II: 1–23. His extraordinarily luxurious palace burnt down during the Congress of Vienna. See Adam Zamoyski, *Rites of Peace: The Fall of Napoleon and the Congress of Vienna* (London, 2008), p. 321 and pp. 383–5.

16 Durylin, 'de Stal'', p. 218.

17 Ibid., pp. 25–6.

18 *Flüchtige Bemerkungen auf einer Reise von St.Petersburg über Moskva, Grodno, Warschau, Breslau nach Deutschland im Jahre 1805. In Briefen von G. Reinbeck, Zweiter Teil* (Leipzig 1806). (month? Publisher = Wilhelm Rein).

19 Friedrich Schiller, *On the Aesthetic Education of Man in a Series of Letters*, eds and trs. Elizabeth Wilkinson and Leonard Willoughby (Oxford, 1967), Letter V, p. 27.

20 Thomas Paine, *Major Works* (lulu.com, 2017), p. 269.

21 S. S. Uvarov, *Esquisses politiques et littéraires*, with an introduction by Louis-Antoine Léouzon Leduc (Paris, 1848), pp. 99–103.

22 Ibid., p. 112. See also Hans Fenske, *Freiherr von Stein: Reformer and Moralist* (Darmstadt, 2012); G. H. Pertz, *Das Leben des Ministers Freiherrn vom Stein*, 4 vols. (Berlin, 1850–5). A. N. Pypin comments on Uvarov's relationship with Stein in *Obshchestvennoe dvizhenie v Rossii pri Aleksandre I* (St Petersburg, 1900), pp. 290ff.

23 Durylin, 'de Stal'', pp. 234–45.

24 Katia D. Hay, 'August Wilhelm von Schlegel', in Edward N. Zalta, ed., *The Stanford Encyclopedia of Philosophy* (Summer 2017 Edition). See in particular sections 3.1 and 6.1.

25 Florence Lotterie, 'Madame de Stael, La littérature comme philosophie sensible', *Romantisme*, No. 124 (2004–2): 23. Downloaded at www.persee.fr/doc/roman_0048-8593_2004_num_34_124_1254.

26 Durylin, 'de Stal'', p. 237.

27 N. V. Riasanovsky, *Nicholas I and Official Nationality in Russia 1825–1855* (Berkeley, CA, 1967), p. 70.

28 Gislain de Diesbach, *Madame de Stael* (Paris, 1983; reissued 2008), p. 419.

29 Ibid., 257, 263.

30 Saint-Julien, 'Hommes publiques russes', p. 485; Bogolyubov, whose father had committed suicide after being found guilty of extortion, was educated in Alexander Kurakin's household. N. I. Grech, *Zapiski o moei zhizni* (St Petersburg, 1886), pp. 410 (412–13), refers to secrets between Uvarov and Bogolyubov, whom he calls a thief.

31 Durylin, 'de Stal'', p. 231. The Soviet critic called Rombecq a *gaiduk* – a 'crude and outspoken woman'. Napoleon pictured her going to St. Petersburg with bottles of Madeira on her back to congratulate the tsar on his military successes. Nesselrode, *Papiers*, III: 203–5 (August 1809).

32 Jean Christopher Herold, *Mistress to an Age: A Life of Madame de Stael* (London, 1959), p. 194.

Chapter 3

1 'Pis'ma V.F. Bogolyubova', *Russkii Arkhiv* 31, No. 11 (1893): 292ff; Vigel', *Zapiski*, II: 59–60 also speaks of Darya Ivanovna's financial difficulties and records her death. SIRIO vols 83 and 89 document plans for staffing the Paris embassy which in Uvarov's case were not fulfilled.

2 'Pis'ma V.F. Bogolyubova', *Russkii Arkhiv* 31, No. 10 (1893): 233–46 (244) (11 April 2008); *Vosem'nadtsatyi Vek*, I: 243. There was perhaps some mischief involving Darya with the Apraksin family. According to Alexander Kurakin 'our uncle' S. S. Apraksin's wife behaved badly (30 October 1800, p. 268) while Darya Ivanovna's morality was 'exemplary'. Vigel's speculation is contained in suppressed passages of the *Zapiski* (Gosudarstvennaya Publichnaya Biblioteka Fond 4, 276/4, pp. 424–6) examined by M. I. Gillel'son, *Molodoi Pushkin i Arzamasskoe Bratstvo* (Leningrad, 1974), p. 23. Stepan Stepanovich

Apraksin (1747–1827) enjoyed a reputation for lavish entertaining at his house in Moscow, particularly around the years 1798–1801, when he 'retired' from service temporarily. The Uvarovs were lodging in Moscow with the Kurakins.

3 Turgenev brothers, *Arkhiv Brat'ev Turgenevykh*, 6 vols. (St Peterburg, 1911–21), II: 416, 420. Whittaker, *The Origins*, p. 19.

4 Vigel', *Zapiski*, II: 58–9 (4 May 1810).

5 Turgenev brothers, *Arkhiv Brat'ev Turgenevykh*, II: 412, 416.

6 Alexander Ivanovich Turgenev (1784–1845) was a liberal in the sense that like the following, better-known generation of 'The Marvellous Decade' he was, through his education and reading, 'imbued ... with both Enlightenment and romantic ideals of liberty and human dignity' (Aileen Kelly, 'Introduction', Isaiah Berlin, *Russian Thinkers*, 2nd revised edn (London, 2008). He was an archivist who published historical documents on Russia, also a civil servant, but chiefly German literature and ideas fascinated him and in the course of his life, much of the latter part spent abroad, he met Schelling and Goethe, as well as de Stael and the later French popularizer of German idealism, Victor Cousin. He was an eternal student, still taking university courses in Halle and Berlin in the last five years of his life. His *Khronik russkogo, Dnevniki 1825-26*, ed. M. I. Gillel'son (Moscow, 1964), reflects the hectic intellectual life of a critical but hopeful Russian mind open to intellectual Europe. His brother Nikolai Turgenev (1789–1871) studied in Göttingen from 1808–11 from where he returned to Russia with an active campaign to abolish serfdom and reform the social structure.

7 'Sehnsucht', in S. S. Durylin, 'Drug Gete', *Literaturnoe Nasledstvo* 4–6 (1932): 186–217. See also Whittaker, *The Origins*, p. 14. Turgenev also enthused over 'Sur l'avantage de mourir jeune', *Arkhiv Brat'ev Turgenevykh* (23 June and 2 August 1810), II: 421–222.

8 Vigel', *Zapiski*, II: 162.

9 Uvarov, 'Iz pisem A. Ya. Bulgakova k bratu', *Russkii Arkhiv* 37, No. 3 (1899): 186.

10 The Razumovskys rose to prominence in the eighteenth century as a reward for their cultural efforts and their military loyalty. Kiril Grigorievich Razumovsky, Uvarov's grandfather by marriage, presided over the Academy of Sciences and advised Empress Catherine. His brother Alexei Grigorievich was a lover of the young empress Elizabeth.

11 Vasil'chikov, *Semeistvo Razumovskikh*, II: 1–23; *Brokgauz*, XXVI: 202–3.

12 Vasil'chikov, II: 140ff; *Arkhiv Dekabrista S.G.Volkonskogo*, I: 17, 69, 101, 136, 337.

13 Whittaker, *The Origins*, pp. 17, 24, is disinclined to believe Uvarov was homosexual. The opposite conclusion is drawn by Simon Karlinsky, *The Sexual Labyrinth of Nikolai Gogol'* (Cambridge, MA, 1976), pp. 56–7. For Uvarov's attitude, see his introduction to *O Grecheskoi Antologii* (St Petersburg, 1820), reprinted in K. N. Batyushkov, *Sochineniya* (St Petersburg, 1834), pp. 237–64 (p. 244).

14 *Projet d'une Academie asiatique* (St Petersburg, 1810), included in Uvarov, *Études de philologie et de critique* (1st edn, St Petersburg, 1843; 2nd edn,

Paris, 1845). Subsequent references are to the 1843 edition. Turgenev's observations in *Arkhiv*, II: 412.

15 Uvarov's appointment became known to Alexander Turgenev early in the New Year, *Arkhiv*, II: 431 (10 January 1811), though M. Stepanov and F. Vermale, 'Pis'ma Zhozefa de Mestra k S.S. Uvarovu', *Literaturnoe Nasledstvo* 29–30 (1937): 677 are misleading, quoting a letter of Turgenev's from 1817, when they say he had already decided Uvarov's sole motive was glory. A. Ya. Bulgakov, however, said the promotion, though warranted, made many people envious, 'Iz pisem', *Russkii Arkhiv* 38, No. 1 (1900): 495. Uvarov was elected a member of the Imperial Academy of Sciences on 16 January 1811 and a Corresponding Member of the Göttingen Learned Society in November 1811 in recognition for his work in Oriental studies.

16 According to Wes, *Classics in Russia*, p. 114, it made him 'world-famous overnight'.

17 Gillel'son, *Molodoi Pushkin*, pp. 157–8; Whittaker, *The Origins*, pp. 19–21. For a mid-twentieth-century view of Russia's inheritance through Byzantium, see Arnold J. Toynbee, 'Russia's Byzantine Heritage', in *Civilisation on Trial* (Oxford, 1948), pp. 164–83. For the letter to Goethe, see 'Goethe und Uwarow und ihr Briefwechsel', ed. Georg Schmid, *Russische Revue* 28, No. 17 (St Petersburg, 1888), pp. 131–82 (p. 144). Uvarov kept the correspondence going spasmodically for the next fifteen years on the basis of such polite, sometimes scholarly but general inconsequential brief exchanges.

18 Uvarov, *Études*, pp. 26–7.

19 Robert Irwin, *Dangerous Knowledge Orientalism and Its Discontents* (Woodstock and New York, 2008), pp. 129–30 and pp. 157–8 spotlights Uvarov's prominent role in the formation of Oriental studies without naming him but referring to the Asiatic Museum opened in 1818 for which *Project* was the blueprint.

20 Durylin, 'Drug Gete', pp. 191ff, argues, 'Uvarov grasped the direction of the external policies of the autocratic, feudal Russian state.' Napoleon asked Langlès for a report; see *Études*, editor's note.

21 Uvarov, *Études*, pp. 10–12 (p. 11).

22 Ibid., pp. 56, 63.

23 Stepanov and Vermale, 'Pis'ma Zhozefa de Mestra k S.S. Uvarovu', pp. 694ff; For the role of de Maistre in Russia, see Berlin, *Russian Thinkers*, particularly pp. 57–65. De Maistre was believed to have helped remove from power Speransky, with whose Westernizing and liberal reforms the young Uvarov was in agreement.

24 V. A. Zhukovsky, *Sobranie Sochinenii* (Moscow/Leningrad, 1959), IV: 481–4. Zhukovsky refers to the extreme nationalist and monarchist Sergei Nikolaevich Glinka (1775–1847), editor of the highly patriotic journal *Russkii Vestnik*, but with no relation to the composer.

25 Compare this worry with Marc Raeff's description in *Imperial Russia* noted above (Preface, note 4) of an autocratic Russian tradition which left its servants feeling the country they administered was unreal.

26 Uvarov, *Études*, p. 31.

27 A. W. Schlegel's concept was itself the product of a halfway house between a Classical and a Romantic outlook, according to Hay in the Stamford Encyclopedia (See Chapter 2, note 24).

28 Ibid., pp. 31ff.

Chapter 4

1 Whittaker, *The Origins*, pp. 62–6. The fundamental Russian source for Uvarov's education policies is S. V. Rozhdestvensky, *Istoricheskii Obzor deyatel'nosti Minsterstva Narodnogo Prosvishcheniya, 1802–1902* (St Petersburg, 1902).

2 For Maistre's influence on Russian education, in the direction of fundamentalism and in opposition to Speransky, see Stepanov and Vermale, 'Pis'ma Zhozefa de Mestra k S.S. Uvarovu', 596–604; Pingaud, *Les Francais en Russie*, pp. 293, 306ff. Under Maistre's championship the Jesuits achieved an unprecedented degree of prominence and autonomy in Russia.

3 Speransky had put forward a plan for state lycees on the French model, teaching classics and philosophy; most recently he had pioneered a statute tying advancement in higher government service to a university education. He had noted the difficulties besetting too much equality too soon in Russia and had encouraged the development of the elite school at Tsarskoe Selo exclusively for the gentry. But he had failed to make adequate provision for Russian and religion. A conspiracy against the power he had amassed as the Tsar's leading adviser from 1809 resulted in his banishment from the court in 1812, on the eve of the French invasion. Speransky became chancellor of the Imperial Alexander University in Turku, Finland and subsequently, what counted as a reprieve, governor of the province of Penza, and then, from 1816, governor-general of Siberia. He returned to power in St Petersburg in 1821 and served Nicholas I as a codifier of Russian law. See Marc Raeff, *Michael Speransky Statesman of Imperial Russia 1772–1839*, 2nd revised edn (The Hague, 1969); Pipes, *Karamzin's Memoir*, p. 66; Whittaker, *The Origins*, pp. 59, 63.

4 Whittaker, *The Origins*, p. 64. Paul R. Sweet, *Wilhelm von Humboldt, A Biography* (Columbus, OH, 1978–80). Uvarov and Humboldt corresponded 1810-1815 when Humboldt was in Vienna; they were also in touch through the Classicists Friedrich Wolf and Gottfried Hermann. GIM, Fond 17, holds an Uvarov-Humboldt correspondence I have not been able to see and neither Sweet nor Whittaker mention, but Alexander von Humboldt suggests it mainly concerned their shared love of Greek and interest in language. Humboldt was working on a translation of Aeschylus" Agamemnon.

5 He had to look past an assumption readily made in ultra-conservative circles, and by Napoleon himself, that Greek literature was republican in sentiment. See Wes, *Classics in Russia*, p. 117.

6 *Project*, p. 23.

7 Note 3 above.

8 Georg Schmid, 'Zur russischen Gelehrtengeschichte: S.S. Uwarow und Christian Friedrich Graefe', *Russische Revue* XXVI (1886): 76–108 and 156–67.

9 Christian Friedrich Mattei (1744–1811). See A. I. Menshikov, *Biograficheskii Slovar' professorov i pripodavatelei Imperatorskogo Moskovskogo Universiteta* (Moscow, 1855), II: 24–41. Uvarov's signed obituary, 'Pis'mo k Izdatel'yu', *Vestnik Evropy* 60 (1811): 59–61.

10 Ghislain de Diesbach, *Madame de Stael* (Paris, 1983, reprinted 2017), p. 410.

11 Ernst Muesebeck, *E.M. Arndt* (Gotha, 1914).

12 Diesbach, *Madame de Stael*, p. 419.

13 *Memoires de Mme de Stael: Dix annees d'exil, ouvrage posthume publie en 1818* (Paris, 1845) does not mention Uvarov. Her knowledge of his plans and thoughts, including the desire to travel abroad again, may have been acquired via her friendship in Sweden with Uvarov's contemporary and fellow litterateur, Dmitrii Blyudov. Stein, one of Russian audience, was delighted by the substance of *De l'Allemagne*, though less so by her extravagant personality. He wrote to Uvarov saying he wished de Stael would stay out of politics. See Durylin, 'De Stal'', pp. 282–4.

14 See above note 2. Maistre sympathized with the Illuminists, who under the inspiration of the mystical Frenchman Claude de Saint-Martin, saw the world as a repository of dark god-given symbols to be interpreted by occult means. For their substantial following in eighteenth and nineteenth-century Russia, see Andrzej Walicki, *A History of Russian Thought* (Oxford, 1980), p. 20. Uvarov implicitly attacked such semi-religious beliefs in his 'Essai sur les mysteres d'Eleusis' (St Petersburg, 1812) and condemned the German philosopher Friedrich Schelling in the same vein. Alekesei Razumovsky's faith in the power of irrational sects, encouraged by Maistre, led him to believe his unbalanced son Kiril had been infected by an outlawed Bavarian Illuminist Society. Vasil'chikov, II: 121ff.

15 M. L. Maiofis, *Vozzvanie ke Evrope,* emphasizes p. 341 that Uvarov's political philosophy needs to be teased out of his minor works and that the *Conservateur impartial* is an important and overlooked source.

16 *Russkii Arkhiv* IX, No. 2 (1871): 132 and X, No. 3 (1889): 545–50, in which P. Bartenev notes Uvarov probably financed the *Conservateur*, for other comments see *Ostaf'evskii Arkhiv knyazei Vyazemskykh*, ed. S. D. Sheremetyev and V. I. Saitov (St Petersburg, 1899–1913), I: 174; Pypin, *Obshchestvennoe dvizhenie*, pp. 281–2.

17 'Eleusis', in *Études*, pp. 67–161.

18 Frederick Copleston, *A History of Philosophy*, vol. I, part II (London, 1946–75), p. 216. Cynthia H. Whittaker, 'Count S.S. Uvarov: Conservatism and National Enlightenment in Pre-Reform Russia', Ph.D. diss., Indiana University, 1971, p. 96, notes that the docrime of the Fall in Uvarov's thinking 'constitutes the primary basis for civic life.'

19 'Eleusis', pp. 81–2.

20 Ibid., pp. 160–1.

21 For comparisons with Hegel see also Whittaker, *The Origins*, pp. 36, 46.

22 Mikhail Bakunin's Introduction to Hegel's Gymnasial Lectures appeared in the *Moskovsky Nablyudatel'* March 1838. For a commentary see Mark Leier, *Bakunin The Creative Passion – A Biography* (New York, 2011), pp. 90–1.

23 *O pripodovanii istorii otnositel'no k narodnomu vospitaniyu* (St Petersburg, 1813). Uvarov to Zhukovsky (6 June 1813), *Russkii Arkhiv* 9, No. 12 (1871): 160.

24 The education ladder was an idea put forward by the eminent Enlightenment figure and early political scientist Marquis de Condorcet in his *Tableau historique des progres de l'esprit humain* (1795). It could be traced back to Plato and in a religious form to Neoplatonism. Copleston, *A History of Philosophy*, p. 215, observes: 'In the system of Plotinus then, the Orphic-Platonic=Pythagorean strain of "otherworldliness", intellectual ascent, salvation through assimilation to and knowledge of God, reach their most complete and systematic expression.' Peter the Great's 'Table of Ranks' which established the model for state service through education and the acquisition of rank on educational merit incorporated the same ideal.

25 *Le Conservateur impartial*, No. 22 (17/19 March 1814).

26 Jacques Delille, 'Les Jardins, en quatre chants' (1780; new edn, Paris, 1801).

27 *Project*, p. 15.

28 Sweet, *Wilhelm von Humboldt*, I: 230.

29 Whittaker, *The Origins*, p. 27.

30 Schiller, *On the Aesthetic Education of Man in a Series of Letters*.

31 G. Schulz, *Schillers Horen* (Heidelberg, 1960).

32 M. I. Gillel'son, 'Pis'ma N.M. Karamzina k S.S. Uvarovu' (21 July 1813), *XVIII vek*, ed. P. N. Berkov (Leningrad, 1969), p. 353.

33 Note 2 above.

34 Karamzin 'paid little attention to the social factor', Pipes, *Karamzin's Memoir*, p. 75.

35 Pipes, *Karamzin's Memoir*, p. 51, discriminates between Shishkov as reactionary and anti-Western and Karamzin as conservative but in favour of a Russia enhanced by Western achievements.

36 'Russko-angliiskie literaturnye svyazi', *Literaturnoe Nasledstvo* 91 (1982): 254, 453.

37 *Russkii Arkhiv* 9, No. 12 (1871): 180 (6 June 1813); V. A. Zhukovsky, *Sochineniya* (St Petersburg, 1902), IV: 472.

38 S. S. Uvarov, 'Pis'mo k Nikolayu Ivanovichu Gnedichu', *Chteniya v Besede lyubitel'ei russkago slova* 13 (1813): 56–8; 'Otvet V.V. Kapnistu na pis'mo ego ob eksametre', *Chteniya v Besede lyubitel'ei russkago slova* 17 (1815): 65.

39 M. N. Longinov, 'Vospominaniye o grafe S.S. Uvarove', *Sovremennik* 53, No. 10 (1885): 120.

40 Zhukovsky, *Sochineniya*, IV: 657.

41 Gillel'son, *Molodoi Pushkin*, pp. 25–6 and *P.A. Vyazemsky, Zhizn' i tvorchestvo* (Moscow, 1969), p. 65; A. F. Voeikov, 'Poslanie k S. S. Uvarovu', *Vestnik Evropy*, No. 5 (1819): 15.

42 *Le Conservateur impartial*, No. 46 (June 1813); Maiofis, *Vozzvanie ke Evrope*, p. 634.

43 Joseph Marie Quérard, *La France littéraire ou dictionnaire bibliographique des savants, historiens et gens de lettres de la France, ainsi que les littérateurs étrangers qui ont écrit en français, plus particulièrment pendant les XVIIIe et XIXe siècles*, 12 vols. (Paris, 1854–9), vol. 11; G. Ghennady [Grigory Nikolaevich Gennadi], *Les écrivains franco-russes. Bibliographie des ouvrages français publiés par des russes* (Dresden, 1874).

Chapter 5

1 'Pis'ma k Zhukovskomu' (17 August 1813), *Russkii Arkhiv* 9, No. 12 (1871): 161.

2 *Éloge funebre de Moreau* (St Petersburg, 1813), pp. 25–6. The essay also appeared in *Le Conservateur impartial* 98 (9 December 1813). I. I. Dmitriev to A. I. Turgenev, 17 January 1814, *Vzglyad na moyu zhizn': Zapiski deistvitel'nago tainago sovietnika Ivana Ivanovicha Dmitrieva, v tryekh chastyakh,* ed. M. A. Dmitrieva (Moscow, 1818), II: 220, commented that it lacked detail on Moreau.

3 Sweet, *Wilhelm von Humboldt,* II: 34.

4 See Chapter 4, note 14.

5 'Pis'mo k baronu Shteinu' (1813), *Russkii Arkhiv* 9, No. 2 (1871): 129–34. French original in Pertz, *Das Lebendes Ministers Freiherr von Stein,* 6 vols. (Berlin, 1851), III: 697–9. Marc Raeff, 'The Russian Autocracy and Its Officials', *Harvard Slavic Studies* IV (1957): 77–91, notes it was quite common for a man to begin as a diplomat then move into a domestic post, but Uvarov, because of his attachment to Europe, felt the change intensely.

6 See Chapter 4, note 3.

7 From Radishchev's appeal to Catherine the Great through to Stalin's telephone conversation with the poet Boris Pasternak, this trope of bewildered dissident loyalty to the autocrat would form part of the Russian political firmament. Cf. Christopher J. Barnes, *Boris Pasternak: A Literary Biography,* Vol. 2 (Cambridge, 2004), pp. 90–2.

8 Uvarov was unwell during the crisis surrounding his resignation as St Petersburg educational superintendent in 1820–1. He had a stroke after the death of his favourite daughter in 1843, and another soon after his wife died, and he had been ousted from office in 1849.

9 'I always used to praise the beauty of the Catholic system to Protestants, I was always demonstrating to them that Protestantism is neither church nor state, only a convulsion of the human mind, and they declared me to be a Catholic. Half-seriously, half-ironically I happened to give the Illuminists some support, and they labelled me a contemporary philosopher and an unbeliever.

Finally, you consider me a Jansenist, because I refuse to anathematize Port-Royal. Quot capita, tot sensus.' (19.6./1 7. 1814), Stepanov i Vermale, 'Pis'ma Zhozefa de Mestra k S.S. Uvarovu', p. 710.

10 4 o.s./16 n.s. 06.1814, in Schmid, 'Goethe und Uwarow', p. 152.

11 de Stael, *Dix années d'exil* [1818], Chs. XIII–XIX.

12 Madame de Stael, *De la littérature*, [1812] édition établie par Gérard Gengembre et Jean Goldzink (Paris, 1991), p. 82 ('De la littérature dans les rapports avec la liberté'): 'L'éloquence, l'amour des lettres et des beaux-arts, la philosophie, peuvent seuls faire d'un territoire une patrie, en donnant à la nation qui l'habite les mêmes goûts, les mêmes habitudes et les mêmes sentiments.'

13 Riasanovsky, *A Parting of Ways*, p. 58.

14 *L'Empereur Alexandre et Buonaparte* (St Petersburg, 1814), p. 23.

15 Ibid., p. 32.

16 Ibid., pp. 36–7.

17 Stepanov i Vermale, 'Pis'ma Zhozefa de Mestra k S.S. Uvarovu', p. 711.

18 *L'Empereur Alexandre et Buonaparte*, pp. 37–8.

19 Ibid., p. 13.

20 Ibid., p. 19.

21 No people, only national pride occurs in *Project*.

22 A. N. Pypin, *Kharakteristiki literaturnykh mnenii: 1820–1850* (St Petersburg, 1906): 'narodnost' offitsial'nayaya'; Riasanovsky, *Nicholas I and Official Nationality in Russia, passim.*

23 *Le Conservateur impartial* 28 (28 January 1813). de Stael, *Dix années d'exil* (Paris, 1966), p. 234 observed strength and a devotion to Russia among its citizens, but with no equivalent intellectual achievement. Karamzin 21 July 1813 wrote to Uvarov (*XVIII vek*, ed. Berkov, p. 353) of 'a time when we Moscow refugees who had lost everything we owned to the enemy and the flames only saved ourselves by our love for the fatherland and by finding friends amongst complete strangers.'

Chapter 6

1 I. I. Davydov, 'Vospominanie o Grafe Sergeii Semyonovichom Uvarove,' *Uchenye zapiski Akademii Nauk*, 3 otd. II (1855): 163–76; P. I. Bartenev, 'Biograficheskii ocherk,' *Russkii Arkhiv* 9, No. 12 (1871): 0133–4; *Ostafe'evskii arkhiv* I: 535–6, V: 77.

2 M. I.Gillel'son's two volumes, *Molodoi Pushkin*, and *P.A. Vyazemsky*, provide excellent material on the leading members of Arzamas. See also E. P. Kovalevsky, *Graf Bludov i ego vremya* (St Petersburg, 1866); L. N. Maikov's biography of Batyushkov is vol I of *Sochineniya*, 3 vols., ed. V. I. Saitov (St Petersburg, 1886–87), reprinted separately as *K.N. Batyushkov:*

ego zhizn'i socihineniya (Moscow, 2001). In English see also Ilya. Z. Serman, *Konstantin Batyushkov* (Woodbridge, CT, 1974). For Zhukovsky's life, see A. S. Arkhangel'sky, 'Biograficheskii ocherk', in V. A. Zhukovky, *Sochineniya*, 12 vols in 2 (St Petersburg 1902), 1; I. M. Semenko also provides an introduction to *Sochineniya* (Moscow, 1954, reprinted 1980). See also A. S. Anusevich, *V mire Zhukovskogo* (Moscow, 2006).

3   See M. S. Borovkova-Maikova, ed., *Arzamas i arzamasskie protokoly* (Leningrad, 1933), with an introduction by D. Blagoi; Aronson and Reisner, *Literaturnye kruzhki i salony*; B. Hollingsworth, 'Arzamas, Portrait of a Literary Society', *Slavonic and East European Review* XLIV, No. 103 (1966). Maiofis, *Vozzvanie ke Evrope* breaks new ground in its particular concern with Uvarov. *Arzamas: Sbornik vo dvukh knigakh* (Moscow, 1994) is a recent collection of documents.

4   Borovkova-Maikova, *Arzamas i arzamasskie protokoly*, p. 59.

5   Ibid., p. 36; Gillel'son, *P.A. Vyazemsky*, p. 102.

6   K. N. Batyushkov, *Opyty v stikhakh i proze*, ed. I. M. Semenko (Moscow, 1977), pp. 34–51. Also at http://batyushkov.lit-info.ru/batyushkov/proza/vec her-u-kantemira.htm

7   Uvarov, 'Literaturnye vospominaniya', p. 38. Uvarov though in retrospect exaggerated the role of Karamzin, calling him its 'guide' and 'leader' to underpin an idea of the group as highly patriotic and give it an ideological unity it did not possess.

8   Vigel', *Zapiski*, II: 63–4.

9   The reference is obscure but may be to Yakob Meshkov, a colonel of the Donsk Military Region (the *Voiska* Donskogo) who was ennobled for his services in 1804. The *Voiska Donskogo* was largely populated by Don Cossacks who were difficult to discipline but whose strength in battle repelling the French in 1812 had become legendary.

10   Borovkova-Maikova, *Arzamas i arzamasskie protokoly*, pp. 179ff.

11   Gillel'son, *Molodoi Pushkin*, p. 81.

12   Vigel', *Zapiski*, II: 63–4.

13   A. D. Bludova, 'Vospominaniya i zapiski', *Russkii Arkhiv* 27, No. 1 (1889): 39–112, also published as 'Vospominaniya I zapiski', *Zarya* No. 3 (1871).

14   Uvarov to Zhukovsky (6 June 1813) *Russkii Arkhiv* 9, No. 12 (1871): 0160–1. In 1815 Uvarov also told Kapnist: 'I expound the theory ... and I am an observer – you are the poet' (Whittaker, *The Origins*, p. 26).

15   Batyushkov, *Sochineniya* (1886–87), I: 251. The lines were part of Batyushkov's 'Ode to Tasso'. III: 439 Batyushkov asked Gnedich to read his poem aloud to Uvarov.

16   The concept distinguishes the tolerance of constitutional monarchy and the institutional church of the moderate position exemplified by Locke and Voltaire from the atheism and republicanism of the radical Enlightenment-inspired Spinoza. See Jonathan Israel, *Radical Enlightenment*.

17   Borovkova-Maikova, *Arzamas i arzamasskie protokoly*, pp. 37, 193–4 ('Rech' N.I. Turgeneva pri vstuplenii v Arzamas'); Aronson and Reiser,

Literaturnye kruzhki i salony, p. 107. Whittaker, *The Origins*, p. 51, suggests Uvarov already thought of Stein's proposed reforms as impractical and Utopian because they advocated the abolition of serfdom.

18 Aronson and Reiser, *Literaturnye kruzhki i salony*, pp. 105–7; Borovkova-Maikova, *Arzamas i arzamasskie protokoly*, pp. 69, 242.

19 For the background to the use of French in Russia, from the mid-eighteenth to the mid-nineteenth century, see Derek Offord's overview, 'Francophonie in Imperial Russia', *European Francophonie: The Social, Political and Cultural History of an International Prestige Language*, eds Gesine Argent, Derek Offord and Vladislav Rjeoutski (Berne, 2014), pp. 371–404. Uvarov is not mentioned.

20 'Eleusis', 123.

21 Nonnos von Panopolis, *der Dichter Ein Beitrag zur Geschichte der griechischen Poesie* (St Petersburg, 1817), also included in *Études*. For passages from the *Dionysiaca* commended by Uvarov, see *Études*, pp. 194–6. The standard English edition is *Dionysiaca*, tr. with a general introduction by W. H. D. Rouse, Mythological Introduction by H. J. Rose (London, 1940; reprinted 1955–56). For a commentary, see Robert Shorrock, *The Myth of Paganism: Nonnos, Dionysus and the World of Late Antiquity* (London, 2012).

22 'Examen critique de la fable d'Hercule, commentée par Dupuis' and 'Memoire sur les tragiques grecs', in *Esquisses*, pp. 143–75 and pp. 177–201 and *Études*, pp. 273–97 and pp. 299–316; 'Über das vorhomerische Zeitalter', in *Études*, pp. 250–71.

23 Wes, *Classics in Russia,* p. 180: 'For the Classical tradition in Russia, it was Uvarov whose activities ultimately brought in the highest returns.'

24 Batyushkov, *Sochineniya* (1886–87), III: 510 (letter dated 'end of June 1818').

25 'Litterature russe: Essai en vers et en prose par M. de Batushchoff [*sic*]', *Le Conservateur impartial* 83 (16 October 1817). The essay is substantially reproduced in Gillel'son, *Molodoi Pushkin*, 98–100, where Uvarov's analysis is called 'subtle and penetrating'. Batyushkov, loved by Uvarov, was a model Romantic figure, having lived the life of a poet in Paris. In 1818, shortly before his mental breakdown, he left for Italy.

26 Zhukovsky himself used the same classifications less successfully in 'O poezii drevnykh i novykh', *Vestnik Evropy* 55, No. 3 (1811): 187–212. For the German view of the world that Zhukovsky instantiated in this journal founded by Karamzin, see Natalia Nikonova and Lidia Dmitrievna, 'Print Media as Socio-imagological tools: German world of V.A. Zhukovsky's Herald of Europe', *Procedia in Social and Behaviour Sciences* 166 (January 2015): 631–4, also at www.sciencedirect.com.

27 Uvarov, 'O Grecheskoi antologii', pp. 241–2.

28 Ibid., p. 244.

29 See Peter Jay, ed., *The Greek Anthology* (London, 1973) for English translations of the poets who attracted Uvarov.

30 J. E. Sandys, *A History of Classical Scholarship*, 2 vols. (London, 1967), II: 389.

Chapter 7

1   Rozhdestvensky, *Istoricheskii Obzor*, p. 70; Whittaker, *The Origins*, p. 66.

2   On primary education, see S. A. Kniazkov and N. I. Serbov, *Ocherki istorii narodnogo obrazovaniya v Rossii do epokhu reform Aleksandra II* (Moscow, 1910), pp. 195–9; Rozhdestvensky, *Istorichesky Obzor*, pp. 122, 131, 145. On teachers' pay ibid., p. 137.

3   For the freeing of Baltic serfs, see David Moon, *The Abolition of Serfdom in Russia* (Harlow, 2001), p. 43.

4   S. S. Uvarov, *Rech' prezidenta Im. A. N. popechitel'ya Peterburgskogo uchebnago okruga v torzhestvennom sobranii Glavnogo pedagogichestkago instituta 22 marta 1818* (St Petersburg, 1818), commented on by Whittaker, *The Origins*, pp. 45–9 and translated by her in 'One Use of History in Education: A Lesson in Patience', *Slavic and European Education Review* 2, No. 1 (1978): 29–38. Referred to subsequently as *Rech'*/Speech.

5   Besides Schiller, Uvarov named as sources Gibbon, Montesquieu, Herder and the Swiss historian who edited Herder, Johannes Mueller.

6   Uvarov, *Rech'*/Speech, pp. 36–7.

7   F. E. Adcock, *Roman Political Ideas and Practice* (Ann Arbor, 1959), p. 16.

8   Uvarov, *Rech'*/Speech, p. 34.

9   Bernard Crick, 'Introduction', *Machiavelli: The Discourses* (Harmondsworth, 1970), p. 58 describes virtù: 'It comes from the Roman "vir" (man) and "virtus" (what is proper to a man). But what is proper to a man? Courage, fortitude, audacity, skill and civic spirit – a whole classical and renaissance theory of man and culture underlies the word; man is himself at his best when active for the common good – and he is not properly a man otherwise; politics is not a necessary evil, it is the very life.'

10 A. P. Kunitsyn, 'Rassmotrenie rechy', *Syn Otechestva* 46 (1818): 136–46, 174–91.

11 *Ostaf'evskii arkhiv knyazei Vyazemskykh*, 8 vols. (St Petersburg, 1899–1913), I: 485. (Karamzin to Dmitriev 29 April 1818).

12 P. A. Pletnev, 'Pamyati Grafa Sergiya Semenovicha Uvarova', *Uchenye zapiski* I (1856): liii–liv; lxii.

13 N. P. Zagoskin, *Istoriya Imperatorskogo Kazanskogo Universiteta*, 4 vols. (Kazan', 1902–1906), III: 308–10. Zagoskin described Uvarov's cause as just and praised his openness. For an overview of the period, see Whittaker, 'From Promise to Purge: The First Years of St Petersburg University', *Paedegogica Historica* XVIII (1978): 148–67; J. T. Flynn, 'Magnitsky's Purge of Kazan' University', *Journal of Modern History* 43, No. 4 (1971): 598–614, and 'S.S. Uvarov's "liberal" Years', *Jahrbücher für Geschichte Osteuropas* 20, No. 12 (1972): 481–91.

14 Whittaker, 'From Promise to Purge', p. 158. Zagoskin, *Istoriya*, III: 386; *Russkii Arkhiv* 31, No. 2 (1893): 131.

15 Batyushkov, *Sochineniya* (1887), III: 618–19 (to S. S. Uvarov May 1819).

Chapter 8

1 'Pis'ma mitropolita Evgeniya Bolkhovitinova', *Russkii Arkhiv* 27, No. 2 (1889): 83.

2 I. I. Davydov, 'Pis'ma I.I. Davydova k A.A. Prokopovichu-Antonskomu', *Russkii Arkhiv* 27, No. 3 (1889): 549–50.

3 A. O. Smirnova, 'A.S. Pushkin po zapiskam A. O. Smirnovoi', *Russkii Arkhiv* 37, No. 2 (1899): 318.

4 Metternich noted to his wife he still regarded Alexander as a threat to his proposals: 'Three weeks at Carlsbad has resulted in something that 30 years of revolution could never produce. For the first time there will appear a group of anti-revolutionary measures, correct and peremptory. What I have wanted to do and what the infernal Tsar Alexander has always spoiled I have now pulled off because he was not present there.' Alan Palmer, *Metternich* (London, 1972), p. 185.

5 Marie-Pierre Rey, *Alexander I The Tsar who Defeated Napoleon*, tr. Susan Emanuel (DeKalb, IL, 2012), p. 319: In 1818 the emperor still believed in the virtue of liberal ideas and of constitutionalism. The speech he gave to the Warsaw diet illustrates a sincere desire to advance along this road … but two years later the text setting out the provisions had changed.' See also Alan Palmer, *Alexander I Tsar of War and Peace* (London, 1974; reprinted 2014), pp. 364–5.

6 *Ostaf'evskii arkhiv* I: 224, 228. 'O novykh pis'makh Vol'tera' was not published until the first collected works of Vyazemsky in 1886. Uvarov's fear was not unusual. Nikolai Turgenev, a man capable of broad sympathies despite his radical liberal politics, said censors generally lived in fear of ruin, *La Russie et les russes*, 3 vols. (Paris, 1847), I: 100.

7 'Memorandum' quoted in Czeslaw Milosz, *The History of Polish Literature* (Berkeley, CA, 1983), pp. 201–2.

8 Quoted in Whittaker, *The Origins*, p. 81.

9 'Poslanie tsensoru', A. S. Pushkin, *Polnoe sobranie sochinenii* [PSS], 4th ed., 10 vols. (Leningrad, 1979), II: 112. For Pushkin's early political poetry, rebellious but not republican, see T. J. Binyon, *Pushkin A Biography* (London, 2002), pp. 23–4 and pp. 51–6, Iurii Druzhnikov, *Prisoner of Russia: Alexander Pushkin and the Political Uses of Nationalism* (Piscataway, NJ, 1999), and *The Pushkin Handbook*, ed. David. M. Bethea (Milwaukee, WI, 2013), pp. 287–8. By the time in 1822 that he wrote this poem, not published in his lifetime, Pushkin had been in exile in the remote south, and finally in the town of Kishinyov, since May 1820. J. Berest, *The Emergence of Russian Liberalism: A. P. Kunitsyn in Context 1783-1840* (London, 2011) establishes the importance of Pushkin's teacher for the political struggle that framed the later period of Alexander's reign.

10 Whittaker, *The Origins*, p. 82.

11 Whittaker, 'From Promise to Purge', p. 161.

12 For a moving account of the professors' personal distress, see A. Nikitenko, *A. I. Galich* (St Petersburg, 1869); I. I. Ivanov, *Istoriya russkoi kritiki*, 4 vols. (St Petersburg, 1898–1900), I: 287–91, and A. Koyré, *La philosophie et le*

problème nationale en Russie au debut du XIX siècle (Paris, 1929), pp. 99–112.

13 Text in French and Russian translation in M. I. Sukhomlinov, *Izsledovaniya i stat'i po russkoi literature i prosveshcheviya*, 2 vols. (St Petersburg, 1889), I: 378–86. This is my translation.

14 Turgenev, *La Russie*, I: 566.

15 Patricia K. Grimsted, *The Foreign Ministers of Alexander I* (Berkeley, CA, 1969), p. 305 notes that the twin influences of the *philosophes* and the anti-revolutionary émigré s on the tsar's upbringing affected his ministers: 'They were caught in the unreconciled dilemma between Alexander's aims, with which they had to sympathize to succeed, and his fundamental quest for peace and social stability – in whose interest he might pursue the most despotic conduct – to which they had to be willing to submit.' Capodistrias, who represented liberal monarchy and was most prominent in Alexander's similarly inclined years 1816–18, was after Alexander tightened the reins obliged effectively to share his portfolio with Nesselrode (Grimsted, *The Foreign Ministers of Alexander I*, p. 252.) Capodistrias and Nesselrode were viewed from Vienna as leading anti- and pro-Metternich factions. See Palmer, *Metternich*, p. 208. Capodistrias voluntarily left Russia in June 1821, the same year as Uvarov resigned as Superintendent.

16 Cf. C. H. Whittaker, 'The Ideology of Sergei Uvarov', *Russian Review* 37, No. 2 (April 1978): 158–76.

17 Uvarov's axiom seems to have been adapted from Sextus Propertius, Elegies, II, x, 5: 'in magnis et voluisse sat est.' [In great endeavours even to have had the will is enough.]

18 Uvarov to Speransky 1.12. 1819 in *V Pamyat' grafa I. I. Speranskogo 1772-1872* (St Petersburg, 1872), pp. 233–4.

19 Cf. Henry A. Kissinger, *A World Restored* (London, 1957), p. 191: 'The conservative in a revolutionary period is always somewhat of an anomaly. Were the pattern of obligations still spontaneous it would occur to no one to be a conservative, for a serous alternative to the existing structure would be inconceivable. But once there exists a significant revolutionary party, even more once a revolution has triumphed, two complementary questions have been admitted as valid, more symbolic in their very appearance than any answer that may be given: What is the meaning of authority? What is the nature of freedom? Henceforth stability and reform, liberty and authority, come to appear as antithetical; the context becomes doctrinal and the problem of change takes the form of an attack on the existing order, instead of a dispute over specific issues.'

Chapter 9

1 P. A. Pletnev, 'Pamyati Grafa Sergiya Semenovicha Uvarova', *Uchenye zapiski* 1 (1856): lxxiv–lxxv.

2 Ibid., p. liv.

3 Whittaker, 'The Ideology of Sergei Uvarov', p. 170.

4 Whittaker, *The Origins*, pp. 122–3.

5 Ibid., p. 124.

6 N. Barsukov, *Zhizhn' i trudy M.P. Pogodina* (St Petersburg, 1888–1910), ix: 308; *Rech'*/Speech, p. 35: 'Providence gave birth in the womb of feudal laws to the means and conditions which would abolish these laws for ever.'

7 *Rech'*/Speech, p. 31.

8 The Soviet economic historian P. I. Lyashchenko, *A History of the National Economy of Russia to 1917* (New York, 1949; reprinted 1970), p. 281, notes this choice of backwardness over instability was typical of Uvarov's class: 'In social-political life a handful of privileged, "Europeanised", sometimes "liberal" aristocrats, despite their European education in liberalism, were fiercely devoted to serfdom. Millions of the submerged, illiterate, impoverished and semi-starved peasantry struggled for freedom and a better existence through persistent uprisings, and represented, despite the lack of organisation, a serious threat to the ruling class.'

9 I. Golovin, *Nicholas I* (London, 1846), 1: 331.ff; Whittaker, *The Origins*, p. 122.

10 *Ostafevskii arkhiv*, I: 438; II: 336, 338.

11 Whittaker, *The Origins*, p. 122.

12 *Ostafevskii arkhiv*, III: 33.

13 *Ostafievskii arkhiv*, I: 357; III: 33, 84, 116, 120, 122, 334.

14 Schmid, 'Goethe und Uwarow', p. 156.

15 Ibid., p. 168.

16 Borovkova-Maikova, *Arzamas i arzamasskie protokoly*, p. 281.

17 Vigel', *Zapiski*, II: 111.

18 The transition from the neoclassical to the romantic aesthetic was brilliantly described in Richard Sennett, *The Fall of Public Man* (Cambridge, 1977), clearly developing the observations of Hannah Arendt, *On Revolution* (revised edition, Harmondsworth, 1973), ch. III *passim*. See also Pipes, *Karamzin's Memoir*, pp. 36, 86–9. That Goethe embraced both old and new age (cf. Sennet, *The Fall of Public Man*, p. 24) was intuitively grasped and revered by Uvarov, just as it was by Schiller, whose major essays, including *The Aesthetic Education of Man in a Series of Letters* [1795], eds and trs. *Elizabeth Wilkinson and Leonard Willoughby*, were informed by the revolution in sensibility and with the consequent desire to retain eighteenth-century 'grace' alongside nineteenth-century sincerity of moral purpose ('dignity').

19 Eleusis, p. 114.

20 Ibid., p. 89.

21 Ibid., p. 103; Cicero, *De Legibus*, II: 14.

22 See 'Greek Tragedians', in *Études*, p. 302.

23 Eleusis, p. 156.

24 Ibid., p. 98.

25 'Prehomeric Age', in *Études*, p. 255.

26 *'V Pamyat' grafa M.I. Speranskogo', XVIII vek*, ed. Berkov, p. 234.

27 Schmid, 'Goethe und Uwarow', p. 155.

28 See note 18.

Chapter 10

1 Uvarov, *Alexandre*, pp. 34–5.

2 Marc Raeff, *The Decembrist Movement* (Englewood Cliff, NJ, 1966), p. 103 quotes from Muraviev's draft constitution for Russia: 'The experience of all nations and of all epochs has demonstrated that autocratic power is equally ruinous for the rulers and for society; it corresponds neither to the teachings of our holy faith, nor to the principles of sane reason. One cannot admit as a principle of government one man's arbitrariness; it is impossible to accept that all rights belong to one side and all duties to the other. Blind obedience can be based only on fear and it is unworthy of both a reasonable ruler and reasonable ministers. By putting themselves above the laws, the sovereigns have forgotten that they are thereby putting themselves outside the law, outside humanity. ... All European peoples are securing laws and freedom. More than any other, the Russian people deserves to have both.'

3 N. K. Shil'der, *Imperator Nikolai Pervyi, ego zhizn' i tsarstvovanie*, 2 vols. (St Petersburg, 1903), 1: 315, 327; W. Bruce Lincoln, *Nicholas I* (Bloomington, IN, 1978), pp. 56, 109.

4 Cf. Raeff, *The Decembrist Movement*, p. 15: 'The Decembrists were ... the only generation in the history of the modern Russian elite to try to lay the foundations for a meaningful, peculiarly Russian, organic synthesis between the political tradition of the eighteenth century and the historicist and nationalist ideas of the early nineteenth century.' Uvarov was distinguished from these men only by his unconditional primary loyalty to the autocracy, which caused him to turn aside from his own ideals. Conversely it was the Decembrists' overwhelming national pride that caused their dissatisfaction with the tsar.

5 Uvarov, *Alexandre*, pp. 35–6. His words echo Deuteronomy IV, 6.

6 Cf. Raeff, *The Decembrist Movement*, p. 28. See also S. V. Mironenko *Aleksandr I: dekabristy i Rossiya v pervoi chetverti XIX veka. Vybor puti* (Moscow, 2016): Despite his carefully modulated Speech Uvarov had been blamed in 1818 over an article that appeared in the press advocating the freeing of the serfs.

7 Shil'der, *Imperator Nikolai*, I: 163, 315, 311; Lincoln, *Nicholas I*, p. 77.

8 Shil'der, *Imperator Nikolai*, p. 314.

9 Ibid., p. 94; Lincoln, *Nicholas I*, p. 98.

10 Cf. Sidney Monas, *The Third Section Police and Society in Russia under Nicholas I* (Cambridge, MA, 1961), p. 145: 'The role of the censor was conceived as that of an amiable legal guardian of letters, a foster father of the arts and sciences. The prevailing moral order ... could not be assailed, but in terms of the new law it could be interpreted with a wider degree of latitude.'

11 Pletnev, 'Pamyati Grafa Sergiya Semenovicha Uvarova', pp. lxxxiii–lxxxiv. Andrea Wulf, *The Invention of Nature: The Adventures of Alexander Von Humboldt The Lost Hero of Science* (London, 2015), pp. 202–16.

12 Louis-Antoine Léouzon Leduc, 'Essai biographique et critique', in Uvarov, *Esquisses*, pp. 58–61.

13 Ibid.

14 Whittaker, *The Origins*, p. 97.

15 Lincoln, *Nicholas I*, p. 76; Raeff, 'The Russian Autocracy and Its Officials', pp. 89–90.

16 Shil'der, *Imperator Nikolai*, p. 297.

Chapter 11

1 Pushkin scandalized his friends and has continued to embarrass scholars with a ferocious celebration of Russia's suppression of the Polish Uprising of 1831–32 in two poems, 'To The Slanderers of Russia' and 'The Anniversary of Borodino'. The poet defended himself in terms of his aesthetic interest in the battle. PSS X: 273 (to Vyazemsky 1.7.1831). Binyon, *Pushkin A Biography*, p. 377 writes: 'Both poems are the expression of the chauvinist, imperialist element in Pushkin'.

2 *Pushkin v vospominaniyakh sovremennikov* (Moscow/Leningrad, 1950), p. 437.

3 Quoted by S. Ya. Shtraikh, in Vigel', *Zapiski*, I: 13–14.

4 In *Sbornik postanovlenii po Ministerstvu narodnogo proshveshcheniya* (Collected Proceedings of the Ministry of National Enlightenment) II, i: 502–32 (4 December 1932).

5 Uvarov, knowing the position of his predecessor, Count Lieven, was shaky, had no doubt risen to the occasion with his trenchantly worded speech. Mikhail Lemke's view that the tripartite slogan was the creation of Nicholas has not found agreement. Cf. M. Lemke, *Nikolaevskie zhandarmy i literatura 1826-1855gg.* (St Petersburg, 1907), p. 81.

6 Plato, *The Republic*, Book 3, 401b–401d. The translation here is by Desmond Lee. [i.e. not specifying a particular edition, but giving the translator if they want to track this particular one down.]

7 *Teleskop* had recently published articles *attacking* the July Revolution and the Polish Insurrection, making Uvarov's repression seem all the more unwarranted. See Lemke, *Nikolaevskie Zhandarmy*, p. 397. But Uvarov may have thought this was a cunning way of drawing attention to these events in Russia.

8 See Lincoln, *Nicholas I*, 203, on Nicholas's own fear of 'all those homeless individuals, men without a country, who have been banished from all well-ordered societies.'

9 *Ostafevskii Arkhiv*, III: 228 (Vyazemsky to A. I. Turgenev 26 March 1833).

10 Uvarov, 'Slovo o Goethe', *Ucheniya zapiski Imperatorskago Moskovskago universiteta* 1 (1833): 74–94, published in French as *Notice sur Goethe* (St Petersburg, 1842) and included in *Études*, pp. 333–53.

11 *Études*, pp. 339–40.

12 Ibid., pp. 342, 345–6.

13 The disillusioned socialist Alexander Herzen came round to Uvarov's conservative point of view after the failure of the 1848 Revolution in France, having as a young man found Goethe's 'egoism' unacceptable. See A. I. Gertsen, *Polnoe sobranie sochinenii*, I: 119 ('Pervaya Vstrecha'), VI: 56 and *passim* ('S togo berega').

14 *Études*, 349. Only Herzen had a grasp of Goethe as a scientist and thinker to rival Uvarov's.

15 Durylin, 'Drug Gete', pp. 208–9.

16 Lesley Chamberlain, *Motherland* (London, 2004), pp. 176–8.

17 'Eleusis', in *Études*, 99. The great mysteries were reserved for a small number of the initiated, because they contained revelations which would have dealt a mortal blow to the religion of the state; the minor mysteries were open to all men.

18 *Rech'/*Speech, pp. 37–8.

19 Adcock, *Roman Political Ideas and Practice*, pp. 12, 16.

20 See Preface, note 17.

21 Uvarov's Official Nationality had far more in common with the practical Roman idea as it entered eighteenth-century French thought than with the Romantic nationality which became its rival. See Arendt, *On Revolution*, p. 37; Andrzej Walicki, *The Slavophile Controversy* (Oxford, 1975), p. 46, contended that the overlap with the Romantic term 'reflected the efforts of the autocratic regime to expand its social base, to rely directly on "the people"'.

22 Michael Cherniavsky, *Tsar and People, Studies in Russian Myth* (New Haven, 1961), traced the growth of the Russian myths of tsar and people from their origins in Byzantium, and showed how closely the Russian ruler has always been identified with the church, to the extent of being considered a 'worker for Christ'. With the splitting off of Orthodox Russia from Constantinople the Russian sovereign was protector of the only Orthodox people and heir to two Roman empires. His religious aspect became accentuated until he was viewed as partly divine, and Russia saw in him its salvation. As a saint of Christ he would save men, as pious tsar he would save his people. He was the 'dear father Tsar', the bridegroom of Holy Mother Russia, with absolute paternal authority. The paternal aspect of the ruler coincided with those Roman notions of authority inherited by Russia. The myth of Holy Russia endured and was coveted in the nineteenth century by nationalists of every stripe. How powerful it was may be seen in the powerful, contradictory feelings aroused by Peter the Great, who was called anti-Christ by the Slavophiles for forcing Russia to move towards the West but was revered by Nicholas I for his might and achievements. Pushkin rejected the idea of

either the tsar or the state being holy, but in 'The Bronze Horseman' hardly
discounted the power of the myth over the ordinary man Yevgeny, whose life
was ruined by the conflicts it created. Cherniavsky concluded, pp. 228–31,
that the tsarist myth destroyed independent thought in those who believed it:
'The overwhelming completeness of the ruler-myth … precluded any theory
of opposition to, or limitation of the ruler within the context of traditional
Russia. Any challenge … was by definition revolutionary. …The power of the
myth was sufficient to make the most intelligent and sophisticated Russian
assign all power and all responsibility to the person of the Tsar.'

23 See Chapter 5, note 21.

24 Walicki, *The Slavophile Controversy*, p. 46, contended that the overlap with
the Romantic term 'reflected the efforts of the autocratic regime to expand
its social base, to rely directly on "the people"'. Uvarov's intentions strike me
as far more disingenuous.

25 Arendt, *On Revolution*, p. 156.

26 Riasanovsky, *A Parting of Ways*, p. 105 calls Uvarov's policy a Russian version
of the Metternich system.

27 N. Barsukov, *Zhizhn' i trudy M.P. Pogodina* (St Petersburg, 1888–1910), IV:
38. Whittaker, *The Origins*, p. 102, observes that in fact Uvarov's views on
serfdom were more moderate than this passage, taken out of context,
suggests. However, here I merely wish to draw attention to the term
'political religion'.

28 Chamberlain, *Motherland*, p. 203; Simon Sebag Montefiore, *Stalin: The Court
of the Red Tsar* (London, 2003), p. 77.

Chapter 12

1 *Ostafevskii Arkhiv*, III: 237 (Vyazemsky to Turgenev 2 June 1833).

2 Vigel', *Zapiski*, II: 323–4.

3 Vasil'chikov, *Semeistvo Razumovskikh*, II: 145; Whittaker, *The Origins*, p. 151;
Belinsky wrote in 'Literary Reveries' (1834): 'Yes, we shall soon have our
own Russian national enlightenment, we shall soon prove we have no need
for foreign intellectual support. It will be easy for us to do when our eminent
high officials, devotees of the Tsar in the difficult field of the government of
the people come amongst the eager young students in the central temple
of Russian education to proclaim to them the sacred will of the monarch
and to show the way to enlightenment in the spirit of Orthodoxy, Autocracy
and Nationality.' V. G. Belinsky, *Polnoe Sobranie Sochinenii* [PSS], 13 vols.
(Moscow, 1955), I: 122. However Belinsky's Soviet editors suggested he was
forced to insert this reverential paragraph.

4 Chapter 9, note 18.

5 N. I. Pirogov, *Russkii Arkhiv* 30, No. 1 (1892): 197; Lincoln, *Nicholas I*,
pp. 57–8, 88, 98. See also Monas, *The Third Section*, p. 10 and compare
N. I. Turgenev, *La Russie*, I: 133. The corollary of Nicholas's effacement of

his ministers' individuality was a stress on acting the part. According to
A. N. Pypin, *Karakteristiki literaturnykh mnenii 1820–1850* (St Petersburg,
1906), p. 101, the bureaucracy had little involvement in the running of Russia,
and functionaries were therefore easily pushed into laziness, boredom and
corruption.

6 G. G. Shpet, *Ocherk razvitiya russkoi filosofii* (Petrograd, 1922), p. 237:
'The Tsar personally did not like Uvarov very much, but gave him authority,
because Uvarov fulfilled his requirements more thoroughly than others, and
was into the bargain an educated man, one of the most educated in the
Russia of his day.' For the tsar's suspicion of educated men, however, see
Lincoln, *Nicholas I*, p. 98; and Raeff, 'The Russian Autocracy and Its Officials'.
Except for those civilian Russians Karamzin recommended, Nicholas selected
mostly military men and foreigners to serve him.

7 Whittaker, *The Origins*, p. 151.

8 Whittaker, 'Dissertation', p. 137, quoting G. Luciani, *Le livre de la genese
du peuple ukrainien* (Paris, 1956), p. 74. Uvarov's predecessor as Minister,
Prince Carl Christoph von Lieven, had noted, 'In the Russian state, where
many merchants and peasants yearly join the ranks of the nobility through
promotion in the army or civil service, the organisation of the schools [on the
class principle] presents great difficulties.' See Rozhdestvensky, *Istorichesky
Obzor*, p. 180.

9 Rozhdestvensky, *Istorichesky Obzor*, pp. 223–4.

10 Longinov, 'Vospominanie o grafe S.S. Uvarove', p. 121.

11 Gertsen, *Polnoe sobranie sochinenii*, VIII: 126–8.

12 Rozhdestvensky, *Istorichesky Obzor*, p. 298; M. K. Vladimirskii-Budanov,
Istoriya Imperatorskogo Universiteta sv. Vladimira (Kiev, 1884), I: 76;
Whittaker, *The Origins*, p. 193 views as poetic the symmetry 'underlining
the essential historical unity and development of the Empire' which resulted.
Kiev enshrined the seat of Orthodoxy, St Petersburg was home to Autocracy
and Moscow enshrined Nationality. Count Alexander von Benckendorff
who at the Third Department headed the tsarist equivalent of the Political
Police of the twentieth century, from the Cheka to the FSB, noted in his
memoirs: 'Kiev was selected as the place for the new university, the city
being, on the one hand, the ancient cradle of Orthodoxy, and on the other,
the headquarters of the First Army, which offered the necessary facilities for
the surveillance of a large gathering of young people.' See Shil'der, *Imperator
Nikolai*, II, appendix.

13 Whittaker, *The Origins*, p. 195; Vladimirskii-Budanov, *Istoriya*, I: 96ff.

14 Henri Troyat, *Tolstoy* (Harmondsworth, 1970), pp. 28, 46.

15 Alexander de Krusenstern, *Précis du système, des progrès et de l'état de
l'instruction publique en Russie* (Warsaw, 1845), pp. 115ff was an almost
contemporary account of how the new regulations affected foreigners
wanting to teach in Russia and Russians wanting to work as tutors. See also
Whittaker, *The Origins*, p. 135.

16 Rozhdestvensky, *Istorichesky Obzor*, pp. 204–5; S. A. Kniazkov and
N. I. Serbov, *Ocherki istorii narodnogo obrazovaniya v Rossii do epokhu
reform Aleksandra II* (Moscow, 1910), p. 210.

17　Whittaker, *The Origins*, p. 147.

18　Rozhdestvensky, *Istorichesky Obzor*, p. 250.

19　See above note 10. The passage is from Herzen's celebrated autobiography *My Past and Thoughts*.

20　Gertsen, *Polnoe sobranie sochinenii*, VIII: 142–3.

21　Kniazkov i Serbov, *Ocherki*, p. 221.

22　*Desyatiletie Ministerstva narodnogo prosveshcheniya 1833–43* (St Petersburg, 1863), pp. 106ff.

23　One of the foreigners, H. H. Hess, a German, discovered four new minerals while working in Russia, and called one of them Uvarovite in tribute.

24　Whittaker, *The Origins*, p. 159.

Chapter 13

1　*Sbornik Proizshestvii Ministerstva Narodnogo Prosvechsheniya*, No. 84 (1828), II, i: 203.

2　Lincoln, *Nicholas I*, p. 226.

3　Rozhdestvensky, *Istoricheskii Obzor*, pp. 223–4. Once Uvarov had been named Deputy Minister of National Enlightenment in 1832, after the July Revolution in France and events in Poland, he redefined the task of censorship with new severity, asserting it was 'to multiply, wherever possible, the number of intellectual dams' against the penetration of destructive Western ideas. A law was passed requiring any new journal to be approved by the tsar; no one person was allowed to edit two journals simultaneously, and for each journal two censors would be appointed.

4　A. V. Nikiten'ko, *Dnevnik*, 3 vols. (Leningrad, 1955), I: 174 (8 August 1835) and p. 135. In fact Grech was himself one of a trio of journalists, with Faddei Bulgarin and Osip Senkowski, whose writing became a symbols for liberal intellectuals of the corruption and arbitrary repressiveness of Nicholas's reign. That the tsar disliked them personally may have motivated Uvarov's choice of example. On one occasion Nicholas had them confined to the guardhouse for attacking his favourite novel. See Monas, *The Third Section*, pp. 120–1.

5　Monas, *The Third Section*, pp. 159–64.

6　Polevoy's love of Europe turned others, including Belinsky, against him. Pushkin called him a Jacobin out of personal dislike, thus aligning himself with Uvarov. Polevoy's opponents then stressed his 'merchant' background as a further negative factor. But Admiral Shishkov, Uvarov's ministerial predecessor but one, admired Polevoy's closeness to old Russian ways. See Monas, *The Third Section*, p. 161.

7　The English royal visitor Frances Anne Vane, Marchioness of Londonderry, came to be known as a well-known judge of the character of Nicholas I and his reign. See *The Russian Journal of Lady Londonderry 1836–7*, eds W. A. L. Seasman and J. R. Sewell (London, 1973).

8 Monas, *The Third Section*, p. 173.

9 Nikitenko, *Dnevnik* (5 April 1834 and 9 April 1835), I: 240–1.

10 See Appendix II.

11 Nikitenko, *Dnevnik*, I: 267.

12 For how these many tensions and feuds allowed good literature to flourish by default, see Riasanovsky, *A Parting of Ways*, p. 276.

13 See note 6.

14 Tatiana Wolff, ed. and tr., *Pushkin on Literature* (London, 1971), p. 307.

15 Vigel', *Zapiski*, I: 13–14.

16 Pushkin, PSS, III: 197. See also L. A. Chereisky, *Pushkin i ego okruzhenie* (Leningrad, 1975), p. 429.

17 Binyon, *Pushkin*, p. 483.

18 Pushkin, PSS, X: 300. Uvarov's version contained, for Pushkin's avowedly chauvinistic line, 'who will survive in the unequal conflict – the arrogant Pole or the true Russian?', the French 'Pour que l'un deux triomphe, il faut que l'autre expire.' That rendered Pushkin's meaning but missed his aesthetic admiration for battle. Chereisky, *Pushkin*, p. 429 follows P. E. Shegolev, *Iz zhizni Pushkina* (Moscow/Leningrad, 1931), pp. 352–6, accusing Uvarov of a tendentious interpretation of Pushkin's ode but this seems to reflect a Soviet unwillingness to endorse Pushkin's enjoyment of war. Lemke, *Nikolaevskie zhandarmy*, p. 496, accepts Pushkin's attitude for what it was and compares it to that of Zhukovsky.

19 Pushkin, PSS, VIII: 34; Nikitenko, *Dnevnik*, I: 241. 'Andzhelo' was based on scenes from Shakespeare's *Measure for Measure*.

20 Pushkin, PSS, VIII: 47; Chereisky, *Pushkin*, p. 429.

21 *Ostafevskii Arkhiv*, III: 277; Lemke, *Nikolaevskie zhandarmy*, p. 520.

22 Pushkin, PSS, III: 316. Translation

23 Gillel'son, *P.A. Vyazemsky*, pp. 256–8; Chereisky, *Pushkin*, p. 429; Monas, *The Third Section*, pp. 223–4. *Sovremennik* was permitted in 1836 not as a journal but as 'a collection of articles', which took away its legal basis for appearing monthly. Pushkin's supporters proposed a second publication to be called *Russkii Sbornik* (A Russian Collection) alongside or in place of *Sovremennik*, to give Pushkin a publication to fall back on, but their requests were ignored.

24 Cf. Wes, *Classics in Russia*, p. 169.

25 Jobard's final legal appeal in February 1836 stated, 'The Minister of National Enlightenment, wanting to destroy me by whatever means he can, first had me declared a criminal, then a madman and a simpleton; refusing once to pay me the high honour of exchanging a few words with me, and not respecting the petitions submitted to him on my behalf by the military governor-general of Moscow [General Golitsyn who brought Jobard from France] on the question of my alleged madness, he ordered me to be certified as to my mental health. This certificate immediately proved he was wrong in that respect too, as I was found by all those who examined me, unanimously, to be in full control of my faculties. But it shows to what degree of arbitrariness he could stoop that he deceived the Committee of Ministers by delivering a distorted report, that he formally lied in his dealings with the Moscow Governor-General, manufactured various excuses and even had the audacity to simulate an order from the tsar, without the tsar's notice, a matter which, bound by my conscience, I have already brought personally to the tsar's attention through the Adjutant-General, Count Benkendorff.' Whatever Jobard's balance of mind these were accusations of a kind frequently levelled at Uvarov by others whose sanity was plain. Jobard, obsessed and choleric, was not mistaken in his assessment. See N. P. Zagoskin, *Istoriya Kazanskogo Universiteta*, 4 vols. (Kazan', 1902–6), IV: 578–61.

26 Monas, *The Third Section*, p. 164.

27 Uvarov's unpublished personal report (in French) on the Chaadaev letter directly connected Chaadaev and the Decembrists. See Gillel'son, *P.A. Vyazemsky*, pp. 248–9. This thinking was typical of conservative opinion, however, and the public was largely against Chaadaev for his deprecation of Russia. For this and Uvarov's zeal, see M. K. Lemke, *Ocherki po istorii russkoi tsenzury i zhurnalistiki XIX stoletiya* (St Petersburg, 1904; reprinted The Hague, 1970), p. 408 and p. 416.

28 *Ostafevskii arkhiv*, III: 334; Pushkin, PSS, III: 321. Binyon's masterly account, pp. 479–90, of their quarrel stresses that Pushkin only harmed himself making such an enemy, but it hardly reflected well on Uvarov either.

29 Lemke, *Nikolaevskie zhandarmy*, p. 522; Chereisky, *Pushkin*, p. 429.

30 Henri Troyat, *Poushkine* (Paris, 1946), pp. 413–14.

31 Monas, *The Third Section*, p. 225; Binyon, *Pushkin*, 632–3.

32 Nikitenko, *Dnevnik*, I: 195.

33 Ibid., p. 199.

34 M. Yu. Lermontov, *Sobranie Sochinenii*, 4 vols. (Moscow, 1961), I: 412–14 ('Smert'poeta', 1837).

35 Belinsky, PSS, XII: 50.

Chapter 14

1 The term, made famous by Isaiah Berlin in *Russian Thinkers* (Oxford, 1976), comes from P. V. Annenkov, *Literaturnye vospominaniya* (St Petersburg, 1909).

2 Not surprisingly a counterbalancing 'ideal personality' was the product of these fresh and marvellous years in Russian literature. E. J. Brown, *Stankevich and His Moscow Circle 1830–1840* (Stanford, CA, 1966) evokes the ethical power of the leading *intelligent* of the 1830s, Nikolai Stankevich. See also Chamberlain, *Motherland*, pp. 20–46, and note 11 below.

3 Belinsky particularly loathed Shevyrev and Pogodin. See PSS, XII: 61–2, and 103, where on one occasion he compared Shevyrev to the second-rate amanuensis Wagner in Goethe's *Faust*.

4 N. G. Ustryalov, *O sisteme pragmaticheskoi russkoi istorii* (St Petersburg, 1836); 'Thus we can say that over the last 10 years , every aspect of our national history has changed. ... Now Russian history is entering a new decade, with a new look at its objects, and is preparing a vast store of information, of which Karamzin could not take advantage.' Uvarov, *Desyatiletie*, p. 94.

5 Ibid., p. 94 and p. 97.

6 Cf. David B. Saunders, 'Historians and Concepts of Nationality in Early Nineteenth-Century Russia', *Slavonic and East European Review* 60, No. 1 (January 1982): 44–62.

7 *Ostaf'evskii archiv*, III: 724, 736–7 (Vyazemsky to Uvarov November 1836).

8 Gillel'son, *P.A. Vyazemsky*, pp. 242–4.

9 B. H. Sumner, *A Short History of Russia* (London, 1943) argued for fundamental continuities between the tsarist and the Soviet regimes, a view with which a year spent living in the Soviet Union in 1978–79 led me wholeheartedly to concur. As Adam Zamoyski more recently observed in *Holy Madness Romantics Patriots and Revolutionaries 1776–1871* (London, 1999), p. 321: 'Uvarov ... held up narodnost as "the last anchor of our salvation and the most secure guarantee of the strength and greatness of our fatherland." The Tsar took his point and ... this stagnant and oppressive self-image crept in everywhere ... . Not surprisingly it was to resurface a century later, under Stalin, as a foil against "rootless cosmopolitanism" in art.'

10 Pypin, *Kharakteristiki*, pp. 103ff; Raeff, 'The Russian Autocracy and Its Officials', p. 86.

11 See above note 1 and Chapter 9, note 18. Arendt, *On Revolution*, III, 'The Pursuit of Happiness' discusses the transition from public to private man, from citoyen to bourgeois, in the early nineteenth century. See also Sennett, *The Fall*, p. 20. The peculiarity of the Russian 'Marvellous Decade' however was the use of new categories of private virtue such as inner harmony, grace and moral good as standards for public life. The new age wanted sincerity and both the Slavophiles with their emphasis on 'the true church' and the Westernizers with their emphasis on personal integrity espoused that hope.

12 In Uvarov's case, where the man and his behaviour were hardly simple, both Russian and Western scholars seem to have followed this liberal ideological impulse and have fought shy of a study of his complex character. For a pioneering exception, see Alexandre Koyré, *La Philosophie et le problème national en Russie au début du XIX siecle* (Paris, 1929).

13 Burke, *Reflections*, p. 94 and p. 100.

14 Edward Crankshaw, *The Shadow of the Winter Palace* (London, 1976), p. 73.

15 Henry Kissinger, *A World Restored: Metternich, Castlereagh and the Problems of Peace, 1812–22* (London, 1957), pp. 8–9.

16 Belinsky, PSS, I: 82 and passim ('Literaturnye Mechtaniya'); pp. 103ff ('O russkoi povesti v povestyakh g. Gogolya'); II: 23 ('Nichto o nichem'); V: 587–8 ('Russkaya literatura v 1841 godu'); X: 95–6 (Pis'ma I). 'You know my nature: It's always at extremes and never finds itself at the centre of an idea.' XII: 66.

Belinsky's essays and letters offer the best access to his personality, but see also E. Lampert's classic study of the mid-nineteenth-century intelligentsia, *Studies in Rebellion* (London, 1957), pp. 46–107. A negative view of Belinsky's influence on Russian literature is Dmitri Chizhevsky, *Gegel' v Rossii* (Paris, 1938), pp. 113–14. The twentieth-century formalist school of criticism which insisted that literature be seen as a means of expression, a device free from social, historical or political connotations, was the first fundamental attempt to provide an alternative to Belinsky's civic criticism in modern Russian literature, In some measure the Formalists returned Russian literary criticism to the apolitical position Uvarov preferred.

17 Marc Raeff, *The Origins of the Russian Intelligentsia: The Eighteenth-Century Nobility* (New York, 1966) remains, together with Pipes, *Karamzin's Memoir*, the best overview of the condition of that class.

18 Lemke, *Ocherki po istorii russkoi tsensury*, p. 444.

19 Whittaker, 'Dissertation', p. 205.

20 Rozhdestvensky, *Istoricheskii Obzor*, p. 224.

21 Saint-Julien, 'Hommes publics russes', p. 501.

22 Belinsky, PSS, XII: 50.

23 St Julien, 'Hommes publics russes'.

24 Pletnev, 'Pamyati Grafa Sergiya Semenovicha Uvarova', pp. cii–cv.

25 On the lack of warmth and imagination in Uvarov's 'museum culture' idea for Nicholas's Russia, compare parallel comments about Soviet Russia in Boris Thomson, *Lot's Wife and the Venus de Milo Conflicting Attitudes to the Cultural Heritage in Modern Russia* (London/New York/Melbourne, 1978). See especially the final chapter, 'Some Properties of Art', on the need for a true culture to live and breathe.

26 See above note 20. William Leatherbarrow and Derek Offord, eds, *A History of Russian Thought* (Cambridge, 2010), pp. 376–7 and p. 379 pioneer mention of Uvarov's significance but did so principally in relation to the twenty-first-century Russia of alternating Prime Minister and President Vladimir Putin. Uvarov's slogan 'in many ways applies just as well to Putin's Russia' and 'the spirit of Count Uvarov's trilogy remains a force to be reckoned with in twenty-first century Russia'. Missing from their account in my view is any analysis of how Uvarov's slogan came into being, with particular reference to the French Revolution. In Cold War times paradoxically many left-leaning Western scholars believed that Soviet Russia was an entirely distinct social and political entity from its tsarist predecessor. Typically Uvarov was ignored *qua* thinker by Andrzej Walicki in the otherwise excellent *A History of Russian Thought* (Oxford, 1980). For Walicki (p. xv) to be a member of the intelligentsia was to fall into an ethical category and/or to take a political position reflecting the standpoint of the unofficial opposition. Again Koyré, *La Philosophie*, pp. 197–207 was unique, half a century earlier, in presenting an inspired reading of Uvarov's complex position, and it is to Koyré that the present author owes her greatest debt.

27 For Pogodin and Official Nationality, see Andrzej Walicki, *The Slavophile Controversy* (Oxford, 1975), pp. 47–65; *Brokgauz i Evron*

Entsyklopedichesky Slovar', vol. 24, pp. 31–33, *Bol'shaya Entsyklopedia* (pre-1917, undated), vol. 15, pp. 305–6; K. N. Bestuzhev-Ryumin, *Biografiya i kharakteristiki* (St Petersburg, 1882), pp. 240ff.

28 S. P. Shevyrev, 'Razgovor o vozmozhnosti naiti edinyi zakon dlya izyashchnogo', *moskovsky vestnik*, No. 1 (1827): 38–49; *Istoriya Poezii* (Moscow, 1835); *Teoriya poezii v historicheskom razvitii u drevnykh i novykh narodov* (Moscow, 1836). For critical commentaries, see Walicki, *The Slavophile Controversy*, pp. 49–51, Brokgauz i Evron, vol. 39, pp. 361–4, and a most detailed and stimulating treatment in Yuri Mann, *Russkaya filosofskaya estetika* (Moscow, 1969), pp. 156–82.

29 Pypin, *Kharakteristiki*, p. 97; Walicki, *The Slavophile Controversy*, p. 46; Koyré, *La Philosophie*, p. 198. For Nicholas, see E. C. Thaden, *Conservative Nationalism in Nineteenth-Century Russia* (Seattle, 1964), p. 23, and Riazanovsky, *Nicholas I*, p. 166. It was a paradox that most of Official Nationality's thought came from abroad. On how men of various persuasions could find themselves being used to further the interests of the autocrat, see Monas, *The Third Section*, p. 152. Pogodin was invited by Benckendorff to choose his reward for an article written in *The Telescope* stressing Russia's historical rights to Lithuania. Since he had had been expressing his own views the bluntness of this positive official reception offended him.

30 See above note 18. Karamzin and the Russian conservative tradition also rejected 'politics', Pipes, *Karamzin's Memoir*, pp. 36–7 and pp. 89–91.

31 D. Magarshak, *Gogol A Life* (London, 1957), p. 131, Whittaker, *The Origins*, p. 120; Durylin, 'Drug Gete', p. 236. On Victor Hugo, see Chapter 17, p. xxx below.

32 'Vues generales sur la philosophie de la litterature', in *Études*, pp. 317–31; penny papers Lemke, *Ocherki po istorii russkoi tsensury*, p. 85, Whittaker, *The Origins*, p. 117; Uvarov quoted by G. P. Volkonsky in Nikitenko, *Alexander I. Galich* (St Petersburg, 1869), p. 276 (7–21 December 1843); Whittaker, *The Origins*, p. 120.

33 I. I. Davydov, 'Vospominaniye o Grafe Sergei Semeonoviche Uvarove', *Uchenye Zapiski Akademii Nauk* (December 1855), pp. 163–76 (p. 167). This attitude to philosophy was also fundamental to Karamzin and immediate conservative reaction to the French Revolution (Pipes, *Karamzin's Memoir*, p. 3) and continued to be the official Russian standpoint for the ensuing anti-revolutionary century. Compare Alexandre Koyré, *L'Occidentalisme d'Ivan Tourgenev* (Paris, 1922), p. 47: 'Philosophy has never been very well regarded in Russia; a foreign product, of recent import and introduced into a country which lacked the primary conditions and the essential bases for its development, it has always a very precarious life, profiting from time to time from an infatuation as superficial as it was widespread, subjected to changes of fashion, though sometimes suspect, often dangerous and always perfectly useless.' See also his entire chapter II, 'La lutte contre la philosophie'. Uvarov was a philosophical pessimist in exactly the opposite way to the optimism of the Slavophiles who believed in the goodness of human nature. However, the Official Nationalists and Pogodin also espoused a pessimistic view of humanity, see Riasanovsky, *A Parting of Ways*, p. 95 and p. 116.

34 Uvarov's colleagues and proteges were not morally well-regarded figures, but they and their work had their uses. For Pogodin's personal reputation, see Bestuzhev-Ryumin, *Biografia*, pp. 240–2. Pogodin's *Moskovskii Vestnik* (Moscow Herald) in the 1820s contained a great diversity of material. His elastic aim as founder had been to 'acquaint curious young compatriots with the latest intellectual efforts in the fields of science, particularly history and aesthetic theory' and he had published many translations of Goethe, the Schlegels and other German Romantic writers, poets and critics. His collaborators included Shevyrev, Khomiakov and Ivan Kireevsky. The periodical was a melting pot for new ideas and it was only ten years later that these hardened into definite ideological standpoints as they cooled. Shevyrev too, though without formal qualifications, was talented. When he returned to Russia in 1832, having published literary articles in his absence and perpetuated the strong reputation he acquired at the Moscow Herald, Uvarov invited him to become a lecturer in the Department of Russian Literary History. In his youth Shevyrev was much admired for his interpretation of Goethe's *Faust Part II* (See Mann, *Russkaya filosofskaya estetika*, pp. 156–61). He was also more perceptive than Belinsky about Gogol, in whose work Shevyrev recognized a poetic definition of the absurdity of life, whereas Belinsky insisted on finding realism there. See Victor Terras, *Belinsky and Russian Literary Criticism* (Madison, WI, 1974), p. 86. Belinsky because of his politics has enjoyed a better press. Shevyrev, essentially a romantic, took as his point of departure on all national questions, whether of Russia or other nations, the notion of the self-conscious, individual national personality. Martin Malia, *Alexander Herzen and the Birth of Russian Socialism (1812–1855)* (Oxford, 1961), p. 60, refers to the popularity of his lectures. In the company of these men Uvarov was essentially a scholar at home with other scholars. He enjoyed his superiority over them, and for the rest was pleased to have some supporters and friends in an otherwise lonely public life, men who were grateful to take advantage of the benefits he offered and who in return willingly served him politically. Riazanovsky, *A Parting of Ways*, p. 126 stresses that he remained ambivalent in his attitude to the true value of things Russian and thus could accommodate himself among the various nationalisms.

35 I. I. Davydov, *Vstupitel'naya lektsiya o vozmozhnosti fifosofii kak nauki* (Moscow, 1826); 'Rech' o zanyatyakh obshchestva lyubitelei rossiiskoi slovesnosti' (1829), in *Russkie esteticheskie traktaty* (Moscow, 1974), II: 539. For commentaries, see Brokgauz, X: 23–4, BE 8:29, Granat 17:494, I. I. Ivanov, *Istoriya russkoi kritiki*, 2 vols (St Petersburg, 1898–1900), II: 296ff. Kireevsky was a Westernizer who would eventually become a Slavophile, the movement for which Khomiakov provided the spiritual inspiration.

36 Vsevolod Setchkarev, *Gogol His Life and Works* (London, 1965), p. 40; Robert A. Maguire, ed., *Gogol from the Twentieth Century* (Princeton, 1995), pp. 121–2 (Valery Bryusov 'Burnt to Ashes'); Magarshak, *Gogol*, pp. 97–101; Wes, *Classics in Russia*, pp. 277–83.

37 Lemke, *Ocherki po istorii russkoi tsenzury*, p. 416. This was the view of the official inquiry into the Chaadaev affair.

38 R. T. Mcnally, *Chaadaev and His Friends* (Tallahassee, FL, 1971), p. 39.

39 Chaadaev/de Maistre in Stepanov i Vermale, 'Pis'ma Zhosefa de Mestra k S.S. Uvarovu', *Literaturnoe Nasledstvo* 29–30 (1937): 618.

40 In a letter written to Alexander Turgenev Chaadaev distinguished his patriotism from the official version: 'A curious movement of minds is taking place with us at the present time. People are trying to fabricate nationality; and since no materials exist for this, the result is of course an entirely artificial product … . It's sad, wouldn't you say, to see that at the very moment when all nations are striving to draw closer to each other, when all local and geographical peculiarities are dissolving, we are turning in on ourselves and appealing to a narrow patriotism?' Quoted in Lemke, *Ocherki po istorii russkoi tsensury*, p. 376. Before Chaadaev Ivan Kireevsky, another outspoken pro-European steeped in German Romanticism, had advanced the idea of spiritual re-marriage with the West in his essay 'The Nineteenth Century'. The censor allowed it to be published in 1831, but when it caught the indignant attention of the tsar it ensured Kireevsky's journal, *The European*, lasted no longer than one issue. Chaadaev had defended Kireevsky (Monas, *The Third Section*, p. 155). The challenge these men presented to Uvarov was far more deeply personal than a mere challenge to Official Nationality.

41 Mcnally, *Chaadaev*, pp. 30–44. Chaadaev's letter did not attack the autocracy, and made a point of praising Peter the Great and Alexander for what they had achieved. It condemned the Decembrist Insurrection as 'an immense calamity which knocked us back half a century', and viewed it as the perverse, almost tragic outcome of Russia's victorious entry into Napoleonic Europe.

42 Mcnally, *Chaadaev*, p. 200 and pp. 212–13, without the final paragraph; the additional sentence is included in the manuscript quoted by Lemke, *Ocherki po istorii russkoi tsensury*, p. 422.

43 Uvarov in *Zhurnal Ministerstva narodnogo prosveshcheniya* (1834), I: v, quoted by Koyré, *La Philosophie*, p. 199. Koyré suggests that in 1834 Uvarov was already thinking of Chaadaev.

44 See Offord et al., *European Francophonie*, pp. 397–8. That Uvarov himself is not mentioned adds weight to the claim that he continues to be extraordinarily neglected as one of Russia's leading intellectuals of the first half of the nineteenth century.

45 Lemke, *Ocherki po istorii russkoi tsensury*, pp. 429–43.

Chapter 15

1 Norman Davies, *God's Playground A History of Poland*, 2 vols. (Oxford, 1981), II: 88.

2 See Appendix 2 for the role Uvarov's policies played in the imprisonment of Joseph Conrad's father, the Polish revolutionary Apollo Korzeniowski.

3 For his own account, see *Desyatlietie*, II: 35–74. For commentaries, see Rozhdestvensky, *Istoricheskii Obzor*, pp. 294ff., Whittaker, *The Origins*, pp. 189–212. Vladimirskii-Budanov, *Istoriya*, I: 76, praised Uvarov's gradual measures to achieve a rapprochement of the Polish/Russian spirit, but says they were misunderstood in both Russia – as lack of action – and Poland.

4 Quoted in Rozhdestvensky, *Istoricheskii Obzor*, p. 301.

5 Zamoyski, *Holy Madness*, p. 321.

6 Milosz, *The History of Polish Literature*, 2nd edn, p. 160. According to Nikolai Turgenev, *La Russie*, I: 516, Karamzin said of Alexander I's idea of giving the Poles a constitution that it would make 'that race' all the more dangerous. Legally constituted as a distinct and sovereign people, Poles would be more dangerous for us than Poles who are Russian subjects. Arguably, Russian oppression generated a distinct streak of Romanticism in the Polish national character.

7 Lincoln, *Nicholas I*, p. 227.

8 Rozhdestvensky, *Istoricheskii Obzor*, pp. 297–8.

9 *Desyatiletie*, p. 36.

10 Ibid., p. 39.

11 Whittaker, *The Origins*, pp. 195–7. Private schools were brought under ministerial control and from 1836 teaching in Polish, except for religion, was banned. In addition each gymnasium was bound to employ two teachers of Russian language and literature. Russian history was taught from the third year and all graduates into the fourteenth rank had to have a 'perfect' knowledge of Russian language and literature.

12 *Desyatietie*, p. 97. David B. Saunders, 'Historians and Concepts of Nationality', *Slavonic and East European Review* 60, No. 1 (January 1982): 44–62 (58–61). To force the peoples closer a union of the Uniate Church in the Western Ukraine with the Orthodox Church was officially proclaimed in 1839. See Thaden, *Conservative Nationalism*, pp. 19–20.

13 Davies, *History of Poland*, II: 88–9.

14 Whittaker, *The Origins*, p. 196; *Desyatiletie*, pp. 39–47.

15 *Desyatiletie*, pp. 65–71; Whittaker, *The Origins*, p. 198; Rozhdestvensky, *Istoricheskii Obzor*, pp. 310–17.

16 Whittaker, *The Origins*, pp. 199–201.

17 *Desyatiletie*, p. 53.

18 *De Bulgariorum utrarumque origine et sedibus antiquissimus* (Dorpat, 1853).

19 Whittaker, *The Origins*, pp. 203–7.

20 Ibid., pp. 207–12.

21 Jacques Droz, *Europe between Revolutions 1815–1848* (London, 1967, reprinted 1985), p. 177.

22 Davydov, 'Vospominanie'; *The Journals of the Marquis de Custine Journey for Our Time*, ed. and trs. Phyllis Penn Kohler (London, 1953, reprinted

1980), p. 219 'I leave you to surmise and appreciate the efforts imposed upon gallant souls and independent minds obliged to resign themselves to enduring a regime where peace and good order are paid for by discrediting the human word'; p. 233 'the artful efforts of people whose profession is disguising the truth'; *ad passim.*

23 'Dlya biografii grafa S.S. Uvarova', *Russkii Arkhiv* 9, No. 12 (1871): 2078–103 (2079) Uvarov to Pogodin, 4 March 1840.

24 Uvarov hoped, as he did in Russia, to keep the middle classes out of higher studies by offering them improved vocational education in secondary schools but everywhere he admitted contradictions. Aware of existing high academic standards, he allowed the increased number of technical schools to teach Latin, Polish and German, as well as Russian and Russian history and practical subjects.

25 *Russkii Arkhiv* 9, No. 12 (1871): 2080 (Uvarov to Pogodin 21 September 1840).

26 Barsukov, *Pogodin*, X: 386–7.

27 Whittaker, *The Origins*, p. 116. *Otechestvennye Zapiski* was founded by A.A. Kraevsky who described its aim as 'to bring to our country's public everything noteworthy and useful and pleasant in literature and life'. With Belinsky as its ideological leader, it attached much importance to philosophy, creative fiction, literary criticism and aesthetics and also offered translations of foreign literature. The critic Igor Panaev in *Literaturnye Vospominaniya* (Leningrad, 1950), p. 267, said all the talented people in Moscow and St Petersburg of the day were drawn to it and its popularity grew and grew. Belinsky eagerly watched the circulation figures approach 1,400 in 1840.

28 Compare above Uvarov to Pogodin 21 September 1840, note 25.

29 I. I. Davydov, 'Vozmozhno li u nas germanskaya filosofiya', *Moskvitanin* 2, No. 3 (1842): 385–401 stressed the inappropriateness of Hegel as a philosopher for Russia, which was Uvarov's official position despite having been strongly influenced by German historicism as a young man.

30 *Russkii Arkhiv* 9, No. 12 (1871): 2083–90 and 2093. Pogodin to Uvarov 28.2. and March 1841.

31 One joke told of a civil servant whose drunken trainees cut off his ear; the other appeared to justify a member of the ministry giving someone a slap in the face: mild stuff for a minister who claimed to admire Gogol nevertheless! This indeed was Pogodin's defence (ibid., p. 2096).

32 Cf. Wes, *Classics in Russia*, pp. 323–55.

33 T. N. Granovsky, *Lektsii T.N. Granovskogo* (Moscow, 1961), particularly pp. 40–9 and p. 91, contains Granovsky's expositions of the World Spirit and the organic development of history. See also A. V. Stankevich, *Biograficheskii ocherk T.N. Granovskogo* and Gertsen, PSS, II: 316–18 (Dnevnik 24 and 28 December 1843).

34 'Vues generales', in *Études*, p. 330.

Chapter 16

1 Saint-Julien, 'Hommes publiques russes', 491ff. St Julien lectured on French literature at St Petersburg University 1833–34 when Uvarov probably first made his acquaintance. He described his subsequent travels in Russia in *Voyages pittoresques en Russie* (Paris, 1854). He wrote a stage comedy which was performed in Paris in 1848 and he was the leader of a literary salon in the mid-1860s. See also W. B. Lincoln, 'The Circle of the Grand Duchess Elena Pavlovna 1847–1861', *Slavonic and East European Review* XLVIII, No. 112 (July 1970): 373–87.

2 Appendix I below.

3 Lincoln, *Nicholas I*, p. 311.

4 On serfdom Uvarov declared (Barsukov, *Pogodin*, IX: 305–8), 'The question of serfdom is closely linked to the question of autocracy and even monarchy. These are two parallel forces which have developed together. Both have the same historical beginning; both have equal legality. Serfdom, whatever one may think of it, does exist. Abolition of it will lead to the dissatisfaction of the gentry class, which will start looking to compensate itself elsewhere, although there is nowhere to look except within the domain of autocracy. … Peter the First's edifice will be shaken. Serfdom is a tree which has spread its roots afar; it shelters both the Church and the Throne.' Uvarov had in fact become more conservative in his view of Russian society than in 1818, the last time he had spoken publicly on question of emancipation.

5 Schmid, 'S.S. Uwarow und Ch. Fr. Graefe', p. 105. Angelo Poliziano (1454–95) was a friend and protege of Lorenzo di Medici and one of the foremost classical scholars of the Renaissance. Having once saved the life of Lorenzo, he entered the Medici house without special duties, and was free to study in the library. He translated the Iliad, wrote fine Latin and outstanding Italian verse. A quarrel with Lorenzo's wife ended his stay. Lorenzo, famous as a patron and lavish host, surrounded himself with artists and good friends in his villas. The circle included his teacher, Pico dela Mirandola.

6 I. I. Davydov, 'Selo Porech'e', *Moskvitanin*, No. 9 (1841): 156–90 and 'Dumy i Vpechatleniya', *Moskvitanin*, Nos. 9–10 (1846): 65–80. Both articles are extensively quoted with additional material in Barsukov, *Pogodin*, V: 33–86; VI: 147ff; VII: 442–51; VIII: 480ff; XII: 60–5; see also Davydov, 'Vospominanie', pp. 163–76.

7 www.nataturka.ru/muzey-usadba/porechie.html (downloaded 12 June 2017).

8 For additional material on the house and its treasures, see P. Leontiev, 'Bakicheskii Pamyatnik Grafa S. Uvarova', *Propilei* I (1851): 135–42; Uvarov, 'Notice sur le monument antique de Poretch', *Bulletin de la classe des sciences historiques, philologiques et politiques de l'academie impériale des sciences de Saint-Petersbourg* IX, No. 8 (1852), cols 113–17; Longinov, *Vospominanie o grafe S.S. Uvarove*, p. 122; *Stolitsa i usad'ba* (1914), Nos. 16–17 'Dvortsy Razumovskogo'.

9 The collection that became famous in his son's name was 20,000 volumes on the occult. See Uvarov (Uvaroff, Ouvaroff), Alexei Sergieevich and Auguste Ladrague, *Sciences Secrètes A Bibliography of the Occult Sciences* (Moscow, 1870).

10 *Russkii Arkhiv* 36, No. 3 (1898): 433, *Russkii Arkhiv* 27, No. 3 (1889): 565.

11 Davydov, 'Vospominanie'.

12 The parallel established between Uvarov's and Putin's Russia, one can't help recalling the life in 1990s Moscow of the intellectual businessman and future dissident Mikhail Khodorkovsky of whom the contemporary historian Masha Gessen has written that despite being 'the most reticent among the oligarchs', choosing not to 'buy yachts or villas on the Côte d'Azur' or to become a fixture of 'the Moscow playboy scene', he did buy 'a gated compound of seven houses on 50 forested acres about half an hour outside Moscow' in the late 1990s, calling it [The] Apple Orchard and housing there leading executives of his firm Yukos, who lived together as 'one large happy family'. His social life consisted mostly of 'Barbecuing for fellow Yukos managers'. At nights he would stay up and 'read until two'. He later wrote that during this period 'I saw business as a game … .It was a game in which you wanted to win but losing was also an option. It was a game in which hundreds of thousands of people came to work in the morning to play with me.' See Masha Gessen, 'The Wrath of Putin', *Vanity Fair*, April 2012. This compound stood abandoned in the new luxurious Moscow suburbs in the early 2000s, after the arrival in power of Vladimir Putin and Khodorkovsky's imprisonment, on false charges, and the state's confiscation of his multimillion dollar business in the post-Soviet oil and gas industry.

13 Nikitenko, *Dnevnik* (16 January 1842), I: 243. Abel-François Villemain (1790–1870) was a French writer, critic, professor at the Sorbonne and Minister of Education 1839–45. A friend of Madame de Stael, he was a literary critic of the French Restoration, steering a course between the remnants of neoclassicism and the less extreme of the views of the Romantics prevalent in his middle years. On 24 April 1814 at the Sorbonne he delivered a public lecture in the presence of Alexander I of Russia, 'On the Advantages and Inconveniences of Criticism' which liberal critics found too complimentary of the Russian emperor and his fellow listener the king of Prussia. Uvarov might well have seen in him his own French counterpart.

14 Belinsky, PSS, XII: 61–2 (3 August 1841 to N. Kh. Ketcher).

15 Nikitenko, see note 13.

16 By comparison, neither Belinsky nor Pushkin was disturbed by Gogol's homoeroticism, and Pushkin went so far as to speculate on possible partners for Vigel'. For Belinsky's notice of the Russian edition of 'Eleusis', see PSS, XII: 322–3.

17 Nikitenko, *Dnevnik* (20 May 1843), I: 267.

Chapter 17

1 *Russkii Arkhiv* 21, No. 1 (1883): 105; *Russkii Arkhiv* 9, No. 12 (1871): 2086.

2 *Desyatiletie*, pp. 106–8.

3 Rozhdestvensky, *Istoricheskii Obzor*, p. 255.

4 Ibid., p. 257.

5 *Lettres et papiers du chancelier Comte de Nesselrode*, XIII: 280–283; *Russkii Arkhiv* 28, No. 3 (1890): 72 and 83.

6 Rozhdestvensky, *Istoricheskii Obzor*, p. 315.

7 Nikitenko, *Dnevnik* (9 April 1834), 1: 140.

8 Ibid., 1: xxx (12 December 1842); Monas, *The Third Section*, pp. 179–81.

9 Magarshak, *Gogol*, pp. 181–2 and pp. 204–7. As an indication of what a sectarian society literary Russia had become Gogol's Slavophile friends were angry he had chosen a Westernizer to help him.

10 Belinsky, PSS, VI: 775; XII: 103.

11 Belinsky, PSS, XII: 108.

12 Magarshak, *Gogol*, p. 209.

13 Rozhdestvensky, *Istoricheskii Obzor*, p. 333.

14 See above Chapter 14, Note 25.

15 Nikitenko, *Dnevnik*, 1: 265.

16 Pletnev, 'Pamyati', p. cxvi.

17 Nikitenko, *Dnevnik*, 1: 267.

18 'Venise' and 'Rome', in *Esquisses*, pp. 249–64 and pp. 265–92 (pp. 291–2).

19 *Esquisses*, p. 284.

20 Saint-Julien, 'Hommes publiques russes', pp. 510–11.

21 See Chapter 3, p. 40.

22 *Esquisses*, pp. 286–7.

23 Ibid., p. 250.

24 Ibid., p. 256 and p. 258; *Journey for Our Time*, p. 63.

25 'Des vues de Napoléon sur l'Italie', in *Esquisses*, pp. 75–92 (p. 81).

26 *Esquisses*, p. 88.

Chapter 18

1 Barsukov, *Pogodin*, VII: 442.

2 Nikitenko, *Dnevnik*, I: 284; Barsukov, *Pogodin*, VII: 452–3.

3 *Ostaf'evskii Arkhiv*, III: 705ff.

4 Nikitenko, *Dnevnik*, I: 276.

5 'Zapiski S.M. Solovieva', *Vestnik Evropy* (1907). Vol. 2 (April), pp. 437–46.

6 See above chapter 13 note 28.

7 Nikitenko, *Dnevnik* (8 May 1845), I: 292.

8 Magarshak, *Gogol*, pp. 230–1.

9 Nikitenko, *Dnevnik* (8 May 1845), I: 292.

10 Whittaker, *The Origins*, p. 126.

11 *Russkii Arkhiv* 30, No. 7 (1892): 351.

12 Metternich resigned on 13 March 1848 after a public march against him turned violent and he found himself under pressure from both opponents within the government and from the people. After his fall from power those who countered themselves victorious included the students and the press, who had campaigned for freedom from censorship.

13 Rozhdestvensky, *Istoricheskii Obzor*, p. 317.

14 Nikitenko, *Dnevnik*, I.

15 *Russkii Arkhiv* 36, No. 3 (1898): 433 ('Rasskazy Grudeva'); *Russkii Arkhiv* 30, No. 7 (1892): 336 and 347– ('Ob ukraino-slavayanskom obshchestve: Iz Bumag D.P. Golokhvastova').

16 Belinsky, PSS, XVIII: 440.

17 A. S. Nifontov, *1848 god v Rossii: ocherki po istorii 40-kh godov*, 1st edn (Moscow, 1931), pp. 181ff. The anonymous critic was possibly Bulgarin.

18 Ibid., p. 203.

19 Whittaker, *The Origins*, p. 225.

20 Nifontov, *1848 god*, pp. 1818–198; *Russkii Arkhiv* 36, No. 3 (1898): 433–4; Prince G. Shcherbatov, 'Student sorokovykh godakh: Knyaz', Grigorii Shcherbatov on Grafe Uvarove', *Sovremennaya letopis'*, No. 6 (1870): 1–5; Nikitenko, *Dnevnik*, I: 311.

21 Whittaker, *The Origins*, p. 227; Rozhdestvensky, *Istoricheskii Obzor*, p. 226; *Russkii Arkhiv* 30, No. 7 (1892): 358.

22 *Russkii Arkhiv* 36, No. 3 (1898): 434.

23 Rozhdestvensky, *Istoricheskii Obzor*, p. 334.

24 Whittaker, *The Origins*, p. 221.

25 Rozhdestvensky, *Istoricheskii Obzor*, p. 261.

26 Shcherbatov, 'Student sorokovykh godakh', 4, col. 1, col. 2.

27 Whittaker, *The Origins*, p. 227.

28 Magarshak, *Gogol*, p. 285; Richard Pipes, 'Introduction' to Giles Fletcher, *Of the Russe Commonwealth* (1591, facsimile edition Cambridge, MA, 1966), pp. 39–40; *Russkii Arkhiv* 28, No. 1 (1890): 251–2.

29 Nikitenko, *Dnevnik* (1 December 1848), I: 312 (24 December 1848), I: 318.

30 'O naznachenii russkikh universitetov i uchasti ikh v obshchestvennom obrazovanii', *Sovremennik* XIV (March 1849), ii: 37–46 (37).

31 Barsukov, *Pogodin*, X: 531.

32 Ibid., Nifontov, *1848 god*, pp. 199–200.

33 Quoted in Droz, *Europe between Revolutions*, p. 189.

34 Shcherbatov, 'Student sorokovykh godakh', 4; Pletnev, 'Pamyati', p. cxxii; Barsukov, *Pogodin*, X: 530–40.

35 Barsukov, *Pogodin*, X: 540–2.

36 Nikitenko, *Dnevnik* (5 May 1853), I: 369–70.

Chapter 19

1 Whittaker, *The Origins*, p. 238.

2 See Chapter 15, note 18.

3 De provinciarum imperii orientalis administrandarum forma mutata inde a Constantine Magno usque ad Justinianum (Dorpat, 1858); 'Marlo, odin iz predshestvennikov Shekspera. Ocherk iz istorii angliiskoi dramy', *Russkoe slovo*, No. 2 (1859): 5–53 and No. 3, pp. 221–84.

4 *Bulletin de la classe des sciences historiques, philologiques et politiques de l'Academie Impériale des sciences* VIII, No. 10 (1851): 147. (Paper read to the Academy on 25 October 1850).

5 Ibid., pp. 147–9.

6 Durylin, 'de Stal'', pp. 233–4 and p. 231.

7 'Os'moe Janvarya 1851 goda', *Sovremennik* 27, No. 6 (1851): 1–6 (1–2).

8 Uvarov, 'Literaturnye vospominaniya'.

9 Uvarov, 'Notice sur le monument antique de Poretch'. See above chapter 17.

10 'Lettre à M. le Secretaire perpetuel de l'Academie Impériale des sciences' (St Petersburg, 1852), subsequently published in Russian as 'Vospominanie ob akademike Fr. Grefe', *Uchenye zapiski Akademii nauk po I i III otd.* (St Petersburg, 1853).

11 V. A. Zhukovsky, PSS (Moscow, 1959–60), IV: 657 (letter of 12/24 September 1847); Barsukov, *Pogodin*, XII: 61 ff.

12 Pogodin, *Russkii Arkhiv* 9, No. 12 (1871): 2107–11 ('Pis'mo k N.N. o konchine Grafa Uvarova' 1855).

13 'À la mémoire de l'Imperatrice Marie' [dated Porechie 19 November 1828] in *Maison impériale de Russie* (Paris, 1831).

14 Pogodin, note 11.

15 Longinov, 'Vospominanie o grafe S.S. Uvarove', pp. 123–4.

16 For the changed character of the ministry under Shirinsky-Shikhmatov see Whittaker, *The Origins*, p. 237; Rozhdestvensky, *Istoricheskii Obzor*, p. 227.

17 *Ostafevskii arkhiv*, III: 497.

18 Chapter 16, note 9.

19 A selection of his works appeared in *Nezabvennoi pamyati Gr. A.S. Uvarova* (Kazan', 1885).

20 Chapter 16, note 7.

Chapter 20

1 Dzhessi Rassel (Jesse Russell), *Uvarova Praskovya Sergeevna* (Book on Demand Pod) (2013).

2 Smith, *Former People*, p. 151.

3 Leatherbarrow and Offord, eds, *A History of Russian Thought*, pp. 376–7 and p. 379.

4 Mikhail Zygar, 'Putin Likes to Pretend 1917 Never Happened How the Russian Revolution became Taboo', *The Atlantic*, 1 April 2017. https://www.theatlantic.com/international/archive/2017/04/russia-putin-revolution-lenin-nicholas-1917/521571/ (downloaded 11 September 2017).

5 Rayymond Williams, *The Long Revolution* (London, 1961), p. 302 was happy to identify the four principles underlying Soviet realism in literature, a cornerstone of the official culture, as 'ideinost, partiinost, typichnost and narodnost'. It's hard to make sense of his parsing of these values today.

6 Personal experience of the author. See also 'Posters Celebrating the Anniversary of the October Revolution', University of Birmingham, Cadbury Special Research Collections Item 24 (1975). The items are listed at www.calmview.bham.ac.uk/Record.aspx?src=CalmView.Catalog&id=XSOVIET+POSTERS%2F789

7 Chamberlain, *Motherland*, p. 112.

Bibliography

A note to the general reader

U varov's writings in French, German and Russian have never been collected in their original form, and only two of his essays have been translated into English, the classical study 'The Mysteries of Eleusis' and the political thesis 'On the Use of History in Education: a Lesson in Patience'. This enormous gap in Russian historiography has recently been filled by *Sergei Uvarov Gosudarstvennie Osnovy* (Moscow, 2015), which is a collection of his political and historical writings in Russian, with a commentary. But this doesn't help the anglophone reader.

Uvarov's conservatism was to blame for the obscurity into which he fell from shortly after his death in 1855 and through most of the twentieth century. Soviet Russian scholars ignored his foundational role in nineteenth-century official Russian culture, and, similarly, few Western historians were drawn to it. In sum, until the end of the Cold War little commentary was available, while most primary sources were published before 1917. The great exception was the pioneering work published in 1978 by the American scholar Cynthia H. Whittaker. Her *The Origins of Modern Russian Education: An Intellectual Biography of Count Sergei Uvarov 1786-1855* is therefore essential reading. Whittaker also translated 'On the Use of History'. For readers of French, however, the Russian émigré philosopher Alexandre Koyré had written an outstanding essay on Uvarov in *La philosophie et le problème nationale en Russie au debut du XIXe siècle* as early as 1929, and it is that essay which inspired the somewhat different approach taken to Uvarov's life and achievements in *Ministry of Darkness*.

Like Whittaker's *The Origins of Russian Education*, *Ministry of Darkness* draws almost entirely on sources published in languages other than English, with the exception of short English-language articles in the academic periodical press. Whittaker also made use of the then Soviet archives of which the present author had only a brief glimpse. Ample material in published sources more than compensated.

After 1991 post-Soviet Russian scholars were once more free, and curious, to turn to the hitherto taboo subject of Russian conservatism, with its roots in the eighteenth century. A 1988 collection of essays by A. A. Zaitsev and his Leningrad collective, *The Book in Russia in the era of the Enlightenment*, set Russian conservatism in the context of the French Revolution. *Rossiiskie Konservatory* (Moscow, 1997), edited by A. N. Bokhanov and including Uvarov as one of its subjects, was one of the first studies openly dedicated to conservatism to appear in the new era. Others are listed below. Whittaker's book was translated into Russian in 1999. In 2013 the masterly Polish-born American historian of Russia Richard Pipes (1923–2018) published as his very last book *Sergei Semyonovich Uvarov: A Description of his Life*. This short monograph however is available only in Russian. Among post-war Western scholars Pipes was for most of the rest of the century rare in his interest in Russian conservatism until the 1990s. After that date many studies, too numerous to list here, were published. Alexander M. Martin's *Romantics, reformers, reactionaries* (1997) covers the early years of Uvarov's career. Older work by Marc Raeff and Nicholas Riasanovsky remains essential reading. The topic of bureaucratism (*chinovnichestvo*) in nineteenth-century Russia, dovetailing with its particular form of conservatism, has also attracted much post-Soviet attention.

It should be noted, finally, that for much of the nineteenth century Uvarov (Ouvaroff) was regarded by the French as a French writer of belles lettres. Any reader inclined to test that assessment would want to begin with his miniature masterpiece, the essay 'Le Prince de Ligne'.

Published works by Sergei Semyonovich Uvarov [Ouvaroff Fr., Uwarow Ger.]

À la mémoire de l'Empereur Alexandre (St Petersburg, 1826).
À la mémoire de l'Imperatrice Elisabeth (St Petersburg, 1827).
À la mémoire de l'Imperatrice Marie (St Petersburg, 1829).
À la mémoire de la Princesse Lieven (St Petersburg, 1828).
Appel à l'Europe (St Petersburg, 1815).
La certitude historique est-elle en progrès? (St Petersburg, 1850).
Desyatiletie Ministerstva narodnogo prosveshcheniya 1833-43 (St Petersburg, 1864).
Éloge funèbre de Moreau (St Petersburg, 1813).
L'Empereur Alexandre et Buonaparte (St Petersburg, 1814).
Esquisses politiques et littéraires, with an introduction by Louis-Antoine Léouzon Leduc (Paris, 1848), contains: 'Des Vues de Napoléon sur l'Italie', 'Stein et Pozzo di Borgo', 'Le Prince de Ligne', 'Examen critique de la fable d'Hercule, commentée par Dupuis', 'Mémoire sur les tragiques grecs', 'Notice sur Goethe', 'Vue génerales sur la philosophie de la littérature', 'Venise', 'Rome'.
Études de philologie et de critique (St Petersburg, 1843; Paris, 1845) contains: 'Project d'une académie asiatique', 'Lettre critique sur ce project, par le

Comte Joseph de Maistre', 'Essais sur les Mystères d'Eleusis', 'Nonnos von Panopolis, der Dichter', 'Über das vorhomerische Zeitalter', 'Examen critique de la fable d'Hercule', 'Sur les tragiques grècs', 'Vues génerales sur la philosophie de la littérature', 'Notice sure Goethe', 'Le Prince de Ligne' 'Rome' in 1845 edition only.

Examen critique de la fable d'Hercule (St Petersburg, 1817).

'K istorii klassitsisma v Rossii: mnenie S.S. Uvarova', *Russkii Arkhiv* 37, No. 12 (1889): 465–8.

Lettre à M. le secretaire perpetuel de l'Académie Impériale des sciences (St Petersburg, 1852), subsquently in Russian as 'Vospominanie ob akademike Fr. Graefe', *Uchenye zapsiki akademii nauk po I i III otd.* (St Petersburg, 1853).

'Literaturnye vospominaniya', *Sovremennik* XXVII, No. 6, ii: 37–42.

'Litterature russe: Essais en vers et en prose par M. de Batushkoff [sic]', *Le Conservateur impartial* 83 (16 October 1817).

Maison impériale de Russie (Paris, 1831) contains: À la mémoire de l'Empereur Alexandre, À la mémoire de l'Imperatrice Elisabeth, 'Le neuf janvier' [on the death of the Queen of Württemberg], À la mémoire de l'Imperatrice Marie, À la mémoire de la Princesse Lieven.

Mémoire sur les tragiques grècs (St Petersburg, 1824).

Mysteries of Eleusis tr. J. D. Price, with observations by J. Christie (London, 1817), reprinted 1992. [Also known as *The Essay on the Eleusinian Mysteries*].

'Pis'mo k izdatel'yu: Nekrolog Khristiana Fridrikha Mattei', *Vestnik Evropy* 60 (1811): 59–61.

Le neuf janvier (St Petersburg, 1819).

Nonnos von Panopolis, der Dichter (St Petersburg, 1818).

Notice sur Goethe (St Petersburg, 1842); in Russian as 'Slovo o Goethe', *Uchenyie zapiski Imperatorskogo Moskovskogo Universiteta* 1 (1833): 74–94.

Notice sur le monument antique de Poretsch', *Bulletin de la classes des sciences historiques, philologiques et politiques de l'Academie Impériale des Sciences de Saint-Petersbourg* IX, No. 8 (1852), cols 113–117.

O Grecheskoi Antologii [With K.N. Batyushkov] (St Petersburg 1820), reprinted in Batyushkov, *Sochineniya v proze i stikhakh*, 2 vols. (St Petersburg, 1834), II: 237–64.

O pripodovanii istorii otnositel'no k narodnomu vospitaniyu (St Petersburg, 1813).

'Osmoe janvarya 1851 goda', *Sovremennik* XXVI, vi (1851): 1–6.

'Otvet V.V. Kapnista na pis'mo ego ob eksametre', *Chtenie v Besede lyubitelei russkogo slova* 17 (1815): 47–67.

'Pis'mo k Baronu Shteinu' (1813), *Russkii Arkhiv* 9, No. 2 (1871): 0129–0134. In the original French in G.H. Pertz, *Das Leben des Ministers Freiherr vom Stein*, 6 vols. (Berlin 1851), 3: 697–9.

'Pis'mo k Mitropolitu Filaretu' (25.11. 1841), *Chtenie v Obshchestve Istorii i Drevnostei Rossiiskikh* No. 1 (1876): 197–8.

'Pis'mo k Nikolayu Ivanovichu Gnedichu o grecheskom eksametre', *Chtenie v Besede lyubitelei russkogo slova* 13 (1813): 56–68.

'Pis'mo k Karamzinu', *Syn Otechestva* 44, No. 8: 79–80.

'Pis'mo k Speranskomu' (1.12.1819), *Russkaya Starina* 27, No. 10 (1896): 158.

'Pis'mo k Speranskomu' (1819) *V pamyat' grafa m. M. Speranskago 1771–1872* (St Petersburg, 1872), 233–4.

'Pis'mo k V.A. Zhukovskomu', *Russkii Arkhiv* 9, No. 2 (1871): 157–70.

Le Prince de Ligne (St Petersburg, 1815).

Projet d'une académie asiatique (St Petersburg, 1810). Translated into Russian by V.A. Zhukovsky, *Sergei Uvarov Gosudarstvennie Osnovy* (Moscow, 2015) [Collected Political and Historical Writings in Russian, with a commentary].

Vestnik Evropy, 1 (1811): 27–52 and 2 (1811): 96–120.

Rech' Presidenta Im. A. N. popechitelya Peterburgskogo uchebnogo okruga v torzhestvennom sobranii glavnogo pedagogicheskogo instituta 22 marta 1818 (St Petersburg, 1818) translated in an abridged version by Cynthia H. Whittaker as '"One Use of History in Education: a Lesson in Patience": A Speech by Sergei Uvarov', *Slavic and European Education Review* No. 1 (1978): 29–38.

Stein et Pozzo di Borgo (St Petersburg, 1846; Paris, 1847), tr. D.F. Campbell, *Stein and Pozzo di Borgo* (London, 1847).

Über das vorhomerische Zeitalter (St Petersburg, 1819).

Primary sources

Arkhiv Brat'ev Turgenevykh, 6 vols. (St Peterburg, 1911–21).

Arkhiv Dekabrista S.G.Volkonskogo (Petrograd, 1918).

Barsukov, N., *Zhizhn' i trudy M.P. Pogodina*, 22 vols. (St Petersburg, 1888–1910).

Bartenev, P.I., 'Biograficheskoe Izvestie', *Russkii Arkhiv* 9, No. 12 (1871): 0133–34, 2104–2107.

Batyushkov, K.N., *Sochineniya*, 3 vols., ed. V.I. Saitov, with a biographical introduction by L.N. Maikov (St Petersburg, 1886–87).

Batyushkov, K.N., *Sochineniya*, ed. Blagoi (Moscow, 1934).

Belinksky, V.G., *Pol'noe sobranie sochinenii*, 13 vols. (Moscow, 1955).

Berkov, P.N. ed., *XVIII Vek* 8 (Leningrad, 1969) [Derzhavin i Karamzin v literaturnom dvizhenii XVIII-nachala XIX veka].

Bludova, A.D., 'Vospominaniya grafina A.D. Bludovoi', *Russkii Arkhiv* 27, No. 1 (1889): 39–112, also published as 'Vospominaniya i zapiski', *Zarya* No. 3 (1871).

Bogolyubov, V.F., 'Pis'ma V.F. Bogolyubova k knyaziyu Aleksandru Borisovichu Kurakinu', *Russkii Arkhiv* 31, No. 10 (1893): 233–46 and No. 11: 257–315.

Bulgakov, A.Ya., 'Iz pisem A. Ya. Bulgakova k bratu', *Russkii Arkhiv* 39, No. 1 (1901): 46–94, No. 2: 260–315, No. 3: 398–469, No. 6: 161–238, No. 7: 339–437, No. 9: 1–43, *Russkii Arkhiv* 40: 42–157.

Buturlin, M.D., 'Zapiski grafa M.D. Buturlina', *Russkii Arkhiv* No. 11 (1901): 384–421.

Le Conservateur impartial, published twice weekly (St Petersburg, 1813–24).

Chaadaev, P., *Polnoe sobranie sochinenii*, ed. M.O. Gershenzon, 2 vols. (Moscow, 1913).

Davydov, I.I., *Chteniya o slovesnosti* (Moscow, 1838).

Davydov, I.I., 'Dumy i vpechatleniya', *Moskvitanin* nos. 9–10 (1846): 65–80.

Davydov, I.I., 'O Naznachenii russkikh universitetov i chasti ikh v obshchestvennom obrazovanii', *Sovremennik* XIV, ii (March 1849): 37–46.

Davydov, I.I., 'Pis'ma I.I. Davydova k A.A. Prokopovichu-Antonskomu', *Russkii Arkhiv* 27, No. 3 (1889): 542–65.

Davydov, I.I., 'Selo Porech'e', *Moskvitanin*, No. 9 (1841): 156–90.

Davydov, I.I., 'Vozmozhno li u nas germanskaya filosofiya', *Moskvitanin* 2, No. 3 (1842): 385–401.

Davydov, I.I., 'Vospominanie o Grafe Sergeii Semyonovichom Uvarove', *Uchenye zapiski Akademii Nauk* 3 otd., II (1855): 163–76.

Davydov, I.I., *Vstupitel'naya lektsiya o vozmozhnosti filosofii kak nauki* (Moscow, 1826).

de Maistre, J., *Essai sur le principe generateur des constitutions politiques et des autres institutions humaines* (St Petersburg, 1814).

Devyat'nadstatyi vek: Istoricheskii Sbornik izdavaemyi po bumagam famil'nogogo arkhiva knyazem Fedorom Alekseevichem Kurakinym (Moscow, 1903).

Dupré de Saint-Maure, E., *Petersbourg, Moscou et les Provinces ou Observations sur les moeurs et les usages russes au commencement du XIXe siècle*, 3 vols. (Paris, 1830).

Durylin, S.N., 'Drug Gete', *Literaturnoe Nasledstvo* 4–6 (1932): 186–217.

Durylin, S.N., 'G-zha de Stal' i ee russkie otnosheniya', *Literaturnoe Nasledstvo* 33–34 (1939): 215–330.

Fletcher, G., *Of the Russe Commonwealth* (1591, facsimile edition with an introduction by Richard Pipes (Cambridge, MA, 1966).

Forster, Robert and Elborg Forster, eds., *The Universities of Goettingen and Vilna' in European Society in the Eighteenth Century, selected documents* (London, 1969), 312–20.

Gertsen, A.I., *Polnoe sobranie sochinenii*, 30 vols. (Moscow, 1954).

Gnedich. N.I., 'Pis'mo k S.S. Uvarovu', *Chteniya v Besede lyubitelei russkogo slova* 13 (1813): 67–72.

Goethe, J.W., *Gedenkausgabe der Werke, Briefe und Gespraeche*, 26 vols. (Zurich, 1949).

Gogol, N.V., *Polnoe sobranie sochinenii*, 7 vols. (Moscow, 1961).

Golokhvastov, D.P., 'Ob ukraino-slavyanskom obshchestve: Iz bumag D.P. Golokhvastove', *Russkii Arkhiv* 30, No. 7 (1892): 334–59.

'Graf S.S. Uvarov Biografichesky Ocherk', *Vsemirnaya illyustratsiya* No. 59 (1870): 123.

Granovsky, T.N., *Lektsii T.N. Granovskogo* (Moscow, 1961).

Grech, N.I., *Zapiski o moei zhizni* (St Petersburg, 1886).

Grudev, G.V., 'Iz rasskazov G.V. Grudeva', *Russkii Arkhiv* 36, No. 11 (1898): 426–39.

Gumbol'dt, A., [Alexander von Humboldt], *Perepiska Aleksandra Gumbol'dta s uchenymi i gosudarstvennymi deyatelyami Rossii* (Mosow, 1962).

'Iubilei prezidenta AN, S.S. Uvarova', *Moskvitanin* 2, No. 3 (1843): 265–86.

Kapnist, V.V., 'O ekzameterakh', *Chtenie v Besede lyubitelei russkogo slova* 17 (1815): 18–42.

Karamzin, N.M., 'Pis'ma N.M. Karamzina k S.S. Uvarovu' (21.7.1813), *XVIII Vek*, ed. M.I. Gillel'son (Leningrad, 1969), 353.

Karamzin, N.M., 'Pis'ma N.M. Karamzina k S.S. Uvarovu', *Syn Otechestva* 44, No. 8 (1818): 79–80.

Kireevsky, I.V., *Polnoe sobranie sochinenii*, 2 vols. (Moscow, 1911, reprinted London, 1970).

Koshelev, A.I., *Zapiski A.I. Kosheleva 1812-1883* (Berlin, 1884).

Kunitsyn, A.P., 'O Konstitutsii', *Syn otechestva* 45 (1818): 202–11.

Kunitsyn, A.P., 'Rassmotrenie rechi', *Syn otechestva* 46 (1819): 136–46, 174–91.

Kurakin, F.A., *Arkhiv F.A. Kurakina* (Saratov, 1874).

Lebedev, K.N., 'Iz zapisok senatora K.N. Lebedeva, 1855', *Russkii Arkhiv* 26, No. 1 (1888): 481–8, 617–28, No. 2: 123–44, 232–43, 345–66, No. 3: 249–70, 455–67.

Leontiev, P., 'Bakicheskii Pamyatnik Grafa S.S. Uvarova', *Propilei* I (1851): 135–42.

Lermontov, M. Yu., *Sobranie sochinenii*, 4 vols. (Moscow, 1961).

Longinov, M.N., 'Vospominanie o grafe S.S. Uvarove', *Sovremennik* 53, No. 10 (1885): 119–24.

Martens, G.F., *Recueil des traites, 1761–*, 7 vols. (Göttingen, 1791–1801).

Martynov, N.S., 'Iz bumag N.S. Marrtynova', *Russkii Arkhiv* 31, No. 8 (1893): 585–606.

Masson, C.F.P., *Mémoires secrètes sur la Russie*, 3 vols. (Paris, 1802).

McNally, R.T., 'Chaadaev's Philosophical Letters written to a Lady and his Apologia of a Madman', *Forschungen zur osteuropäischen Geschichte*, vol. 11 (Berlin, 1966).

Menshikov, A.I., *Biograficheskii Slovar' professorov i pripodavatelei Imperatorskogo Moskovskogo Universiteta*, 2 vols. (Moscow, 1855).

Mercier-Dupaty, C.J.M.B., *Lettres sur l'Italie en 1785* (Rome, 1788).

Ministerstvo narodnogo prosveshcheniya. *Sbornik postanovlenii po Mininsterstvu narodnogo prosveshcheniya* [SPMNP], 15 vols. (St Petersburg, 1875–1902).

Nesselrode, K.V., *Lettres et papiers du chancelier Comte de Nesselrode*, 11 vols. (Paris, 1904–1907).

Nikitenko. A.V., *Dnevnik*, 3 vols. (Leningrad, 1955, reprinted Moscow 2005).

Nonnos, von Panopolis, *Dionysiaca*, tr. and intr. W.H.D. Rouse, Mythological Introduction by H.J. Rose, 3 vols. (London, 1940).

Ostaf'evskii Arkhiv knyazei Vyazemskikh, 8 vols. (St Petersburg, 1899–1913).

'Ouvaroff' (par Rumelin) *Biographie universelle* 31 (Paris, 1843): 517–18.

Ouvaroff, Alexis, *Sciences secrètes: bibliothèque Alexis Ouvaroff* (Moscow, 1870, facsimile ed., Paris 1980).

'Ouvaroff, Sergius-Semenovitch, comte', *Larousse dictionnaire du XIX siècle* (Paris, 1866–76), 1591.

Panaev, I.I., *Literaturnye vospominaniya* (Leningrad, 1950).

Pletnev, P.A., 'Pamyati Grafa Sergiya Semenovicha Uvarova', *Uchenye zapiski* I (1856): liii–cxxv.

Pletnev, P.A., *Sochineniya i perepiska*, 3 vols. (St Petersburg, 1885).

Pogodin, M.P., 'Dlya biografii grafa S.S. Uvarova', *Russkii Arkhiv* 9, No. 12 (1871): 2078–107.

Polevoy, K.A., *Zapiski* (St Petersburg, 1888).

Pushkin, A.S., *Polnoe sobranie sochinenii*, 4th ed., 10 vols. (Leningrad, 1979).

Pushkin v vospominaniyakh sovremennikov (Moscow/Leningrad, 1950).

Reinbeck, G., *Travels from St Petersburgh through Moscow, Grodno, Warsaw, Breslau etc. to Germany in the year 1805, in a Series of Letters*, tr. from the German (London, 1807).

Reinbeck, G., *Sämmtliche dramatische Werke*, vol. 2 (Heidelberg/Frankfurt am Main, 1818).

Saint-Julien, Charles de, 'Hommes publiques russes, Le Comte Ouvaroff', *Revue de Paris* 15 (October 1868): 481–512.

Shcherbatov, Prince G., 'Student sorokovykh godakh: Knyaz' Grigorii Shcherbatov o Grafe Uvarove', *Sovremennaya letopis'* (1870), nos. 5–7.

Schiller, F., tr. and intr. E.M. Wilkinson and L.A. Willoughby, *On the Aesthetic Education of Man in a Series of Letters* (Oxford, 1967).

Schlegel, A.W., *Kritische Schriften und Briefe*, 7 vols. (Stuttgart, 1966).

Schmid, G., 'Goethe und Uwarow und ihr Briefwechsel', *Russische Revue* 28 (St Petersburg 1888): 131–82.

Schmid, G., 'Zur russischen Gelehrtengeschichte: S.S. Uvarow und Christian Friedrich Graefe', *Russische Revue* 26 (St Petersburg 1886): 76–108 and 156–67.

Shevyrev, S.P., *Istoriya poezii* (Moscow, 1835).

Shevyrev, S.P., 'Razgovor o vozmozhnosti naiti edinyi zakon dlya izyashchnogo', *Moskovskii Vestnik* No. 1 (1827): 38–49.

Shevyrev, S.P., *Teoriya poezii v istoricheskom razvitii u drevnykh i novykh narodov* (Moscow, 1836).

Shevyrev, S.P., 'Vzglyad russkogo na sovremennoe obrazovanie Evropy', *Moskvitanin* No. 1 (1841).

Smirnova, A.O., 'A.S. Pushkin po zapiskam A.O. Smirnovoi', *Russkii Arkhiv* 27, No. 6 (1889): 310–99.

Soloviev, S.M., *Moi Zapiski* (Moscow, 1914).

Stael-Holstein, A.L.G. de, ed. Simone Bellaye, 2 vols, *De l'Allemagne* [1813] (Paris, 1967).

Stael-Holstein, A.L. G. de, édition établie par Gérard Gengembre et Jean Goldzink, *De la littérature* [1799] (Paris, 1991).

Stael-Holstein, A.L.G. de, ed. Simone Balayé et Mariella Vianello Bonifacio. *Dix années d'exil* [1818] (Paris, 1996).

Stepanov, M. and F. Vermale, 'Pis'ma Zhozefa de Mestra k S.S. Uvarovu', *Literaturnoe Nasledstvo* 29–30 (1937): 577–726.

Sukhomlinov, M.I., *Issledovaniya i stat'i po russkoi literature i prosveshchenii*, 2 vols. (St Petersburg, 1889).

Turgenev brothers. *Arkhiv Brat'ev Turgenevykh*, 6 vols. (St Petersburg, 1911–1921).

Turgenev, A.I., ed. M.I. Gillel'son, *Khronik russkogo, Dnevniki 1825–26* (Moscow, 1964).

Turgenev, N.I., *La Russie et les russes*, 3 vols. (Paris, 1847).

Uvarova P.S., *Byloe : davno proshedshie schastlivye dni* (Moscow, 2005).

Vane, Frances Anne, Marchioness of Londonderry, *The Russian Journal of Lady Londonderry 1836–37*, eds. W.A.L. Seasman and J.R. Sewell (London, 1973).

Vigel, F.F., *Zapiski*, 2 vols. (Moscow, 1928, repr. 1974).

Vosem'nadtsatyi vek. Istoricheskii Sbornik izdavaemyi po bumagam famil'nogo arkhiva knyazem Fedorom Alekseevichem Kurakinym (Moscow, 1904).

Voeikov, A.F., 'Poslanie k S.S. Uvarovu', *Vestnik Evropy* No. 5 (1819): 15.

Volkonsky, S.G., *Arkhiv Dekabrista S.G. Volkonskogo* (Petrograd, 1918).

Vorontsov family. *Arkhiv Knyazya Vorontsova*, 40 vols. (Moscow, 1870–1895).

Vyazemsky, Prince P.A., *Polnoe sobranie sochinenii*, 10 vols. (St Petersburg, 1886).

Zhukovsky, V.A., 'O poezii drevnikh i novykh', *Vestnik Evropy* 55, No. 3 (1811): 187–212.

Zhukovsky, V.A., *Sobranie sochinenii v 4 tomakh* (Moscow /Leningrad, 1959).

Secondary sources

Adcock, F.E., *Roman Political Ideas and Practice* (Ann Arbor, MI, 1959).

Aleshintsev, I. *Istoriya gimnasichestkago obrazovaniya v Rossii* (St Petersburg, 1912).

Amburger, E., *Beiträge zur Geschichte der deutsch-russischen kulturellen Beziehungen* (Giessen, 1961).

Annenkov, P.V., *Literaturnye vospominaniya* (St Petersburg, 1909).

'Apraksiny', *Brokgauz* 1a (1890): 927–30.

Arendt, H. *On Revolution*, revised ed. (Harmondsworth, 1973).

Arndt, E.M., *Erinnerungen aus dem ausseren Leben* (Leipzig. 1840).

Arkhangel'sky, A.S. 'Biografichesky ocherk', Zhukovsky, V.A., *Sochineniya*, 12 vols. in 2 (St Petersburg, 1902), vol. 1.

Aronson M. and S. Reiser, *Literaturnye kruzhki i salony* (Leningrad, 1929).

Barante, Claude de, *Souvenirs du Baron de Barante*, vol. 5 (Paris, 1900).

Bartenev, P. *Rospis' soroka knigam Arkhiva knyazya Vorontsova* (Moscow, 1897).

Barycz, H., *The Development of University Education in Poland* (Warsaw, 1957).

Berlin, I, *Vico and Herder* (London, 1976).

Berlin, I., intr. Aileen Kelly, *Russian Thinkers* (London, 1978).

Bestuzhev-Ryumin, K.N., *Biografii i kharakteristiki* (St Petersburg, 1882).

Binyon, T.J., *Pushkin A Biography* (London, 2002).

Bokhanov, A.N, et al. *Rossiiskie Konservatory* (Moscow, 1997).

Borovkova-Maikova, M.S., ed., *Arzamas i arzamasskie protokoly* (Leningrad, 1933).

Brown, E.J., *Stankevich and His Moscow Circle 1830-1840* (Stanford, 1966).

Bruford H., *Culture and Society in Classical Weimar* (Cambridge, MA, 1962).

Bruford, W.H., *The German Tradition of Self-Cultivation* (Cambridge, 1975).

Burke, E., ed. Conor Cruise O'Brien, *Reflections on the Revolution in France* [1790] (Harmondsworth, 1968).

Catalogue of the Humboldt Library (London, 1858).

Chamberlain, Lesley 'New Eurasians', *Times Literary Supplement*, 13 May 2015.

Chereiskii, L.A., *Pushkin i ego okruzhenie* (Leningrad, 1975).

Cherniavsky, M., *Tsar and People, Studies in Russian Myth* (New Haven, CT and London, 1961).

Chizhevsky, D., *Gegel' v Rossii* (Paris, 1938).

Clark, R.T., *J.G. Herder, His Life and Thought* (Berkeley, CA, 1955).

Copleston, F., *A History of Philosophy*, 9 vols. (London, 1946–75).

Crankshaw, Edward, *The Shadow of the Winter Palace* (Harmondsworth, 1973).

Danilevsky, R. Yu., *Molodaya Germaniya i russkaya literatura. Iz istorii russko-nemetskikh literaturnykh otnoshenii pervoi poloviny XIX veka* (Leningrad, 1969).

Davies, N., *God's Playground: A History of Poland*, 2 vols. (Oxford, 1981).

'Davydov, I.I.' *Entsikopedicheskii Slovar' Brokgauza i Evrona*, 86 vols. (St Petersburg, 1890–1907).

de Krusenstern, A. *Précis du système,des progrès et de l'état de l'instruction publique en Russie* (Warsaw, 1845).

Dmitriev, S.S., *T.N. Granovsky, Bibliografia (1828-1867)* (Moscow, 1969).

Droz, J., *Europe between Revolutions 1815-1848* (London, 1967).

Fenske, Hans, *Freiherr von Stein: Reformer and Moralist* (Darmstadt, 2012).

Flynn, J.T., 'Magnitsky's Purge of Kazan' University', *Journal of Modern History* 43, No. 4 (1971): 598–614.

Flynn, J.T., 'S.S. Uvarov's "liberal" Years', *Jahrbuch für Geschichte Osteuropas* 20, No. 4 (1972): 481–91.

France, P., *Politeness and its Discontents* (Cambridge, 1992).

Galaktionov, A.A., and P.F. Nikdandrov, *Russkaya filosofiya XI-XIX vekov* [Leningrad, 1970] 2nd ed. (Leningrad, 1989).

Gennadi, G, *Les ecrivains franco-russes: Bibliographie des ouvrages francaises publies par des russes* (Dresden, 1874).

Gete Bibliograficheskii ukazatel' russkikh perevodov i kriticheskoi literature na russkom yazyke 1780-1971 (Moscow, 1972).

Gillel'son, M.I., *P.A. Vyazemsky: Zhizn' i tvorchestvo* (Moscow, 1969).

Gillel'son, M.I., *Molodoi Pushkin i Arzamasskoe bratstvo* (Leningrad, 1974).

Golovin, I., *Nicholas I*, 2 vols. (London, 1846).

Gooch, G.P., *Germany and the French Revolution* (London, 1920).

Jay, Peter, ed., *The Greek Anthology* (Harmondsworth, 1981).

Grimstead, P.K., *The Foreign Ministers of Alexander I* (Berkeley, CA, 1969).

Hans, N., *History of Russian Educational Policy 1701-1917* (London, 1931).

Harder, H., *Schiller in Russland: Materialien zu einer Wirkungsgeschichte 1789-1814* (Bad Homburg, 1969).

Haumant, E. *La Culture francaise en Russie* (Paris, 1910).

Hérold, J.C., *Mistress to an Age. A Life of Madame de Stael* (London, 1959).

Hollingsworth, B., 'Arzamas, Portrait of a Literary Society', *Slavonic and East European Review* XLIV, No. 103 (1966): 306–26.

Istoriya Akademii nauk SSSR, vol. 2 (Moscow, 1964).

Istoriya biblioteki Akademii nauk SSSR 1714-1964 (Moscow, 1964).

Istrin, V.M., 'Russkie studenty v Gettingene v 1802–1804 gg.', *ZMNP* 7 (1910): 80–144.

Ivanov, I.I., *Istoriya russkoi kritiki*, 4 vols. (St Petersburg, 1898–1900).

Ivanov, O.A, *Ideologiya 'Pravoslavie, Samoderzhavie, Narodnost' S.S. Uvarova: Konservatizm v Rossii i v mire: proshloe i nastoyashchee*, Vyp.1 (Voronezh, 2005).

Kamensky, Z.A., *Filosofskie idei russkogo prosveshcheniya* (Moscow, 1971).

Kamensky, Z.A., ed., *Russkie esteticheskie traktaty pervoi treti XIX veka*, 2 vols. (Moscow, 1974).

Karlinsky, S., *The Sexual Labyrinth of Nikolai Gogol* (Cambridge, MA, 1976).

Kissinger, H.A., *A World Restored* (London, 1957).

Kniazkov, S.A., and N.I. Serbov, *Ocherki istorii narodnogo obrazovanii v Rossii do epokhu reform Aleksandra II* (Moscow, 1910).

Kohler, Phyllis Penn, ed. and tr. *Marquis de Custine, Journey for Our Time* (London, 1953).

Kostka, E., *Schiller in Russian Literature* (Philadelphia, PA, 1965).

Kovalevsky, E.P., *Graf Bludov i ego vremya* (St Petersburg, 1866).

Koyré, A., *L'Occidentalisme d'Ivan Tourgeneff* (Paris, 1922).

Koyré, A., *La philosophie et le problème nationale en Russie au debut du XIXe siècle* (Paris, 1929).

Kozmin, N., *N.I.Nadezhdin, zhizn i nauchno-literaturnaya deyatel'nost' 1804–1836* (St Petersburg, 1912).

Kuleshov, V.I., *Literaturnye svyazi Rossii i zapadnoi Evropy v XIX veke* (Moscow, 1965).

Kurakin, A.B. *Russky biografichesky slovar*, ed. Vengerov (St. Petersburg, 1896). 'Kurakiny', *Brokgauz* 17: 61–62.

La Harpe, Frédéric-César de, *Correspondence de Frédéric-César de La Harpe, et Alexandre 1er suivi de la correspondence de Frédéric-César de La Harpe avec les membres de la famille imperiale de Russie* (Neuchatel, 1980).

Lampert, E., *Studies in Rebellion* (London, 1957).

Leatherbarrow, William, and Derek Offord, eds., *A History of Russian Thought* (Cambridge, 2010).

Lemke, M., *Nikolaevskie zhandarmy i literatura 1826-1855 gg.* (St Petersburg, 1907).

Lemke, M., *Ocherky po istorii russkoi tsenzury i zhurnalistiki XIX stoletiya* (St Petersburg, 1904).

Lincoln, W.B., 'The Circle of the Grand Ducheess Elena Pavlovna 1847-1861', *Slavonic and East European Review* XLVIII, No. 112 (July 1970): 373–87.

Lincoln, W.B., *Nicholas I* (Bloomington, IN, 1978).

Ludwig, A., *Schiller und die deutsche Nachwelt* (Berlin, 1909).

'Lunin, Mikhail Sergeievich', *Russkii biograficheskii slovar'*, vol. 'Labzina-Lyashenko', 742–4.

Lyashchenko, P.I., *History of the National Economy of Russia* (New York, 1949, reprinted 1970).

Magarshack, D., *Gogol A Life* (London, 1957).

Maguire, R.A., ed., *Gogol from the Twentieth Century Eleven essays* (Princeton, NJ, 1974).

Maiofis, M.L., *Vozvanie ke Evrope Literaturnoe obshchestvo 'Arzamas' i rossiiskii modernitzatsionnyi proekt 1815-1818 godov* (Moscow, 2008).

Malia, M., *Alexander Herzen and the Birth of Russian Socialism 1812-1855* (Oxford, 1961).

Mann, Yu., *Russkaya filosofskaya estetika* (Moscow, 1969).

Martin, A., *Romantics, Reformers, Reactionaries: Russian Conservative Thought and Politics in the Reign of Alexander I* (DeKalb, IL, 1997).

Masulin, S., *Vienna in the Age of Metternich* (London, 1975).

McClelland, J.C., *Autocrats and Academics: Education, Culture and Society in Tsarist Russia* (Chicago, IL, 1979).

McNally, R.T., *Chaadaev and His Friends. An Intellectual History* (Tallahassee, FL, 1971).

Meinecke, F., *Weltbürgertum und Nationalstaat* (Munich, 1928).

Milosz, C., *The History of Polish Iterature*, 2nd ed. (Berkeley, CA, 1983).

Monas, S., *The Third Section: Police and Society in Russia under Nicholas I* (Cambridge, MA, 1961).

Montefiore, Simon Sebag, *The Romanovs* (London, 2016).

Muesebeck, E., *E.M. Arndt* (Gotha, 1914).

Mylonas, G.E., *Eleusis and the Eleusinian Mysteries* (Princeton, NJ, 1961).

Nifontov, A.S., *1848 god v Rossii: ocherki po istorii 40-kh godov* (1st ed. (Moscow, 1931)). The 1st edition contains material on Uvarov dropped from 2nd ed. (Moscow, 1949).

Nikitenko, A., *Aleksander I. Galich* (St Petersburg, 1869).

Nisbet, H.B., *Goethe and the Scientific Tradition* (London, 1972).

Offord, Derek,, Lara Ryazanova-Clarke, Vladislav Rjeoutski, Gesine Argent, eds., *French and Russian in Imperial Russia* 2 vols. (Edinburgh, 2015).

Palmer, A.W., *Alexander I Tsar of War and Peace* (London, 1970).

Palmer, A.W., *Metternich* (London, 1972).

Pertz, G.H., *Das Leben des Ministers Freiherr vom Stein*, 6 vols. (Berlin, 1851).

Petukhov, E.V., *Imperatorskii Yurevskii, byvshii Derptskii, Universitet*, 2 vols. (Iur'ev, 1902).

Pingaud, L., *Les Francais en Russie et les Russes en France* (Paris, 1886).

Paips, R. [Richard Pipes], *Sergei Semyonovich Uvarov: Zhizneopisanie* (Moscow, 2013).

Pipes, R., *Karamzin's Memoir on Ancient and Modern Russia: A Translation and Analysis* (Cambridge, MA, 1959).

Pipes, R., *Russian Conservatism and Its Critics A Study in Political Culture* (New Haven, CN, 2005).

Pipes, R., *Russia under the Old Regime* (London, 1974).

'Pogodin, Mikhail Pavlovich, '*Entsiklopedicheskii Slovar'*, *Brokgauza i Evrona* 24: 31–33.

'Pogodin, Mikhail Pavlovich, *Bol'shaya Entsyklopedia* 15: 305–306.

'Pogodin, Mikhail Pavlovich, *Entsiklopedicheskii Slovar'*, *Granat* 32 (Moscow, 1910–17, 1922–48): 402–406.

Pypin, A.N., *Istoriya russkoi etnografii* (St Petersburg, 1891).

Pypin, A.N., *Kharakteristiki literaturnykh mnenii:1820-1850* (St Petersburg, 1906).

Pypin, A.N., *Obshchestvennoe dvizhenie v Rossii pri Aleksandre I* (St Petersburg, 1900).

Pypin, A.N., *Religiosnye dvizheniya pri Aleksandre I* (Petrograd, 1916).

Quénet, C., *Tchaadaev et les lettres philosophiques* (Paris, 1931).

Quérard, J.M., *La France litteraire ou Dictionnaire des Savants, historiens et gens de lettres de la France ainsi que des litterateurs étrangers qui ont écrit en francais*, 12 vols. (Paris, 1854–59).

Raeff, M., *The Decembrist Movement* (Englewood Cliffs, NJ, 1966).

Raeff, M., 'The Enlightenment in Russia and Russian Thought in the Enlightenment', *The Eighteeenth Century in Russia*, ed. J.G. Garrard (Oxford, 1973).

Raeff, M., *Imperial Russia 1682–1825: The Coming of Age of Modern Russia* (New York, 1971).

Raeff, M., *Michael Speransky, Statesman of Imperial Russia 1772-1839*, 2nd revised ed. (The Hague, 1969).

Raeff, M., *Origins of the Russian Intelligentsia The Eighteenth-Century Nobility* (New York, 1966).

Raeff, M., *Political Institutions and Ideas in Imperial Russia* (Boulder, CO, 1994).

Raeff, M., 'The Russian Autocracy and its Officials', *Harvard Slavic Studies* IV (1957): 77–91.

Ragsdale, H, ed., *Paul 1 of Russia: A Reassessment of His Reign* (Pittsburgh, PA, 1979).

Ragsdale, H., ed., *Tsar Paul and the Question of Madness* (Westport, CN, 1988).

'Razumovsky, Graf Alexei Kirillovich', *Brokgauz* 36: 202–203.

Reed, T.J.. *The Classical Centre: Goethe and Weimar 1775–1832* (London, 1980).

Reizov, B.G., 'Madame de Stal', 'Frantsiya i Germaniya', *Mezhdu klassizmom i romantizmom-* (Leningrad, 1962).

Riazanovsky, N.V., *Nicholas I and Official Nationality in Russia 1825–1855* (Berkeley, CA, 1967).

Riazanovsky, N.V., *A Parting of Ways Government and the Educated Public in Russia 1801-1855* (Oxford, 1976).

Riazanovsky, N.V., 'Pogodin and Ševirev in Russian Intellectual History', *Harvard Slavonic Studies* IV (1957): 149–67.

Riazanovsky, N.V., *Russia and the West in the Teaching of the Slavophiles. A Study of Romantic Ideology* (Cambridge, MA, 1952).

Rosenberg, H., *Bureaucracy, Aristocracy and Autocracy: The Prussian Experience 1660-1815* (Boston, MA, 1966).

Rozhdestvensky, S.V., *Istoricheskii obzor deyatel'nosti Ministerstva narodnogo prosvenshcheniya* (St Petersburg, 1902).

Russkaya periodichestkaya pechat' (Moscow, 1959).

'Russko-angliickie literaturnye svyazi', *Literaturnoe Nasledstvo*, 91 (1982).

Sakulin, P.N., 'Russkaya literatura vo vtoroi chetverti veka', *Istoriya russkoi literatury XIXv.*, ed. O.N. Ovsyanikov-Kulikovsky (Moscow, 1910).

Sandys, J.E., *A History of Classical Scholarship*, 2 vols. (London, 1967).

Saunders, D.B., 'Historians and Concepts of Nationality in Early Nineteenth-Century Russia', *Slavonic and East European Review* 60, No. 1 (January 1982): 44–62.

Sbornik russkogo istoricheskogo obshchestva [SIRIO] (St Petersburg/Leningrad, 1872–1927), vols 83 and 89.

Schadewaldt, W., 'Goethes Begriff der Realität', *Goethestudien, Natur und Altertum* (Zurich, 1963).

Schulz, G., *Schillers Horen* (Heidelberg, 1960).

Sennet, R., *The Fall of Public Man* (Cambridge, MA, 1977).

Setchkarev, V., *Gogol His Life and Works* (London, 1965).

Seton-Watson, H., *The Russian Empire 1801-1917* (Oxford, 1967).

Shebunin, A.N., *Dekabrist N.I. Turgenev* (Moscow, 1936).

Shebunin, A.N., *Nikolai Ivanovich Turgenev* (Moscow, 1925).

Shevchenko, M.M, *Sergei Semyonovich Uvarov: Protiv techeniya; istoricheskiye portrety russkikh konservatorov pervoi treti XIX stoletiya* (Voronezh, 2005).

'Shevyrev, Stepan Petrovich', *Entsiklopedicheskii Slovar' Brokgauza i Evrona* (St Petersburg, 1890–1904), 39: 361–4.

Shil'der, N.K., *Imperator Nikolai Pervyi: ego zhzin' i tsarstvovanie*, 2 vols. (St Petersburg, 1903).

Shpet G.G., *Ocherki razvitii russkoi filosofii* (Petrograd, 1922).

Simenov P.P *Zhivopisnaya Rossiya Otechestvo nashe v ego zemelnom, istoricheskom, plemennom, jekonomicheskom i bytovom znachenii*, 18vols. (Moscow, 1896).

Simmons, E.J., ed., *Continuity and Change in Russian and Soviet Thought* (Cambridge, MA, 1955).

Simmons, T., *The Russian Landed Gentry* (Cambridge, 1968).

Stankevich, A.V., *Biograficheskii ocherk T.N. Granovskogo* (Moscow, 1914).

Stieda, W., *Deutsche Gelehrte als Professoren an der Universität Moskau* (Leipzig, 1930).

Stolitsa i usad'ba Zhurnal krasivoi zhizni (Moscow, 1914), Nos. 16–17 'Dvortsy Razumovskogo'.

Storch, H., *Russland unter Alexander I* (St Petersburg/Leipzig, 1804–8).

Strich, F., *Goethe und die Weltliteratur* (Berne, 1946).

Sushkov, N.V., *Moskovskii Universitetskii Pansion* (Moscow, 1858).

Sweet, P.R., *Wilhelm von Humboldt A Biography*, 2 vols. (Colombus, OH, 1978–80).

Terras, V., *Belinsky and Russian literary criticism The Heritage of Organic Aesthetics* (Madison, WI, 1974).

Thaden, E.C., *Conservative Nationalism in Nineteenth-Century Russia* (Seattle, 1964).

Thomson B., *Lot's Wife and the Venus de Milo Conflicting Attitudes to the Cultural Heritage in Modern Russia* (London, 1978).

Toynbee, A.J., *Civilisation on Trial* (Oxford, 1948).

Troyat, H., *Poushkine*, 2 vols in 1 (Oxford, 1946).

Troyat, H., *Tolstoy* (Harmondsworth, 1970).

Unbegaun, B.O., *Russian Versification* (Oxford, 1956).

Ustryalov, N.G., *O Sisteme pragmaticheskoi russkoi istorii* (Moscow, 1836).

Ustryalov, N.G., *Russkaya Istoriya*, 2nd ed. (Moscow, 1839).

Uvarov, A.S, *Nezabvennoi pamyati Gr. A.S. Uvarova* (Kazan, 1885).

'Uvarov, Alexei Sergeevich', *Entsiklopedicheskii Slovar' Brokgauza I Evrona* 34: 418–19.

'Uvarov, Alexei Sergeevich', *Bolshaya Sovietskaya Entsiklopedia* 26 (1977): 438.

'Uvarov, Alexei Sergeevich', *Bolshaya Entsyklopedia* 18: 711.

'Uvarov, Fyodor Semyonovich', *Entsiklopedicheskii Slovar' Brokgauza I Evrona* 34: 420.

Уваров, Сергей Семенович, граф, 1786-1855 Sergeĭ Semenovich Uvarov, graf, 1786-1855 author.

Moskva: Institut russkoĭ t͡si͡vilizat͡sii, 2014. Москва: Институт русской цивилиз ации (2014).

Vasil'chikov, A., *Semeistvo Razumovskikh*, 6 vols. (St Petersburg, 1859–1900).

Veselovsky, A., *Zapadnoe vliyanie v novoi russkoi literature*, 2nd revised ed. (Moscow, 1916).

Vlasov, V.A., 'Radetel' Rossiiskoi Samobytnosti' Graf Sergei Semyonovich Uvarov', *Zhurnal isvestiya Penzenskogo gosudarstevennogo pedeagogichestogo universiteta im. V.G Belinskogo*, No. 9 No. 13, 2008, downloaded on 07/12/2018 at https://cyberleninka.ru/article/n/radetel-rossiyskoy-samobytnosti-graf-sergey-semyonovich-uvarov.

Vladimirskii-Budanov, M.F., *Istoriya Imperatorskogo Universiteta sv. Vladimira* (Kiev, 1884).

von Gronika, A., *The Russian Image of Goethe Goethe in Russian Literature of the First Half of the Nineteenth Century* (Philadelphia, PA, 1968).

Vucinic, A.S., *Science in Russian Culture*, 2 vols. (Stanford, CA, 1970).

Vrangel, Baron N.N., *O.A. Kiprensky v chastnykh sobraniyakh* (St Petersburg, 1899).

Walicki, A., *A History of Russian Thought* (Oxford, 1980).

Walicki, A., *The Slavophile Controversy* (Oxford, 1975).

Waliszewski, K., *La Russie il y a cent ans, le règne d'Alexandre*, 3 vols. (Paris, 1923).

Webster, C.K., *The Foreign Policy of Castlereagh*, 2 vols. (London, 1925).

Wes, Marinus, *Classics in Russia 1700-1855: Between Two Bronze Horsemen* (Leiden, 1992).

Whittaker, C.H., 'The Ideology of Sergei Uvarov: An Interpretive Essay', *Russian Review* 37, No. 2 (April 1978): 158–76.

Whittaker, C.H., *The Origins of Modern Russian Education An Intellectual Biography of Count Sergei Uvarov 1786-1855* (DeKalb, IL, 1984); in Russian as *Graf Sergei Semyonovich Uvarov i ego vremya* (St Petersburg, 1999).

Winter, E.J., *August Ludwig von Schloezer und Russland* (Berlin, 1961).

Wischnitzer, M., *Die Universität Göttingen und die Entwicklung der liberalen Ideen in Russland* (Berlin, 1907).

Wulff, O. *Die Neurussische Kunst, im Rahmen der Kulturentwicklung Russlands von Peter dem Grossen bis zur Revolution* (Augsburg, 1932).

Zablotskii, A.P., 'Russkoe geograficheskoe obshchestvo', *Vestnik russkogo geograficheskogo obshchestva* 15, otd. 15 (1855): 13–18.

Zagoskin, N.P., *Istoriya Kazanskogo Universiteta*, 4 vols. (St Petersburg, 1902–1906).

Zaitsev, A.A. et al., eds., *Kniga v Rossii v ėpokhu prosveshcheniia: sbornik nauchnykh trudov* (Leningrad, 1988).

Zamoyski, A., *Holy Madness: Romantics, Patriots and Revolutionaries 1776–1871* (London, 1999).

Zamoyski, A., *Rites of Peace: The Fall of Napoleon and the Congress of Vienna* (London, 2008).

Zhirmunsky V., *Gete v russkoi literature* (Leningrad, 1937).

Zverev, N.A., *Obshchestevenno-politicheskie vzglyady S.S. Uvarova* (Volgograd, 2005).

Index